ucap,ustx GN 21.L37C64 1975b
Leakey's luck :
3 9153 01288459 1
W9-CCX-847
DISCARD

Leakey's Luck

by the same author

The Prehistory of East Africa
Counterfeit
The Neolithic Revolution
Races of Man
Animal Ancestors

Frontispiece
Louis was never happier than when exploring: here he is on a fossil-hunting expedition to Kenya's northern frontier. 'Happy memories of Muruorot, Feb. 1951, Louis' refers to Muruorot Hill near Lodwar, which produced fossils nearly twenty million years old

Sonia Cole

Leakey's Luck

The life of
Louis Seymour Bazett Leakey

1903-1972

Harcourt Brace Jovanovich
New York and London

Copyright © 1975 by Sonia Cole

All rights reserved. No part of this publication may be reproduced or transmitted in any form or by any means, electronic or mechanical, including photocopy, recording, or any information storage and retrieval system, without permission in writing from the publisher.

Printed in Great Britain

ISBN 0-15-149456-8

First American edition

B C D E

Contents

Illustrations

Acknowledgements

When Dr Mary Leakey did me the honour of inviting me to write a biography of her husband my immediate reaction was to say that it would be so much easier if she were dead, to which she replied 'I'm not going to die just to please you.' In all other ways she has been most co-operative.

Obviously this book could not have been written without her help and that of other members of the family. She allowed me to see the unpublished MS of the second volume of Louis's memoirs, *By the evidence*, and with even greater generosity let me read her own unpublished book, *Valley of the wild sisal*, from which I have skimmed a large amount of cream for my chapter on Olduvai. I must thank her also for much hospitality both at Olduvai and at her house at Langata; for letting me browse through the files in her office at the National Museum in Nairobi; and for her help in blowing clouds of insecticide on the inmates of half a dozen tin trunks containing Louis's correspondence going back to the 1920s. Above all, I am grateful to her for patiently correcting the drafts of this book and filling in gaps.

Her son Richard also proved an excellent critic and gave me a lot of his time, and I should like to thank him and his wife Meave for a memorable trip to East Rudolf. My thanks also to Jonathan and Mollie Leakey for information and for having me to stay at their beautiful home on Lake Baringo. Other members of the family who have helped enormously are Louis's sisters, Mrs Julia Barham and Mrs Gladys Beecher; his first wife, Mrs H. W. (Frida) Leakey, and her son and daughter, Dr Colin Leakey and Mrs Priscilla Davies.

The last few chapters concerning Louis's involvement with California owe much to the great kindness of Mr Allen O'Brien, founder and first president of the Leakey Foundation, and to the

Foundation's secretary, Mrs Joan Travis, who gave unsparingly of their time and made my visit to Los Angeles both rewarding and enjoyable. I am also greatly indebted to Miss Cara Phelips, Louis's secretary during the last two years of his life, whose account of the traumatic experiences of his illnesses I have quoted extensively.

I should also like to thank the following for Leakey stories and other material: Mrs Pat Barrett, Mr Robert Beck, Dr W. W. Bishop, Mrs Miles Burkitt, Dr Gertrude Caton-Thompson, Dr Alan Charig, Dr Glyn Daniel, Professor Michael Day, Mrs Marjorie Firth, Miss Dian Fossey, Mr Ed N. Harrison, Dr Glynn Isaac, Professor F. Clark Howell, Mr Malcolm MacDonald, Dr Kenneth Oakley, Dr C. G. Richards, Mrs Shirley Coryndon Savage, Lady Shaw, Professor Phillip Tobias, Dr Alan Walker and Dr E. Barton Worthington. My thanks also to Mr N Fedha, chief archivist of the National Archives of Kenya, and his cheerful assistants; and to Miss Rosemary Keen, archivist of the Church Missionary Society in London.

For permission to reproduce National Geographic Society's photographs I am immensely grateful to the Society's president, Dr Melvin M. Payne, and to Miss Joanne Hess, secretary of the NGS lecture committee, for the great trouble she took in connection with them. Acknowledgements to others who have so kindly allowed me to use their photographs are made with the captions.

1 Preview

Louis Leakey did not quite reach his three score years and ten, but he packed more into his sixty-nine years than ten ordinary men would in their combined lifetimes. He was one of the most versatile scientists of his generation, even in an age when specialization had not yet become the god that it is today and it was still possible to be archaeologist, anthropologist, anatomist, palaeontologist and zoologist all at the same time. He was renowned in each of these roles but they by no means exhausted his repertoire: he threw himself into anything that aroused his curiosity, which was just about everything that lived or had once lived.

Few men can have been more obsessively committed to the search for man's origins; but more than anything else East Africa – its past, present and future – was his consuming passion. He was an authority on its animals, extant as well as extinct; curator of Nairobi's National Museum; founder trustee of Kenya's National Parks. He had an unrivalled knowledge of the Kikuyu people, their culture and customs, language and beliefs. The son of missionary parents, he was born in the heart of Kikuyuland at a time when there was only a handful of European settlers in Kenya. His boyhood friends were Kikuyu, and during those formative years he learnt to 'think African'. Louis always took a pride in regarding himself as more of a Kikuyu than an Englishman.

This background explains much of the strength as well as the conflicts in his life. From his parents he inherited missionary zeal and dedication to a cause, as well as devotion to African people and a faith in God and humanity. Yet his scientific intellect made him rebel against their limited horizons and their adherence to Christian dogma. His close association with the Kikuyu made him appreciate that the missionaries were undermining tribal structure, and he expressed these views forcefully. As a result, he came to be mistrusted by the British community in Kenya – but throughout most of his career Louis found himself a misfit.

After sixteen years of thoroughly happy home life in Africa he was plunged head first into an English school, and then into Cambridge. For the first time he had to adapt and conform – as far as it was ever possible for him to conform. The struggle had begun. His companions were not at all impressed by his adventures in the bush, while he regarded their interests as childish; the more he boasted, the more unpopular he became. His poverty, the absence of a conventional education before adolescence, and the lack of communication with his English contemporaries all reinforced Louis's inherent ambition and his determination to prove himself.

Africa, as we now know, was the homeland of our earliest ancestors; yet until very recently its past was shrouded in as much mystery as the geographical features of its interior were in the nineteenth century. When the Royal Geographical Society awarded Louis their Founder's Medal in 1964 the citation read: 'For as long as Livingstone or Baker are remembered for their geographical explorations, Dr Leakey will be remembered for his scientific explorations.' When he began his research half a century ago the prehistoric map of East Africa was practically a blank. As a young man with a double first from Cambridge but no other assets except eagerness and optimism – and against the advice of his superiors – he embarked on the great adventure of filling in that map. He was convinced that somewhere in that virgin territory he would find the first traces of emergent humanity. The story of how this came about is one of persistence and courage, an endless struggle to raise funds, trackless country crossed in unreliable transport, shortage of water, tropical diseases and many other hardships.

The first ten years of his scientific career, from the mid 1920s to the mid 1930s, were a period of exploration and reconnaissance during which he pinpointed most of the major sites which were to make him famous. By the time he was thirty years old he had managed to scrape up funds to lead four archaeological expeditions to East Africa, but the success he might have enjoyed was impaired by two unfortunate scandals. One was matrimonial, the other scientific, and each took a long time to live down. Their effect was to make him intensify his efforts even further.

The trail ended more than thirty years later with a skull embedded in the side of a canyon. Of all the Leakey discoveries the one best known is 'Nutcracker Man', or 'Zinjanthropus'. *Australopithecus boisei*, to give him his proper name, was found at Olduvai Gorge, Tanzania, in 1959. That he was actually discovered by Louis's second wife, Mary, is irrelevant, for the family always worked as a team, with Louis the acknowledged leader. Subsequent discoveries at Olduvai showed that 'Zinj' was our distant cousin rather than a direct ancestor, which is perhaps comforting in view of his frankly forbidding features. That famous skull, with gorilla-like crest surmounting a low vault, was pictured in almost every newspaper at the time; it brought the Leakeys fame and changed the course of their lives.

As a colleague said in connexion with another find, 'Zinj' was launched by the power of Louis's personality. But although Louis was ambitious he had a genuine love of science and a consuming desire to make contributions to it for its own sake; at the time 'Zinj' seemed a fulfilment scientifically as well as personally. Louis was a great believer in popularizing science through the media, above all in lectures. He was a showman and loved the limelight, and his seeking after publicity has been freely criticized. But to do him justice he had to make the very most of each new find in order to raise the money to carry on.

In the early days, as well as launching expeditions on a shoestring, Louis had to fight other battles. He had to persuade his scientific colleagues to accept his conclusions, which often differed fundamentally from their own. As the years went by, and he made more and more revolutionary discoveries, the conflict with orthodox opinion only intensified. He was like a needle embedded in the armchair of the 'experts', whose universe was centred on western Europe.

When Louis set off on his first expedition in 1926 the accepted view was that man had arisen in Asia, and from there the main cultural stream had flowed inexorably towards the Atlantic. No academic was prepared to concede that anything significant could ever emerge from barbaric Africa. Louis had the vision that others lacked; he was determined to prove them wrong and he did so. This did not make him any more popular.

Throughout his long quest to solve the mystery of human origins, Louis clung tenaciously to two main evolutionary theories. One was that man arose in Africa – and on present evidence it is impossible to argue convincingly that hominid* fossils of comparable age have been found elsewhere. His second theory is still disputed by some of his colleagues, although they seem to be outnumbered: this is that the australopithecines were an unsuccessful sideline which left no descendants. Louis believed that 'Zinj', as well as others of his ilk, less specialized, less gorilla-like, lived at the same time as our true ancestor. Similarly he was convinced that the heavy-browed Java Man, Neanderthal Man and their African equivalents were aberrant offshoots of the main stem leading to modern man.

Essentially, however, Louis was a discoverer, and probably he found and named more fossil 'firsts' than any other palaeontologist who ever worked in Africa. Nobody disputed the importance of these discoveries nor his flair for making them, although quite a few questioned his interpretations of their status and the new names that he bestowed on them so lavishly. A new species attracts funds, further examples of known species do not; this was certainly part of the reason for this incurable habit of his, but it was not the whole reason. Louis became tremendously excited over his finds and was often completely carried away by his enthusiasm.

When 'Zinj' was discovered he claimed that it was *the* oldest tool-maker; but when a more human-looking hominid from Olduvai assumed this role soon afterwards Louis had to eat his words. When he saw that he had been wrong he was quite ready to retract; but if he felt he was right he would never budge, even if the evidence against him seemed overwhelming. One of his secretaries tells a story of him dictating a letter in which he mentioned 'the 600-odd miles from Mombasa to Kisumu'; this she questioned, and on checking found the distance to be 515 miles. 'Oh well', said Louis, not at all put out, 'split the difference.'

*Terms not explained in the text may be found in the glossary.

Someone who talked as much as Louis would not be expected to make a good listener, and he was apt to be dogmatic and intolerant of criticism. This is evident from the irate letters he sometimes wrote to *Nature* and other scientific journals in reply to those who questioned his findings. All his life he provoked controversy, and this he thoroughly enjoyed; but he liked to have the last word.

Whatever the merits or otherwise of Leakey theories, scientists freely admit that he produced an unparalleled amount of material for them to study. Many of his other finds were just as important as 'Zinj', some probably even more important from a scientific point of view. In the pre-Leakey era, for example, fossil apes were known merely from a few scraps of jaws, a handful of isolated teeth. In western Kenya, Louis and Mary found the remains of *hundreds* of early Miocene apes twenty million years old, including an almost complete skull. This was the first skull of a fossil ape of any age known from anywhere in the world. And the value of the bones of these apes, which may have included members of our own ancestry, was enhanced by previously unknown details of their ecological setting: the mammals, reptiles and fish which lived with them, even fossil insects, seeds and fruits. It is no exaggeration to say that the evolutionary panorama unfolded by the Leakeys in East Africa revolutionized knowledge of early man, his contemporaries and his forerunners.

How did a man with no money, who blotted his scientific copybook almost at the outset of his career, achieve so much? By sheer persistence he managed to raise funds for four expeditions, but he could not go on doing so indefinitely. There came a nasty moment when it seemed that he might have to abandon prehistory and – worse – abandon East Africa. Instead he benefited from his unique knowledge of the Kikuyu, and spent nearly two years collecting an enormous amount of information on their customs. Circumstances then forced him to deviate once again from prehistory, and during the second world war he did intelligence work (as he did also during the Mau Mau emergency in the 1950s); this satisfied his love of intrigue and interest in all kinds of people. In his spare time, such as it was, he did voluntary work at the Coryndon – now the National – Museum in Nairobi, and in 1945 he was appointed full-time curator. For the first time in his life he had an anchor and a salary. During the twenty-three years that he held this post he built the Museum up until it became one of the finest in Africa. His drive and imagination and his love of educating the public made him an excellent curator, but he never became bogged down with administrative duties and always found the time and the means to get into the field.

Soon after Louis became curator he initiated the first Pan African Congress on Prehistory, which was held in Nairobi in 1947. Not only was this a milestone in the study of man's past in Africa, but as a direct result he obtained funds to launch a series of expeditions to collect Miocene fossils in western Kenya. The next decade, 'the Miocene years', was probably the peak of Louis's career. Overlapping to a certain extent were 'the Olduvai years', culminating on that historic day, 17 July 1959, with the discovery of 'Zinj'. 'Zinj' was only one of a series of hominids to emanate from Olduvai, and the hominids were only a small part of the Gorge's almost limitless supply of fauna.

So began the Leakeys' connexion with the National Geographic Society of Washington, who thereafter publicized their finds and subsidized their work. The tremendously detailed excavations which went on at Olduvai during the 1960s were left largely to Mary, the expert on stone tools, while Louis spent more and more time in the United States raising funds to enable her to carry on.

By this time he was beginning to pay the price for obstinately neglecting his health, and he was forced to switch from the field-work he so much enjoyed into other projects. To house his bulging collections, and to make them available to others for study, he founded a Centre for Prehistory and Palaeontology adjoining the Museum in Nairobi; but the Museum was in no way responsible for financing and staffing it, and Louis did this entirely by his own efforts. Not content with one research centre he set up another for the study of living monkeys; again he had to find the funds to keep it going, which he did at great cost to his health. Next he launched Jane Goodall into the field to study chimpanzees, followed by other students to make long-term observations on gorillas and orang-utans. And, as if he had not got enough on his hands already, he became involved in raising money for excavations in Israel and California.

All this involved strenuous lecture tours, and during the last ten years of his life Louis spent nearly as much time in the USA as he did in Africa. There he received all the adulation he had ever craved. Dr Leakey the dedicated scientist, the champion of African causes, became Dr Leakey the star. The reasons why he allowed this to happen had a good deal to do with his deteriorating physical condition, but they were far more complex and went much deeper than that.

So much for the moment for Louis the scientist; what of Louis the man? We may begin with a picture of the explorer in his element at some new site. His eyes sparkling with excitement, he would scurry rather than walk, as though there was not a moment to be lost. His head would be thrust forward so as not to miss a single bone or stone, but at the same time he would never fail to take in the significance of some geological formation far away on the horizon. Even when completely absorbed in fossil-hunting he would always notice an animal hiding in the bush, or its tracks, or its dung; he had a passion for wildlife, and his knowledge of animal habits was legendary. His powers of observation and his extraordinary memory made a powerful combination on which he could draw when writing a book, delivering a lecture, or simply entertaining a companion.

So many adjectives can be applied to Louis – and most have been: energetic, exhilarating, effervescent, ebullient. Enthusiasm is a most infectious disease, and one of his greatest gifts was to inspire others to take up the projects in which he was so interested. He had an especially remarkable way of getting through to the young, but he could talk to any age group or educational level and hold them spellbound: five-year-olds, teenagers, Kikuyu elders, university dons, even heads of state. Louis was a catalyst, and Walt Disney's reply* to a small boy who asked what he actually *did* expresses this well: 'Sometimes I think of myself as a little bee. I go from one area of the studio to another and gather pollen and sort of stimulate everybody.'

*David Robinson in *The Times*, 14 December, 1973

Louis's love of children and young people was just one of the endearing and essentially African qualities in his make-up. His soft voice with its sing-song inflexions was also typically African – and his laugh was as characteristic as his voice, quiet and staccato, like a bronchitic gasping for breath. Like the members of his adopted tribe, the Kikuyu, he loved an audience, taking a delight in performing conjuring tricks or demonstrating the endless permutations of string figures (cat's cradles) at which so many African tribes used to be expert.

For all his apparent complexities Louis enjoyed the simple things of life. He would throw himself with as much energy into cooking a soufflé as he put into solving a scientific problem. In the face of practical difficulties such as a mechanical breakdown he was invariably good-humoured: he looked upon adversities as a challenge, and the more he had to exercise his ingenuity the happier he became. Perhaps his delight in cooking, entertaining children, fixing a Land-Rover, all stemmed from his need to be loved and admired, but certainly he never seemed to be bored by menial tasks.

In spite of his love of theorizing, Louis took nothing for granted and always put everything to practical test. He became an expert flint-knapper, and would use the stone tools he had made to skin and chop up animals. Even this was not enough: to prove that man had to be a tool-maker to survive, he tried unsuccessfully to skin animals with his teeth.

Louis could show amazing patience if necessary, but by nature he was impetuous. His inclination was to get on with the next job rather than slog over tiresome details. Although temperamentally unsuited to making detailed excavations or minute studies of fossils he did both successfully; he had tremendous self-discipline and would cheerfully work all night if necessary. He was never good at working with other people, especially with men, and always wanted to tackle everything himself.

Although always an individualist and happiest in the bush, he was stimulated by company and blossomed at conferences. He was very adaptable and, curiously, when he lived in Nairobi he enjoyed such suburban pursuits as pony clubs, dog shows and breeding tropical fish. Not gardening, however: this would have been too slow, and for relaxation he preferred to clean a fossil.

Louis was used to doing without luxuries, as every cent he earned went back into research; but he was too efficient to put up with discomfort if it could be avoided, and his camps were always well run. He much enjoyed good food, although he bolted it as if he could not afford the time to linger over meals. From early middle age he had a weight problem which he tackled with his usual determination. He dieted for the sake of his health and to keep his mobility, certainly not out of vanity: he wore his clothes until they fell off, after which he used them for wrapping up fossils. His favourite outfit was a boiler suit bleached by the sun, devoid of buttons, with baggy knees and bulging pockets.

Louis had a great ability to make complicated subjects seem straightforward; he loved to share his encyclopedic knowledge, and however tired he might be he would respond to an intelligent question. His finds brought him fame in scientific circles, but his way of talking about them made them – and him – known to a much wider public. His frequent appearances on the lecture platform and television screen in the USA, and the articles about him in the *National Geographic*, brought him an enormous fan mail. He tried to answer all these letters personally, often arranging to meet the writers if he felt their interest was genuine, and he would go to endless trouble to help anyone he thought worthy of encouragement.

Louis used to refer to 'Leakey's luck', but that is only a small part of the story. He was certainly lucky to have a completely unknown territory to investigate, a land of desert and lakes, rifts and volcanoes, which proved to have a combination of unique circumstances. The climate and topography of East Africa provided an ideal setting for emergent humanity. Huge herds of herbivores grazed on the steppe or browsed on the savanna, coming down to drink at streams flowing into the Rift Valley lakes where early hunters lay in wait for them. Man's camping places were then sealed over by silt and volcanic ash preserving every tool in place and many bones intact. No prehistorian could ask for more.

Luck must always play some part in fossil-hunting, but it is largely a question of knowing where to look and then going on looking, again and again. Leakey's luck, in fact, was largely the outcome of a touch of genius and persistence in the face of difficulties which to almost anyone else would have been insuperable.

Towards the end Louis was a very sick man, slowed down by a severe head operation, several heart attacks, a semi-paralysed hand and a plastic hip. Yet he never let up on his exhausting programme of lectures, and just before his death he was planning to take part personally in an expedition to unexplored, inaccessible, and for him frankly impossible desert country in northern Kenya. This is characteristic of the courage and determination with which he tackled every obstacle throughout his career. At a time when most men have retired, he drove himself harder than ever.

Louis died of a coronary on 1 October 1972. He had just arrived in London, hot foot on his way to the United States to embark on an even more exhausting itinerary than usual. No man could have gone on at such a pace, even one half his age and in robust health. Perhaps it was as well that he did not live any longer; he would have become increasingly frustrated by his inability to work as hard as he had done all his life, and he could never have become adapted to inactivity.

He died a happy man. Only a few days before, his son Richard had shown him a skull found on his latest expedition east of Lake Rudolf which seemed to bear out all Louis's favourite theories on human evolution. It more than fulfilled his expectations: it was the oldest, the biggest, the greatest. . . . Here was the large-brained ancestor which Louis had been expecting for at least forty years, ever since he himself had found a certain contentious jaw which had blighted his budding scientific career. He was not the sort of person who would have said *nunc dimittis*, but if ever there was a reason for saying so this was it.

Complete dedication to a cause must involve sacrifice, but it also brings results; Louis would certainly not have thought the cost too great. He expected his family to endure as much as he did in the cause of science, hence the failure of his first marriage and the success of his second. In Mary he found not only an outstanding scientist but also a remarkable complement to his own character and a restraining influence on his impetuosity. Louis led the kind of life he loved, in the country he loved, and his wife and sons became as committed to Africa and the wide open spaces as he was himself. He solved to his own satisfaction the questions he set out to answer regarding the origins of man, and he inspired many others to ask more questions. One of these was Richard Leakey, whose involvement with prehistory led directly to international expeditions which have opened the door to the distant past even wider than Louis would have dreamt possible. If the most that a man can hope to achieve is to increase the sum of human knowledge, then Louis achieved it in full measure.

2 Initiation

When the Rev. Harry Leakey landed on African soil for the first time in January 1902, he settled the destiny of his son Louis who had not yet been conceived. Leakey was thirty-four and had just been accepted by the Church Missionary Society to take up a post in the heart of Kikuyu District in Kenya, which at that time was part of the East Africa Protectorate. Two and a half years before his arrival the railway, that backbone of the country, had been completed as far as Kikuyu Station, nine miles west of the brash shanty town of canvas and corrugated iron which was Nairobi. He was therefore able to travel by rail to within six miles of his future home at Lower Kabete, and the three-hundred mile journey from Mombasa up the steep gradient to the highlands took only about twice as long as it does today. Before the building of the railway an earth road had been constructed all the way from the coast to Lake Victoria, but it was suitable only for bicycles or bullock wagons; it was the *only* up-country road in the whole Protectorate. The line of this historic Sclater's Road, which runs within a few miles of the mission station at Lower Kabete, is followed by its tarmac successor to this day.

From Kikuyu Station Harry proceeded for six miles by footpath up and down the steep slopes. The Kikuyu villages were hidden in the bush to escape the attention of Masai warriors; but as Harry approached them he was inspected closely by his future parishioners, whose greetings and comments he could not understand. When at last he arrived at the house he was to occupy he must have got a shock. It had been hastily run up by the incumbent, Mr MacGregor, a bachelor who had been there for less than a year and was about to move on to open up a new mission station. Although it was slightly better than the Kikuyu huts in having several rooms and being smoke-free, in one important respect it was far worse: the thatch roof leaked like a sieve. The Kikuyu builders were expert at making a round hut waterproof but they had no idea how to cope with a rectangular house – nor had Mr MacGregor. This was the home to which Harry was proposing to bring his wife and two baby daughters, who were to sail from England and join him as soon as he was established.

'At least', he wrote in his first letter to the CMS, 'I found the Natives excessively friendly; much credit is due to Mr MacGregor for the way he had won their regard and esteem.'[1] Thereafter the 'annual' letters which he was supposed to write to the CMS were few and far between; Harry Leakey was no writer, and in any case he was far too busy.

He had wanted to be a missionary for some years, but as the youngest of four brothers and three sisters he had been unable to leave his widowed mother; and he had also been forced to earn enough by teaching to pay back the loans which had enabled him to go to Peterhouse, Cambridge, from 1888 until 1891. The family came originally from Devon, but Harry's father, James Shirley Leakey, was a founder partner in a firm of solicitors, Leakey, Chapman and Clarke of Lincoln's Inn Fields, which formed a branch in Paris and thereafter James lived in France. After contracting tuberculosis in Paris he moved to Le Havre where the work was less arduous, and just before his death he acted as a civil umpire in the treaty following the end of the Franco-Prussian war. His youngest son Harry was born on 11 March 1868 at 73 Grande Rue d'Ingouville, Le Havre, and James died when the child was only three years old. His widow, Emma Elizabeth Payne Leakey, was left very badly off – one of her daughters said that in the interests of economy they were instructed to rub soap only on the front of their hands. Harry's mother ran a school at Le Havre, and later at Brighton, to help to support her large family. The boys were educated at first in France, and in 1876 Harry went to school in England. By the time he was sixteen he was earning his board and ten pounds a year by teaching French at Reading Grammar School.

Also living in Reading at the time were some friends of the family called Bazett. Of Huguenot extraction, they had fled from persecution in 1695 and went to St Helena in the service of the

British East India Company, moving to England in 1789. Colonel Bazett had retired to Reading after serving in the Indian Army. His wife, who came from South Africa, had married when she was fifteen and produced thirteen children; among them was Harry's future wife Mary, whom he had known since he was about twelve. She was about a year older than Harry and, like him, had a call to become a missionary. They had already fallen in love when at the age of twenty-one Mary, as well as two of her sisters, wanted to respond to an appeal from Bishop Parker in Mombasa for three unmarried women to go out and help in the work there. However, Colonel Bazett insisted that they were too young and they had to wait for another five years before they could embark for East Africa.

The first missions to be established there were the Church of Scotland, followed by the Church Missionary Society and then the Catholic White Fathers, all in the Kiambu District of Kikuyuland. Of the CMS missionaries the first to penetrate the country were two Germans, Ludwig Krapf and Johann Rebmann, who established a station at Rabai, near Mombasa, as early as 1845. They are remembered for being the first Europeans to set eyes on the snows of Kilimanjaro and Mount Kenya, and they also performed a valuable service by compiling a Swahili dictionary.

Thirty years after Krapf and Rebmann landed at Mombasa, Stanley's famous appeal in the *Daily Telegraph* urged the Churches to send missionaries to Uganda. He despatched this letter by a young Belgian who was murdered on his way up the Nile, and a punitive expedition found it tucked away in the dead man's boot. It was forwarded to General Gordon at Khartoum and from there it ultimately reached London. As a result of its publication £24,000 was subscribed by the public, and a year later the first ill-fated missionary expedition was on its way to Lake Victoria. In October 1885 the world was horrified to learn of the murder of Bishop Hannington, whose last words to his spearmen were 'Go tell Mwanga I have purchased the road to Uganda with my blood.' He purchased far more than the road with his blood, for his death, and the danger in which his fellow missionaries found themselves, led to the establishment of a British Protectorate over the country in 1894. In the meantime more than two hundred Christians were martyred, twenty-two of whom were canonized by the Pope at Kampala in 1964.

Perhaps it is not surprising that Colonel Bazett was not keen on allowing his daughters to go to East Africa, even though Mombasa was a very different proposition to Kampala. However, the girls never wavered in their determination and after their father's death in 1889 they achieved their goal. In spite of Mary's attachment to Harry, she and her elder sister Louisa ('Lou') and younger sister Sibella ('Sibbie') were prepared for their mission at the CMS training college in London. They eventually arrived at Mombasa on 24 November 1892 when Mary was twenty-six. For three years she worked among the Moslem women of Mombasa – it is hard to believe there were many converts – while her sisters ministered to the children of freed slaves. Mary also started a boys' school, later to be called the Buxton High School.

In 1898 another former Miss Bazett, Ellen ('Nellie'), set forth on an even greater adventure than her sisters. She had married the Rev. Cyril Gordon, a relative of Bishop Hannington and a member of the Bishop's 1882 expedition. After Hannington's murder Cyril was summoned by the infamous King Mwanga and for some time he was the only CMS missionary in Uganda. Nellie accompanied her husband there, travelling by rail for the first two hundred miles and then for the next five hundred miles in a hammock – a means of travel which she preferred to the only alternatives, a donkey or a bicycle. Louis liked to embroider this story, making out that she walked the whole way in her bloomers, scaring off lions by means of an alarm clock and defending herself with an umbrella. Whatever her methods of defence against lions and other hazards, they were evidently effective. This indomitable lady lived to the ripe old age of ninety-three.

After three years in Mombasa Mary's health broke down and she was forced to return to England, where she was told by her doctor that she must never go back to the steamy heat of the East African coast. Harry in the meantime had worked off his debts by teaching, specializing in preparing boys for public schools and for the Royal Navy. He then went to a theological college, was ordained in 1899, and became curate at St James's Church at Hatcham in south-east London. At last he and Mary were able to get married. Soon after, Harry's mother died and he and his bride offered themselves again to the Church Missionary Society.

When Mary returned to East Africa to rejoin her husband two years after her marriage, four months after his arrival there, it was not to the humid heat she had known at the coast but to a leaking house with mud floors at an altitude of 6,000 feet. She arrived in April, the rainy season, accompanied by her small daughters Julia and Gladys and by Miss Oakes, a 'lady nurse'. The paths to the mission station were awash and the ladies and children were carried in hammocks by Harry's Kikuyu neighbours. Many years later the East African Women's League commissioned a series of tapestries depicting the early history of various districts; one of these commemorates the arrival of the Leakey family at the stream below the mission and shows porters wading across with a curtained hammock.

In June, Mr MacGregor went off to prospect for a site for a mission station near Fort Hall, and Harry Leakey was left on his own. His most immediate problem was to patch up the house; his other main difficulty was the language. Most Kikuyu living around Kabete knew a little Swahili and, as Harry wrote in his letter to the CMS, 'this little, which is grammatically atrocious and abominably pronounced, they insist upon airing; so that I find myself practically struggling with three languages, viz. good Kiswahili, which it is important to know to arrive at the formation of the native language; bad Kiswahili, which I hear spoken at every turn and which I am learning against my will; and Kikuyu, the language proper of the people.'[2]

'Bad' Swahili, as every settler knows, is very easy; 'good' Swahili, as spoken at the coast, is fairly difficult; Kikuyu is extremely difficult. No wonder, then, that when Harry Leakey had a severe nervous breakdown three years later the Bishop of Mombasa attributed it mainly to his hard work on the language, with the altitude and the atrocious accommodation as contributing factors. Harry did indeed work hard at Kikuyu and was ready to sit for the special CMS examination just before his breakdown; but, as was to be the case also with Louis when he took Kikuyu in his modern languages tripos at Cambridge, no one competent to examine him could be found.

Bishop Peel came to inspect the 'atrocious accommodation' himself[3] and was much disconcerted by the jiggers – burrowing insects which are particularly fond of laying their eggs between human toes. Difficulties in obtaining sanction to rebuild the house dragged on for over two years, and things only began to move after a cable was sent to CMS headquarters in London: 'Leakey's house urgent.' After that, a stone house with an iron roof was completed within a few months. The Bishop might have added financial worries to the causes of Harry's breakdown: he had had to spend £25 of his private money on house repairs, a sum which he could ill afford.

Meanwhile, the ladies busied themselves in the dispensary and Harry Leakey struggled to teach a class of forty boys in 'bad' Swahili. Within a year he had mastered enough Kikuyu to embark on what he described as aggressive evangelism, 'itinerating' (the official CMS term) on horseback. Mrs Leakey, on the rare occasions when she left the mission, continued to proceed by hammock. She was never much of a walker and took little part in the outdoor activities which her husband so much enjoyed, like keeping cows and chickens and a well-stocked vegetable garden. Mary was a good housekeeper and sang beautifully, and she always remained thoroughly English, preferring neat fields and hedgerows to the exuberant vegetation of the tropics. During the years when she worked in Mombasa she had passed her Swahili exams with flying colours, but she never mastered the Kikuyu language with any great proficiency. She taught Swahili in Harry's school, at first only to the men as the women were not allowed to come by their parents and husbands. Eventually a few girls were brave enough to turn up and she began to teach them also. When the Leakeys returned after their first home leave Mary started a small school for women and girls which expanded greatly in the years to come: she was, in fact, one of the two great pioneers of women's education in Kenya; the other was her sister Sibella.

Before the end of her first year at Kabete Mary was pregnant; and on 7 August 1903 Louis Seymour Bazett Leakey made a premature appearance. He was named after his Leakey uncle Louis (pronounced 'Lewis' in spite of the family's upbringing in France) and his Bazett uncle Seymour. A Mrs Watson of the Church of Scotland Mission at Kikuyu, seven miles away, acted as midwife; the puny baby was immediately wrapped in cotton wool in lieu of an incubator, while his mother had to endure the heat from a tin filled with charcoal under her bed.

Louis began life, as he ended it, as a VIP. He was the first white baby the Kikuyu had ever seen, and everyone within walking distance came to inspect the phenomenon. As soon as he was strong enough to lie in a basket on the verandah he was subjected to their gaze and their spit (the German missionary Rebmann called it 'the saliva of peace'). In his autobiography *White African* Louis insists that they sprinkled him liberally to ward off the evil eye, but I am assured by his sister Julia (Mrs Lawrence Barham) that their mother did her best to keep him out of range and a sponge was always at hand in case of accidents.

Harry's breakdown came the following year, and the family went with him on sick leave to England. They were accompanied by a Kikuyu boy named Stefano, one of the only two baptized so far by Harry. The object was for Stefano to help Harry with the Kikuyu language, and at the same time learn English himself so that he could assist in the missionary's intended work of translating the Bible into Kikuyu. Harry was rapped over the knuckles by the CMS for this typical example of Leakey unorthodoxy: he was told that it was completely against the Society's policy to introduce African converts to an alien way of life. In fact Harry took great care to see that Stefano was not spoilt by his experiences and the experiment proved a great success. Stefano was quick to master English and learnt the Bible almost by heart, so that by the time Harry was able to tackle the translation after his return from leave Stefano's services were invaluable. Harry eventually completed this monumental work; the family all subscribed to buy him a typewriter, and this historic machine is preserved by the Bishop of Nairobi as a museum piece. As for Stefano, he went from strength to strength, eventually becoming interpreter to the High Court in Nairobi.

By the time the family got back to Kabete, just before Christmas 1906, they found that the hut built by Mr MacGregor which had served as a church was a tumbled-down hovel; two of their most trusted helpers had decamped; and two others, who had been imported to carry on with the teaching, were in disgrace for unseemly behaviour.[4] Harry had completely recovered his health and he threw himself into the task of rebuilding, restoring order, and gathering his straying flock together. He had brought back with him from England materials with which to build a new church; and he had also brought with him a nephew, Gray Leakey, who was a skilled amateur builder. The original little corrugated iron church which they constructed is still used today as a parish hall, dwarfed by its new neighbour St Paul's, or as the Kikuyu call it, the 'Mother Church'. Built in memory of Canon Harry Leakey, the foundation stone of St Paul's was laid by his son-in-law Bishop Leonard Beecher in 1956. Not far away, on the site where the mission station once stood, is the Mary Leakey Girls' Secondary School, named after the woman who did so much for the primary education of girls.

Soon after his return from leave Harry wrote one of his spasmodic 'annual' letters to the CMS reporting most encouraging progress: he was beginning to baptize adults as well as boys, and his wife had collected a dozen girls for tuition. It was slow work, but at last the dividends were beginning to come in.

By now the Leakey children were completely bilingual, and this thorough knowledge of the Kikuyu language was to be invaluable to Louis in later years. The children also learnt French from their father. He insisted that they should speak it at meals, allowing English only on Sundays; but the conversation was rather one-sided, especially as Mary spoke French with difficulty, and the rule was often broken.

The last member of the family, Douglas, was born in 1907. A Kikuyu nurse was engaged to look after him, and she used to tell the children African folk tales which Louis remembered all his life and told to his own sons in due course. The Leakeys seldom went away from home – they were too busy – and on the few occasions when they had a holiday in some house lent by other missionaries or by cousins the children were always happy to get back to the familiar surroundings of Kabete. Expeditions to Nairobi, however, were always an adventure and these they thoroughly enjoyed. When they were small they travelled by rickshaw with their mother, while Harry rode behind them on a horse; later the rickshaw was replaced by a pony trap, and eventually the children graduated to bicycles. Gladys (Mrs Leonard Beecher) remembers how she and Julia sat on either side of their mother in the rickshaw, while Douglas lay on Mary's lap and Louis perched on a footstool at her feet. One man ran between the shafts, five or six others pushed from behind, singing as they ran, and a fresh relay took over half way. The first call was generally to the house of 'Uncle George' and 'Aunt Sibbie', near where the Norfolk Hotel and the University buildings now stand; Sibella had married the Rev. George Burns and they had transferred to Nairobi from the coast in 1906. As a special treat the children were sometimes taken to the Commonage, now part of the Nairobi National Park; it was mainly here that Louis developed his abiding interest in wildlife.

On Boxing Day 1910 the family went to England for their second leave. Missionaries were normally given a year at home after a spell of four years abroad, but only six weeks in the beginning and six weeks at the end were holidays; the rest of the time was spent on 'deputation' work, giving the supporting churches an account of how their money was being used. As it turned out, the Leakeys stayed in England for two years because the CMS was short of funds and could not afford their passage back to Kenya. Under such circumstances missionaries were encouraged to get a temporary job so that the Society should not have to pay them an allowance, and Harry returned to his old work of teaching.

They arrived at Mary's old home in Reading on a Friday, and on Monday morning Louis was plunged into his first school. But he did not stay there long. With some money that Mary had inherited Harry bought a house at Boscombe, near Bournemouth, so that the family should have a home to go to on their leaves. Some friends living near by started up a prep school, Gorse Cliff, and invited Harry to help with the teaching. Louis and three other boys were the first pupils, and by the time the school expanded he had grown used to mixing with others, so the experience was not too alarming. Louis was now seven and up till then his only playmates had been his sisters and Kikuyu boys.

After the Leakeys returned to Kabete early in 1913 the children's education was put in the hands of a series of governesses. In spite of the distraction of birds and chameleons, which they could see from their schoolroom on the verandah, the children were made to work very hard. The fifth governess, Miss Broome, was their favourite as she was a keen naturalist and was young enough to enjoy taking part in birds' nesting and butterfly collecting. The rich red soil around Kabete is well watered by a network of rivers; most of it was under cultivation, with patches of maize, beans, sweet potatoes and bananas (nowadays there is a profusion of coffee bushes). But there were also strips of forest along some of the streams, and the children's nature walks were assisted by a pointer named Dan who rounded up duikers, bushbuck and other animals for their inspection. Their favourite excursion was to some waterfalls, reached by crossing the Gitengeti stream on slippery stones, and it was here that Louis was to make his first archaeological excavation.

Harry Leakey took a great interest in natural history, inherited no doubt from his father, James, who was a life member of the Zoological Society of London and who had also published a book on birds which gained him and his seven children free entry to the Paris Zoo. As a young man Harry had been tutor to the sons of English landowners, on whose estates he became a good shot and horseman, as well as cultivating his interests in birds and beasts. He built an aviary at Kabete and the family always kept innumerable pets – monkeys, bush-babies, tree hyraxes, serval cats, genets, and various kinds of buck.

There is no doubt that Louis was profoundly influenced by his father, that kindly man whom the Kikuyu affectionately called 'Giteru' – big beard. Most of Louis's tastes and interests came from Harry and in many ways they were alike in character. For example, both were devoted to children and in teaching them nothing was too much trouble. Louis's daughter Priscilla remembers her grandfather giving her a practical scientific demonstration when she was only four years old: having failed to convince her that a stream which disappeared beneath a road emerged on the other side, he plunged into the water and crawled through the culvert.

Harry was always in a hurry and the days were never long enough to get through half the things he wanted to do. Among his many activities he found time to teach the Kikuyu boys carpentry, so of course Louis joined the class and, like his father, became a good handyman. In due course Louis built himself a succession of huts, each more ambitious than the last, until by the time he was fourteen he had made himself a real mud-and-wattle house with two rooms. In one room he housed his natural history collections and the other was his bedroom: although his parents kept a firm hand on him they did not restrict his independence, and sometimes he was allowed to sleep in his hut and cook for himself.

Louis spent nearly all his leisure time with Kikuyu contemporaries, learning their games and organizing them into a barefoot football team. Kikuyu children mature more quickly than Europeans because from an early age they are given more responsibility: small boys herd the goats, while their sisters help their mothers in the fields and look after younger brothers and sisters. There is always work to be done and nobody has the time to entertain children; but by seven in the evening it is dark all the year round, and then the boys and girls listen to the conversation of their elders as they sit round the fire. Through his contemporaries Louis learnt the wisdom of the elders and gained unique knowledge – for a white man – of Kikuyu customs and lore. When he was thirteen he took part in some of the initiation ceremonies and, although he did not go through the full ritual – which included circumcision – his friends agreed that he should be considered a member of their age group, the Mukanda. He was thus adopted into the Kikuyu tribe as a junior warrior and was always proud to call himself a 'white Kikuyu'.

Several members of the Mukanda age group still live in the Kabete area and remember well the barefoot football team captained by Louis. There are even some who claim to have held Louis in their arms when he was a baby. One such is Solomon Ng'ethe, who says he is ninety; exceptionally tall for a Kikuyu, though now slightly bent, he still works hard in his fields. He was the third convert to be baptized by Harry Leakey and helped to build the original church at Kabete. Close by lives Chief Josiah Njonjo, a wealthy landowner, good-looking and vigorous, who claims to have been born in 1885. He speaks of Harry Leakey with great affection: 'Light of the Kikuyu, we call him,' he said, adding, 'the Leakey family are like our brothers.' Judging by the excitement and pleasure with which the Kabete people greeted Gladys Beecher when she took me to visit them, there is no doubt that they look on her as a sister. Another neighbour is Ernest Bacha, a schoolteacher who also runs the local coffee co-operative, and a member of the Mukanda age group. He used to play in Louis's football team, as did Bishop Obadiah Kariuki, first Bishop of Mount Kenya, who consecrated the new church of St Paul's at Lower Kabete in 1961. Many of these contemporaries of Louis, as well as older men, remained his friends all his life. One member of the Mukanda age group, Heselon* Mukiri, became a scientific colleague as well as a friend and shared in many of Louis's most important discoveries.

Louis's favourite occupation as a boy was hunting and trapping birds and small animals. His teacher, Joshua, was a man whom Louis suspected of having 'Ndorobo blood, although this is denied by Chief Josiah Njonjo. The 'Ndorobo, of whom few now survive, were indigenous hunters and food-gatherers when the Kikuyu arrived in the country about four centuries ago; the Kikuyu themselves, who were agriculturalists and stock-keepers, rarely took any interest in hunting. Joshua taught Louis the habits, calls and tracks of every creature in the neighbourhood: duiker, dikdik, mongoose, genet, porcupine, antbear, jackal and hyena. Through Joshua Louis learnt two essentials which contributed to much of his subsequent success as a fossil hunter – observation and patience. Writing in the *National Geographic* after he became a celebrity he said: 'My Kikuyu training taught me this: if you have reason to believe that something should be in a given spot but you don't find it, you must not conclude that it isn't there. Rather, you must conclude that your powers of observation are faulty.'[5]

Like many hunters who turn conservationist, Louis freely

*Louis invariably spelled the name 'Heselon'; but 'l' and 'r' are interchangeable in Kikuyu and other Bantu languages, and Heselon himself used to sign his letters 'Hezoron'.

admitted that as a boy he had a passion for hunting and that the biggest thrill of his life was when he eventually managed to stalk and capture a duiker in his bare hands. With the money he made from selling skins he paid for the materials and labour used in building his house: wages were then only about six shillings a month. He got his friends to help, so labour was not a very large item, but poles were rather expensive at about a shilling each. He also earned small sums now and again by trapping animals and birds for zoos, something of which he disapproved strongly in later life. At this time he also experimented with beekeeping under the instruction of a renowned local professional well versed in the elaborate Kikuyu etiquette and ceremony involved in this art.

Apart from his father and the few Europeans he had met during his brief schooling in England as a child, Louis had never known the influence and friendship of an older man of his own race; but now, when he was in his teens, one appeared on the scene who did much to shape his future career. Arthur Loveridge arrived in Nairobi in 1915 from the National Museum of Wales to act as the first paid curator of the small museum run by the East Africa and Uganda Natural History Society. In that very year it is recorded that 'the Committee beg to tender their thanks to Master Lewis [*sic*] Leakey for his kindness in presenting the Nairobi Museum with the specimens enumerated below.' These included three snakes, a live horseshoe bat, a porcupine, a melanistic genet cat, and various birds. Loveridge, who became the world's leading expert on African snakes and eventually Professor of Herpetology at Harvard University, was a knowledgeable ornithologist who channelled Louis's enthusiasm for trapping birds into classifying them scientifically. For the rest of his life Louis retained this interest, and thought seriously about becoming an ornithologist until quite suddenly he developed an entirely new interest.

An aunt in England had sent Louis a simple book on the stone age of Britain, and he immediately began scouring the country for 'flints', which in fact did not exist in Kenya. The local equivalent was obsidian, a black volcanic glass with a homogenous composition like flint and equally suitable for tool-making. Louis soon collected a mass of flakes made of this rock; he was under the impression that it was flint, and it says much for his powers of observation that he recognized human flaking in artifacts so different from the ones illustrated in the book. Diffidently he showed his collection to Arthur Loveridge, who not only enlightened him about flint but, to his immense delight, told him that among the flakes there were some actual tools. From that moment Louis became addicted to prehistory. Loveridge produced other books on the subject from the small library which he kept in his office at the museum, and Louis read avidly. Soon the shelves in his hut were overflowing with what the Kikuyu called 'spirits' razors'. Obsidian could be flaked to produce an edge sharp enough to be used as a razor – Louis tried this out as soon as he was able to grow a beard – and the Kikuyu believed that storm spirits hurled them from the sky. This was reasonable, since obsidian artifacts are noticeable after a rainstorm, when they are washed out of deposits on to the surface. Less romantically, Louis's family referred to his pieces as his 'broken bottles'.

All these occupations which were to mould his career – natural history and prehistory, as well as the study of Kikuyu customs – were made possible as a result of the First World War which, paradoxically, was one of the earliest manifestations of Leakey's luck. The war prevented him from going to school in England and, mainly because of the danger of floating mines, the family remained in Kenya until 1919, when Louis was sixteen. 'Otherwise,' he wrote in *White African*, 'I would have become a typical product of the public school system.'[6] Probably the statement is not strictly true: it would have been an exceptional school that could have shaped him into any semblance of orthodoxy.

To the family's great sorrow, their governess Miss Broome left to nurse the wounded from the campaign in German East Africa, and Arthur Loveridge also joined the forces. Louis did his bit of war work from 1917 onwards by helping to recruit Kikuyu volunteers for the Volunteer Carrier Corps, which was organized mainly by missionaries to take the place of the conscripted Carrier Corps of the early years of the war. Miss Broome had given the Leakey children a good groundwork in several subjects, particularly Latin and mathematics, but above all she inspired them with the wish to learn. After her departure in 1916 they taught themselves, supervised by their father when he could spare the time; Louis also helped Harry in the boys' school, thus gaining useful experience in handling a class.

Harry Leakey, who was made a canon in 1916, needed all the help he could get. His congregation was increasing fast and the church was now filled with young people. A few old women came too, but most of the men were permanently drunk on *pombe*, a local concoction made from sugar cane. Julia and Gladys gave stalwart support in the girls' school, for Mary Leakey was often seriously ill. She was forty when her last child, Douglas, was born, and her health began to deteriorate soon afterwards. Then for years she was prostrated by appalling haemorrhages associated with the menopause, and was nursed devotedly by Julia.

After seven years without leave, in 1919 the Leakeys were at last able to return to their house at Boscombe. The following January Louis entered Weymouth College, Dorset, and began the most traumatic experience of his life. He had always enjoyed a good deal of freedom; he had been the leader of a group of Kikuyu youths; and his best friend, the same age as himself, was already engaged to be married. Louis felt completely adult and the boys at Weymouth seemed utterly childish; no doubt when he boasted of his experiences it did not go down too well, and they soon set about reducing this uncouth white African to size. They promptly locked him in a coal hole and generally made his life a misery. Worst of all, he was made to fag for a boy who, in Louis's words, 'in both years and experience' was younger than himself. The rules at Weymouth seemed quite incomprehensible: he had to get a pass for shopping, when he was used to roaming where he liked in the African bush; and he had to go to bed at a definite time, after having done as he pleased in his own house.

Louis must indeed have seemed strange to his fellow pupils. His sister Gladys tells how one of their aunts in England met a boy from Weymouth and asked if he knew her nephew: 'Oh', was the reply, 'you mean that chap who walks with his feet in front of him.' Anyone who knew Louis will recognize this very apt if somewhat puzzling description, and I was amused to find the explanation for this characteristic walk on re-reading his book *Kenya: Contrasts and Problems* (1937): 'One of the curious things about Africans is that they walk in such a way that each foot is placed almost exactly in front of the other instead of slightly to one side. As a natural consequence, African footpaths are very narrow indeed and many Europeans find them difficult to walk along in comfort.'[7] I had always assumed that the walk was adapted to the width of the paths but, as a physical anthropologist, Louis should surely have known his anatomical facts. Did he himself learn to adjust his walk to the width of the footpaths round Kabete, or did he imitate the stride of his Kikuyu friends?

The barefoot team at Kabete had certainly not prepared him for the refinements of rugby football, and nobody at Weymouth bothered to enlighten him on the rules. However, he mastered them and came to enjoy the game very much. Cricket was a different story, and he never lost his hatred of it; it was, he said contemptuously, fit only for a 'typical Englishman'[8] and obviously was quite unsuited to his quick temperament. The abilities he had, such as tracking animals or building huts, were completely useless in such a place as Weymouth. 'I often used to wonder why I fitted in so badly,' he wrote, 'why I made so few friends, why I was so unpopular. . . . I was not understood as an individual, and so I was not happy.'[9] Alas, poor Louis! If ever anyone wanted to be admired, loved and treated as an individual it was he. Another story told by his sister Gladys illustrates this. Louis was not a natural athlete, but everything he attempted had to be done with every ounce of his energy: after a race at Weymouth he collapsed and, on opening his eyes, the first thing he said to his father, who was watching, was 'I did win, didn't I?'

Because of his advanced years – sixteen and a half – and the fact that his father and Miss Broome had grounded him so well in Latin, French and maths, he was put into the fifth form. There he had to contend with Greek, of which he knew nothing at all, and the situation in English was almost as desperate: his master simply could not believe that he really had no idea what it meant to write an essay. Also, some of the subjects set were completely out of his ken, for example 'A visit to the theatre' – Louis had never been to one.

Somehow the two years passed. This unhappy period at least toughened his character and, if it did not stamp out his bumptiousness, it may have sobered him a little and taught him that, to a certain extent at least, it was necessary to conform. Louis worked hard, for he was determined to get into Cambridge. He was not in the least interested in academic knowledge, but he was shrewd enough to realize that if he were to confound the scientific world with his discoveries, as he fully intended to do, he would have to get a degree in order to be taken seriously.

The trouble was that his total resources amounted to £60 and he was too old to sit for a scholarship. At his father's old College, Peterhouse, he was told that his financial situation made acceptance out of the question. Luckily he also had a letter of introduction to Ernest Benians of St John's, later Master of that College, who must have recognized Louis's exceptional qualities. Benians gave him every encouragement, then and throughout his subsequent career at Cambridge.

Apart from the question of money, there was another problem. Louis could take anthropology only as the second part of a tripos, and something else had to be found for Part 1. Because of his knowledge of French, modern languages seemed a possibility; but two languages were needed. To Benians's utter horror, Louis proposed Kikuyu as the second. According to a newspaper report some thirty years later, the Cambridge authorities tried to exclude Kikuyu on the grounds that it was not a written language and had no literature, but had to give way when Louis protested that the Bible had been translated into Kikuyu by his father.[10] In any event, the University could not get round the fact that it was a modern language, spoken by a large number of people, and by their own rules (which were subsequently changed) they were forced to accept it.

A loophole was also found in the matter of a grant: although ineligible for a scholarship, Louis could sit for a 'sizarship', which in effect is a mini-scholarship. Four subjects were required for the examination, or alternatively three plus a certificate of 'competent knowledge'. Louis had no difficulty in producing a certificate testifying to his competence in Kikuyu; one of his sponsors was Dr J. W. Arthur, head of the Church of Scotland Mission at

Kikuyu, and for the other who better than a Kikuyu chief? The document, signed with the thumbprint of Senior Chief Koinange, became a legend which is remembered in Cambridge to this day. At the same time Louis had the foresight to put his own name down as being competent in Kikuyu at the School of Oriental Studies (now the School of Oriental and African Studies) of London University, thus ensuring that there was at least one qualified examiner in that language in Britain. He began his Cambridge career, as he was to continue it, with flamboyance.

In the summer of 1922 he passed the sizarship exam with flying colours and was awarded the princely sum of £40 which, together with the £60 his father had been able to scratch together, was just enough to see him through. In October he went up to St John's, which was to be his home and anchor for many years.

The purgatory of Weymouth was soon forgotten in the joy of having his own rooms. They contained only the bare essentials, notably a large table piled with books, papers and natural history specimens, and rows of shelves to hold his 'broken bottles' and other treasures; but the freedom was what mattered, and he was able to cook for himself to eke out his meagre resources.

Kikuyu, obviously, presented no problem, except in the matter of finding a tutor. W. A. Crabtree of St Catharine's came to the rescue; he knew no Kikuyu, but he was proficient in Luganda and at least knew the general grammatical form of Bantu languages. Louis proceeded to teach his tutor Kikuyu, paying him the normal supervision fee for the privilege. French literature was quite another matter, as Louis knew nothing about it and cared less. Probably the only benefit he got from this subject was a chance side-line: during his enforced study of medieval texts he became something of an expert on graphology. It was never good enough for Louis to be told something, he always had to prove it for himself; and so, when his French tutor said that certain emendations had been added later by another hand, Louis carefully studied the author's handwriting until he was satisfied of the truth or otherwise of the statement. Some twenty years later he was to put this knowledge to good use in helping the police with criminal investigations: another of Louis's characteristics was that he never forgot anything he learnt.

At the end of the first year he failed in French literature, and this put paid to any hope of a scholarship. However, his sizarship of £40 was renewed, and he also managed to get grants of £15 per term from the Towers Trust, a fund set up to help missionaries' sons who themselves hoped to become missionaries. Although by this time he knew that his career would be wedded in some way to prehistory, the grants were not obtained entirely under false pretences. He could have been a part-time archaeologist or palaeontologist, like his friend Archdeacon Owen who comes into this story later, or as many a French priest had been from Teilhard de Chardin down to the Abbé Breuil (who was far more prehistorian than priest). In *White African* Louis says that he did not give up all idea of being a missionary until the summer of 1925.[11] He could never have gone through with it – he was far too ambitious – but he always had a strong streak of militant zeal. At Cambridge Louis used to address prayer meetings and would burst into the rooms of acquaintances and launch into religious arguments. Earlier still he had preached from a soapbox in the streets of Boscombe.

Weymouth had not managed to tame Louis and Cambridge did not either. Throughout those formative years he remained brash and, as one of his contemporaries described him, 'very self-confident, very bright, not at all self-critical, and not particularly popular with his colleagues.' Another contemporary, a woman this time, says she first met him in 1923 'when he called, out of the blue, one night after dinner, on a sudden impulse we thought, as he was dishevelled and even untidier than usual. I was engulfed in a flood of excited talk about his projects in Kenya. I got the impression that, though likeable, he was overcharged and unbalanced, and unlikely to make good. This impression was not changed when, later on, he leapt on to a bicycle and tore about eighty miles in order to propose to . . . and presumably returned a disappointed man. She always claimed she hardly knew him.'

Louis was good looking, tall and lean, with high cheek bones and a long nose, and very dark eyes set rather too close together. His enthusiasm was infectious, but his unconventional ways did not go down too well in the 'twenties, and well brought up Cambridge bluestockings were apt to be alarmed by his impetuosity. Also, English girls were a completely new experience for him and he had no idea how to handle them. He was undoubtedly a show-off and one of the ways in which he could become the centre of attention was by performing conjuring tricks. He became a member of the Magic Circle and never enjoyed himself more than when he sawed a woman in half. At the Leakeys' house at Langata, near Nairobi, there are still relics of false bottoms and other props mouldering in trunks.

For relaxation Louis also enjoyed playing erratic tennis: he was the first ever to appear on the courts in shorts and was ordered off, being told that they were indecent. But his greatest sporting ambition, perhaps to compensate for his early humiliation on the field at Weymouth, was to be a rugby Blue. His chance came one day in October 1923 when he was playing for the College XV. The University captain was watching, and Louis put on the performance of his life. Probably as a result of doing something foolish, he was kicked on the head; and after a few minutes unwisely returned to the field only to receive a second kick. That evening he tried to work and had a very bad headache, and the next morning it was worse. He was forced to see a doctor, who ordered complete rest for ten days. When Louis got back to his books he found he was suffering from loss of memory, and this time the doctor said he must spend a whole year away from Cambridge, preferably in the open air.

This was a severe blow to his ambition to obtain a degree as quickly as possible and launch into archaeological work in Kenya. But, as so often happened, Leakey's luck took over, and the enforced sabbatical proved to be a most valuable experience which turned his attention from stones to fossil bones. He spent the next eight months digging for dinosaurs in Tanganyika.

Louis's first thought was that, in spite of his lack of academic training, he might be able to start right away on archaeological explorations; but he was told that it would be quite out of the question to obtain a grant. He discussed his problem with Mr

C. W. Hobley, a distinguished administrative officer who took a keen interest in prehistory and had found many stone tools during his tours round Kenya. Hobley told Louis that the British Museum (Natural History) was looking for someone with experience of Africa to go on a fossil-hunting expedition to south-eastern Tanganyika. Before the 1914 war a German expedition had found remains of many gigantic reptiles dating from the late Jurassic and early Cretaceous periods at a remote spot named Tendaguru Hill. Sir Arthur Smith Woodward, Keeper of Geology at the Natural History Museum in London, had persuaded the trustees to launch a British expedition to this place under the leadership of Dr William Edmund Cutler, who was famed for his dinosaur collections in Canada. Some of his finds can be seen in the Natural History Museum, including an armoured dinosaur with a cast of the skin preserved which is one of the star exhibits of the fossil reptile gallery today. Cutler, a Canadian, had never been to Africa and needed someone with a knowledge of the local people and their languages.

Louis applied for the job, and in January 1924 he was accepted. His duties were to deal with the labour force, to whom he would be able to speak in Swahili, and to collect small mammals and birds for the Museum, for which he was well qualified after his youthful experiences at Kabete. He was to be paid a salary of £7 a month and was granted an outfit allowance of £25.

Cutler and Louis sailed on the last day of February and, as representatives of the British Museum, they travelled first class – certainly the first and probably the last time Louis had such an experience. He stopped off at Mombasa and paid a short visit to his parents before rejoining Cutler in Dar es Salaam. Owing to a dock strike in London much of their equipment had been held up, so Cutler decided to wait until it arrived and sent Louis on ahead to find the site of the old German excavations and set up camp.

At the small port of Lindi, not far north of the Mozambique border, Louis engaged porters and, by an incredible stroke of luck, found a headman from the Tendaguru district about to return home. They set off together, at first following a path but later having to thrash their way through thick elephant grass and thorn-bushes. Tendaguru Hill is some 56 miles inland from Lindi, unmarked on any map, and if it had not been for his guide it would have taken Louis a long time to find the old German camp. This they did on the third day of the march, and Louis proceeded to get his men to clear the high grass, make a track, build houses and organize food supplies – one shilling for a hundred eggs or for a hundred and fifty bananas. Louis was in a high state of excitement to be back in the bush and to have so much responsibility.

Nearly two months went by before Cutler was ready to join him. In the meantime he gave instructions in a letter: 'You will be sure to write me a full and lucid classified description of how roads, camps, stores, hindrances, floods, men, porters, game and fevers are developing. . . . Best of luck to you and believe that I feel a bit shabby at leaving you so long. If, however, you can make out, you will be proving yourself of real value and mettle.' While Cutler was lingering to investigate fossils in the hinterland of Dar es Salaam, Louis constructed a road through to Lindi. This was very necessary because, apart from anything else, no less than 2,600 lbs of plaster of Paris had to be transported to deal with the dinosaur bones they hoped to find. When it was time to meet Cutler at Lindi Louis was justifiably proud of what had been accomplished.

Cutler was a rather sour character aged forty-six; Louis was twenty, brimming with confidence, holding forth about the fauna and flora, chattering with the natives, picking up artifacts along the road. ('I think them chipped by the heat of grass fires,' noted Cutler sceptically.) Cutler was forced to lean heavily on his young assistant, and it was hardly surprising that he resented it. Reading between the lines in his diary it is clear that the more Louis laid himself out to be helpful the more Cutler withdrew into his shell. It was not a happy partnership, but fortunately all their energies were absorbed in their work.

The fossil sites were more than three miles from camp, and the whole area had to be cleared with billhooks, as the elephant grass was too wet to burn. In places where bones appeared on the surface, trenches were dug down to the main fossil level, which was usually at a depth of about eight feet. The trenches were up to fifty feet long and twenty-five feet wide, and during the season about fourteen of these monster excavations were completed. The bones were first exposed by picking round them carefully with small tools, and Cutler would then select the ones to be removed. Usually they were in a friable condition and had to be hardened with shellac before being coated with plaster of Paris.

Louis was fascinated by this operation and must have longed to try his hand, but Cutler made a mystique out of it and insisted on keeping a monopoly on this one task. Evidently he succeeded in impressing his pupil with its difficulty, for Louis wrote later in the *Illustrated London News*: 'Plastering was never done by anyone but Mr Cutler himself, as several years practical experience are needed to make a successful plasterer.'[12] In fact, although irreparable damage could be done to a delicate skull by an inexperienced person, the extraction of a hefty dinosaur bone could be done perfectly well after only a few hours' experience.

Tendaguru was famous for its remains of *Brachiosaurus*, which had been discovered by the German expedition and taken to Berlin. This was one of the biggest land animals that ever lived, and the ambition of the BM and of Cutler was to find a complete skeleton of this beast – or for that matter a whole skeleton of any of these huge reptiles dating from about 150 million years ago. In this they were disappointed, nor were complete skeletons ever likely to turn up at Tendaguru. The dinosaurs would have fed on lush vegetation beside the delta of a great river; as they wallowed in the mud their great weight would cause them to sink, and eventually their bloated carcases would be carried downstream to the Indian Ocean. As the bodies decomposed, first one limb would become detached then another, until finally the whole skeleton would fall to pieces and be scattered over a wide area. Obviously the heavier bones would be more likely to survive than the relatively fragile skulls, which at Tendaguru were extremely rare and always fragmentary.

Some of the bones which Cutler extracted were colossal, but he does not always seem to have been as conscientious as his previous high reputation would lead one to expect: in his diary he records that some of the best bones were extracted without the ends which, judging by the clean look of the fractures, must have been present[13] – a clear admission of lack of supervision.

However, allowance must be made for the fact that both Cutler and Louis were constantly suffering from malaria, dysentery and other tropical ailments. Tendaguru is only seven hundred feet above sea-level and extremely unhealthy; water was obtained from three foul pools several miles away from camp, and the expedition had only the most rudimentary medical supplies. Cutler's diary is full of comments such as 'Leakey very low with malaria, temperature 104°'; 'Leakey still has malarial symptoms and a temperature of 102°, but he superintended ditches 4, 5 and 6 all day'; and of himself he wrote 'Passing blood and vomiting.'[14] On one occasion a runner was despatched to obtain drugs and advice from the doctor at Lindi, and returned bearing 'a bottle of brandy, a hundred cigarettes, some tonic medicine and a bedpan.' The men also suffered, showing 'subnormal temperature, headache, bad stomach and aching bones', and Louis ran a daily clinic.

They were bothered by every kind of insect pest, especially mosquitoes, and also termites which undermined the buildings and ate the spare bedding and mosquito nets. The grass round the base of the hill was burned regularly to keep scorpions and snakes at bay, but they had many narrow escapes. Once Louis was nearly bitten by a deadly green mamba eight feet long, and Cutler only just avoided treading on a couple of puff adders. One day Louis brought back to camp a python nearly thirteen feet in length; he had stunned it, but it took several days to die. 'It is very active and vicious,' notes Cutler, 'and strikes although its back is broken. I pierced the basi-occiput with a pick point and it is quiet. I put two half hitches around its head and ditto round a tree, the blacks were horrified to see me handling it.' After three days the python at last expired and they had soup and chops: Cutler found it pleasant meat, though tough.

Cutler had a streak of cruelty towards animals – so unlike Louis, who was constantly collecting pets and was heartbroken when they died, as when his baby baboon was taken by a leopard. One particularly horrible incident reported in Cutler's diary must have caused Louis great distress: 'A man brought in a large hornbill and after hanging by the neck with 40 lbs of rock to its feet for forty minutes, it still lived. I then pierced it below the sternum and in the eye socket with no apparent harm and lastly I pierced its skull with a steel point; it then cried out and soon died.'[15]

Every morning they had roll call at 5.30 and the men stopped work at 2.30 p.m.; then, after a meal and a short rest, Cutler and Louis would go their separate ways. Cutler was an ardent butterfly collector and must have decimated the Lepidoptera population of Tendaguru: each day he recorded the running total of his catches, and three months after his arrival they amounted to no less than seven hundred specimens, of two hundred different species. Louis, with a local assistant, trapped a good many small mammals and birds for the Natural History Museum. Cutler was particularly interested in a giant shrew with a long snout, whose teeth were very like those of early Cretaceous mammals more than a hundred millions years old.

When the men were on short rations, which happened frequently, they would go hunting after the day's work was over. The labour force numbered more than fifty and Cutler would have liked to take on more, but he dared not because of the difficulty in obtaining food. At times the local people had nothing to sell and the situation in camp became desperate. On Sunday mornings Louis used to go hunting for the pot, often returning with nothing, or at the most a guinea fowl or a couple of pigeons. Game was very scarce, but the commonest antelopes were eland and the magnificent sable, both of which are now quite rare even in the national parks. When Louis managed to bag one of these noble animals there was great rejoicing, and another favourite item on the menu was warthog.

On 7 August 1924 Louis celebrated his twenty-first birthday. Perhaps 'celebrated' is not quite the right word, for it is unlikely that Cutler did anything about it. On his own birthday, however, he mentions in his diary that Louis presented him with a box of chocolates; they must have been obtained at Lindi and were no doubt stale, but the gesture is typical of Louis's thoughtfulness.

By the end of October Louis packed up, as he wanted to spend a little time with his parents before returning to Cambridge. On arrival at Lindi he discovered that the regular steamer to Dar es Salaam had boiler trouble and he had only twelve days to catch his boat to Mombasa. There was nothing for it but to walk the 269 miles, in a temperature of nearly 100°F. He engaged fourteen porters to carry his numerous loads, which included a monkey in

1. Louis first went to England as a two-year-old in 1905 when his father was on leave from Kenya. 2. *Below* Ten years later the family poses outside their mission station at Kabete in Kikuyuland. Canon Harry Leakey stands between his younger daughter Gladys and Louis; his wife Mary sits beside Douglas and Julia

Overleaf

3. *Inset* Louis was the first to appear in shorts on the tennis courts of Cambridge as an undergraduate in 1923 – and was ordered off for indecency. 4. A year later he was digging for dinosaurs at Tendaguru in Tanganyika; his studies had been interrupted as a result of concussion, but meanwhile he learnt valuable lessons in the art of extracting fossil bones

a large cage; but even so he had to leave some of the heavier boxes of bones and stones to be forwarded later. The march was arduous, but he reached Dar in good time.

Cutler meanwhile was missing his assistant. Part of Louis's job had been to construct at least thirty crates strong enough to bear the weight of the dinosaur bones in their encasing plaster and, as Cutler confesses in his diary, 'I was never any good at carpentry.' However, the only mention he makes of Louis's departure is to ask 'I wonder how the magnificent L.S.B.L. is faring? He is sure to be blowing his trumpet hard.'[16] From Cutler's correspondence with people at the Natural History Museum it is clear that he was extremely jealous of anyone stealing his thunder, and he tried hard to prevent Louis from writing or lecturing about his experiences at Tendaguru.

Louis, in fact, was given permission to write some articles, including the one for the *Illustrated London News* already mentioned, in which he pays tribute to Cutler's skill in plastering and modestly sums up his own tasks as 'the making and labelling of parcels'. As he often said later, he had learnt a great deal by watching Cutler's techniques, which were to be invaluable when he began to excavate fossils himself. He also obtained useful experience in running a camp and organizing a large labour force, as well as coping with a variety of the men's ailments. Otherwise Tendaguru was not a success. On the whole, the dinosaur remains were of no very great interest – to this day some of them have never been cleaned or even unpacked. Also, Cutler himself came to an unfortunate end.

After Louis left, Cutler engaged another young assistant whose main task was to make boxes. He was slow and inexperienced, and for a long time was out of action with a badly poisoned leg. Cutler was obviously exhausted by the heat and recurring fever; he began to lose all sense of proportion, sacking the men for supposed insolence and even firing the cook for making 'murderous bread'. He hung on for nearly a year and then, on 21 August 1925 he recorded in his diary: 'Owing to fever I stay in and only visit the ditches late. Upon returning home, feeling weak and horrible, found my temperature to be 104° so went to bed.' This was his last entry: as a consequence of repeated bouts of malaria and excessive doses of quinine, Cutler had blackwater fever. Nine days later he was dead.

After having skipped a whole academic year, Louis returned to Cambridge in January 1925 to be faced with the same old problems: lack of money, and his old enemy French literature. He tackled the first by lecturing and writing about his experiences at Tendaguru, but he was only allowed to keep half of the proceeds, the other half going towards the expedition's funds. Moreover, he had to obtain written permission from the British Museum for each article he wrote and for each lecture he gave.

His very first public lecture was delivered to an alarming audience of academics at the Guildhall in Cambridge; he had to borrow tails for the occasion and admits he was terrified. After the first slide went on, showing reconstructions of dinosaurs from the film of Conan Doyle's *Lost World*, his panic vanished and he began to feel the thrill of holding an audience. From the financial point of view the lecture was not exactly a success. Receipts amounted to just over £18, but by the time he had paid for the hire of the hall, printing, billposting and the services of one fireman (five shillings), there was a debit of 5/4d. However, the experience was valuable.

Louis then began to write to the better known public schools asking if they would like a lecture on 'Digging for Dinosaurs'. The response was encouraging, and he got a fee of six guineas per lecture plus expenses, with fifteen shillings extra if the film of the *Lost World* was thrown in. He hired the film from First National Pictures Ltd for the sum of 10/6 and he also had seventy lantern slides which he could show if the extra charge for the film was thought too exorbitant. His lecture bookings were helped greatly by a testimonial written, at Louis's request, by the president of the Natural History Society of Wellington College: 'Mr Leakey's lecture cannot fail to interest all boys whether they are interested in natural history or not. . . . After his lecture here I heard nothing but favourable criticism, and about 400 boys were delighted with it. Mr Leakey knows how to talk to boys.' Evidently Louis's power to hold the attention of a young audience goes back to the time when he was only a few years older than some of the boys himself.

In this modest way Louis began nearly half a century of public speaking. During the last few years of his life he could command a fee of $1,500 on the platforms of the United States; but in 1925 he was obviously not going to be able to support himself by lecturing or writing, and he had to think of other ways to make money. One source of income was a large collection of carved ebony walking sticks which he had brought back from Tendaguru; these he sold to a tailor, and the proceeds at least kept him in clothes.

In his penniless state the vacations were a problem, but fortunately he had a swarm of cousins with whom he sometimes stayed. The complications of the Leakey family were exceeded only by those of the Bazetts; and to make matters worse three Leakeys married Miss Bazetts, including not only Canon Harry Leakey of Kabete but also his first cousin once removed, Canon R. H. Leakey of the CMS in Uganda. Needless to say they were always getting each other's letters, and in conversation it did not help when people said 'I mean the Canon Leakey who married a Bazett.' In 1969 there was a grand reunion of the clan and nearly seventy of them appear in the photograph taken on that occasion. The cousins made a great difference to Louis, who missed his parents and sisters a great deal; they were a stimulating bunch, who widened his social contacts and intellectual horizons. One in particular, Mrs Lillian Ridge, tried to make a home for Louis and his brother Douglas while they were at Cambridge; she was a daughter of Harry Leakey's brother Arundell and sister of Gray, who had helped to build the church at Kabete. Before the Tendaguru expedition Louis had spent the summer with the Ridges at Portmadoc in North Wales, earning his keep by cooking. On other occasions he joined the cousins at seaside camps – they indulged in *mixed* bathing, which was considered most irregular for the children of clergy, as so many of them were. These camps were often in East Anglia, where Louis made the most of his time by studying prehistoric sites and learning the art of flint knapping from the professionals who made gun flints at Brandon.

Louis spent much of his time during the vacations working, and for Easter 1925 he went to Boulogne for coaching in French literature. There his headaches returned – ever since his kick on the rugby field he had felt the effects of concussion when he overworked – and he collapsed one day while out walking. However, the coaching was worth while, and in May he got a first in Part I of the tripos: French, including the hated literature, and of course Kikuyu. The authorities at Cambridge had written to the University of London asking for help in finding a suitable examiner in Kikuyu; the School of Oriental Studies consulted their files and produced the names of G. Gordon Dennis, a retired missionary, and L. S. B. Leakey! Inevitably this gave rise to the story, told with especial relish in Oxford, that Leakey had been his own examiner and – when the results came through – that he awarded himself a first; he became known as the 'senior wangler'. In fact by that time Louis's tutor-pupil W. A. Crabtree had learnt enough Kikuyu to be able to help prepare the examination papers.

As a result of his first St John's rewarded him with a scholarship, and the worst of his financial troubles were over. At last he could get down to anthropology and archaeology for Part II of the tripos. The reader in anthropology, Dr A. C. Haddon, FRS, was an inspiration to Louis and a loyal friend in the years to come, when he recommended him for many grants. He had been one of the three who had started the anthropological tripos at Cambridge, together with Sir William Ridgeway (a classical archaeologist) and Anatole von Hügel, founder and first curator of the Museum of Archaeology and Ethnology in Downing Street, which now houses many of Louis's finds. The succeeding curator was Louis C. G. Clarke, who on several occasions was to make generous personal contributions towards Louis's expeditions. Pioneering on the archaeological side as Secretary to the Board of Studies was Miles Burkitt, who was paid the handsome sum of £10 a year for arranging the course. Little osteology was taught in those days, although the practical work of one term was devoted to craniology; otherwise anthropology was concerned with material culture only. The complete course included the races of man, general ethnology and technology, social anthropology and primitive religions, with prehistoric archaeology as a somewhat incongruous side-line. Only about half a dozen students were doing the anthropological tripos, of whom Louis was undoubtedly the brightest.

Haddon therefore took a special interest in him, inviting him to

Sunday afternoon 'at homes' and lending him books from his private library. Haddon was often bluff to the point of rudeness – he loved to shock people with the less refined aspects of primitive tribes revealed by anthropological research; but inside he had the proverbial heart of gold, and would do anything to help those whom he thought worthy of encouragement. He taught Louis string figures, which were to become of absorbing interest to him later on and enabled him to break the ice with various tribes that he encountered on his wanderings through Africa. He also stimulated Louis into making his first contribution to ethnological knowledge. During one of Haddon's lectures on the classification of African bows and arrows, based on the work of a German ethnologist, Louis spotted errors concerning some areas that he knew personally. He therefore spent his Christmas vacation studying specimens in museums on the Continent with a view to making a new classification. He obtained a small grant from the College council towards his expenses, but he also had to sell his precious motor bicycle to pay for the trip. In the museum at Hamburg he found three thousand bows and arrows, all of which had to be sorted according to tribes and pinpointed on a map. Louis then went on to the Tervuren Museum at Brussels to see their marvellous collection from the Belgian Congo; and thence to Paris, but he was disappointed in what the Musée de l'Homme had to offer. The results of these labours were published in the *Journal of the Royal Anthropological Institute* in 1926, Louis's first scientific paper.[17]

His finals came up in the summer of 1926, the year of the general strike. He worked in a signal box on the Cambridge to Ely line, studying between trains; if there were any crashes as a result, history has not recorded them. With his tremendous interest in anthropology and archaeology it is not surprising that he got another first; but a double first in a tripos with such an unheard-of combination of subjects was a real achievement and is probably unique. If some had thought that Part I of the tripos had been a fiddle, they could hardly accuse him of this in Part II. St John's again rewarded their brilliant scholar, this time with a research fellowship. Normally this is held for three years only, but in Louis's case they made an exceptional concession in extending it for a further three years; by the time it elapsed he had launched his fourth archaeological expedition. During these six years Louis had a base at St John's, with room to house his ever-growing collections and facilities to work on them, and for the rest of his life he was grateful and devoted to his old College.

The results of the finals were indeed amazing for someone who had had very little schooling and who had missed a whole year as a result of concussion – and who still sometimes felt its effects. In addition, during the last few months before the finals Louis's mind was preoccupied in making plans for the archaeological expedition to Kenya that he was determined to make that summer, a project which had spurred him on ever since he came up to Cambridge. As usual he was penniless and he knew his chances of getting a grant were slim unless he got a first, so he had to curb his impatience and concentrate on his books. As a result of the first he obtained not only the research fellowship from St John's but also grants from the Percy Sladen Memorial Trust, the Royal Society, the Kenya Government, and Sir John Ramsden, a wealthy Kenya landowner: quite an achievement for a young man of twenty-three proposing to investigate the totally unknown.

3 Reconnaissance

When Louis embarked on his first archaeological expedition to Kenya in 1926 he was starting almost from scratch. That eminent geologist Professor J. W. Gregory, FRS, who was the first to make peaceful contacts with the Kikuyu, was also the first to recognize stone tools in Kenya, in 1893. Perhapse 'recognize' is hardly the right word, for he thought the flaked pieces of obsidian he found were gun flints, dropped along the caravan route by traders from Zanzibar. Later, however, he realized the significance of his finds. The man who really put the palaeolithic on the map of East Africa, E. J. Wayland, did not appear on the scene until 1919. His discoveries in Uganda, and above all his means of dating them, laid the foundations for Louis's research in Kenya.

Wayland came to Uganda as 'government geologist expert', but he lost no time in dropping the 'expert' from the official title. His appointment was for two years, and he stayed for nearly forty. As soon as he arrived he started pushing for the formation of a Geological Survey, which was duly established under the sympathetic reign of the Governor, Sir Robert Coryndon. As the newly appointed Director of this one-man team, Wayland set out on a reconnaissance of his territory. Within four months he had walked nine hundred miles, as well as travelling over three hundred miles by canoe. A publisher once asked him to write a book about his adventures, but Wayland replied 'I had none; only incompetent people have adventures.' As a mineral prospector in Ceylon, Wayland had recognized stone tools among the gravels; when he subsequently saw flaked pebbles in the Kafu valley of Uganda he therefore felt he was on familiar ground. He duly described the 'Kafuan', which was thought to be the earliest pebble culture in the world; it was not for another forty years that other geologists decided that the pebbles had been flaked by nature and not by man.

E.J., as he was always known to his friends, was solid and square-shaped, usually rather silent, occasionally garrulous in congenial company, invariably voluble in correspondence. He was always generous in sharing his knowledge with anyone who showed the slightest interest in his discoveries, and desperately wanted to persuade a prehistorian to tackle the work for which he had so little time and so few qualifications. After his marathon walk, Wayland wrote in his first annual report (1920): 'One may conclude that Uganda has been inhabited by people in various stages of savagery and civilization for a very lengthy period, indeed probably quite as long as Europe has.' This caused quite a sensation, for up till then practically nothing was known about prehistory anywhere in the continent outside South Africa.

Louis had followed Wayland's discoveries with the greatest interest and corresponded with him from Cambridge, but they did not meet until 1927, when Louis went to Entebbe to see Wayland's collections. Already Wayland had a great many stone tools of various cultures and ages, which at least gave Louis some idea of what he might expect to find in Kenya. (By the time Wayland left Uganda he had amassed some 30,000 artifacts, which he housed in a shed attached to the Geological Survey. After the Second World War the shed was needed, and 'old Wayland's stuff' was shoved in boxes, where the labels and catalogue were eaten by white ants. Louis was invited to take his pick of the tools, after which most of the rest were tipped over a cliff.)

As well as encouraging Louis to search for traces of early man, Wayland influenced his whole thinking in the matter of dating the finds. This was some twenty years before the development of radiometric dating techniques, and only two methods were available: by correlation of fossil fauna, if any; or by evidence of past changes of climate. As Wayland found little in the way of fossil fauna, he pinned his faith on a climatic framework. He became completely obsessed by the need to establish a sequence of pluvial and interpluvial periods, i.e., times of greater and lesser rainfall, which could be correlated with the glacials and interglacials of Europe.

His evidence was based mainly on traces of terraces high above the level of the present lakes, obviously left when the lakes were much deeper and – he thought – presumably as a result of higher rainfall during the Pleistocene. The ice ages must have profoundly affected the climate all over the world, and Wayland assumed that a pluvial in the tropics corresponded with a glacial in higher latitudes. He dated his finds on that basis, and until some independent means of dating could be found his theory could be neither proved nor disproved.

By the time Louis embarked on his first archaeological expedition he had been thoroughly indoctrinated by Wayland's published views on climatic changes and was determined to look for similar evidence in Kenya. In the years to come critics were to dispute many of these interpretations; but it was the Waylands and the Leakeys who set up all the coconuts for others to knock down, and in the meantime the coconuts served their purpose well enough.

The grants which Louis had managed to scrape together totalled £850, of which nearly half came from the Percy Sladen Memorial Trust. This trust was formed in memory of Walter Percy Sladen by his widow Constance in order to promote the scientific objects in which he was interested, particularly snakes and starfish – a far remove from prehistory. In fact, Mr Sladen would have been interested in Louis's work as he was distantly related to the Uganda branch of the Leakey family. The second largest grant, £200, came from the Royal Society. The grand total was just enough to finance Louis and one assistant, a student from Selwyn College, Cambridge, named Bernard H. Newsam. Newsam was taking a history tripos and after this trip to Kenya he proposed to do anthropology and prehistoric archaeology for Part II, just as Louis had done. (In fact, he went on to a theological college and was later ordained.)

In July 1926 the two young men sailed for Mombasa under the high-sounding title of the East African Archaeological Expedition. They spent the first month staying with Louis's parents at Kabete, where they dug a trench in a cave by the waterfall which Louis and his sisters had named 'Gibberish' when they were children. Louis recruited several members of his Kikuyu age-group to dig, including Heselon Mukiri, but the results were not very exciting – some bits of pottery and a few obsidian tools – so Louis left his brother Douglas to continue the excavations while he and Newsam proceeded up the Rift Valley to Nakuru.

This was long before Italian prisoners of war constructed the all-weather road which now hugs the eastern wall of the Rift. Below, on the floor of the valley, are lakes threaded like beads between volcanoes. There are steam jets and hot springs, and the soil is full of minerals which make it wonderful cattle country in spite of the frequent droughts which reduce it to a dust bowl. Nakuru, beside the lake of the same name which is always pink with flamingoes, is the former capital of the 'White Highlands'. A thriving market town, it is in marked contrast to most of the other townships which are still much the same as when Louis drove past them in 1926 – a hideous collection of *dukas* (shops) with corrugated iron roofs.

The immediate object of the East African Archaeological Expedition was the farm of Major J. A. MacDonald, just south of Nakuru. In 1923 he had written to the *East African Standard* describing stone bowls and other objects which he had found, and Louis had cabled begging him to stop digging until he could get there and make a 'detailed examination' himself. Rather surprisingly, the Major complied.

Louis and Newsam set up camp at the site, where they found a mass of rocks piled up against the face of a lava cliff. Within a fortnight they discovered some broken human bones among the rocks; and by the time they moved on, two months later, they had excavated parts of ten skeletons. Only one was complete, with knees tied up to the chin and covered with red ochre. The bones of nine others were scattered, and Louis speculated that these represented either wives or slaves, sacrificed when the main character was buried. This type of burial, the first of many to be found in later years, was associated with hundreds of stone tools and Louis named the culture 'Gumban B': the Gumba were a semi-legendary people who, according to the Kikuyu, were living in holes in the ground when they themselves arrived.

It was during these excavations that Louis scandalized the local settlers, not for the last time, by actually sharing in manual labour.

He and Newsam used to carry four-gallon cans of water along with the African staff – Louis would have enjoyed flouting convention, but on this occasion probably his only reason for doing so was to speed up the proceedings. He was anxious to get on, for he had another objective in mind. As a fifteen-year-old in 1918 he had attended a lecture given by Professor Gregory in Nairobi and, while he was talking to the great man afterwards, they were joined by a Mr W. S. Bromhead. He told Gregory about human remains he had found in a cave near Elmenteita, to the south of Nakuru, and ever since Louis had wanted to see 'Bromhead's site'. Now at last he was able to do so. He was the proud possessor of a T model Ford, which transported him along the dusty track to the farm of Mr A. Gamble, brother-in-law of the man who had owned the property where the skeletons were found. When Mr Gamble showed him the place Louis noticed another skull sticking out of the face of the cliff. Work was speeded up at Nakuru and in January 1927 he and Newsam moved camp.

Bromhead's site was close to the Makalia River, so there was no need for water-carrying parties and they could also bathe. They lived in relative comfort in a disused and airy pigsty. After they had cleared the bush and begun to dig they found a second skull; and by the time they had finished no less than twenty-eight skeletons had been unearthed. The people buried at this site were tall, with long heads and long faces; in the anthropological literature they came to be known as the 'Elmenteitan type' after the small township and lake of that name. Various authors were to describe them as 'Caucasoid' or 'Mediterranean', and Louis stressed that they were essentially 'non-Negroid'. Theories of migrations from the north were propounded, but until quite recently neither Louis nor any other anthropologist thought of looking nearer home: in fact the 'Elmenteitans' were no more exotic than other tall, lean Africans such as the Masai, or the Tutsi of Rwanda.

Sometimes at weekends Louis would play tennis with Mr Gamble, and one day his host showed him two rock shelters on his farm which Louis thought looked distinctly promising. Gamble's Cave I and II, as they came to be called, are about four miles from Bromhead's site; the second one proved to be extremely important and was to occupy Louis for most of the time during his second expedition.

Before the end of the 1927 season he dug a trial trench in the first shelter. One day while Louis was in camp packing up specimens, Newsam came across a human skeleton more than four feet below the surface. But, as Louis noted with disgust in his field diary: 'Newsam took same out without any shellac or proper tools and brought it home, all fragments bundled on top of each other any old how.' It appears that Newsam decided the skull looked 'Negroid', unlike the Elmenteitans they had been finding, and therefore it must be recent and was not worth bothering about.

However, in the second shelter they discovered three fragmentary skeletons at a depth of fourteen feet, much deeper and obviously older than Newsam's specimen, which Louis now suspected was a later intrusion. Pompously he notes in his diary: 'Unfortunately I was not present when the skeleton was found and cannot say if the soil above showed signs of disturbance, and Mr Newsam does not seem to have taken very precise notice of the matter.'[1]

Louis now had to turn his attention to yet another site. Named Willey's Kopje, it was on the slopes of Eburru mountain, a dormant volcano whose steam jets are used by local farmers for their water supply. Some Africans sent by one of these farmers to collect stone thought they had found an easy way of doing this by removing rocks from a cairn when, to their horror, they saw human bones. They fled, leaving the mound disturbed and with bones sticking out of its side. By the time Louis got there the bones had almost disintegrated, but he found skeletons in two other mounds. There were no stone tools, but sherds of pottery were scattered round the kopje, and near the toe of one skeleton was an iron ring. Rather than accept the obvious conclusion that the burials were iron age, Louis referred to the culture as neolithic: he consistently over-estimated the age of his finds to fit in with his pluvial-glacial correlations.

His very first climatic clue had been the discovery of fish bones near the Nakuru site, three miles from the shore of the present alkaline and fishless lake; and he also found a terrace 145 feet above it. From the great thickness of lake deposits in the Nakuru and Elmenteita basins it seemed that there was plenty of evidence of past pluvial periods, and these he tried to link with the dated sequence of Europe. This may seem very far-fetched, but it must be stressed again that there was no alternative; somehow Louis had to build a framework to determine the relative age of his finds. If he had left it at that, instead of trying to give them *absolute* ages, he would have avoided much criticism in the years to come.

Wayland came to see the evidence and was excited to find that it seemed to tie in nicely with his Uganda terraces. He also put Louis in touch with the geologist Dr Erik Nilsson, a Swede with a limited command of English who was doing some detailed levelling in the Rift Valley with a view to proving pluvial hypotheses. In spite of the language difficulties Nilsson gave Louis a great deal of help, and made him realize that on his next expedition he must have a surveyor and a geologist.

On 16 July 1927 Louis's paper 'Stone age man in Kenya Colony' appeared in *Nature*[2] – the first of some forty articles and letters that he was to publish in that learned journal. By this time funds had run out, and, accompanied by more than a hundred crates of bones and stones, Louis and Newsam sailed for England.

The specimens were distributed among different authorities: the human bones went to the foremost expert on fossil man, Sir Arthur Keith, FRS, at the Royal College of Surgeons; the animal bones were sent to Arthur Tindall Hopwood, who was in charge of fossil mammals at the British Museum (Natural History). The artifacts Louis took with him to St John's, where the returning hero had been provided with a 'commodious set of rooms' in which to work. For the next nine months he divided his time between Cambridge and London, where Sir Arthur Keith supervised the cleaning of the skeletons and taught Louis a great deal.

At the same time Louis was planning his next expedition, and it was clear that he would need far more money than he had had before. Early in 1928 he wrote to another Sir Arthur, Sir Arthur Smith Woodward, who had been keeper of geology at the Natural History Museum ever since 1901. He was a former trustee of the

Sladen Fund, and Louis asked if he would back an application to them for £3,000. He did not get the whole of this sum from the Sladen Fund, but all the bodies which had supported him for the first expedition did so again. He also succeeded in getting a number of new benefactors, including the Rhodes Trust and the Royal Geographical Society. With the assistance of Dr Haddon, he also obtained a senior studentship from the commissioners of the Royal Commission of the 1851 Exhibition – funds left over from the Great Exhibition which had been put into research studentships. As a result he had a certain income of £400 per annum for the next two years, which made all the difference.

In the summer of 1928 Louis got married. For the background we must return to the time when he was excavating at Bromhead's site and living in a pigsty. The social life was extremely limited, so that it was quite an event when a couple named Keeling living near Elmenteita invited Louis to meet a visitor. She was a good-looking young woman called Henrietta Wilfrida ('Frida') Avern, nearly two years older than Louis, rather tall, with dark eyes and dark hair cut in a short bob, an alert expression and a charming smile. After graduating from Newnham in modern and medieval languages, she had taught for two years at Benenden School in Kent and then decided to see the world. Accompanied by another girl she had toured East Africa for eighteen months, and was on the last lap of her journey when she stayed with the Keelings at Elmenteita.

Louis, who had not seen an educated woman for some time, was tremendously excited to have an intelligent and attractive audience to talk to about his discoveries and gossip about mutual acquaintances in Cambridge. He lost no time in inviting her to dine with him in the pigsty. Frida remembers that although the equipment was rudimentary and the meal unmemorable the decor was remarkable. A python skin was drying outside and the crude mud hut was full of bones of all sorts, as well as drums and other African musical instruments. Louis even laid on a cabaret in the form of his Kikuyu labourers singing Moody and Sankey hymns. The next day Frida was shown the Nakuru burial site, with a picnic beside the hippo pool in Lake Nakuru. It was all very romantic: the glorious surroundings, the flamingoes, and this strange man, so unlike anyone Frida had come across before. With his usual impetuousity Louis proposed almost at once, and Frida went back to England to think it over.

She was the third daughter of Henry Avern, a merchant of Reigate in Surrey who owned cork forests in Spain and Portugal. Frida had had a thoroughly conventional middle-class upbringing, which perhaps was one of the main stumbling blocks to a successful partnership with Louis. In the years to come she was torn in two directions: she enjoyed the mental stimulus and adventure that Louis provided, and yet, conditioned by her background, she needed routine, a base, a settled environment for her children, none of which Louis could supply. Another factor that doomed the marriage was Frida's character, intelligent and talented, practical and capable, dominant and obstinate – far too like Louis himself. He could never have tolerated a wife who was not his intellectual equal, but Frida was sometimes tactless enough to disagree with him in public. Curiously enough they were alike not only in character but also in appearance; in middle age, long after they had parted, with their white hair, dark eyes and rather stout figures they could have been taken for brother and sister. Frida should have made the perfect wife for an archaeologist: she was prepared to undertake anything, even learning to draw stone tools adequately; and she had the great advantage of having an income of her own, which she generously put into the kitty for Louis's second archaeological expedition.

Two months after their marriage they were off to Kenya with the rest of the party that Louis had collected. One of these was an undergraduate of Trinity named Donald MacInnes, who had sought Louis's advice on the restoration of some very broken skulls he had found near Cambridge. Louis was so impressed with his skill in putting them together that he promptly invited him to be a member of his expedition. So began a symbiotic partnership which lasted for many years. Louis gave Donald the opportunity to work in Africa and subsequently got him involved with the Miocene fauna (Chapter 7) which was to be the subject of his thesis; in return, Donald taught Louis all he knew about vertebrate anatomy and restored the human and other mammalian remains that he found. They were a perfect foil: Donald had immense patience and was extraordinarily skilful with his hands, but completely lacked the drive and ambition which Louis possessed in such full measure. At times he was a restraining influence on Louis's 'intuition', a Sancho Panza who turned Louis's giants back into windmills.

A second member of the expedition was Louis's younger brother Douglas, who had gone up to St John's in the autumn of 1927 and was reading geography, with a special interest in geomorphology. His supervisors encouraged him to put in a year's practical work before sitting for his degree, and thus Louis had the surveyor whom he needed so badly to level the lake terraces.

Douglas, who eventually joined the Forest Department in Kenya, had the disadvantage of following in the wake of his brilliant brother both at Weymouth and at St John's. Like all the Leakeys he was a strong individualist, and he disagreed with many of Louis's interpretations and intuitions. He recognized Louis's incorrigible tendency to over-estimate the age of his finds, and disapproved strongly of his brother's headlong rushes into print and the consequent limelight and publicity.

Apart from a surveyor, Louis needed a geologist; but he could not find one prepared to come for the limited fee he was able to offer. As extra pairs of hands he took on three people who would pay their own expenses – £10 a month each. One was Tom Powys Cobb, an undergraduate of Trinity whose home was in Kenya. The other two were students from Girton, Mrs Cecely Creasey and Miss Elizabeth Kitson, both of whom attended Louis's lectures. To increase his income and because he loved teaching, he had been coaching for the anthropology tripos. There were no formal lectures: the students perched on packing cases, listened to him talking on every conceivable subject, were given implements to sort, and watched him chipping flints. When no flint was available he would demonstrate on potatoes: it is said that a musty odour pervaded the room, emanating from potato chips lodged in the crevices of an ancient sofa.

Douglas Leakey went on ahead to set up house – literally 'house', for they were to be in the relative comfort of a disused farmhouse instead of the pigsty which Louis and Newsam had occupied in 1927. The comfort to which they had been looking forward, however, proved to be a disappointment, for the house was full of holes, giving free access to rats, and the bachelors were better off in their tents. Louis, Frida and Donald MacInnes sailed in August to join Douglas, while the other three came out later.

Louis, as always, first visited his parents at Kabete and introduced his bride, whom they loved as a daughter immediately. By this time Julia and Gladys had founded one of the first girls' intermediate schools in the country; they worked unceasingly and Frida described them as 'heroines'. After the war, while Louis was at Weymouth, Julia had done a course in parish work at Bristol for two years, joining the CMS in 1924. Gladys, after doing a correspondence course, went to Cheltenham Ladies' College and then University College, London, where she took a degree in English and French. She also did a teacher training course and then, as a CMS missionary, returned to Kenya in 1927. The house where the sisters lived, close to their parents' home, and the building where they ran their school still stand. The style is unmistakably of the 'twenties, contrasting strongly with the modern classrooms and dormitories which surround them today. One of their pupils was Grace Wahu who, in 1920, had married a young man from the nearby Scottish mission school called Johnstone Kamau, better known under the name he assumed later: Jomo Kenyatta.

While Louis was in England he had left in charge of the pigsty a man he had taken on to help at the Nakuru burial site, Juma Gitau bin Sharrifu. Juma had been an officer's orderly in German East Africa, but in spite of this he did not much fancy domestic work; instead, in Louis's words, he proved to be a 'born scientist'.[3] He also had plenty of initiative. During Louis's absence he had excavated a cairn near the camp and extracted a human skeleton. Not only did he write and tell Louis about it, but he also managed to find someone to photograph the bones before he removed them. When Louis returned the following year, rather to his surprise he found the skeleton in perfect condition. 'He had done the work every bit as well as I would have done it myself,' he said.[4]

The site became known as the Makalia burial site, and this is where Louis began work in 1928, postponing the excavations at Gamble's Cave while he extracted two more skeletons at Makalia. They were in a semi-crouched position and in each case the two central incisors had been extracted before death, perhaps a practice connected with initiation ceremonies. Louis was reminded of the Willey's Kopje skeletons found in the previous year, but again there were no accompanying artifacts.

While the rest of the party worked on their various assignments, Juma preferred to go off exploring. Apart from his dislike of routine jobs, Juma had two main disadvantages: the number of wives and camp followers he seemed to collect and, as a devout Mohammedan, his strict observance of Ramadan. Like Louis, he seemed to have a nose for likely sites that seemed almost to smack of the supernatural. Before long he had added further glory to himself by locating another site at Stable's Drift, a crossing place over the Nderit River. There were hundreds of sherds of a most unusual kind of pottery, with an all-over decoration like basket-work on the outside and deep scratches on the inside. There had been similar fragments at Willey's Kopje and clearly there was a connection between all three sites – Willey's, Makalia and Stable's. Louis named the culture Gumban A, believing it to be earlier than the Gumban B from the Nakuru burial site.

Donald MacInnes, with his penchant for palaeontology, spent most of his time searching for fossils in the ancient lake beds and had a site named after him. Douglas continued the levelling work begun by Erik Nilsson, a very difficult task which he performed with great skill: the line of the old terraces was often obscured by *leleshua* bushes, which had to be cut down along the line of sight, and the only fixed points were along the railway which was often many miles away. He also charted the depths of Lake Nakuru, said to be 'bottomless' according to local opinion but which he found nowhere exceeded nine feet.

Louis, as the boss of the first team he had ever had under him, was in his element and tireless in his energy. Once he began the main work at Gamble's Cave he found it was more than a full-time occupation, but nevertheless he had to supervise the activities of Donald and Douglas, as well as following up Juma's leads and his own hunches. He also ran a daily clinic for the locals, as he had done at Tendaguru and as he was to do throughout his career. Frida was equally busy, supporting him all day long at Gamble's Cave and in the evenings marking up the innumerable specimens they found. She also ran the housekeeping efficiently, but shops were some distance away and there was not much to be bought in them anyway. Game, on the other hand, was plentiful, and Louis had obtained permission to shoot for the pot. Although the men did the actual killing, when it came to cutting up the carcases they always seemed to be occupied with some more important matter and Frida had to act as butcher; this was one task that she really disliked.

The honeymoon couple were undoubtedly happy. Louis was at the top of his form, adored by his wife and doing the work that he so much enjoyed; the possibility that he might be more in love with his work than with Frida would not have occurred to her, nor perhaps to him. Scratching in the dust of a rock shelter all day long and sharing camp life with others was not the way she would have chosen to begin married life, but she accepted it as a necessary prelude to their eventual return to Cambridge and a home of her own.

The excavations at Gamble's Cave were begun at the end of September and continued until the following April; although so time-consuming, they proved to be far more worthwhile than anything that Louis had tackled before. He took enormous care, insisting that all soil from the occupation levels should be riddled so that every tiny artifact and scrap of bone would be recovered. By the end of the first month he was collecting up to seven hundred implements and thousands of flakes every day, all of which had to be numbered and catalogued. By the time they had finished they had dug through twenty-eight feet of deposits, of which the last ten were almost solid with tools.

Beneath the two prehistoric occupation levels located in 1927 there were two more. The uppermost level contained artifacts and pottery like those associated with the Elmenteitans of Bromhead's site. The industry from the second level was somewhat scrappy, and it turned out that the three fragmentary skeletons found in 1927 had not come from the base of this level, as Louis had thought, but from the underlying one. Both this third level and the fourth were chock full of artifacts which seemed to resemble those of the Aurignacian culture of Europe, so at first Louis called this industry the Kenya Aurignacian.

In December they unearthed another skeleton; and the last one, making five altogether, turned up in March 1929. These were in a far better state of preservation than the three excavated in 1927. The bodies had been placed with their backs against the wall of the shelter, with the knees drawn up, and traces in the surrounding soil showed that originally they must have been covered with red ochre – perhaps to resemble blood, implying the continuation of life after death.

The bones had to be uncovered with great care, and Louis may well have been the first to pioneer the use of that invaluable implement, the dental pick, for this purpose. A newspaper correspondent called while this delicate operation was in progress and, misinterpreting Louis's excited flood of words, reported: 'Mr Leakey discovers the first dentist.' As a result more than two hundred visitors crowded round to see the prehistoric 'dentist', causing considerable disruption to the work.

To prevent damage in transit, a good deal of rock had to be left surrounding the skeletons. The whole huge block was encased in plaster, and the result was something like a gigantic egg with the skeleton curled up inside like an unhatched chick. Each block weighed about 3 cwt, and eight men were needed to carry it down the steep slope back to camp; it was nearly as bad as transporting dinosaur bones at Tendaguru, but the technique was the same and Louis had cause to be grateful to Cutler.

The artifacts from the two lowest ('Aurignacian') levels included a variety of obsidian tools, delicate awls made from bird bones, and ostrich eggshell beads. But the biggest excitement – and Louis was to make the most of it – was two sherds of coarse pottery: not all that thrilling, one might think, but in an 'Aurignacian' context, believed to date from about 20,000 B.C., it was revolutionary. In those days pottery was unthinkable before the neolithic, about 5,000 B.C.

Louis had based his date of about 20,000 years, inevitably, on climatic correlations. Underlying the occupation levels in the rock shelter was an ancient beach, more than 500 feet above the present level of Lake Nakuru, which he attributed to the time of the pluvial which he called the Gamblian and which he correlated with the last maximum of the ice age in Europe. The 'Aurignacian' appearance of the tools fitted in well with such an age. Later on he recognized that they were more like those of the much later Capsian culture of North Africa but, although he changed the name from Kenya Aurignacian to Kenya Capsian, he never budged over the date.*

In abandoning the term Aurignacian, Louis may have been influenced by the views of his Cambridge supervisor Dr Haddon who, in May 1929, wrote: 'I strongly advise you to give up using the term "Aurignacian". It seems to me to be rash and in every way undesirable to employ terms of Western European cultures or industries for those found elsewhere. . . . Also I think it somewhat dangerous to rely too much on typology. . . . I hear you are probably going to the British Association meeting in South Africa. If you do, I entreat you to be careful what you say. Naturally you will tell them of what you have found, but do not go in for wild hypotheses. These won't do your work any good and it's foolish to try to make a splash.' Haddon certainly knew his Louis!

Louis did, in fact, attend the British Association meeting, as mentioned later, and probably because of Haddon's advice he was fairly guarded in his pronouncements. Wayland also delivered a warning, written in the very same month as Haddon's letter, in connection with something that would certainly carry a great deal of weight in restraining Louis's impetuousity at this time: the possibility of a Fellowship from St John's. 'Harm is done to the cause,' wrote Wayland, 'by over-emphatic comments with regard to these correlations at this date. (Strictly between you and me and the gatepost, I found it necessary to defend your work . . . for the benefit of some folks at Cambridge who are interested in the bestowal of Fellowships.) Believe me you will serve archaeology, the expedition and yourself best by maintaining a strictly scientific attitude. You have the chance of making yourself, in time, one of

*In the 1970s dates of around 6,000 B.C. were obtained for Gambles Cave by C14 and also by the method based on the racemization of amino acids in bone. Such a date is still early for the appearance of pottery, however.

the leaders of archaeological thought – don't spoil your chances, for by so doing you will unintentionally let the science down. I must ask you to forgive the sermon, it is delivered in all friendship.' Wayland, like Haddon, was a wise old bird.

In the intervals of his work at Gamble's Cave, Louis had been trying to puzzle out the meaning of various sediments in exposures cut by rivers through the ancient lake beds. Obviously he had to have a qualified geologist, and he appealed for help to the Governor of Kenya, Sir Edward Grigg, with the result that he got a grant-in-aid of £1,000. He cabled to Dr Haddon 'Find me a geologist', which resulted in the arrival of John Solomon early in 1929.

Solomon was a large, shambling, gentle man who played the flute and sang beautifully – not at all one's idea of a tough geologist; but although he was not a pioneer by nature, he was extremely competent. During the few months he was in the Rift Valley he managed to sort out many conundrums of relevance to the pluvial problem. His main contribution was to recognize that the thick series of lake deposits attributed by Gregory to the Miocene was actually Pleistocene. Louis was elated: he now had evidence of an earlier and mightier pluvial than his Gamblian. Gregory had named these sediments Kamasian after a range of hills further north, near Lake Baringo, so Louis called his new pluvial the Kamasian.

As proof of the Pleistocene age of these sediments, Solomon found some magnificent Acheulian handaxes sticking out of the side of a cliff above the Kariandusi River, which flows into Lake Elmenteita. The cliff was of pure white diatomite, composed of the skeletons of microscopic organisms which had once lived in the lake. In stone age times a handaxe must have served as many purposes as its invaluable modern equivalent the *panga*, without which life in East Africa would be unthinkable: pick, trowel, wedge, axe and knife, it can be used to hack a way through the bush, dig up potatoes, or skin an antelope. Its prehistoric forerunner in Africa was usually made from some kind of lava but never, except at Kariandusi, of obsidian. This material was widely used for the smaller tools of the middle and later stone age, but hardly ever during the earlier stone age. Nearly all the obsidian tools in Kenya whose chemical composition has been tested can be traced to two mines: one on the slopes of Eburru mountain, the other in Njorowa Gorge, a former outlet of Lake Naivasha. On Eburru there are steaming fumaroles and a strong smell of sulphur; at Njorowa are towering lava cliffs where lammergeyers soar and nest, a place with an oppressive sense of doom which earned it its popular name of Hell's Gate. The whole of this area has been subjected to volcanic outpourings and earth movements, which perhaps explains why the source of the Kariandusi obsidian has never been found: it may have been buried. The instability of the Rift Valley also explains the eventual foundering of much of the pluvial hypothesis: high terraces could have been left by much deeper lakes, but they can also be the result of tectonic upheavals.

In June, not long after the discovery at Kariandusi, the members of the expedition dispersed. It had been a most successful season, providing Louis with enough material to fill two books – one on the stone tools, one on the human remains – and to get his research fellowship renewed in November 1929 as well as his doctorate in the following year.

Louis and Frida, together with John Solomon and Elizabeth Kitson, headed south to attend the British Association's meeting in Johannesburg. They travelled by truck, which was quite an undertaking in the 'twenties. Camping every night, the journey took them six weeks; the slowness was partly due to the fact that Louis was always shooting off to look at sites, but mainly it was due to the appalling condition of the roads. The Great North Road, embryo of the Cape to Cairo route, was little more than a track cleared of the worst of the tree stumps, plunging down steep gullies and crossing rivers by the flimsiest of bridges. Both Louis and the Kikuyu he took with him were good mechanics, and the Chevrolet stood up well to its battering. (On his return to Kenya Louis sold it for £20.)

Probably the worst section of the road was near the Kenya-Tanganyika border, but there was another very bad patch near Livingstone. According to a newspaper report on the epic journey: 'Here the mica hills had to be crossed and projecting knife-edges of rock, combined with the sheer, ungraded ascent, made terribly heavy going for the loaded vehicle. An eighteen inch slit in one of the tyres and a smashed rear spring told their own tale of the difficulty of this part of the route. Mr Leakey was enthusiastic about the climbing powers of their six-cylinder Chevrolet truck. Without the fourth gear with which the latest models are equipped, they would have experienced great trouble crossing the hills, he said.'

In Tanganyika (Tanzania) they made a detour to see the rock paintings near Kondoa and Louis resolved to study them in detail one day. They also made a pilgrimage to Broken Hill (Kabwe) in Northern Rhodesia (Zambia), the lead and zinc mines where the famous skull of Rhodesian Man was found in 1921, and actually managed to trace the miner who had discovered it. Another highlight of the trip was a visit to Zimbabwe in Southern Rhodesia, where Miss Gertrude Caton-Thompson had recently established beyond doubt the 'medieval' date of the most imposing part of those controversial ruins.

The total cost from Nairobi to Johannesburg for the five people amounted to just over £87, of which half was spent on petrol. Only four nights were spent in hotels, which accounted for a mere £14 for the whole party. Not only was the journey by truck the most economical means of travel, but it had enabled Louis to see many prehistoric sites outside his own territory; altogether it had been a most valuable experience.

He broadened his horizons still more at the British Association's meeting in Johannesburg, where all the leading lights in African prehistory had gathered. They included the two pioneers of South African archaeology, Professor C. ('Peter') van Riet Lowe and Mr John Goodwin; and Professor Raymond Dart, whose first australopithecine skull, found at Taung in 1924, was rejected as a mere ape by nearly all his colleagues. Louis's contribution to the meeting, 'An outline of the Stone Age in Kenya',[5] was later expanded into his first book, *The Stone Age Cultures of Kenya Colony* (1931).[6] He had taken Haddon's warning to heart and made a good impression, and Haddon wrote to him afterwards: 'Someone kindly sent me the Johannesburg *Star* with a full account of your report and I congratulate you and Solomon on the work you have done, which appears to have been well received in South Africa. I have had a letter from Fleure [grand old man of prehistoric archaeology, Professor H. J. Fleure, FRS] in which he expressed his appreciation of your diggings and their results. I asked him to write me a letter on the subject which I could enclose with a covering letter to the Master of St John's. This he did immediately and I at once forwarded it and received the assurance from the Master that it would be considered at the next Fellowship elections. So I have done all I can for you in that matter.'[7] He had indeed, and the outcome was successful.

The immediate result of Louis's report to the British Association was a proposition which he received with mixed feelings. A large party of participants returning to England decided they would like to break their journey in Kenya and see Louis's sites for themselves. Delighted as Louis was at the prospect of showing off Gamble's Cave to such distinguished visitors, it meant that he was unable to see any of the South African sites as he had planned. It also meant covering the 3,000 miles, which had taken them six weeks on the way south, in fifteen days in order to be back in Kenya in time to receive the party.

On arrival at Gamble's Cave they had to quickly unpack the cases of specimens which were ready to be shipped to England, remove the boards which covered the excavations in the shelter, and expose some more artifacts for the visitors to see *in situ*. One of those who came was Sir Julian Huxley, who remained Louis's lifelong friend and champion. For Louis, the rush to get back from South Africa had been well worth while: altogether about sixty scientists came to see Gamble's Cave, and after they got home they spread the word that Leakey had done good work.

After their departure Louis had planned to do a little quiet digging at the Kariandusi handaxe site, but it was not to be. Instead he and Frida were summoned to spend a night at Government House – they had hastily to borrow some clothes suitable for the occasion – and Sir Edward Grigg asked Louis to serve on a committee to report on the Kikuyu system of land tenure. He could hardly refuse, and in any case it was a matter on which he had very strong feelings. From his close contacts with the Kikuyu he knew a good deal about their grievances. The basic facts, as he was to explain many years later in his book *Mau Mau and the Kikuyu* (1952), were as follows.

Owing to a misunderstanding, when the first settlers began to arrive in Kenya in 1902 they were under the impression that they had bought land in Kikuyu territory. In fact, outright sales to outsiders were invalid by Kikuyu law and custom. In some cases owners parted with pieces of land in the belief that it was only on a temporary basis, in other cases the 'sales' were made by tenants of the real owners who had moved to other parts of the country. The period of European settlement happened to follow a series of disasters: smallpox, rinderpest among the cattle, drought and famine. Land formerly under cultivation returned to bush, although it was still grazed by goats and sheep; but the fact that it was apparently idle did not affect ownership. Payments were made for such disused land, and naturally the purchasers regarded themselves as the outright owners.

After the railway was built food could be brought to areas stricken by famine, the principles of hygiene were taught, the Masai were tamed – and their traditional enemies the Kikuyu multiplied. Early in the 1920s the first political organization was formed with the aim of getting back the land which the white man had 'stolen'. The Kikuyu were regarded as tenants on Crown land and they clamoured for title deeds, or 'tiddlydee' as they called them.

Louis spent three exhausting weeks on the 1929 committee of enquiry acting as interpreter to evidence taken from Kikuyu elders. It was at this time that he earned his Kikuyu name 'Wakaruigi', meaning 'son of the sparrow-hawk', since not much escaped his keen powers of observation and, as one of the elders observed, 'he asked many questions.' The report was completed in November and it opened the eyes of the Government about Kikuyu views on land ownership. Three years later the Carter Land Commission went into the whole question very thoroughly, and in some cases compensation was made either in cash or in the granting of more land. Unfortunately the Kikuyu Central Association made such outrageous claims that they killed the goose before many golden eggs were laid. The grievances simmered for another twenty years and then erupted in Mau Mau.

By the time the committee of enquiry was over Louis had had enough and decided it was time to get back to Cambridge. After spending the whole of the first year of her marriage in camp Frida was looking forward to setting up a home at last. On their way back from South Africa they had got into conversaton with a man whose sister had a cottage to let at Foxton, a few miles south of Cambridge, and they had arranged to rent it. It was a delightful little oast house, with no mod. cons. whatever, but with a rent of only five shillings a week. Fortunately Louis's fellowship had come through, so he had three rooms at St John's in which he could work – he needed them, with another sixty cases of artifacts to add to the collections which were already there from the previous expedition.

The human skeletons from Gamble's Cave in their egg-like shell of plaster went to the Royal College of Surgeons. There Louis was given space in the basement, which contained grim exhibits of plastic surgery dating from the 1914–18 war. As he had to be in London so much he also rented a small flat in Chancery Lane. It took a long time to extract the Gamble's Cave skeletons from their matrix, but fortunately Louis had the help of Donald MacInnes who was studying at London University. A picture of Sir Arthur Keith and Louis 'unwrapping' one of the skeletons – rather as though it were a mummy which could be unwrapped in a matter of minutes – appeared in *The Times* of 28 December 1929, and an exhibition of the material was put on at the Royal College of Surgeons.

Louis had little time to spend at Foxton. Even when he was not in London he often used to sleep in the kitchen of his rooms at St John's so that he could work until the early hours. He was desperately anxious to publish the results of his first two expeditions before embarking on the third, as he would be unlikely to get more money until his benefactors could see what he had achieved with their previous grants. It took him eighteen months to get all the material in order; but in the end he decided to publish only the stone tools and hold over the skeletal descriptions, hoping to get more on his next expedition – which indeed he did. In the meantime, to help him in the formidable task of getting his skulls illustrated, Louis turned inventor. With the aid of a colleague named Harper, he produced a device called the Leakey-Harper drawing machine, a Heath Robinson-like contraption which was described in *Nature* in August 1930, and exhibited at a Royal Society conversazione earlier in the year. His book on the artifacts, *The Stone Age Cultures of Kenya Colony*, was published by Cambridge University Press in 1931 and was well received by both reviewers and scientific colleagues. It included a most valuable appendix on the geology by John Solomon, in which he distinguished two pluvial periods – Kamasian and Gamblian – followed by two post-pluvial wet phases – Makalian and Nakuran – and in which he also lists the heights of the terraces levelled by Douglas. Louis's team had done good work, but by far the most important outcome of the expedition had been the results which he himself had obtained by his painstaking excavations at Gamble's Cave. Louis had established, for the very first time in East Africa, a sequence of stratified industries. And another important result of his work was that he was awarded his PhD degree at a meeting of the Board of Research Studies at Cambridge University on 14 October 1930.

While Louis was in England his younger sister Gladys became engaged to the Rev. Leonard Beecher, and the wedding took place on 7 October 1930. It was something of an occasion and must be described in the words of Harry Leakey, who sent a letter for circulation among the many relations in England:

> Owing to the fact that both my sons were born at Kabete, and Julia and Gladys arrived here at about twenty months and eight months respectively, the people naturally look upon them as almost belonging to them. We decided therefore to make the wedding able to be appreciated by our African friends as well as our European guests, and so to start with we determined to have the service in the Kikuyu language. This of course made it rather a unique affair, as it's fairly uncommon for two English people to be married in an African tongue. But it was not a foreign tongue to any of us, of course, as we are accustomed to have daily prayers as well as services every Sunday in it, year in and year out. However, when some of our friends heard of it, and somewhat exaggerated reports of what we were going to do

at the wedding, they began to get alarmed and were inclined to censure us. As we are pretty used, as a family, to doing things in eccentric ways it did not worry us much, and we just carried on with our plans, and since the wedding we have had nothing but congratulations from all sides as to what a charming and delightful wedding it was.

Leonard once thought of having a very nice young African teacher of mine as his best man, to match Gladys's two Kikuyu bridesmaids, but this boy got married himself and settled that matter for us. So instead he chose a very nice young clergyman friend of ours, Mr E. L. Barham, a Cambridge man. He was working as curate in my old parish of St James, Hatcham, when Julia was there during her training in 1925. He now works in the CMS Ruanda Mission. The bridesmaids looked quite sweet; but they were rather a queer couple in a way, for one suffers badly from elephantiasis in both feet, and has one foot nearly as big as a baby elephant! And the other is thought to be suffering from TB which we hope to check, and was only brought out from Nairobi by the matron of the hospital and rushed back before it became too cold. All sorts of things had to be considered in the choosing of these maids, or *terrible* jealousy would be caused, and their lives might be made a burden to them afterwards by the other girls. If they had been chosen for their pretty faces (for some, not many, are really very pretty), or their neat figures, it would never have done. So Gladys chose her namesake Gladys of the elephantine feet, a very keen Christian girl, on the grounds that though she is now one of our most senior hostel members no one else has, or is ever likely to choose her as bridesmaid. It was fully agreed upon by the other girls that this was very fair and all were pleased with the arrangement. The other is our eldest girl teacher, baptised in infancy, and quite obviously had a right to be selected.

As the bride approached the chancel steps, a Kikuyu hymn well known to the people was sung lustily. Then the service was conducted by me in Kikuyu. . . . Tea was provided for over 500 guests, all invited by written invitations. We knew the women would keep to themselves, but we arranged for some of the best educated men – clergy, head teachers, Government chiefs etc. – to mingle somewhat with the Europeans with the intent of breaking down some of the racial segregation which is essential when the Africans are barbarians but is unchristian when they get a certain amount of education and have learnt cleanliness and good manners. With this intent we warned the very few old friends from amongst the settlers who were invited, as having known the bride all her life, what they might expect and begged them not to come if they minded having tea with people who might have been their servants at some time. But they all insisted on coming all the same. The great bulk of European guests were fellow missionaries of our own and other Protestant Societies.

One of the very nice features of the wedding was that several of our old dormitory girls now married (one with nine children) insisted upon undertaking all the tea making for the crowds of native guests and even brought bunches of bananas and extra firewood to help. When we thanked them they said how could one of their 'children' be married without their helping . . . Gladys looked exceedingly nice in her very simple white silk frock she made herself.

Canon Harry then added a postscript: 'Today, October 9th, I have to announce the engagement of Julia to Rev. Edward Lawrence Barham, who is spoken of as best man. They have been great friends for over five years.' He had already proposed several times, and perhaps it was the atmosphere of her sister's wedding that made Julia accept; it proved a very happy marriage. Mr Barham was to become Bishop of Rwanda and Burundi 1964–66, afterwards Assistant Bishop of Southwark, and then Suffragen Bishop of Wimbledon. Gladys's husband, Dr Beecher, became Bishop of Mombasa and, in 1960, Archbishop of East Africa.

While all these family excitements were going on in Kenya, Frida was pregnant. In April 1931 Louis became a father for the first time. The baby was named Priscilla Muthoni: in Kikuyu 'Muthoni' means a relation-in-law and is used as a term of affection. The stem *thoni* signifies 'shyness', because an engaged girl was not allowed to speak in the presence of her future parents-in-law. As it turned out, a more inappropriate name for Priscilla could hardly have been chosen; like both her parents she is extremely talkative and anything but shy. The cottage at Foxton, with its almost complete lack of facilities, was no place for a newborn baby, so Frida went to her mother's house at Reigate for the event.

Louis at that time had been having disturbing symptoms; a specialist's report to his doctor, dated 13 April 1931, tells of the diagnosis: 'His attacks are typically epileptic . . . I think they are the result of an old cerebral contusion due to his accident in the rugby match in December, 1923. When he was in East Africa he had, as you know, malaria, dysentery and fever, and had one of his attacks there . . . I would not look upon his case as a severe one and I think there is a good chance of the fits being checked with moderate doses of sedative. All the attacks have occurred in the morning before 11 o'clock, and one of them was when he was doing hard physical work in Africa and two when he was tired. I would suggest that you put him on Luminal gr. 1 to be taken at bed time and again on awakening. He ought to take it at any rate for a year. If free from attacks, he could then drop the evening dose, but ought to keep on with the morning dose for two or three years. . . . He must quite definitely give up driving a car.'

Needless to say, nothing would induce Louis to give up driving a car and he continued to do so for the next forty years. He also continued to have fits occasionally when he was over-tired, although he would refer to them as a 'collapse'; there seems little doubt that they were provoked by sheer exhaustion.

After Frida and her baby returned to Foxton from Reigate in April, Louis paid them a few flying visits, and then, at the end of June, he was off to Kenya again to prepare the way for his third and most ambitious expedition. His parents suggested that Frida should use their home as a base when she came out to join him, but that he should build a small separate bungalow for his family. This he did, for a total cost of £36. Frida and Priscilla sailed in September and, as an infant was accepted for one-sixteenth of an adult fare, Priscilla was transported all the way from Southampton to Mombasa for the sum of £3.15.0.

4 Bones of Contention

The excavations at Gamble's Cave, although arduous, had at least been in the heart of what was then known as the White Highlands, close to roads and shops and within a couple of hours' drive from Nairobi. Louis's third expedition was to take him far off the beaten track, and he was also to get involved with material infinitely older than anything he had encountered so far. The involvement was to prove time-consuming and, in one case, extremely distressing. In western Kenya a certain human jaw was to cause Louis more excitement and trouble than any other fossil that ever crossed his path; it involved him in a battle with scientific establishment and taught him an unforgettable lesson on how exigent was the discipline he had chosen for his career.

But the main object of the 1931 expedition was to try to settle the vexed question of the age of 'Olduvai Man', through whom Louis was introduced to the site which, more than any other, brought him fame: Olduvai Gorge. This controversial skeleton had been found as long ago as 1913 and was, in fact, the first prehistoric human remains known from Africa south of the Sahara. Its discoverer was a Berlin geologist, Professor Hans Reck, who was at that time a member of the Geological Survey of German East Africa. His brief was to investigate the structure of the continent between the Indian Ocean and the central African lakes – quite a tall order. He was also to study volcanic formations in the Rift Valley, and in passing he was to examine a spot known to the Masai as *ol duvai*, 'place of the wild sisal'.

The story of the discovery of this place is almost too good to be true, involving the classic joke of the absent-minded professor armed with a butterfly net. In 1911 an entomologist from Munich called Kattwinkel was intent on pursuing an alluring specimen when he almost fell three hundred feet down a spectacular gorge. Unlikely as this may sound it is by no means impossible: Olduvai is indeed invisible from the plains above until one is standing almost on its very edge. Kattwinkel took enough time off from his butterfly collecting to pick up a few of the fossil bones he saw all around him in the eroded gullies and took them back to Germany. There they aroused great interest among palaeontologists, for amongst them was an unknown species of three-toed horse and other extinct beasts whose presence in East Africa was completely unsuspected. Hence the official request to Reck to locate Olduvai and collect more fossils. About all the information he had was that somewhere in the plains west of the Rift Valley there was this great gash. With a hundred porters, Reck struggled up the trackless highlands to the rim of the great caldera of Ngorongoro, descended to the Ol Balbal Depression and at last, after enduring great hardships and difficulties, reached his goal.

During the three months he spent at Olduvai Reck collected hundreds of fossils and worked out the basic geology without too much trouble. It was obvious that there were four main beds, which he labelled I to IV, composed mainly of lake sediments and volcanic tuffs – ash laid down in water and then consolidated. In places they were overlain by other deposits, but before these had been laid down tectonic movements had caused the formation of the gorge. This had then been deepened by erosion, exposing the earlier beds most beautifully in its sides.

Reck was almost ready to leave when one of his workmen came across a human skeleton, apparently lying in Bed II. This he proceeded to excavate and took it back to Berlin. It was unquestionably *Homo sapiens*, buried in the crouched position, and practically complete. Its apparent association with extinct species of mammals which were almost certainly Lower Pleistocene in age was extremely puzzling, as a far more primitive type of man would have been expected; however, from its position Reck had no doubt that it must be contemporary with these animals. He published his finds in Berlin, as well as in the *Illustrated London News* of 4 April 1914, only to receive a barrage of criticism: many of his scientific colleagues said that the body must be that of a recent Masai, buried into a much older deposit.

To try to settle the matter the Kaiser himself supported the launching of a second expedition to Olduvai under Reck's leadership. Others promptly jumped on to the bandwagon, and no less than three other expeditions set out; but none of them got there, for war was declared. Reck stayed in German East Africa as Government Geologist, but in 1916 he was taken prisoner and spent the rest of the war interned in Egypt. When Britain was granted a mandate over Tanganyika Territory after the armistice Reck's cherished hope of getting back to Olduvai was shattered.

Louis, of course, had heard about the Olduvai skeleton, and when he was studying bows and arrows in museums in Germany in 1925 he took the opportunity to call on Reck. Hans Reck, who was born in 1886, was a Bavarian, tall and fair, with blue eyes; he was described as of a sunny disposition and upright character, incapable of an ungenerous thought or act.[1] He collected Arab art, was a gifted pianist, and one of the world's leading authorities on volcanoes. He and Louis struck up a friendship at once, and throughout the remaining twelve years of Reck's life they corresponded regularly. Reck had also worked for a time at Tendaguru in 1912, so at this first meeting they were able to swap dinosaur stories as well as discussing the remarkable Pleistocene fossils that Reck had collected at Olduvai. From that moment the place was never far from Louis's mind and he determined to get there; but he had to wait another six years before he managed to raise enough money to do so.

Louis was not able to see the Olduvai skeleton when he visited Reck in 1925 as it was in Munich being studied by Professor Theodore Mollison. But he went to Munich in 1927 and again in 1929, when he was able to examine it carefully and compare it with his Gamble's Cave skeletons. Not only had the bodies all been buried in the crouched position, but there was a close resemblance in the actual skulls. Louis was convinced that Olduvai Man and the Gamble's Cave people must be of the same general age, about 20,000 years according to his reckoning, and that Reck must have made a mistake in thinking it contemporary with the extinct fauna. There and then he invited Reck to accompany him to Olduvai in 1931 – long before he had obtained the money to get there – and Reck accepted with delight.

Sure enough when the time came Louis was successful in raising funds. As on his first two expeditions he got money from the Royal Society and the Percy Sladen Trust, as well as other sources. In writing to the secretary of the Sladen Trust he asked for £450 towards the expedition and £150 for Reck's passage money, explaining that if Reck's expenses were paid he was willing to renounce all claim to any new species from Olduvai.

To the Master of St John's he applied for – and got – a grant from the Taylor Fund; in his letter he gives as his target £2,500, listing the money already at his disposal which included £350 from 'self and wife'.[2] It seems unlikely that 'self' could produce much and presumably most of it came from 'wife'. A new contributor was the British Museum (Natural History) who agreed to Louis's suggestion that A. T. Hopwood should accompany the expedition to collect fossil mammals. Reck had obtained a number of interesting specimens on his 1913 expedition, including a new species of elephant which was named *Elephas recki* in his honour, and the BM was keen to add some of these exciting creatures to its own collections. The bargain was that the BM should have the fauna, while any human remains and artifacts should be the property of the East African Archaeological Expedition.

Hopwood had already been involved in the study of fossil mammals from East Africa. Not only had he described the relatively late and mostly rather dull specimens which Louis had produced from his Rift Valley sites, but also some much earlier extinct species found by Wayland at Kaiso, near Lake Albert. Hopwood was particularly interested in investigating some even older fossil beds, of Miocene age, which had been reported from western Kenya; he therefore arrived in East Africa some weeks ahead of Reck, and Louis deposited him near the shores of the Kavirondo Gulf of Lake Victoria to search for fossils.

Louis then despatched Captain J. H. Hewlett to prospect a route to Olduvai: no one had yet attempted to get anywhere near the place in a vehicle, but Louis had no intention of following in Reck's footsteps with a hundred porters. Apart from his known skill in cross-country driving, Hewlett, ex-Indian Army, had the reputation of being one of the best shots in Africa. He had accompanied the Prince of Wales (the late Duke of Windsor) on his shooting safari and, although his services were somewhat costly as a result, Louis was taking no chances with the safety of his party.

Olduvai is on the eastern edge of the Serengeti Plains which, as George Schaller put it so poetically in his book *Serengeti – A Kingdom of Predators*, 'is an area throbbing with an inexhaustible vigour of life, a Pleistocene vision of immense herds'.[3] Where there are half a million wildebeest to be eaten, inevitably there are also many lions; Hewlett did, in fact, have to shoot two lions to protect other members of the expedition, and Louis had to kill a wounded rhino which charged him.

For the first hundred miles out of Nairobi there was a road of a sort, and for the next hundred there was a track used occasionally by Indian traders. After that it was a question of bushwhacking for another hundred miles, up incredibly steep gradients and across deep gullies – the beds of streams which might flow only once or twice in a man's lifetime. Hewlett did his reconnaissance well and managed to beat a trail right up to the edge of the gorge. For most of the way his pioneer track is followed by the tourist route from Arusha to the Serengeti today; but the journey from Nairobi to Olduvai by car now takes seven hours instead of four days as it did in 1931. Fifty miles south of Arusha, the main town in northern Tanzania, a side road passes Lake Manyara and winds up the flank of thickly wooded slopes to the splendour that is Ngorongoro. This caldera, twelve miles across and 2,000 feet deep, is the largest of the volcanoes of the Crater Highlands, volcanoes which once ejected the ash which has preserved the fossils so well at Olduvai. The Crater Highlands form a barrier between the Rift Valley to the east and the vast Serengeti plains, which continue for a hundred and fifty miles to Lake Victoria in the west. From the lush forest 8,000 feet up on the rim of Ngorongoro the road descends to the coarse brown grass and dust of the plains, which are green for only a few weeks in the year after the rains. Olduvai is twenty-five miles from Ngorongoro, and a further thirty miles brings one to the boundary of the present Serengeti National Park.

After Hewlett returned from his pioneer trek and Hopwood got back armed with Miocene fossils from western Kenya, Louis met Reck at Mombasa. Then, accompanied by eighteen Africans, the party set off at the end of September 1931. They had three trucks and one car, with as much equipment, food, and above all water, as could possibly be squeezed in. During the last part of the journey they often had to crawl along at five miles an hour, with the radiators boiling furiously. Louis, who loved a challenge, wrote forty years later: 'I still look back with pleasure at the hardships of that trip and would gladly endure them again for the mere satisfaction of achievement in the face of so many difficulties.'[4]

Reck's emotion at seeing Olduvai again after so many years can be imagined, but he was faced with an immediate and urgent problem. In 1913 he had been lucky in finding a pool of water in the gorge, a most rare occurrence; but now there was none. He set off at once with Hopwood to look for a waterhole he remembered on the slopes of Olmoti, an extinct volcano about twelve miles away. When darkness fell and they still had not returned Louis sent out a search party, but it came back without finding them. Lions were roaring round the camp and Louis had visions of the two most important members of the expedition coming to an untimely end on their very first day at Olduvai. However, at one o'clock in the morning they turned up unscathed: they had waited for moonlight to guide them back to camp, but that night there was an eclipse and they got no light until midnight.

They had set up camp on the edge of the gorge quite close to the site of Reck's 'Olduvai Man', and at first light Louis was off to search for stone tools. Incredible as it may seem, during the three months that Reck had spent at Olduvai in 1913 he had never found a single artifact. It transpired that he had been looking for *flint*, just as Louis had done as a boy at Kabete. Unlike Louis at that time Reck did know what flint looked like – after all, he was a geologist – and when he failed to see any he assumed there could be no stone tools. The handaxes he had seen in Europe were all made of flint, and the idea that they might be made from other kinds of rock had simply never occurred to him.

Louis felt sure that the Olduvai beds must be of the same general age as the 'Kamasian' deposits at Kariandusi, and therefore assumed there should also be handaxes at Olduvai. He made a bet with Reck that he would find one within twenty-four hours of his arrival; the wager was for £10, 'a not inconsiderable part of my research funds for that year', said Louis. He won the bet by a handsome margin. Not only did he find a handaxe but it was actually *in situ*, sticking out of the grey cliff of Bed IV just below the camp. 'I was nearly mad with delight,' he wrote in his book *White African*.

However, he had to tear himself away from Olduvai almost immediately in order to meet Frida and Priscilla, who were due to arrive from England. One can imagine his impatience to get back to this incredible site and with what enthusiasm he proposed that Frida should go there with him only three days after her arrival. But he came smack up against a hurdle which was certainly one of the major causes of the ultimate failure of the marriage. Frida was far too English really to enjoy life in the bush; she was quite prepared to endure it herself, but when it came to taking her baby to a dangerous and waterless camp she put her foot down. Nor could Priscilla be left in the care of others until she had been weaned, and for this lengthy process it was essential for her to have a roof over her head. The roof was only a piece of corrugated iron covering a home-made shack, but it was preferable to canvas with lions scratching at the flaps. So Frida stayed in the bungalow which Louis had built adjoining his parents' house, and he returned to Nairobi to collect two more members of his expedition. These were Donald MacInnes, who had come out for the summer vacation, and a young geologist from St John's called E. V. ('Bunny') Fuchs, later to become Sir Vivian Fuchs of Antarctic fame. Fuchs had recently taken part in the Cambridge expedition to the East African lakes and was ill in hospital in Nairobi, so the party's departure for Olduvai was delayed until 10 October.

The next six weeks was perhaps the most exciting period in Louis's life so far, a period of exploration and discovery with unknown and unlimited possibilities. He and his colleagues could cover only a fraction of the ground, for the sites are spread over some fifteen miles of the main gorge and about three miles of the side gorge which joins it. The search had to be carried out both in a horizontal plane, weaving in and out of countless gullies, and also in a vertical one, up and down sheer cliffs. The camp was situated on the north side of the main gorge, and most of the discoveries made that year were within five miles to the west, towards the junction with the side gorge. Those who were not engaged in puzzling over 'Olduvai Man' (to which we shall return presently) went exploring in different directions, and every evening when they returned to camp, hot and exhausted, they each had something exciting to report.

The sites were named *korongo*, the Swahili word for gully, usually prefixed by the initials of the discoverer, and this tradition has been carried on ever since. Thus the site of Reck's 1913 skeleton was named 'RK', Reck's Korongo, and the place where Louis found the first handaxe in Bed IV became 'CK', Camp Korongo. Then Fuchs and Reck simultaneously found artifacts in Bed II, so the spot was called 'EF-HR' (Evelyn Fuchs-Hans Reck). At MK, MacInnes's Korongo, Donald MacInnes discovered the first remains of aquatic creatures such as hippo, crocodiles and fish, implying the existence of a former lake and giving a boost to Louis's pluvial hypothesis.

During the two months they were there the team accomplished a great deal. They discovered tools in all four main beds, handaxes in Beds II–IV, and 'pebble tools' of a culture which was to be named the Oldowan in the oldest bed, Bed I. After Wayland's 'Kafuan' culture of Uganda was proved to be of natural origin, the Oldowan became the earliest known culture in the world. The first Oldowan artifacts to be found *in situ* came from a site which was named after the absent Frida, FLK; and it was here, within a few yards of the small trial excavation that Louis made in 1931, that the famous '*Zinjanthropus*' skull was discovered by his second wife, Mary, in 1959.

On his pre-war expedition Reck had not found any fossils in Bed I, but the party now discovered plenty. The most sensational was a partly articulated skeleton of *Deinotherium bozasi*, a bizarre relative of the elephant with downward-sweeping tusks in the lower jaw. This beast was well known from Miocene deposits in Europe and Asia, but here it was in the Pleistocene, contemporary with man – an African anachronism. This discovery supported the first hints, deduced from the three-toed horse recovered by Kattwinkel in 1911, that animals long extinct in other continents survived much later in Africa.

But we must return to that human skeleton of Reck's which was, after all, the main purpose of the expedition. Compared with the other discoveries made in 1931 its dating was of minor importance, but this they did not know at the time. If Reck had been right about its position it would indeed have been little short of a miracle: a complete, articulated skeleton of early Pleistocene man – and a man of completely modern appearance! Reck would not budge from his contention that it was *in situ* in Bed II, and after all he was the only person who had witnessed its original position.

Unfortunately the skeleton's resting place was in an area where the geology is particularly misleading. The whole of Bed IV, as well as the conspicuous red bed, Bed III, had been removed by erosion; but just above where the skeleton had lain was a reddish deposit which, very naturally, Reck had taken to be the remains of Bed III. Overlying this reddish pocket is a bed which Reck called Bed V, capped by a crust of hard limestone which formed quite recently. This at least seemed to refute the argument of Reck's critics that the burial was that of a modern Masai, since it seemed very unlikely that anyone would have gone to the trouble of hacking through this very hard crust.

Owing to the presence of that misleading pocket of red, Reck, Louis and the rest of the team dismissed a third possibility, which was in fact the right one. Wily old Wayland hit the nail on the head when he visited Olduvai for a few days in 1932: he concluded that the most likely time for the burial was *after* the formation of Bed IV, when parts of Bed II had been exposed as a land surface as a result of earth movements, and *before* the formation of Bed V and its later limestone capping. In a report of his impressions he wrote: 'Were I compelled to bet, I would put my money on Olduvai Man as a contemporary, more or less, of the Aurignacian people of Elmenteita.'[5] (By 'Elmenteita' he was referring to the general area, but he meant the people of Gamble's Cave.) This was exactly Louis's impression when he saw the Olduvai skeleton in Munich.

However, Reck managed to persuade Louis otherwise – he must be one of the few people who succeeded in swaying Louis once his mind was made up. The other members of the expedition also agreed with Reck, as well as the Director of the Geological Survey of Tanganyika, Sir Edmund Teale, who came to see what was going on in his territory. Within only a few days of their arrival at Olduvai a letter signed by Reck, Louis and Hopwood was despatched to *Nature* confirming Reck's original impression of the great age of the skeleton.[6]

Louis followed this up by articles in *The Times* in which he was rashly dogmatic. The expedition, he said, had established 'almost beyond question that the skeleton of a human being found by Professor Reck in 1913 is the oldest known authentic skeleton of *Homo sapiens*.' (One wonders what he meant by 'authentic', more than twenty years before the debunking of Piltdown!) The age, Louis surmised, must be about the same as that of Peking Man, nearly half a million years.

Having settled, as they thought, the question of Reck's skeleton, the expedition could concentrate on the more rewarding matters already mentioned. Every ten days a truck would go to Nairobi laden with crates of fossils, and by the time the party left at the end of November about a hundred boxes had been despatched. The truck would return with food and petrol, of which they used a great deal in fetching water. Most of it went in plastering fossils and little could be spared for washing. The fine black volcanic dust, blown by the almost continuous strong wind, clung to perspiring skins and everyone was permanently dirty.

The members of the expedition also suffered from cuts and scratches caused by scrambling up and down gullies on hands and knees in search of fossils – Louis once said that he must have spent most of his working life on his knees. Also, the xerophytic vegetation adapted to this dry country is notoriously prickly, particularly the wild sisal that gives Olduvai its name. Wayland, after his first visit there the following year, described it in his usual graphic style: 'Every step is challenged by bayonets of sisal and a hundred other needle points impede one's progress. Almost every vegetative organ that can be so modified to minimise water loss by transpiration has become a thorn. The tough-skinned rhino appear to revel in this, but to the mere human, dermally defenceless, it is another matter.'[7]

By the time the expedition packed up at the end of November,

Louis must have known that at Olduvai he had a site with more than enough work to last him a lifetime.

We now turn to an even more contentious bone, the Kanam jaw, which was to make the ramifications of the Olduvai skeleton seem straightforward by comparison. In March 1932 Louis and Donald MacInnes began exploring the southern shores of the Kavirondo Gulf, an eastward projection of Lake Victoria which extends into the Kavirondo country of western Kenya. Their object was to investigate some early Pleistocene fossil beds discovered in 1911 by Dr Felix Oswald, who had been sent to East Africa by the British Museum (Natural History) to collect in Miocene beds further south. Louis's appetite had been further whetted in 1930 when he had been sent some fossils by an indefatigable collector, the Venerable Archdeacon Owen of the CMS at Maseno, Kavirondo, who had re-located some of Oswald's sites. The fossils were from a place called Kanjera, and it was here that Louis and MacInnes set up camp, three miles from the shore in an unsuccessful attempt to avoid mosquitoes.

They collected many fossils in the ancient lake beds and were excited to find that some, such as Reck's elephant, *Elephas recki*, suggested that the deposits were of the same age as at least part of the Olduvai sequence; and this was further confirmed by the presence of handaxes. Then MacInnes picked up a piece of human skull and, after a thorough search, they collected some more fragments of the same skull cap and two bits of a second one. These were all on the surface, but a hundred yards away they found two pieces of a third skull *in situ* in the lake beds, and nearby on the surface a human femur. The first finds included some scraps from the region of the forehead, which was quite smooth as in *Homo sapiens*. The age of the Olduvai skeleton might still be in doubt but here, it seemed, was certain evidence of a modern type of man in early Pleistocene deposits. Peking Man, with his hefty brow-ridges, had been discovered only three years previously: the Kanjera skulls, it seemed clear to Louis, suggested that the human stem had split in two directions. Here at Kanjera he had the true ancestor of modern man.

Elated with success they moved on to Kanam, three miles to the west near the foot of Homa mountain. Here they attained one of their main objects by finding a tooth of *Deinotherium*, the elephant-like beast which they had found only in the lowest bed at Olduvai. It seemed, therefore, that the Kanam deposits were older than those of Kanjera, and this was later confirmed by the presence of other archaic mammals and also by Oldowan-like tools.

One of the assistants whom Louis had taken with him was that observant collector Juma Gitau. On 29 March Juma brought over to Louis another *Deinotherium* tooth which he had dug out of the side of a gully at Kanam West; Louis was busy excavating the jaw of an extinct pig, so he told Juma to go on searching. Hacking into the same cliff, Juma then dislodged a large block which he proceeded to break up with his pick. One of the pieces contained some teeth, which he showed to Donald MacInnes who was working further up in the same gully. Obviously they were human, and Donald called to Louis to come over. They searched hard for more pieces but in vain.

Back in camp they cleared off some of the surrounding rock and found they had part of a human jaw, much damaged and weathered, with all the teeth broken off except for two premolars. If only Louis had left his pig and gone to the spot straight away he would have saved himself untold worry in the years to come. But why should he? Juma was perfectly capable of following up a *Deinotherium* tooth unaided. On 19 April Louis wrote off to *Nature* describing the Kanam mandible, and within a month it was published.[8]

In June, after finishing work in the Kanam-Kanjera area, Louis went on to Entebbe to invite Wayland personally to visit Olduvai. According to his account in *White African*, he took with him the Kanjera skulls and Kanam jaw to show to his colleague. On the return journey his lorry skidded and overturned. His first thought, apparently, was not for the widow and child he might be leaving behind but 'Will anyone discover and recognise the precious specimens which we have on board and recover them?'[9]

Louis had to spend a month recovering from the accident, and from a bout of malaria which came on at the same time. He then went to the worst possible place for convalescence, a rock shelter some twenty miles north of Olduvai in completely waterless country. The Masai call it Nasera, but Louis always referred to it as Apis Rock. The name owes its origin to a remark made by the late H. J. Allen Turner, who had been connected with the East Africa and Uganda Natural History Society, and with the little museum it ran in Nairobi, ever since 1911. He accompanied Louis and Donald MacInnes on a reconnaissance to Nasera, and Louis was in a state of great excitement at finding a stagnant pool at the rock shelter. 'There's water,' he cried. Turner looked at it with distaste and said 'That's not water, that's ape's piss.' And Apis Rock it has been called ever since.

The shelter, for all its lack of facilities, is a most impressive place. About fifty feet high, with a large overhang, it is still used by Masai warriors for meat feasts. Probably it has been used for the same purpose for thousands of years – at any rate, Louis's excavations proved that it had been occupied spasmodically for a very long time. It was an act of real heroism for Louis and MacInnes to persist in their work for two months. A few weeks after their arrival Louis wrote to Hopwood: 'The water problems are worse than ever and our present drinking water is so vile that for half an hour after drinking it either with lemon or in tea or coffee one feels sick as a dog. It's drier than I could ever have believed and in the gorge [Olduvai] there is not a rhino, not a lion, not even a hyena, only dikdik and hares which do without any water at all . . . I'm too tired to write much.'[10]

Apis Rock proved to have five prehistoric occupation levels: the finds have been described by Louis in his book *Stone Age Africa* (1936). One of the industries appeared to be similar to the 'Magosian', first described by Wayland in 1926 from a waterhole called Magosi in Karamoja, eastern Uganda. When Wayland accepted Louis's invitation to visit Olduvai, therefore, he was particularly interested to see the Magosian of Apis Rock. They then spent three days at Olduvai, collecting fossils and tools but mainly going over the problem of Reck's skeleton. Wayland's impressions have already been quoted, and Louis was half persuaded; but he was reluctant to go back on his support for Reck's original dating within a year of the publication of their views in *Nature*. There was by now also an even weightier reason for hoping that Olduvai

Man was as ancient as Reck had at first believed. At Kanjera Louis had found skulls of apparently modern type associated with extinct fauna; a modern-looking man with similar associations at Olduvai would obviously help to confirm the dating and validity of his Kanjera skulls. He was thus torn in two directions: he *wanted* the Olduvai skeleton to be early Pleistocene, yet he was haunted by his first impression that it was of the same age as his Gamble's Cave skeletons. And now Wayland was supporting this view.

To finish this long story of Olduvai Man to the bitter end, we must go forward to the following year, 1933, when Louis made yet another pilgrimage to Munich – his third – in order to see the skeleton. He found it bore no resemblance whatever to his Kanjera skulls. Moreover, Professor Mollison, who had been studying Olduvai Man for so many years, had now examined it under ultra-violet light: he found a great contrast between it and very recent bones on the one hand and the fossil fauna from Olduvai Bed II on the other. There was nothing for it but to go back to Olduvai and find out where they had gone wrong in interpreting the field evidence. In 1934 Louis was accompanied there by Professor P. G. H. Boswell, FRS, who features prominently later on in this chapter. Boswell collected samples of the red deposit overlying the site of the skeleton, which the members of the 1931 expedition had taken to be the remains of Bed III. He tested them by his pet method of heavy mineral analysis and proved conclusively that the sample contained minerals which were not present in Bed III, nor in Bed IV, but were present only in the overlying deposits. The skeleton, in fact, could not be contemporary with Bed II, but had been buried into it after the formation of Bed IV. In the early 1970s a radiocarbon date on part of one of the ribs of the Olduvai skeleton gave an age of about 15,000 B.C.*

Louis's first impressions had been right after all. Wayland had been right and Reck had been wrong. Louis and Reck had to eat

*On the dating, the skeleton is correlated with a site in what is now called the Naisiusiu bed, the equivalent of the later part of Reck's 'Bed V'. In 1931 Louis dug a small trial trench in this bed and found artifacts rather like those of Gamble's Cave, but which are now known to be much earlier. Reck's Olduvai Man, in fact, must have been one of the makers of the earliest microlithic – 'small tool' – industry in East Africa.

their over-hasty words in *Nature* and at long last, after twenty years in limbo, this time-wasting skeleton was relegated to its rightful resting place. Underneath 'H1' on the concrete slab marking the site of the first human remains discovered at Olduvai someone should write 'RIP'.

From Apis Rock, Louis had written to Hopwood: 'I've put all our passage money into this trip, hoping to get enough back from the sale of the lorries and cars when the time comes.'[11] Poor Frida, who had been waiting patiently all this time, let us hope that she did not know that their passage money was in jeopardy. But evidently the sale of the vehicles was successful, for they were able to return to England towards the end of 1932.

They still had the little oast house at Foxton, but Frida decided it was no place in which to bring up her daughter and that it was time they had a proper home. So with £1,800 of her own money she bought a fairly large house called 'The Close' at Girton, on the outskirts of Cambridge, after which she never moved again. (Eventually she made over the house to her son Colin and built herself a cottage in the orchard, where she still lives today.) Louis kept on the Foxton cottage as a base, sharing the rent of five shillings a week with Dr E. Barton Worthington and his wife. After his return from an expedition to the East African lakes to study fish, Dr Worthington was almost as penniless as Louis. 'We could just afford half a crown a week each,' he says, 'and the box and cox arrangement lasted a year or so. Needless to say, much of the oast house was occupied by boxes of stone tools and fossils.'

In fact, Louis spent very little time either at Foxton or The Close; as before, he worked and often slept in his rooms at St John's, with many visits to London. He was busier than ever, studying his collections of tools, making restorations of the Kanjera skulls, and preparing these and his other human remains for publication. The Kanjera skulls with their smooth brows were unprecedented in such an early context, but the even older Kanam jaw was still more puzzling. According to the then accepted pattern of Piltdown, a human jaw of such venerable age was expected to have a receding chin; instead, the contour in the Kanam mandible was almost vertical. (A bony growth on the inside had exaggerated the prominence of the chin, but this was not realized at first.) Before Louis left East Africa Hopwood had written to warn him of the reception he was likely to get if he claimed such a great age for specimens with so modern an appearance: 'I'll tell you the main question raised in regard to your discoveries up to now and then you can set about answering it in advance. Can you disprove the assertion that your specimens may have slipped in during falls of cliff, or that you may have found them in rain-wash? The latter is a very dangerous form of criticism which is always being pushed at me with great vigour. All I can do is to say "Wait and see" and extol your virtues as a careful and conscientious collector. Your job is going to be all the harder because you have no geologist with you. Well, I go on fighting for you as best I can and you have other allies as well. So long as you have plenty of evidence, checked and cross-checked, there will be eventual triumph ahead of you.'[12]

The triumph was a very long time in coming – if indeed it ever did so far as the Kanam jaw was concerned – and, although Louis himself thought his evidence was watertight, unfortunately it had *not* been checked and cross-checked sufficiently.

In order to satisfy themselves about the provenance of the Kanam and Kanjera finds, the human biology section of the Royal Anthropological Institute decided to convene a conference at St John's on 18-19 March 1933. Presiding over a learned bunch of twenty-eight scientists was Sir Arthur Smith Woodward, and among those who served on the various committees were Dr A. C. Haddon, Professor P. G. H. Boswell, and four members of Louis's expeditions: Hopwood, Fuchs, MacInnes and Solomon. Louis first gave a talk on his evidence for the dating of the finds. This was followed by a general discussion and the appointment of committees to consider the geological, palaeontological, anatomical and archaeological evidence. That evening, Louis was 'at home' in his rooms at No. 1 New Court, where he exhibited material from Olduvai, Kanam and Kanjera, and those members of the conference who were staying in College dined with the Fellows in Hall. The next day, a Sunday, the sub-committees met in the morning, and in the afternoon the whole conference assembled to hear their reports and draw up a statement.

The geological committee agreed that, from the evidence presented, the Kanam mandible had come from the horizon which yielded *Deinotherium* and other Lower Pleistocene fauna. The anatomical committee concluded that the appearance of the human jaw was not inconsistent with the high antiquity assigned to it, and they were 'unable to point to any detail of the specimen that is incompatible with its inclusion in the type of *Homo sapiens*.' (These two statements seem somewhat contradictory, but in referring to its appearance the committee were presumably referring to the state of mineralization of the jaw.) With regard to the Kanjera skulls, the anatomical committee were unable to exclude the possibility of some distortion in the reconstruction, but nevertheless they could not call them anything other than *Homo sapiens*.

In general the conference 'accepted the reports, congratulated Dr Leakey on the exceptional significance of his discoveries, and expressed the hope that he may be enabled to undertake further researches, seeing that there is no field of archaeological enquiry which offers greater prospects for the future. It especially urges the organization of another expedition.'[13] So far, very good; but the triumph was short-lived.

For the next six months peace reigned, at least on the surface. Louis exhibited the Kanam jaw at a Royal Society conversazione on 17 May, and for a month it was on show at the British Museum (Natural History). At a meeting of the Royal Anthropological Institute in October Louis announced that he had decided to create a new species, *Homo kanamensis*, mainly because of certain features of the pulp cavities in the roots of the cheek teeth. (Palaeoanthropologists and palaeontologists are divided into two camps, the lumpers and the splitters; Louis was an incorrigible splitter.) But, as though to get the best of both worlds, Louis also emphasized that the Kanam jaw 'approached primitive *Homo sapiens* very closely.'[14] What was this 'primitive *Homo sapiens*'? At that time no such example was known from the fossil record, so presumably he was referring to modern 'primitives' such as the Australian aborigines.

Amid the general congratulations which followed his talk at the RAI one sour note was struck. The striker was Professor Boswell, who had already put his name to the conclusions of the geological committee at the Cambridge conference. Having brooded over the matter since then, he now stressed the advisability of obtaining further geological evidence from Kanam. He did not let the matter rest, but continued to voice his misgivings to such an extent that Louis persuaded the Royal Society, of which Boswell was a senior Fellow, to pay for him to go to Kenya and study the evidence for himself. How often in the months to come Louis must have wished he had kept his mouth shut; for the Battle of Boswell, fought on the field of Kanam in January 1935, was to prove disastrous.

Percy Boswell, Professor of Geology at Imperial College, is said to have had a somewhat contradictory character, emotional, inclined to be humorous, almost obsessively concerned with professional conduct. He came from a poor background and may have suffered from the proverbial chip on his shoulder even after he had risen to the dizzy heights of FRS. He had been to Gamble's Cave on his way back from the British Association meeting at Johannesburg in 1929, so he should have gained a favourable impression of Louis's methods of excavation. On the debit side, however, Louis had gained a black mark by his over-hasty letter to *Nature* on the antiquity of the Olduvai skeleton, which Boswell had always believed to be more recent. His vendetta against the Kanam mandible – and against Louis – was no doubt prompted mainly because of his insistence on scientific exactitude, but perhaps jealousy was another motive. In addition, Boswell championed the Piltdown mandible and so was unable to accept a jaw with a chin in the Lower Pleistocene.

Louis had no doubt whatever that Boswell would be convinced once he had seen the evidence at Kanam, but the prospective visit could not be arranged before January 1935. In the meantime Louis knew that at all costs he must find a geologist and a surveyor, so he had to raise more funds than ever for his fourth expedition, and it was not until the autumn of 1934 that the party got away. As geologist he took a young man called Peter Kent from the University of Nottingham, and he could not have made a better choice: Sir Peter Kent, FRS, was to have a distinguished career and eventually became British Petroleum's exploration manager. The post of surveyor was filled by Sam White; and a zoologist, Peter Bell, also joined the expedition to collect for the Natural History Museum.

They went straight to the Kanam-Kanjera area where Kent was kept busy trying to work out the very complicated geology. At a nearby site called Rawi, Louis and his African staff soon began to find quantities of fossils, including a gigantic tortoise with a femur as big as that of a buffalo. The indefatigable Juma discovered the skull of a new species of giraffe which was named after him, *Giraffa jumae*. On one occasion the entire labour force went on strike because they said the foreman had given them an impossible task to complete and told them they could not eat until they had done it. Louis hurried over to Rawi and, he wrote in his diary:

> While sullenly watched by some of the staff, Ndekei and I alone cleared the so-called too big set task in twenty minutes. So that eight men (who were on that particular job) could have cleared it easily in ten or even five minutes. I gave them a piece of my mind and made them really afraid they would all lose their jobs, and then forgave them and they went off to work cheerfully once more.[15]

If only industrial relations were so easily solved nowadays!

In January 1935 Louis left the others to continue their work while he went to Nairobi to meet Boswell. He was not looking forward to this visit and he had invited his ally Wayland to come and lend his support. The events which followed were recorded in Louis's field diary:

> January 16. Spent day at Kanjera with Wayland, the Professor, [i.e. Boswell] Kent and White and we went over the area with my book and with my photos etc. but I could not place the site of Kanjera No. 3 exactly after the lapse of time, though I placed it within ten yards or so to my satisfaction. . . . Then White found a piece of fossilized bone (apparently human parietal bone) on the surface. I spent the rest of the day riddling the surface and getting quite good material (small fragments which fitted).

Next day he notes that they started digging and:

> Juma found a bit of human skull very heavily mineralized within

> thirty feet of where I claim the Kanjera skull to have been before it was eroded away . . . and I found a second bit. It is nineteen paces to the SSW of point 7 on the map. Its position has been marked.[16]

The map refers to one made by White on the present expedition; none had been made in 1932 when the skulls were found – and this was the cause of all the trouble to come.

At Kanam the auspices were far from good. In 1932 Louis had marked the spot where the human jaw was found with iron pegs; but in the intervening years the local Luo fishermen had taken advantage of this windfall and removed the pegs to make into harpoons and spear-heads. To make matters worse the rainfall had been heavy and there had been much erosion: it proved impossible to pinpoint the exact spot where the mandible had been found. All this was bad enough but there was worse to come. In 1932 Louis had photographed the spot where Juma's *Deinotherium* tooth had lain, and which led to the discovery of the human jaw; but his ancient camera had an unsuspected hole in the bellows, and the film was a complete blank. However, someone else had taken some photos at the time. This was Miss Kendrick, a friend of Frida's who had been staying at Limuru to share in the baby-sitting (in fact Frida seems to have done most of the sitting, while Miss Kendrick did most of the travelling). When Louis found that his own photos had not come out he borrowed some of hers. One was marked on the back 'Site of the *Deinotherium* tooth', and this had been displayed beside the human jaw at the Royal College of Surgeons. For the events that followed, we may return to Louis's diary for 18 January.

> Professor Boswell, Wayland and Kent spent the day at Kanam West [Louis himself was at Kanjera, searching for more skull fragments] and they say – and I suppose they are right – that they have located the exact position of Miss Kendrick's photo and that it was not Kanam West main gullies at all, but is Kanam West Fish Cliff gullies. This is serious because in all good faith I have published the photo of Miss Kendrick's as being Kanam West main gullies. I've cabled to the Press to hold up distribution of my book pending insertion of an erratum notice. [This was *The Stone Age Races of Kenya*, to be published by Oxford University Press.] The Professor is in a bad humour over it. Apart from the absence of trees and of details in the

> gullies, it is terribly like Kanam West and the mistake is not surprising though very regrettable.

Next day Boswell and Wayland had to leave. The visit had been a disaster from start to finish, and as Louis was ill with fever at the time he may have been more argumentative with Boswell than he might otherwise have been. The affair of the unfortunate photograph might be thought to be more of a molehill than a mountain, yet because it had such an effect on Louis's reputation it is important to get the facts straight. Miss Kendrick's picture, in fact, showed the site where the *first* of the *Deinotherium* teeth had been found, some four hundred yards from the place where Juma found the second *Deinotherium* tooth and the human jaw. Boswell was already put out when Louis could not pinpoint the exact spot where the Kanjera No. 3 skull was discovered; when he heard of the mix-up over the Kanam photograph he was doubly suspicious that the whole thing had been framed.

When Miss Kendrick gave Louis the photograph she is said to have remarked 'I am not sure that this is the exact spot,' to which Louis is supposed to have replied 'Near enough.' However, from the extracts from his field diary, which was for his own use and certainly not intended for posterity, it seems clear that he had no intention of deliberately cooking the evidence. To him the matter of a few hundred yards was quite unimportant, and it took this affair to teach him that in science even a few inches are vital.

In his diary for 16 March 1935 Louis wrote: 'A letter from Dr Haddon which is very disturbing. In it he suggests that Boswell's findings may ruin my career. Apparently he has reported most unfavourably to the Royal Society and is writing to *Nature.*' In his letter Haddon had said:

> I have been shown Boswell's report to the Royal Society and also your field report, December 24–January 24, and I must confess that I am disappointed at the casual way in which you deal with the matter. So far as I can gather it is not merely a question of a mistaken photograph, but a criticism of all your geological evidence at Kanam, Kanjera and Oldoway. The conference at Cambridge had to rely implicitly upon your statements, and from what I hear there is much annoyance in view of recent developments. It seems to me that your

future career depends largely upon the manner in which you face the criticisms. I am not in a position to know to what extent they can be rebutted by you with scientific evidence, but if you want to secure the confidence of scientific men you must act bravely and not shuffle. You may remember that more than once I have warned you not to be in too much of a hurry in your scientific work as I feared that your zeal might overrun your discretion and I can only hope that it has not done so in this case.[17]

Dr Haddon was always among the first to congratulate his gifted pupil on his achievements but, because he took such an interest in him, he never hesitated to try to pull on the reins when necessary. Louis had a great deal of respect for his old supervisor personally, but Haddon also stood for St John's and for Cambridge, and Louis minded very much indeed what Cambridge thought of him. As Haddon said in his letter, on this occasion as on so many others Louis had been in too much of a hurry. After the Kanam jaw was found in 1932 he had wanted to get back to Olduvai and to excavate at Apis Rock. He should have stopped to make some geological maps, although neither he nor MacInnes were properly qualified to do so; and he should have made sure his own photographs had come out and, if necessary, returned to take more – but it is easy to be wise after the event.

Boswell's bombshell appeared in *Nature* on 9 March 1935[18] but Louis did not receive a copy until 28 March, when he wrote in his diary: 'Got a copy of Boswell's attack in *Nature*, to which I must reply when I calm down. At present I'm so angry that I'd probably say things which I'd regret afterwards.'

In this letter to *Nature* Boswell said: 'Unfortunately, it has not proved possible to find the exact site of either discovery [i.e., Kanam and Kanjera] since the earlier expedition neither marked the localities on the ground nor recorded the sites on a map.' This was not true, as Boswell knew very well: the spot had been marked with iron pegs, which the Luo fishermen had removed. Boswell, of course, also brought up the matter of the photograph and made a serious allegation not only of cooked evidence but also of geological incompetence.

Moreover, the photograph of the site where the mandible was found, exhibited with the jaw fragment at the Royal College of Surgeons, was, through some error, that of a different locality; and the deposits (said to be clays) are in fact of entirely different rock (volcanic agglomerate).

Boswell then turned his attention to Kanjera, pointing out that the photograph labelled as the horizon from which Kanjera No. 3 was obtained proved to be a picture of a cliff of volcanic ash some distance away. He next referred to the excavations made in 1934, just before his arrival, 'at sites which, one hoped, were close to those of the original finds.' They 'revealed the fact that the clay beds . . . had frequently suffered much disturbance by slumping. The date of entombment of human remains found in such beds would be inherently doubtful, and careful investigation of the deposits by an experienced geologist at the time of discovery would therefore be essential.'

In conclusion he wrote: 'Thus, in view of the uncertain location of the Kanam and Kanjera sites, and in view also of the doubt as to the stratigraphic horizons from which the remains were obtained and the possibility of distortion of the beds, I hold the opinion that the geological age of the mandible and skull fragments is uncertain.'

This attack, in the glaring spotlight of one of the world's most esteemed scientific journals, came as a complete shock to Louis. In his fifth monthly field report for February-March 1935 (these reports were circulated to fund-giving sources and colleagues) Louis wrote: 'Professor Boswell explicitly told me . . . that he proposed to publish *nothing* until the Expedition returned to England.' Boswell was swift to repudiate this statement, and in Louis's combined ninth and tenth field reports he had to make amends:

> I most certainly never intended making an unjustified accusation of bad faith against Professor Boswell. . . . In his letter to me Professor Boswell implies – but does not actually state – that he had told me he was going to publish a criticism in *Nature* or elsewhere, but from what he says in a letter to one of my colleagues I understand that he says that he told me on January 18th. I can still say quite frankly that I have no recollection whatever of his saying so . . . I am, of course, fully prepared to accept Professor Boswell's word that he did tell me that he was going to write to *Nature* on his return to England . . . and

I sincerely apologise for having mistakenly made an unfair accusation of bad faith.

Meanwhile Louis had been composing a lengthy reply to *Nature*, but his first effort was too long-winded and was turned down by the editor. The amended version was not published until the following year, 1936.[19] After giving his explanation of the photographs, claiming that he had only used them to show the general nature of the sites, he went on to say that Boswell's remark about the geological context had been widely interpreted as meaning 'Leakey does not know the difference between a clay and a volcanic agglomerate.' Although Louis had had no formal geological training, his long experience in the field had certainly made him capable of distinguishing between the two; whatever the merits of Boswell's other accusations, this one was unjustified.

There was never any question that the jaw had come from within a few feet of the spot pointed out to Boswell; but no scientist had actually seen it *in situ*, and the Professor would not accept Juma's word for it – Louis's description of Juma as a 'born scientist' would have cut no ice at all. Whether the mandible was actually *in situ* in the beds containing early Pleistocene fossils, notably the *Deinotherium* tooth, was another matter. The block containing the human jaw might have been of a later age, washed down into the gully, and this is the explanation offered by some authorities today.

If only Louis had had the courage to own up that he just *could* have been wrong, and that the jaw *might* not be as old as he thought, he would have been forgiven; but he would never admit that there could be any possibility of a mistake. He had already committed himself too deeply in *The Stone Age Races of Kenya*, which could hardly have come out at a more unfortunate moment. In it he wrote: 'The importance of this Kanam mandible lies in the fact that it can be dated geologically, palaeontologically and archaeologically, and that it represents the oldest known human fragment yet found in the African continent. . . . It is not only the oldest known human fragment from Africa, but the most ancient fragment of true *Homo* yet discovered anywhere in the world.'[20]

Louis soon abandoned the specific name *kanamensis* and

reverted to *sapiens*, which only made matters worse in the eyes of his critics: if the jaw was that modern in appearance, they said, then it must have got into the wrong layer. In the years to come the jaw was to be called by as many names as a much-married film star. There were as many different opinions about its age as there were about its taxonomic status, but uranium tests carried out at the BM in 1962 seemed to suggest Upper rather than Lower Pleistocene.

Louis thoroughly enjoyed crossing swords in the esoteric pages of *Nature* when he felt he was right; but on this occasion, although convinced that his evidence was watertight, he knew he had been slipshod in putting it across. This was one controversy that he had *not* enjoyed.

Boswell's report had a profound psychological effect on Louis, who for the rest of his life was haunted by the spectre of that jaw. It taught him a lesson he never forgot. Henceforward he drove himself harder than ever in order to prove himself, but he never again made the mistake of not checking, cross-checking, and then rechecking his evidence.

Many people thought that Boswell's attack was unjustified in its intensity and that it might have been made less blatantly than in the pages of *Nature*. Ironically, Nemesis caught up with him in a cruel way: he was accused of the very same charge that he had levelled against Louis – incompetence in geology. At a meeting of the Geological Society in London, Professor O. T. Jones made mincemeat of a paper that Boswell had given on tectonic structures in Wales, implying that he did not know the elementary principles of structural geology. As a result Boswell resigned his professorship, and had a nervous breakdown from which he never recovered.

5 Louis and Mary

If Louis had made a mistake over Kanam, he made an even bigger one when he married Frida. This was through no fault of hers, for she had excellent qualities and she truly loved him; but she could no more confine Louis to conventional home life than he could make her adapt to his nomad wanderings. Probably she had already faced up to the fact that the marriage had foundered when she bought The Close at the end of 1932. The appearance of Mary Douglas Nicol on the scene some six months later merely hastened the inevitable.

Mary had prehistory in her genes. Her great-great-great-grandfather on her mother's side, John Frere, was the first Englishman to recognize a flint implement for what it was: in 1797 he said about some handaxes he had found at Hoxne, Suffolk, that they must have been used by 'a people who had not the use of metals' and that they belonged to 'a very ancient period indeed, even before that of the present world.' Mary herself made her debut in archaeology at the age of eleven when she was taken to the Dordogne by her father, Erskine Nicol, a landscape painter. While he stood in front of his easel his daughter was introduced to prehistory by the Abbé Lemozi, who was excavating at Cabrerets at the time.

Mary had been to various schools in France, but her parents had never stayed in one place long enough for her to remain anywhere for more than a few terms. Before the birth of their only child in 1913 they had lived on a houseboat on the Nile, and then, during the war, they had rented cottages in England for short periods. After the war was over they travelled in France and Italy, returning to England only briefly each summer while Erskine Nicol held an exhibition of his somewhat Turneresque paintings. After he died in 1926 his widow Cecilia, who was a Roman Catholic, sent Mary to a succession of convents from which she was regularly expelled for unruly behaviour. She also spent a few terms in village schools, and occasionally she had a governess.

After this sketchy education, Mary could not hope to read for a university degree; but ever since her introduction to the fabulous caves of the Dordogne she was determined to study prehistory, and she therefore went to lectures on archaeology and geology at University College, London. At the same time she was developing an exceptional talent for drawing, inherited from her father. From an early age she had copied engraved stones and other artifacts for her own amusement, and through a chance introduction she now got an opportunity to put this hobby to practical use. A friend had written to the archaeologist Dr Gertrude Caton-Thompson telling her of Mary's interest in prehistory and suggesting that she might like to encourage her. When Dr Caton-Thompson saw Mary's drawings she was so impressed that she invited her to illustrate stone tools for her book *The Desert Fayoum.*[1] Mary had no training in this difficult art, but she had one most important qualification: an understanding of the way in which the tools were made.

Dr Caton-Thompson also introduced Mary to Louis. He was giving a talk about Olduvai at the Royal Anthropological Institute and she invited Mary to come along. Afterwards some of the Fellows dined together at a hotel near the RAI's offices in Bedford Square; Louis was surrounded by people wanting to ask more questions about his wonderful site, but Mary's fairy godmother arranged that she should sit next to him. Louis was at his best, the centre of attention, and with an intelligent and attractive girl to listen to his excited talk. In spite of their difference in age and experience – or perhaps because of it – they clicked at once. Louis was not quite thirty, Mary was just twenty; she was flattered by his attention and completely bowled over by his charm.

Louis had nearly finished writing a 'popular' book on prehistory, *Adam's Ancestors,* and badly needed someone to draw stone tools for it; when Mary showed him the drawings she had done for *The Desert Fayoum* he promptly offered her the job. She accepted with delight, and so they were thrown together by their work as well as by mutual interests and attraction for one another. Mary did most of her drawings at the British Museum in Bloomsbury, where Louis's collections were housed; but he also kept artifacts in his rooms at St John's, and he asked Frida if he could bring Mary to stay for a few days at The Close so that she could draw them. Frida had not been at all well and was expecting her second child very soon, but she agreed. The two women were completely unlike, both in appearance and character: Frida tall, big-boned and dark, Mary relatively short, slight and blue-eyed; Frida bustling and talkative, Mary quiet and methodical. They met for the first and last time. Frida was quite unaware of the possibility that Louis's feelings for Mary were getting deeper every day; in fact she did not appreciate the situation until after the birth of her son, Colin Louis Avern, on 13 December 1933.

Parents are usually the last people to hear about events that affect them so closely, and Canon and Mrs Leakey were no exception. They had just retired to a farm at Limuru, not far from the mission station at Kabete, where the Canon proposed to grow pyrethrum and plums as well as continuing his translation work. At a meeting of the executive committee of the Church Missionary Society in Nairobi in November 1933 the Society's indebtedness to the Leakeys was recorded in the following minute:

> On the occasion of the retirement of Canon and Mrs Leakey from active service in the Mission, this executive committee of the Kenya Mission of the CMS desires to place on record their keen appreciation of the very earnest and consistent work which they have done since their first coming to Kenya, Canon Leakey in 1902 and Mrs Leakey as long ago as 1892. Their devotion to the cause of Christ, and to the uplift and evangelization of the African, have been greatly used in the advancement of the Kingdom of God. The wonderful growth and development of the work at Kabete under their direction and the valuable translation work done by Canon Leakey are greatly appreciated by the Committee, and they pray God that in their retirement they may still have many years of happy and useful service. They especially trust that Canon Leakey's great linguistic gift may still be used to the benefit of the Kikuyu tribe.

This tribe paid 'Giteru', as they called him, an even more touching tribute when the members of the Loyal Kikuyu Patriots of Kiambu presented him with a silk square on which were printed these words:

> We, members of Loyal Kikuyu Patriots, wish to express our gratitude to you, Mr Leakey, for the great work which you have performed amongst us during 16 years. We are sorry that you are leaving us, we shall miss you very much. Your ability, patience, endurance and enthusiasm in your work among the Kikuyu have influenced many souls and have won the confidence of all in you. We are glad to say that your sociability, courtesy, humility and spirit of perfect leadership have made you a successful bridge between black and white. We cannot express the feeling in our hearts, either verbally or in writing, owing to the fact that we know that you would not like the praise of men; but let us assure you that we men and women, old and young, are thankful indeed.

At the same time, they presented Canon Harry with a silver tray 'as a token and memento of our love, confidence and esteem towards you.'

In May 1934 Louis's parents went on a holiday to England. They still did not know of Mary's existence, nor even that Louis had left Frida, as is clear from a letter Canon Harry wrote to Louis from the Red Sea:

> *Dear Old Man* . . . It was only when the breeze dropped that Mother began to melt badly. She dreamt the other day that she was entreating someone just to leave her quietly alone and she would be a little pile of melted butter in the morning! But she's all right, and still quite solid, and I am absolutely amazed, and so, so thankful, to find what her head can stand now as compared with years ago when she used to be so delicate. . . . We are longing to see you all four again – or rather Colin for the first time. Heaps of love from your loving old Daddy,
>
> *Harry Leakey*.[2]

Some time during their visit to England that summer Louis had to tell his parents that his marriage to Frida had broken up; but he did not introduce Mary to them, and they did not hear about her until the following year.

Meanwhile Mary was doing her first important archaeological excavations, at Hembury Fort in Devon. The leader, Miss Dorothy Liddell, was well ahead of her time in methods of excavation and she taught Mary many techniques which were to be invaluable in her work later on in East Africa. Then, in September 1934, Mary was for the first time her own boss on an archaeological dig, cooperating with Kenneth Oakley who did the geological side of the work. At that time he was working for the Geological Survey, and he had obtained a grant from the British Association for the Advancement of Science to try to settle the vexed question of the place of the Clactonian culture in the British sequence. This they succeeded in doing as a result of their excavations at Jaywick Sands, near Clacton in Essex, and they subsequently published a joint report – Mary's first scientific paper.[3] Louis was particularly interested in the Clactonian, which he later investigated himself at Swanscombe in Kent, so he had a genuine excuse to visit Mary frequently at weekends in the bungalow rented by her mother near Jaywick Sands.

Soon after, Louis left for East Africa on his fourth expedition. In January 1935, while he was having his traumatic experiences with Boswell at Kanjera and Kanam, Mary went to South Africa to look at prehistoric sites; and in April she was to join Louis at Olduvai.

Louis, with Sam White the surveyor, left for Olduvai on 13 April, the beginning of the season known in East Africa as 'the long rains'. Camping only a few miles along the road, next morning they got away by 8 o'clock and by dusk they had accomplished exactly twelve miles. The road was ghastly: 'Never,' wrote Louis in his diary, 'have I known worse all my time out here. Had to take off mudguards as mud was pure gum – every hundred yards had to take out mud with hands.'[4] The next day they left camp at 7.30 a.m. and by midday had covered only two hundred yards. Louis was getting frantic, as Mary's plane from South Africa was due at Moshi, near Arusha, on 18 April. However, after that the road improved and they arrived in plenty of time. From Arusha Sam White went on to Ngorongoro Crater with the lorry, while Louis took the car to Moshi to meet Mary.

She was to have a tough introduction to Louis's way of life, and if she had ever had any doubts about wanting to share it with him the events of the next few days would have been enough to put her off.

On the way to pick up a geologist named Sam Howard who was

to work at Olduvai they were chased by a rhino and broke a spring. At the foot of the scarp up to Ngorongoro they stuck and had to sleep the night in a damp hut abandoned by road-makers. It rained all night, and the following day they made exactly three miles' progress. They managed to get a message through to White, who was waiting on the rim of the Crater, and he sent some men to push; but they had first to unload the vehicle and carry all the equipment on their heads. The clutch was ruined, and for the second night in succession they had to sleep in a cold, damp hut. They left early next morning and by nightfall just managed to reach White's camp at Ngorongoro, eleven miles away. It had taken three and a half days to cover sixteen miles. After that, although the clutch was slipping badly, they descended on to the plains and reached Olduvai with no further trouble.

The annual rainfall at Olduvai averages twenty-three inches, and nearly all of it must have fallen just before they arrived. But surface water does not remain long on parched soil, which soaks it up greedily like a sponge, and already the river in the gorge had subsided, leaving only dirty pools. Two days after their arrival Louis wrote: 'Spent afternoon trying to make a filter as the water is *vile*.'[5] And next day: 'The waterhole is drying up. I'm feeling very unfit.' The filter was not a success, but worked better after he had collected some clean sand: 'After filtering, the water is a little less smelly and makes drinkable tea or coffee. It will be awful as plain water I fear.' (They still had some drinking water that they had brought with them and were trying to eke it out.) About a fortnight later it rained again and the river in the gorge was raging; Louis records that he actually swam three strokes in one of the pools.

Naturally Louis was anxious for Mary to be impressed by Olduvai – who could fail to be? – and he could not have chosen a better time to show it to her than after the rains. It was looking its very best, with green grass and abundant wildlife; it was difficult to imagine that for the rest of the year the plains above the gorge would be brown as far as the eye could see and for hundreds of miles beyond. They camped further west than the place where Louis and Reck had pitched their tents in 1931, still on the north side of the main gorge but close to its junction with the side gorge.

The side gorge had not yet been explored, and this was the main object of the present expedition.

After Peter Kent joined the party he began to work on the geology of the side gorge – on one occasion he had a nasty encounter with nine lions there – and in later years, when the geology had been studied in more detail, an explanation was found for the abundance of prehistoric sites in this area. The side gorge follows the line of the shore of the early Pleistocene lake, and this is where the hominids camped and ate their meals, scattering debris for the Leakeys to uncover. During that 1935 season Louis and his team found at least twenty promising sites. One of them, MNK – Mary Nicol Korongo – was named in honour of Mary, who discovered a scrap of human parietal bone there; this became H2, the second hominid from Olduvai. There had been an interval of twenty-two years since Reck unearthed the first, and another twenty years were to go by before the discovery of the third.

Louis made at least a few exceptions to the general rule of naming sites after their discoverers: in a surge of patriotism he called one GRK to commemorate King George V's jubilee which took place that year; and another was named NBG – it proved to be No Bloody Good, but in fact the letters stood for Nobody's Gully.

Until a thorough survey had been made Louis resisted the temptation to do more than a few trial excavations. Only after exploring more than a hundred miles of exposures methodically would it be possible to decide on the most promising sites for digging. He had been impatient at Kanam with most unfortunate results, and he was not going to take any chances at Olduvai – the most magnificent site that had ever fallen into the lap of any prehistorian. If it had not been for the First World War he would never have got it: Reck would certainly have claimed it for Germany. And if it had not been for the Second World War Louis would have come to grips with it much sooner. The treasures which Olduvai was to yield had lain buried for up to two million years, and another twenty years would not make any difference; but the temptation to dig must have been almost impossible to resist, and the fact that he did resist is a tribute to Louis's tenacity. No one could be more impatient over little things than he, but over really important matters he could show incredible patience. In the meantime both he and Mary were gaining valuable experience for their work in the years to come.

The next adventure was an unpremeditated trip into completely trackless country, south of Olduvai and north-west of Lake Eyasi. It was prompted by a visitor, half Masai and half Kikuyu, who announced that he knew of stone-like bones similar to those they had been finding at Olduvai at a place called Laetolil, and he volunteered to guide them there. It proved to be beside a stream which the Germans had named the Vogel River, and the deposits, in heavily eroded 'bad lands', were different from those of Olduvai. In fact they were terrestrial rather than lacustrine, and contained many land tortoises and fossil rodents, but lacked aquatic animals such as hippos which were abundant at Olduvai. Eventually it was found that they were older than Bed I at Olduvai – a lava flow covering the deposits has now been dated to more than two million years.

After this brief reconnaissance they returned to Olduvai to find that the pool which they had been using for their water had turned to mud and become the property of a resident rhino, who used it for his daily ablutions. Worse still, in order to keep the wallow moist he urinated into it freely. More inviting water supplies were available both at the spring at Olmoti and at Ngorongoro, but petrol was too short to be used for this purpose. They tried to collect rain water off the roofs of the tents, forgetting that the canvas had been impregnated with insecticide; there were dire results, and all the party were violently ill after drinking the water.

By this time they were also running short of food. Sam White and Peter Bell were due to return to England, and the lorry taking them back to Nairobi was to bring much needed supplies to the garrison at Olduvai; but it never returned. For the next fortnight Louis and Mary's diet consisted almost entirely of rice and sardines. An even greater hardship was the lack of cigarettes, and they had to resort to picking up fag ends scattered round the camp.

When the lorry failed to appear after two weeks they set out to look for it. At one point they had to turn back as the road was in such a terrible state, and they spent the rest of the day helping to extract Indian traders' lorries from the mud. Their reward was a little flour and sugar, but they were still very hungry. Next their own car overturned in a gully, and they spent a whole day trying to extricate it with a plate and some spoons. (The lack of proper tools seems curiously uncharacteristic of Louis, who was usually so efficient.) Watching their efforts was a crowd of supercilious Masai warriors who considered it beneath their dignity to do any manual labour. It was just as well that Louis did not try to press them: almost at that very moment the District Commissioner at Narok was being murdered by Masai for ordering them to help with road work. Louis and the Masai treated each other with mutual respect, and many of them had cause to be grateful for the treatment they received at the clinics he ran at Olduvai.

The lorry turned up just in time to pull the car back on to the road – its delay had been caused by clutch trouble. (By a curious coincidence the man who mended the clutch at the Motor Mart in Nairobi became Mary's nearest neighbour at Olduvai thirty-five years later: he is George Dove, a 'character' with magnificent waxed moustachios who ran a delightful little tourist lodge at Ndutu, some thirty miles from Olduvai, in the early 1970s.) The car itself was in far worse condition than the lorry had been, with the whole of the bodywork damaged, but amazingly it was still able to run. Louis and Mary returned to Olduvai to pack up before setting off for their next target, a place called Engaruka.

Reck had been to Engaruka in 1913 and told Louis of burial mounds there, and in Arusha Louis had heard reports of a mysterious 'ruined city' capable of housing a million people; there were even rumours of 'inscriptions' (which in fact consist of some pecked lines and marks which mean nothing in any known language). When he was asked by the Tanganyika Government to make a report, therefore, he willingly agreed and set out full of curiosity and anticipation.

Engaruka is about forty miles from a village with a colourful market known as Mto wa Mbu, 'River of mosquitoes', where everyone stops on the way to Olduvai to buy tomatoes and bananas.

Engaruka itself is in the middle of nowhere, on the floor of the Rift Valley between Lakes Manyara and Natron. There is a track of sorts leading to it, but even today it is one of the dustiest in East Africa, which is saying a good deal, and the only landmarks are the occasional magnificent baobab tree. When Louis and Mary went there in 1935 the track was almost invisible. Suddenly, with no apparent reason, in the middle of the bush there is a cluster of huts; but in fact there is a very good reason for their presence, for just behind them a glorious stream of clear water cascades down the scarp of the Rift. That is why a settlement existed at Engaruka in iron age times, and why there is one there today.

On the slopes above the present village is a huge complex of stone walls, hut floors and cairns, now known to spread over ten square miles. By building a system of terraces and ditches, crops could be irrigated from the river (by damming the stream it is still possible to divert water along the ancient channels). Louis and Mary excavated a couple of cairns but were disappointed to find no burials in them. They also dug beneath a hut floor, where they found only a few potsherds, beads and scraps of iron.

In his estimate of the number of huts in the hill ruins, which he put at 6,000–7,000, Louis exaggerated. Allowing for five people per house this would give a population of some 30,000, with another 3,000 or so living in the valley ruins below. 'There is a vast job to be done here,' he concluded. 'The surveying alone would take one man about two years to do really properly.'[6] However, he decided that this was protohistory, not prehistory, and he was not the man to do it. It was another thirty years before anyone tackled Engaruka.

Peter Kent had accompanied Louis and Mary to Engaruka to map some of the ruins before leaving for western Kenya. On the way he stayed with Canon and Mrs Leakey at Limuru, and wrote to warn Louis that they were planning to visit him. 'I have told them to let you know in advance,' he said 'because you might be out on safari. They asked me (twice at least) whether I had left you alone and I said yes – with a face (almost) like an angel. But it seemed rather rotten to be like that and then afterwards join in family prayers. If they eventually hear all about it, please convey my apologies for such conduct.'[7]

Obviously Louis's parents had heard that a female student was among the party, and Harry was prompted to write at length to Louis about their feelings on the subject of Frida; his letter is dated 11 August 1935, a week after Kent's warning. Some extracts will convey the extent of their distress:

> Since you told us a year ago about your feelings with regard to Frida, Mother and I have hardly ceased to think about the matter, and it has been like a millstone around our necks. Never has a day passed that we have not prayed God to show you your error and so change your heart that you must feel that, cost what it may, you simply cannot carry on with such a dreadful plan. For your sake, and because we love you so much, we have accepted Frida absolutely as a daughter and love her almost exactly as we do Julia and Gladys. And as for our dear little grandchildren, Priscilla and Colin, whom you have given to us, we love them more dearly than we can describe. Cannot you understand what it means to us to think of the life before all these three if you are divorced?

Although Louis did not share his parents' beliefs on divorce, he loved them deeply and hated to hurt them. However, he knew he could never make Frida happy, nor she him, and in Mary he found a perfect partner to share his interests and his way of life. By this time they had been living together for more than a year, although only the other members of the expedition and a few friends and colleagues in England were supposed to know about it.

After drafting his report on Engaruka for the Tanganyika Government, in which he strongly recommended its preservation, Louis took Mary for the treat she had been promised: a look at the cave paintings near Kondoa in southern Tanzania. Louis had seen some of them very briefly on his way to the British Association meeting in Johannesburg with Frida in 1929, since when he had always meant to return. Mary had been fascinated by prehistoric art ever since her introduction to it in the Dordogne as a child, and she had recently visited some of the famous rock paintings in South Africa which she was anxious to compare with the ones in Tanganyika.

Their camp near the rock shelters at Kisese, north of Kondoa, was a change from conditions at Engaruka, for they were able to buy local luxuries such as mangoes and tomatoes. They spent ten days exploring the steep cliffs, covered with thick bush and the refuge of many snakes. The Government's recent attempts to clear the bush in their tsetse control campaign had been unfortunate: they had managed to eliminate most of the game, but the tsetse merely flew on to pastures new.

During their brief stay Louis and Mary concentrated on three shelters at Kisese and a particularly interesting one at Cheke, about ten miles further south. Among the paintings there is a beautiful naturalistic frieze of elands and giraffes, and an elephant surrounded by human figures who seem to be vaulting over its back in the manner of Minoan bull-dancers. Many of the paintings at Kisese have been damaged by the local inhabitants, who chip off fragments of red paint with which to make magic. A charming scene which has survived shows a female rhino pursuing a male – a rhino's usual method of courtship.

Mary courageously tackled the problems of recording rock art, perched on a ladder with tracing paper flapping in the wind. Some of the results of her labours were reproduced in Louis's book *Stone Age Africa*; the text was based on the Munro Lectures which he gave in Edinburgh in February 1936 – he was the youngest scientist ever invited to deliver these prestigious lectures.

On their return to England in September 1935, Louis and Mary lived together at Steen Cottage in a village with the unfortunate name of Nasty, near Great Munden in Hertfordshire. Situated approximately half-way between Cambridge and London it suited Louis admirably. This little sixteenth-century cottage, like his previous one at Foxton, totally lacked modern conveniences: no running water or inside lavatory, no electricity or telephone. However, after the rigours of the past few months it was luxury.

They lived on less than a shoestring. Louis gave the facts to Sir Henry Dale, Secretary of the Royal Society, when he applied for a grant to enable him to work on the material from his last expedition. After paying bills, his credit balance would amount to eleven pounds; and he had to produce £42 for his life assurance, which was an education policy for Colin. 'If I can't get a grant somehow,' wrote Louis, 'I shall have to stop my research work for a bit and write my "life" which a publisher wants and is prepared to pay for, but I don't want to do that yet.'[8]

He goes on to list his prospects for the next twelve months: an honorarium of £200 for the Munro Lectures which he was to give in February 1936, £50 from other lectures, £20 due on articles he had written, £50 advance royalties for a forthcoming book (*Kenya: Contrasts and Problems*), and £10 royalties due on a book already published (*Adam's Ancestors*).

In response to this *cri de coeur*, Sir Henry Dale replied that the

> Council took note of the difficult position in which you are placed as regards personal support while you are working up the materials from your last expedition. They decided that they would do something immediately to relieve the situation by a grant of £100 from the Mond Fund to enable you to continue your work on the collections already made.[9]

How appalled the Council of the Royal Society would have been if they had known that they were 'relieving the situation' in Steen Cottage.

Divorce proceedings were begun in January 1936: 'The petition of Henrietta Wilfrida Leakey sheweth . . . that the Respondent has frequently committed adultery with Mary Nicoll [*sic*]. . . . That from about the month of November 1935 up to the present time at Steen Cottage, Great Mundon [*sic*] the Respondent has lived and cohabited as man and wife with the said Mary Nicol' – and so forth. Frida obtained a decree nisi with costs on October 19 1936; naturally she was given custody of the two children and she claimed maintenance for them, but not for herself 'until Dr Leakey's financial position improved'.

There were the inevitable headlines in the press: 'Told his wife about the other woman', 'Archaeologist and student'. Of course the Kenya papers also printed the story, which came as a great shock to Louis's parents as they had read it before receiving Louis's letter telling them that the divorce was through. 'We have suffered but not with any anger', wrote Mrs Leakey to Louis, 'and we freely forgive you; and as God when he forgives also forgets, so will we try to do, though of course the consequences to other lives must live on.'[10]

Louis and Mary were married at a registry office in Ware on Christmas Eve, 1936. It was a cold day, and just as they were starting out from Steen Cottage it was discovered that Mary's Dalmatian had chewed a scalloped edge round the hem of Louis's overcoat. The bride, who wore a regulation coat and skirt of sensible tweed, cooked the lunch before the ceremony. The wedding guests consisted of Mary's mother and her Frere aunt Mollie. There were no representatives of the Leakey family, but there was one other guest at the wedding. This was Peter Mbiyu Koinange (now Minister of State in President Kenyatta's Government), son of senior chief Koinange who had thumb-printed his testimony to Louis's competence in Kikuyu for his sizarship at St John's. Mbiyu Koinange had just obtained a degree at Columbia University, New York, and Louis had arranged for him to spend a year at St John's on a grant from the Rhodes Trust. In the meantime he had been staying at Steen Cottage and was under the impression that Louis and Mary were already married: the wedding came as quite a surprise.

The divorce had a very bad effect on Louis's image in Cambridge, where Frida was well liked and had many friends. Louis maintained that the attitude taken by his colleagues there turned him against conventional Christianity; but they were merely conforming to the moral judgements of the '30s, and it would have been strange if they had not given him the cold shoulder. Frida, with her conventional upbringing, felt the stigma of divorce particularly deeply. She insisted that Louis should not see the children again until they were grown up and could choose for themselves. She never mentioned their father's name to them, although curiously enough she left his photograph in the sitting room of The Close for two years after his remarriage, after which it was removed at the suggestion of a governess. Frida and Louis did not meet again for another thirty years, by which time the wounds had healed.

About this time Louis was engaged in writing several books.

Adam's Ancestors, his first 'popular' book, is probably his best known. The suggestion for a general account of prehistory had come from Dr E. V. Rieu, managing director of the publishing firm of Methuen's. Just six months after Dr Rieu had made the suggestion in November 1933, the book appeared in print. Louis wrote very quickly, as he did most things. Reviewing it in the *Sunday Times*, Sir Arthur Keith called it 'a romance of modern science.'[11] ('A good selling phrase', commented Dr Rieu, 'and we are putting a yellow band bearing this review on all future copies.') Sir Arthur also wrote to Louis personally in warm terms: '*Adam's Ancestors* made its appeal to me because of many things: its title, its get up, its matter and its author – the last being first.'[12] In general, it was extremely well received and was chosen by the Scientific Book Club of America for October 1934.

Soon after, Louis acquired a literary agent. He used them for more than twenty years, in spite of his constant irritation over what he took to be their dilatoriness in forwarding royalties, which he always needed badly. He also used to get annoyed over their failure to place some of his excursions into fiction and playwriting. Occasionally he got short stories published under the pen name of Ellis B. Tookey, which sounded near enough to L. S. B. Leakey, but to his bitter disappointment nobody would put on his play 'Eve's Children'. The theme was to a certain extent autobiographical, centering on a professor and his wife and students who were excavating a rock shelter in Tanganyika and were transported back into stone age times by some sort of time-machine process. Thirty years later Louis was still trying to plug this play, and a friend even tried to interest Dame Flora Robson in it, but without success: dialogue was not Louis's strong point.

These excursions into fiction were partly to amuse himself, partly to make money. He also wrote an account of the first thirty years of his life, *White African*, which was published by Hodder and Stoughton in 1937; the motives were mainly financial, but his parents were worried by what seemed to them to be an attempt at self-glorification. He had asked them to supply him with certain facts about his childhood, and his mother wrote to him:

At first I felt very against your writing an autobiography at all. It

> seemed to me very conceited to want to do it or to think of yourself as anyone worth seeking such publicity . . . I pray you once again give God the praise for any success or any gifts you have (and you have we know been endowed with special brain power) and don't be like Nebuchadnezzar who took all the praise to himself and ignored God.[13]

On the ship returning from Mombasa to Marseilles in September 1935 Louis had tossed off another short book, *Kenya: Contrasts and Problems* which caused his parents far more distress: in it he attacked not only settlers and administrators, but also missionaries. Most of the views he expressed they knew only too well as they had been the subject of many long arguments between them; but it was one thing to voice them in private and quite another to flaunt them in print. They differed fundamentally on the question of polygamy, and on the Kikuyu practice of female circumcision, or cliteridectomy. This was of fundamental significance to the tribe, and the Church of Scotland's firm stand against it in 1929 had caused great resentment among the Kikuyu. The missionaries' disapproval was more on medical than religious grounds, since often the mutilation was so severe that the scar tissue caused much trouble in childbirth.

Louis fully appreciated that the operation should be performed with skill to avoid such complications, but he did not agree that it should be abolished altogether, as the missionaries insisted. The reasons for its significance to the Kikuyu, which he had outlined in a paper published in the *Journal of the Royal Anthropological Institute* in 1931, were too fundamental to be thrown over completely, he said.[14] A few years after he had written this paper, he heard that Jomo Kenyatta was going to discuss the subject at one of Professor Malinowski's seminars at the London School of Economics. Basically they were in agreement, but they differed over matters of detail; as Jeremy Murray-Brown relates in his biography *Kenyatta*, there was a heated argument which was lost on the rest of the class as Louis and Kenyatta shouted at each other in Kikuyu.[15]

Owing to his upbringing, Louis knew his facts about missionaries and their teachings. He had not been deceived by prospective 'converts', whose only reason for attending school was to learn to read and write in order to better themselves. The missionaries taught them that many of their own customs and beliefs were wrong, which made them lose respect for their elders; but comparatively few of the pupils really absorbed the fundamentals of the new faith, and they were left in a vacuum. The Government was only too thankful to leave education to the missions, and could hardly be expected to foresee the problems that would result. In *Kenya: Contrasts and Problems* Louis did praise as well as criticize the work of the missionaries, however: 'Of all the Europeans living in Kenya there can be no doubt that the missionaries are the ones who are the most trusted and most loved by the Africans, "heathen" and Christian alike. . . . In Kenya the missionaries have always been champions of the natives.'[16]

Louis's own championship of 'the natives' and his unconventional ideas had never made him popular among European settlers, who regarded him as a traitor to the colour of his skin. This book, however, was the last straw. After admitting that there were exceptions, Louis wrote: 'In my own experience I think it is fair to say that as a whole the settler community is disliked and certainly distrusted by the African.'[17] Worse still, he concluded that in the end Kenya would not prove to be a 'white man's country'. The indignation was as great among reviewers in England as it was in Kenya itself. Here is an example from the *Sunday Times* of 2 February 1936:

> Dr Leakey's heart is with the Kikuyus and native tribes; he is more concerned for their welfare than for the future of the European settlers who have risked their all to establish in the heart of Africa a home for white men. . . . He anticipates that the black races are to develop more and more. . . . Is it possible to build up a society in which the distinct and unequal races are to remain separate and move forward on terms of equality? Must not the race which is superior in qualities be given superiority in power?

The reviewer was an anthropologist: none other than Louis's old champion Sir Arthur Keith, who had given *Adam's Ancestors* such unstinted praise.

A reviewer in the *East African Standard* of 7 March 1936 was particularly scathing: 'I rather gather the impression that he suffers from a very common complaint of youth, namely an almost aggressive assurance and self-confidence in his own views and judgments. . . . But he will mellow, like all of us, with age.' (Louis was thirty-two!) However, African opinion was very different; Mr Eliud W. Mathu, who was to become the first African member of the Kenya Legislative Council in 1944, wrote in the same paper three days later:

> Here is a revelation at long last of one great scientist of great repute who 'thinks black' and who really understands the native point of view. I trust that the book will have the widest circulation among all Kenya communities for I believe this is the type of book that would aid in the clearing of misunderstandings.

Probably today many people would agree that if at least parts of the book had been given more attention at the time, a number of misunderstandings might have been avoided. Thirty-six years later Louis's son Colin praised his father's grasp of the merits of Kikuyu agricultural methods, which government officials tended to decry. Colin was then reader in the department of crop science at Makerere University in Kampala, and in a lecture he gave to the Uganda Society on 9 February 1972 he said that Louis

> wrote of the technical advantages and excellence of the Kikuyu mixed cropping system of agriculture. Two essential requirements were fulfilled which alternative systems favoured by government officials at that time might have thrown overboard. The Kikuyu system assured an abundant and varied supply of food at all times of the year and also afforded protection of the soil.

Louis's attack on the settlers was perhaps more justified than his criticism of administrators and missionaries for their lack of understanding of the mental and social background of the people they were trying to govern and reform. Both these groups were constantly struggling against lack of funds and, in the case of the civil servants, the lack of an effective policy from Britain. Missionaries at least had the advantage of being left in one district for many years so that they could master the local language and really get to know the people, but administrative officers were constantly being shuffled around. The idea was to allow them to gain wide experience, and to discourage sentimentality towards any particular tribe; but these incessant moves to different districts did not make for a better understanding of the people they were supposed to help.

As well as being engaged on these various literary productions, Louis also had to write up his scientific finds. His preliminary conclusions about the archaeological side of his work, which he had published as long ago as 1931, had been updated to a certain extent in *Stone Age Africa.* His next major preoccupation was to get the archaeological results from Olduvai written up, and fortunately he had Mary to illustrate the tools. For the book that he planned he also needed a chapter on the geology by Reck, and a description of the fossil mammals by Hopwood. Louis was so accustomed to working flat out himself that he could not understand why his colleagues should appear to be so dilatory; it never seems to have occurred to him that they might have other things on their minds besides the work they were doing for him.

As the years went by Hopwood became slower and slower over describing Louis's material. To do him justice he was inundated by it; and, as the fossils were so often new species, he had little or nothing with which to compare them. It is said that his heart was never really in the identification of fossil bones, and that he was far more interested in observing the mating behaviour of the snails which he kept in his room at the Museum. He was, in fact, in a wrong niche and would have been much better as a teacher, which is what he became after retiring from the Natural History Museum in November 1957. Hopwood was a curious character, deeply religious, lugubrious in appearance and rather forbidding, although basically kind. He and Louis had a sort of love-hate relationship and kept up a long correspondence over the years. Louis would lay his finds excitedly at Hopwood's feet and anxiously await descriptions, which were postponed indefinitely; or he would turn up in the department in his usual tearing hurry and expect long-forgotten specimens to be produced from the basement at the drop of a hat. 'Hopwood couldn't even find the skull of *Hippopotamus gorgops*', Louis once complained. (This was a fine skull of the 'hippo with the periscopic eyes' discovered at Olduvai in 1935.) 'They've lost it, a *hippo* skull! You wouldn't think a thing of that size could disappear even at the BM.'

If Louis thought Hopwood had been slow over producing his chapter for the Olduvai book, Reck was even slower. Reck's speciality was volcanology, and for years he had been working on a monumental account of the Santorin volcano on the island of Thera in the Aegean. In 1936 he suffered a series of heart attacks while working for the Geological Survey in South Africa – he had had a weak heart even at the time of the 1931 Olduvai expedition – and Louis could press him no further. On 4 August 1937 Reck died in hospital in Lourenço Marques on his way back to Germany, and his widow, who was heartbroken, was unable to find the notes he had meant to incorporate in his chapter for the Olduvai book. This was the second time that Reck's valuable notes on the geology of Olduvai were lost: all his original notebooks disappeared during the First World War. There was nothing for it but for Louis to write what he could from the material he had already gathered from Reck. By this time he also found that other alterations and additions to the text were necessary, and the book was not ready for the press until 1938. Louis could not raise the sum needed to publish it at that time, after which there was no hope of obtaining funds until the war was over.

In preparation for the Munro Lectures which he was to give in Edinburgh in February 1936 Louis had had to study stone tools from all over Africa in the collections of various museums. While he was engaged on this at the Pitt Rivers Museum in Oxford, a chance remark led to what many people regard as one of the most important projects of his career. At a dinner at New College, some anthropologists suggested that he ought to record in detail the customs of the Kikuyu before memories faded and all the old men died. Unknown to Louis, these anthropologists later approached the Rhodes Trust who, much to his surprise, offered to guarantee his salary for two years if he would undertake the work. It was a difficult decision to make as it would mean abandoning prehistory for the time being. However, the project was too close to his heart to refuse and, in addition, an assured income for the next two years would certainly be a welcome change.

When Louis and Mary began their married life the financial situation, as we have seen, was desperate, and Louis had already been considering jobs in various parts of the world. There was no immediate prospect of security in East Africa, for as yet there was no university and the Coryndon Museum in Nairobi already had a curator. There had been talk of an Archaeological Survey, and in fact Professor C. van Riet Lowe, director of the Archaeological Survey of South Africa, had spoken to General Smuts about the need to have one in Kenya. 'He is keen,' wrote van Riet Lowe to Louis, 'and had me thoroughly on the mat about you. As your territory is the only gap in the African chain he would like to see it bridged.'[18] But Government purse strings were tied tightly and nothing came of it. The position in Tanganyika was just as bad as it was in Kenya: the Chief Secretary informed Louis that the Governor had concluded that 'expenditure by Government on pure archaeological research would not be justified in the present financial circumstances of the Territory.'[19] Louis put in applications for various jobs in Africa and England: he even wrote to the Vice-Chancellor of Cambridge University saying he wished to be a candidate for the William Wyse professorship of social anthropology – an astonishing move, since he must have known that he was *persona non grata* in Cambridge after the Kanam affair and still more so after the divorce. In the following year he considered applying for the Disney professorship in prehistoric archaeology at Cambridge, but a colleague told him quite plainly that he was unlikely to get a post at his old University.

After these discouraging experiences it seemed best to accept the Rhodes Trust's offer of £500 per annum for two years. In January 1937, within a few weeks of their marriage, Louis and Mary embarked for Kenya to begin the monumental task. Louis was by no means starting from scratch: he had been taking notes on Kikuyu customs for many years. When he was working in western Kenya in 1935 he brought some Kikuyu elders with him and used to pick their brains in camp every evening. Not only did he record what they told him, but he also had practical demonstrations of how to sacrifice and cut up a sheep in the proper way.

When Louis arrived in Kenya early in 1937 he went straight to Kiambaa, not far from his childhood home at Kabete, to consult his old friend Koinange, senior chief of all the Kikuyu tribes. The chief summoned about a hundred elders to a meeting at which Louis explained the purpose of his study. The project would have been quite impossible if he had not been a recognized member of one of their age groups already; now, as he was married and had children, he was eligible to be made a first grade elder. After paying the usual fee he was duly initiated as such. Even so, some of the elders regarded the project with typical Kikuyu suspicion, but Koinange persuaded a group of nine to act as advisers. Louis had to sift through many conflicting statements, especially when he needed information from women: even though he was an adopted member of their tribe it was difficult for them to accept intimate questioning by a man with a white skin.

The preliminary outline of the study was drafted at Kiambaa, and Louis realized that it would run into three volumes. The first would be concerned with the history of the Kikuyu; the second with the life of an individual; and the third with social organization.

Chief Koinange's hospitality had solved the immediate problem of where Louis and Mary were to stay. In the past Canon and Mrs Leakey had enjoyed having Frida in the little house that Louis had built adjoining their own; but now somehow they had to adjust to her successor. Quite apart from their private feelings, they had to consider the effect on their flock: Canon Harry had always taken a strong line on monogamy and the sanctity of marriage, and now here was his eldest son flaunting divorce.

Mary's introduction to her parents-in-law took place at Kiambaa, where she got double pneumonia. For such kind-hearted people it was impossible not to sympathize with their pathetic, feverish little daughter-in-law, and their sympathy soon turned into affection.

By the autumn of 1937 Louis had completed the first draft of a good part of the Kikuyu book. They then moved to Nakuru, where Mary was anxious to excavate a site known as Hyrax Hill just outside the town. While she was digging, Louis continued his writing and questioning with the aid of his two senior advisers. There was still much work to be done, and he pursued his enquiries with great thoroughness. For example, he recorded the

Kikuyu names of all the numerous plants used for medicine, witchcraft and ceremonial purposes. He worked at Nakuru for a whole year, and then returned to Kiambaa to check on various points with Chief Koinange and his other advisers.

Mary meanwhile was kept busy at Hyrax Hill, which proved to be a most interesting and demanding site. The hill, a lava ridge about half a mile long, got its name from the numerous hyraxes that live in fissures in the rock. The whole area, which is in a commanding position overlooking Lake Nakuru, had been occupied over and over again. Burial mounds and settlements dating from the neolithic and the iron age were excavated, and Mary also made a thorough survey of those she did not tackle. Her findings were eventually published in 1945 in the *Transactions of the Royal Society of South Africa*, taking up more than a hundred pages.[20] The Kenya Government declared Hyrax Hill an Ancient Monument, and many years later a 'museum on the spot' was opened for visitors.

Although Louis helped at Hyrax Hill when he could spare the time, this was Mary's site and her skill in dealing with it was recognized in scientific circles; from then on she was accepted as a professional archaeologist in her own right.

During the Christmas holiday of 1937 Louis and Mary also undertook joint excavations at the Njoro River Cave, some fifteen miles to the west of Nakuru, on the farm belonging to Mrs Nellie Grant, mother of Elspeth Huxley. The site was far smaller than Hyrax Hill and was confined to one period, but the finds were more spectacular. There were nearly eighty partially cremated burials, and many perishable objects such as basketwork and a carved wooden vessel had been turned into charcoal and so preserved. Njoro River Cave was the first site in Kenya to be dated by radiocarbon, which gave an age of about 960 B.C.

Before Mary became immersed in the palaeolithic at Olduvai she was more interested in neolithic and iron age artifacts. Louis, on the other hand, always preferred bones to stones, and the earlier the better. He was therefore happy to find an excuse to take a short break from Kikuyu customs and neolithic sites and get back to skulls. The opportunity was provided by a find made in 1935 by a German ethnologist. Dr L. Kohl-Larsen, on the northern shore of Lake Eyasi in Tanzania. Reck had asked him to keep an eye open for fossils while he was visiting his son who had a farm nearby, and he discovered both tools and fauna as well as a fragment of mineralized human skull. He returned the following year and found further pieces, and in July 1936 Louis went to Berlin to see the skull. It had heavy brow-ridges like Rhodesian Man, and Louis was determined to see the site and if possible establish its age.

The Royal Society acceded to his modest request for a grant of £60, and in November 1937 Louis and Mary went to Eyasi. Having learnt his lesson at Kanam, Louis got a geologist, Dr W. H. Reeve, to accompany them. They found that the fossil mammals were scrappy and few, but clearly they were of two different ages: the older ones were heavily rolled, the later group consisted of species still living today. The artifacts were rather nondescript, but certainly no older than middle stone age. Louis and Reeve presumed that the human skull fragments must belong with them and with the later group of fauna, probably early Upper Pleistocene.

Louis also took the opportunity to study the local population, the Hadza, whom he found more intriguing than the fossil site. This small group of hunters and food-gatherers was hardly known at that time, and Louis used to go out with them and was fascinated by their methods and equipment. He was particularly impressed by their fire-drills, nearly six feet long, with which they could make a flame in about thirty seconds; he had practised the art of fire-making himself, but he could not rival their speed.

After Louis and Mary finished their work at Nakuru and he had collected the final bits of information from Chief Koinange, they rented a house in Nairobi. Here he completed his third manuscript draft of the Kikuyu book, which ran to more than 700,000 words. The first volume described Kikuyu history and tradition and their way of life: systems of land tenure, village and homestead, agriculture and livestock, food and drink, crafts, industry

5. After taking his finals in the summer of 1926 (and getting a double first) Louis led his first archaeological expedition to East Africa. 6. *Inset* There he met Frida Avern, also a Cambridge graduate; they were married at Reigate, Surrey, in June 1928

7. Louis and Mary at Olduvai in 1935, the year before his divorce and marriage to her, with the geologist Peter Kent. 8. *Below* Members of the 1931 expedition to Olduvai: Vivian Fuchs, A. T. Hopwood, Sir Edmund Teale, Louis, Hans Reck, Donald MacInnes

and trade. The second part traced the life of an individual from birth and 'rebirth' through initiation, the novice stage, warriors and maidens, sex and kinship, to death and disposal of the dead. The third volume was concerned with social organization: law and justice, religious beliefs, warfare and raiding, magical practices, witchcraft and black magic, ceremonial purification, and ceremonies connected with the handing over from one generation to the next. There were also a number of appendices listing, among other things, occasions for the sacrifice of a sheep or a goat – 172 times in a man's lifetime; occasions for ceremonial sexual acts; taboos; plants used for medicinal and magical purposes.

The Rhodes Trust had not bargained for such zeal; having financed the project for two years, they now said they were unable to bear the cost of publishing the results. Louis was utterly appalled. He was already trying to raise the money to publish his Olduvai book, and he now had a 700,000-word monograph on his hands as well. He tried to interest various publishers, both in the UK and the USA, but they all said the same thing: the work must be severely cut. This Louis refused to do, and the manuscript remained in a safe for more than thirty years.

6 The Curator

When the two years' grant from the Rhodes Trust came to an end in January 1939, Louis had no plans for the immediate future. He was thirty-five, an age at which a scientist was expected to hold a comfortable post at a university or museum. Prospects of raising money for archaeological and palaeontological work were dim, especially with the threat of war looming. Ironically, it was the political situation in Kenya and the subsequent outbreak of war which solved his problem.

The Kenya Government was worried about fifth columnists spreading anti-British propaganda; Louis, because of his great knowledge of the Kikuyu and their language, was asked to search for the ringleaders. He was paid a small allowance to travel round the country picking up gossip, an assignment which suited him down to the ground. He was also able to kill two birds with one stone by wholesale distributing to isolated Kikuyu shops, thus augmenting his meagre income and at the same time keeping his ears open.

When war was declared Kenya found herself sandwiched between two territories harbouring potential enemies. To the south was the mandated Territory of Tanganyika where there were many German settlers, while to the north were the Italians in Abyssinia, Eritrea and Somaliland. Fortunately an efficient intelligence service had been built up in Kenya, and Nazi supporters were promptly interned. Louis was drafted into the civilian side of the African Intelligence Department, Special Branch 6, with a salary of £600 a year.

He soon heard allegations that the Kikuyu Central Association was plotting with the Italians and was engaged in various forms of subversion. This Association had been formed as long ago as 1922, mainly in connection with land grievances; it was the first political organization in Kenya. In May 1940 it was proscribed – of which

Louis did not entirely approve – and its leaders were detained. The CID went through the papers found at the KCA's headquarters, and Louis was given the task of trying to establish who had written them. For this he drew on his experience with medieval manuscripts at Cambridge, since when he had kept up his interest in handwriting.

Louis had to travel round the country persuading local chiefs to hold meetings at which he could explain the war news and counteract rumours; and he also tried to whip up volunteers for the King's African Rifles. One of his main tasks, however, was to build up a network of informers all over Kenya – real cloak and dagger stuff, with mysterious characters turning up in the middle of the night. Cryptic messages would arrive, if not actually in a cleft stick at least secreted on the person of curious intermediaries, often scribbled almost illegibly in Kikuyu and other vernacular languages. From these scraps Louis would compile reports to the Director of Intelligence.

Much of the information was passed on verbally, but notes have survived which give some idea of the sort of news Louis was collecting. As an example:

> A Kikuyu whom I found at Machakos was telling the Kamba that they were fools to be recruited for the Army. He told them that in Kikuyu country the young men were much wiser and were taking to the bush fully armed with pangas and swords. Also that these young men were soon to kill any chiefs or headmen who tried to get them for conscription.

One agent who seems to have been particularly active reported that a Somali prostitute in Nairobi collected information from the troops and passed it on to a contact in Mombasa, who in turn gave it to the Japanese. It appears that before the war a certain village on the coast had been used as a base for Japanese 'fishermen', whose task was to cut channels through the reef with depth charges. These channels were later used by submarines, which called to collect messages and supplies from the local headman. Louis went personally to investigate, using a bird-collecting trip as cover, and was able to confirm the truth of the story.

Louis's family knew practically nothing about his war-time

activities; he was constantly disappearing to unknown destinations and, quite apart from the security aspect, he loved to make a mystery of his movements. Apparently he spent a good deal of time on the northern frontier, gun-running, it is said, to arm the Abyssinians against the Italians. At the same time he kept his eyes open for prehistoric sites, and located several.

During these trips he made extensive enquiries about his cousin Nigel, son of Gray Leakey, presumed killed but whose body was never found. On 19 May 1941 Sergeant Nigel Leakey of the King's African Rifles leapt on top of an enemy tank at Colite in Abyssinia and wrenched open the turret. He shot the crew with the exception of the driver, and then charged across the ground which was being swept by machine gun fire. Again he jumped on to a tank and opened the turret, killing one man; but he himself was shot by another member of the crew. In 1945 Nigel was awarded a posthumous VC. The citation reads: 'His determination and initiative were entirely responsible for the breaking up of the Italian tank attack. . . . Had they succeeded the result would have been the loss of a most valuable bridgehead.' Nigel's younger brother Robert, incidentally, survived three flying crashes, three motor cycle and two car crashes, as well as five bullets which passed through his clothes, a Japanese ambush, a diving accident, a caving accident and a fall into a crevasse – from all of which he emerged with one broken arm and a broken back. He recovered.

Another of Louis's war-time jobs was to make weekly broadcasts in Swahili and Kikuyu and, with the help of interpreters, in Kikamba and Luo. Very few Africans at that time owned radios, but loudspeakers were installed in chiefs' *bomas* (enclosures) and in the marketplaces, for the Government was very anxious that wild rumours should be counteracted and that the people should be kept in touch with what was really happening. The first-ever broadcast for African listeners was made from Kabete in August 1939. The Director of Medical Services inaugurated it and, after a summary of the week's news, the District Commissioner of Kiambu gave a short pep talk; Louis then told a folk tale, and Chief Koinange gave an address. Louis found that these weekly broadcasts took up a lot of time, and he asked for the assistance of his brother-in-law, the Right Rev. Dr Leonard Beecher.

Eventually, as Louis became more and more involved with other work, he left the broadcasts entirely to Dr Beecher and various African assistants. This was the start of vernacular broadcasting, which from then on became part of the normal service of VOK – Voice of Kenya.

Louis's routine during the war years was to do intelligence work all day and voluntary work at the Coryndon (now the National) Museum in Nairobi until late at night. Ever since the end of the first world war the curator had been Dr Vernon van Someren, a former dentist and a long-standing supporter of the East Africa and Uganda Natural History Society; but soon after the outbreak of the second world war he resigned owing to a difference of opinion with the Museum trustees, of whom Louis was one. The assistant curator at that time was Donald MacInnes, who was soon called up and spent a rather uninspiring war controlling mosquitoes in military camps. For a short time the Museum was in the sole charge of its botanist, Peter Bally, who was a Swiss non-combatant, and Allen Turner, who was too old for war service. Louis's offer to act as honorary curator was therefore thankfully accepted by the trustees. So began his twenty-one years' service to the Museum, five years in an honorary capacity followed by a salaried post from 1945 until 1961.

The original museum dates back to 1911, when the East Africa and Uganda Natural History Society housed its collections in a building in the centre of Nairobi leased to them for a nominal rent by an Indian philanthropist, Mr Jivanjee. The first paid curator was Louis's boyhood friend and mentor, Arthur Loveridge. In 1921 the museum moved to a building in Kirk Road, which later was to house the criminal records section of the CID. The present museum was a memorial to Sir Robert Coryndon, Governor of Kenya from 1922 until his death in 1928 and a great supporter of the EA & U Natural History Society. It was built by public subscription and a government grant on a magnificent fifteen-acre site on Ainsworth Hill, on the western outskirts of Nairobi, and was opened by the succeeding Governor, Sir Edward Grigg, in 1930. The EA & U Natural History Society relinquished control to a board of trustees and handed over its collections – Louis presented his archaeological collections at the same time.

When van Someren resigned Louis and Mary moved into his house near the Museum. For the first time since their marriage they had a home of their own. It was an old government building made of corrugated iron, in very bad repair and harbouring every form of insect life. It did have certain compensations, however; it was peaceful, high above the main road running westwards out of Nairobi, and surrounded by trees and shrubs full of birds and butterflies. Towards the end of the war this historic but impractical house was pulled down and replaced by a modern bungalow with very small rooms, which seemed even smaller because of the boisterous pack of Dalmatians which occupied every chair and sofa.

The first change that Louis made in the Museum was to open it to all races; incredible as it may seem, it was the first public institution in Nairobi to throw its doors open to Asians and Africans as well as Europeans. Discrimination was apparent only in the entrance fees: one shilling for Europeans, fifty cents for Asians, ten cents for Africans. This was about a tenth of what many Africans earned for a whole day's work, and it is a tribute to the quality of the exhibits that they began to flock into the Museum. Considering the little time that Louis had to spare for his curatorship during the war years, it is amazing how much he achieved. He arranged a new temporary exhibit every week, organized monthly competitions on the identification of specimens to encourage observation, and persuaded the pitifully few members of the staff to guide school parties round the collections. By the end of the war 50,000 visitors were recorded in one year; by 1947 there were 102,000. The attendance, in fact, more than doubled as soon as Louis was able to devote full time to his curatorship. Today the Museum is believed to be the only one in the world to be open eleven hours a day, 365 days a year.

The botanist Peter Bally married Joy, now famous under the name of her third husband George Adamson, and Louis soon recognized her great talent as a painter. He helped to launch her by commissioning her to paint a series of pictures of indigenous plants, which are still one of the highlights of the Museum. She later depicted representatives of many tribes in their traditional costumes for the Kenya Government, some of which also adorn the Museum while others now hang in State House. Joy also painted some of the colourful fishes of the Indian Ocean, while Allen Turner prepared casts of them with great skill. After the war Louis persuaded the trustees to add an ornithologist to the staff: this was John Williams, now well known for his books on birds and animals in the National Parks. The Museum now had an excellent team with wide-ranging interests.

On 23 June 1940 Canon Harry Leakey died at his home at Limuru, aged seventy-two. Paris had just fallen, but the family kept the news from him during his last illness as he had had such a great love for the city he had known as a boy. Although he was only three when the Franco-Prussian war ended, he used to declare that he could remember the sound of the guns of Paris. He was buried at the little church of All Saints, Limuru, and the pall-bearers were Louis, his brother Douglas, and four African clergy. Altogether he had spent forty years of his life working for the Kikuyu, for his work had by no means ended with his retirement. For several years he was their sole representative on Legislative Council – the first African member was not appointed until 1944.

A few months after Canon Harry's death, on 4 November 1940 Louis and Mary's first son was born. He was named Jonathan Harry Erskine, the second and third names being after his two grandfathers. The baby was quickly weaned so that Mary could go and look at some burial mounds at Ngorongoro Crater. She was accompanied by an anthropologist, the late Dr Jack Trevor, who never produced his description of the skeletons they found; and so Mary's report on the archaeological contents of the mounds, which probably date from about 700 B.C., did not appear until 1966. While she was away, a nurse was left in charge of Jonathan by day; Louis took charge at night. Although already doing more than a full-time job, Louis took bottle feeding and nappy changing in his stride – in fact he rather enjoyed it. Frida had been too possessively maternal to allow him to play much part in Priscilla's upbringing even when he was there, which was seldom, and by the time Colin was born Louis was out of the picture. Mary, on the other hand, was always far more enthralled by prehistory than infants, and left a good deal of the mothering to her husband.

Mary was much occupied at this time in writing up her finds from Hyrax Hill and the Njoro River Cave, while Louis described the skeletons. As if this was not enough, just before Jonathan was born they had had to do an urgent rescue operation at a new site. The railway at Naivasha station was to be realigned at the foot of a cliff where Louis had noticed artifacts washing out, and he had persuaded the railway authorities not only to delay their work but also to put up £400 to enable Mary to investigate. In one trial trench she retrieved nearly three million artifacts and waste flakes! Then, just when she thought she had finished, a skeleton turned up and had to be extracted; from its geological and archaeological context it appeared to be slightly more recent than the people of Gamble's Cave. Louis was fortunate to be able to leave such jobs in the hands of his wife, for all his time was taken up by his CID duties and museum work.

In the following year, 1941, Louis and Mary took a few days off to look at some exciting discoveries in western Kenya. Louis had to make one of his vernacular broadcasts to the Luo, so he and Mary stayed with their friends Archdeacon Owen and his wife at their mission station, Ngiya, near Maseno. For some time the Archdeacon had been wanting to show them a completely unknown kind of pottery he had found nearby. It was known as 'dimple-based' because of a characteristic hollow in the base of many of the pots, and it also had elaborate and unusual decoration round the rims. Owen and the Leakeys produced a joint paper on the 'Dimple-based pottery of Central Kavirondo' which was published in 1948.[1] At the time they did not appreciate its significance. In later years this kind of pottery was found in many parts of eastern and central Africa, dating from the fourth century A.D. onwards. It proved to be particularly important because it was associated with the earliest evidence of iron working, and was probably made by Bantu agriculturalists who at that time were expanding from the west.

Walter Edwin Owen had known Louis for many years and collaborated with him – and had occasionally been in conflict with him – in a great many palaeontological and archaeological finds. Owen joined the Church Missionary Society in 1903 and in the following year went to Uganda to work under Bishop Tucker. His energy was legendary: building churches, mastering a number of African languages, and making contacts with people all over the country. In 1918 he was appointed Archdeacon of Kavirondo in western Kenya, a post which he held until 1944 when he resigned after several heart attacks. The Bishop of Mombasa then appointed him Archdeacon Emeritus in recognition of his outstanding services – 'I could not bring myself to call you by any other designation' wrote the Bishop.

Soon after he came to Kavirondo there was an outbreak of bubonic plague; the Archdeacon is said to have inoculated 11,000 people with his own hands and constantly visited the sick and dying, thereby winning the affection of the Luo for all time. He soon began to bombard the Government and the press with letters demanding reforms on taxes, on unpaid labour, on education and, above all, on forced marriages: Owen and his devoted wife Olive were the pioneers of Women's Lib in western Kenya, just as Canon Harry Leakey and his wife and daughters were in Kikuyuland. He also founded the Kavirondo Taxpayers' Welfare Association whereby sources of discontent, which might otherwise have provided ammunition for political agitators, were diverted into constitutional channels. During the Kakamega gold rush in 1933 he drew up a petition to the House of Commons and managed to get better compensation for the people whose land was exploited.

In the early '30s a petition from 'Kenya natives' was submitted to the House of Commons. The Colonial Secretary, Philip Cunliffe Lister, noted that the majority of complaints 'appear to be connected with a certain Archdeacon Owen's mission. The Archdeacon, I may say, seems to have ample time to devote to matters which are only remotely connected with his spiritual charge.' A letter from Charles Roden Buxton to the *Spectator* broke into verse on the subject of the Colonial Secretary's remarks; the first and last verse read as follows:

Yes, Philip, you may read of them in novels –
A poor Black folk who seldom brush their hair –
The kind of ignorant folk that merely grovels
Until they find a powerful friend is there;
And this same Owen treats them in their hovels
As you might treat the ladies of Mayfair;
Yes, Philip, you must do your best to weaken
The elbow of this dangerous Archdeacon.

A man who knew not when he was defeated
Or whether he was kicking o'er the traces
Was sometimes, I admit, a trifle heated
And thought but little of the airs and graces,
But when plain truths had got to be repeated
Stood up and told the rulers to their faces –
A man who risked his job to serve the weak
And blurted out what toadies feared to speak.

Because of his lifelong struggle for African rights the Archdeacon was not popular with European settlers, who referred to him as the 'Archdemon'; and because he was something of a free-thinker he was not always too popular in ecclesiastical circles either. In fact he had a good deal in common with Louis, although they differed fundamentally on such questions as polygamy.

The Owens had met Mary for the first time in 1937, while Louis was writing his Kikuyu book. However unorthodox the Archdeacon may have been in many respects, his initial reaction to the proposed visit of Louis and his new wife was stuffy. 'With regard to Mrs Leakey,' he wrote to Louis, 'she has not the claims which are, without question, yours. My own wife never accompanies me on these expeditions, for conditions are rough and men are freer to carry on according to the exigencies of the work when matters are not complicated (say regularity at meals) by wives. I would prefer that you came alone, but if you decide to bring Mrs Leakey I will, of course, give no cause of offence by word or deed. She will understand, I am sure, that such courtesy cannot be regarded as indicating that a man in my position could approve of conduct contrary to the Church's (and if I may add, though you disagree, our Saviour's) teachings.'[2] The Archdeacon soon learnt that Mary accepted the exigencies of the work as well as any man, and that she was not at all concerned by such matters as regularity at meals. From that time on, Owen and the Leakeys did many expeditions together.

The Archdeacon had been one of the very few who took any interest in East Africa's past before Louis put it on the prehistoric map. Geology was his particular hobby, and he was a keen fossil collector. An indefatigable walker, he knew every inch of the country; like Louis he had endless patience and tenacity, but he could also be intolerant and obstinate. He was a man with a

Archdeacon Owen

striking presence, tall, with a large head and penetrating eyes, humorous and witty in conversation, with an amazing memory for facts.

He had extended his interest in fossils to stone tools as a result of a visit from Cecely Creasey (now Lady Shaw), who had been one of the members of Louis's second archaeological expedition. After the Gamble's Cave excavations in 1929 she stayed with the Owens in connection with anthropological studies she was proposing to make on the Luo, and her account of Louis's finds fired the Archdeacon with enthusiasm. He began to search for artifacts with as much vigour as he had done for fossils, and with equal success. 'I have three thousand,' he wrote to Louis in that same year, 'how many do you want?' In the margin of this letter Louis scribbled 'Said send tools. *Don't excavate.*' He often repeated this exhortation in the years to come, but the Archdeacon seldom heeded it. Mr H. J. Allen Turner, the Museum's preparator who had so aptly named Apis Rock, once said in a letter to Louis that Owen 'will never stop digging and accumulating. His verandah at Maseno is a marvel. He has tons of stones and bones in heaps and such a good memory that he can give full details of every fragment. I am afraid that nothing is safe in Uganda or Kavirondo while he is active.'[3]

Before long Owen was finding new industries all over the place. He found one similar to the 'Tumbian' of the Belgian Congo and the joint paper he wrote on it with Louis was published in 1945 as the first Occasional Paper of the Coryndon Museum. Louis was quite happy so long as Owen confined his attention to tools, since it was impossible to do much damage to them; but when it came to fossil bones amateur digging could do a lot of harm, and Louis and the Archdeacon crossed swords over many a Miocene fossil (Chapter 7). In spite of this, their many mutual interests bound them together in a friendship that lasted until Owen's death.

The Archdeacon had just finished correcting the typescript of his joint paper with the Leakeys on dimple-based pottery when he died, on 18 September 1945. He was buried at All Saints, Limuru, where Canon Harry Leakey's grave was and where Louis himself was to be laid to rest twenty-seven years later. Owen died at the age of sixty-six, Louis at sixty-nine, both after repeated heart attacks, both worn out by ceaseless struggles and controversies in their various fields. Owen's burial service was conducted by the Bishop of Mombasa, assisted by Louis's brother Dr Leonard Beecher, who later became Bishop of Mombasa himself and eventually Archbishop of East Africa. Owen had been much loved and there were innumerable tributes, but perhaps the most touching was addressed to him a few days before he died. It came from Joseph William Shyeyo wa Sakwa, a Muluhia from North Kavirondo, and it ends:

> Thank God to have blessed you to have a such a uncommon spirit. You have always been polite and kind to we poor Africans – God bless all your ways. I call you 'Our White Shield', a true Christian fellow, full of mercy and kindness, etc. Because you have always been protecting the weak Black skinned.

Louis and the Archdeacon argued incessantly over religious dogma and many other subjects, but they stimulated each other intellectually and enjoyed each other's company. As Mrs Owen noted, the Archdeacon was interested in *everything*: 'A native game, a spider, a Luo word or expression he had not heard before – he noticed and questioned and rejoiced in everything.' This might well have been a description of Louis. I was also amused to see that a tribute to Mrs Owen might apply equally to Mary Leakey: 'Although she supported him loyally in the causes he championed, she did not hesitate to criticize when necessary, or to apply the brake of a more even temperament when Owen's enthusiasm was in danger of outrunning his judgement.'[4]

Considering that Mary was tied to a certain extent by young Jonathan, and still more so by petrol rationing, she had managed to get in quite a lot of archaeology during the first two years of the war: the Ngorongoro burial mounds, the Naivasha Railway site, a trip to Olduvai, and one to western Kenya to look at 'dimple-based' pottery. Her next excursion into prehistory was spectacular, and happened quite unexpectedly as the result of an outing on Easter Monday 1942.

The Leakeys set out in their ancient car along the bumpy, dusty track which skirts the present Nairobi National Park and leads to Lake Magadi. After about forty miles they turned off into the bush in the direction of an extinct volcano, Mount Olorgesailie. In that short journey the altitude decreases by two thousand feet from the foot of the Ngong Hills – Karen Blixen's country – to the floor of the Rift Valley. The view is magnificent, with immense purple shadows from the clouds dappling the flatness below, and there are always animals to be seen: perhaps a whole herd of giraffes, twenty to thirty of them; or sometimes a gerenuk, looking like a miniature caricature of a giraffe, standing upright to reach the tender shoots of the thorn bushes. Suddenly the brown earth gives way to the white of ancient lake beds, strangely incongruous in this parched landscape.

Somewhere in this area, in 1919, Professor Gregory had made finds which aroused the Leakeys' curiosity: 'Mr Hobley and I,' he wrote in *The Rift Valleys and Geology of East Africa*, 'found independently near our camp at the Ol Kejo Nyiro, at the northern foot of Mount Ol Gasalik [now spelled Olorgesailie] some roughly chipped axes. . . . The specimens collected were lying on a bank of white diatomaceous earth.'[5] Gregory had no map on which to record the spot in more detail, and there was mile after mile of 'white diatomaceous earth'; so far the Leakeys had been unsuccessful in their explorations of the area.

On that Easter Monday the heat, as usual, was intense, and the glare from the white earth dazzling. Louis and Mary, with an Italian technician from the Museum and two African members of the staff, spread out and began to walk in line over some ground they had not covered before. Almost simultaneously Louis and Mary called to each other: he had just spotted some handaxes and was reluctant to leave his finds, but her voice was so urgent that he hurried over. She was standing transfixed beside such an unbelievable concentration of handaxes that Louis could not believe his eyes. Nowhere else in the world, not even at Olduvai, have they been found in such profusion.

The discovery was so exciting that it took all the Leakeys' scientific discipline to make them stick to their original plan and spend their leave that year working on the Miocene deposits of Rusinga Island (Chapter 7). Olorgesailie had to wait until August 1943, when Louis managed to get away for eighteen days and, after he had to go back to Nairobi, Mary and two-year-old Jonathan stayed on for another six weeks. Although excavations were to continue for several years, many of the most important finds were made in that summer of 1943.

In spite of the intense heat and absence of water, Olorgesailie is an idyllic spot; it is almost impossible to believe that Nairobi with its parking meters and its Hilton is within an hour's drive (the road has improved greatly since the Leakeys first went there).

For most of the year no one ever comes near Olorgesailie; only after the infrequent rains do the occasional Masai herdsmen with their cattle and goats momentarily disturb the peace. At dawn and dusk the silence is broken by a chorus of cicadas, and quite often by the roar of lions; but in the middle of the day every living thing finds a patch of shade under a thorn bush and sleeps.

In Pleistocene times Olorgesailie must have been even more idyllic because of the presence of a lake. Here was more grist to the mill of Louis's 'pluvial' hypothesis, but in fact the whole basin has been tilted towards the south-west since Pleistocene times so that it no longer holds water – and this applies to the hypothesis as well as to the basin. The Acheulian hunters camped along the banks of streams flowing into the lake, and also on a rocky peninsula projecting through the surrounding swamp. All they had to do was to lie in wait for animals coming down to drink and drive them until they became bogged, when they could hasten their end by bombarding them with rocks and clubs. Louis was a firm believer in the bolas as a hunting weapon – three stone balls of different weights enclosed in leather bags and tied together with thongs of different lengths, which would be hurled at running animals and become entwined in their legs. The use of this weapon implies co-operative hunting, with a team driving the animals past other men waiting in ambush. Certainly there seemed to be convincing evidence of the bolas at Olorgesailie, for several groups of three stone balls in close proximity were discovered. Some people were inclined to be sceptical and attributed the grouping to chance, but Louis was never afraid of voicing such imaginative theories.

As the work progressed it became clear that there were occupation sites or 'living floors' at about ten different levels. This was the first time that the actual places where Acheulian man had camped had been found, for as yet no excavations had been made at Olduvai. Unlike Olduvai, however, the sites did not span a long period of time. The handaxes and other tools were similar to those of Bed IV at Olduvai, and belonged to a late, evolved stage of the Acheulian. As a possible age Louis suggested about 125,000 years, and at the time many prehistorians thought he exaggerated the antiquity of the deposits. Twenty years later, when they were dated by potassium/argon, the age turned out to be around 400,000 years. For once Louis had been cautious.

The deposits at Olorgesailie consist of clays, diatomites, silts, sands with pumice, and volcanic tuffs derived from forerunners of the present extinct volcanoes of Suswa and Longonot; as also at Olduvai, it is these tuffs that can be dated by the potassium/argon method. Clay and fine-grained silt must have been laid down in fairly deep water, diatomite in shallower water, and sand around the shores of the lake. Obviously it is no use looking for signs of human occupation in deposits which must have formed in the middle of the lake, and it takes a trained geological eye to spot the irregular lines which mark the position of former land surfaces. The Acheulian hunters camped on these surfaces after the rains and moved away during the dry season; as the lake rose once more during the next rains, the bones and tools left behind by the hunters were covered and sealed. Hundreds of thousands of years later some were exposed by erosion, and others were uncovered by the Leakeys' excavations.

Most of the fossil bones were fragmentary, because Acheulian gourmets had bashed in skulls to get at the brains and smashed long-bones to extract the marrow. Many of the beasts were gigantic: pigs the size of a rhino, and horses (or zebras – we do not know if they had stripes) as big as a cart-horse. One small site produced the remains of more than eighty baboons of an extinct species more massive than the modern Gelada baboon of Ethiopia; they were armed with formidable teeth, and their flesh might not be to everyone's taste, but evidently they were appreciated by the Acheulians. In the *Illustrated London News* of 5 October 1946 there was a lurid reconstruction of hairy Acheulians hurling bolas at giant baboons, accompanying an article by Louis entitled 'A prehistorian's paradise in Africa'. Evidently Olorgesailie was also an Acheulian's paradise.

As a result of Mary's preliminary work in 1943 it became clear that there was a great deal to be done, and that the site was too important to leave until the war was over and Louis could devote his time to it. He solved the problem by recruiting a number of Italian prisoners, who were only too delighted to be put on parole and taste the freedom of unfenced Africa. They could, of course,

9. The first Pan African Congress on Prehistory was held in Nairobi in January 1947. Delegates include (front row) Professor Raymond Dart, discoverer of the first australopithecine; the South African geologist Dr Alex du Toit; Abbé H. Breuil, expert on prehistoric art; Dr Robert Broom, palaeontologist extraordinary; Mary and Louis. Back row, left, is the youngest delegate, Wendell Phillips from California

10. *Above* The 'cat walk' at Olorgesailie spans the biggest known concentration of handaxes in the world: every stone is an artifact

11. *Below* Returning from Tanganyika after the 1947 congress, delegates encountered unprecedented floods

12. *Above* Dr Broom; nearly eighty and dressed as always in blue suit a stiff collar, paddled happily throug the torrent

have escaped, although it would have been a long, hot walk; but in fact they were blissfully happy at Olorgesailie, digging trenches and pits, making paths through the handaxes and doing other jobs under the Leakeys' supervision – Mary, at least, tried to get down at frequent intervals, and Louis came whenever he could get away.

The foreman of this band, Della Giustina, was a competent and delightful man, always laughing and singing. When at last the day for repatriation came he begged to be allowed to stay; with the rank of assistant warden, he remained at Olorgesailie for many years. In such an isolated place there is much to be said for mixing men of different races and tribes. They quarrel less, perhaps because they understand each other's languages too imperfectly to appreciate the finer insults. The Italians got on well with Louis's work force, who were mainly Kikuyu. Undisputed boss, as always, was Heselon Mukiri; dignified and rather unapproachable but with a well-developed sense of humour, he was respected by the others. Few could rival his eye for a fossil or his skill with plaster-of-Paris; Louis owed a great deal to this faithful man, who stuck to his master for thirty-eight years. With such a team Louis and Mary felt quite happy in leaving them to get on with it, visiting them from time to time to check progress and plan future strategy.

The most urgent need was to protect the fossils, many of which must have been ground to dust by the feet of Masai cattle and itinerant rhinos. Apart from the most important specimens, Louis did not intend to remove them but to leave them where they were found in a 'museum on the spot'. The Government agreed that the site should be protected, and they also employed two guards to control visitors and prevent the pocketing of 'souvenirs'. The next step was to obtain the co-operation of the Masai who owned the land, and a *baraza* (meeting) was arranged on 20 October 1943 to discuss ways of achieving this. It was attended by the officer in charge of Masai at Ngong, two Masai chiefs and about a dozen elders. After explaining the importance of the site, Louis told them he would like their permission to enclose an area of less than half a square mile, which would belong to the people of Kenya as a whole. In exchange he promised to give them a borehole.

With the Masai's agreement, an electric fence surrounded by a thorn barricade was then erected round the main site, after which it was necessary to hold another meeting. Louis was in the middle of a lesson in elementary physics when a Masai warrior leaned his spear nonchalantly against the wire. He leapt several feet into the air, giving such a convincing demonstration of the properties of the electric fence that there was no need to continue the lesson. Many a rhino was to receive a nasty surprise on his nose, which is extremely sensitive – unlike the rest of his hide – and giraffes were apt to show their disgust by breaking the wire with a mighty kick. Luckily one of the Italians happened to be an electrician, so any damage was soon repaired.

The finds were widely reported in the Press, and even the Secretary of State for the Colonies showed an interest. In a telegram (18 May 1944) addressed to the Officer Administering the Government of Kenya he remarked: 'Dr Leakey's discoveries have aroused considerable interest. Story was printed in *Times*, *Telegraph*, *Mail*, *Manchester Guardian*, *Birmingham Post* and *Scotsman* of May 6 and *Illustrated London News* printed four photos.' Olorgesailie was declared a scientific reserve – eventually it became a National Park – and Louis took steps to make it attractive for visitors. The tents in which he and his family had sweltered were replaced by thatched rondavels, and others were added so that people could stay the night and tour the site in the cool of the evening and early morning. The excavations were roofed over to provide shade both for the excavators and for the visitors, and to afford protection for the fossil bones. After the war was over Louis added a fairly large building to the amenities, furnished with a table and benches for picnics and a number of showcases with exhibits. He also constructed a spectacular bridge on stilts known as the 'cat walk' spanning the biggest concentration of handaxes. It served the dual purpose of allowing visitors a bird's eye view and preventing them from trampling on the artifacts.

While Louis was supervising the construction of these amenities I accompanied him to Olorgesailie in his ancient Chevrolet, whose name was Laura. It was through Laura that I learnt my first word of Kikuyu, *huha*. On every hill, Laura would splutter and stop, whereupon Louis's factotum would descend and blow vigorously into the petrol tank, while Louis sucked violently at the carburettor end. Both of them were so used to this procedure that no words were needed, but every now and then, between spits of petrol, Louis would gasp '*huha*'. It is the Kikuyu for 'blow', and repeated forcibly and often it is most expressive. For at least twenty years Louis had to contend with prehistoric cars like Laura and, although he rather enjoyed exercising his ingenuity with bits of string and chewing gum, it took up a lot of valuable time. On this particular occasion no amount of *huha*-ing had any effect – a sad blow to Louis's pride – and four of us had to bed down for the night on Laura's far from luxurious upholstery.

Leakey expeditions were always stimulating, not least because Louis would actively encourage questions even while busy excavating. About this time I came to watch, learn and if possible help in the extraction of a neolithic skeleton near Nakuru. Louis held forth on every conceivable subject to the Scottish foreman of a Public Works Department road gang, who had reported the presence of the bones in a quarry. This man kept his horse saddled all day long, and at intervals he would canter off, take a look at his gang, then return and bombard Louis with more questions. One hot afternoon I was taking a short break in the shade when the Scotsman reined in his horse beside me.

'What, not working?' he said, looking at me very intently. 'Ye won't mind me asking, but are ye *really* interested in those old bones? I used to be an undertaker meself, mind, but I never could see much in them. Well, it seems strange for a young lady like yourself. Now if it was *gold* ye were after. . . .'

I felt lazy and disinclined to enlarge on the significance of those particular bones, which in any case Louis had already explained in some detail. So I agreed that it would be indeed better if we were digging for gold. His puzzled face brightened immediately.

'I'm delighted to hear ye say that,' he said. 'There's no doubt that the best thing in the world is making money. Of course the girls are more fun' – this rather doubtfully, with his head on one side. 'Ah but making money's the best of all.'

Having settled this to his satisfaction he cantered away for a hundred yards or so and then pulled his horse sharply round.

'Mind you, although I'd rather be making money, it must be

wonderful to have the whole *universe* at your finger tips like Dr Leakey.'

After the end of the war the Leakeys at last managed to get some overseas leave, and Christmas 1945 was spent with Mary's mother and aunts in London. Mary was able to show off her two sons, for an addition to the family, Richard Erskine, had been born on Christmas Eve 1944. A year earlier Mary had had a daughter, Deborah, but she died from enteritis when only a few weeks old.

Louis had had to fight for this leave. In May he had been offered the job of permanent curator of the Coryndon Museum; in accepting the post, he asked if he might first take some leave. 'I have now been in Kenya for eight years and four months without long leave,' he wrote to the Secretary of the trustees, 'and during that time have only once had more than ten days' consecutive holiday. During the past four years and four months I have devoted an average twenty hours a week in my spare time to running the Museum for the trustees, and this has made me more than ever in need of leave.'[6] He added that he must get to England to complete arrangements for the publication of his Olduvai book, and to try to find money for the publication of this three-volume work on the Kikuyu. Also, he told the trustees, he had to pack up his scientific collections and library at Steen Cottage, which had been let all this time and had now been sold.

The reply to this letter stated that leave was not granted until earned by service; a long-term agreement could be entered into after his leave, but in the meantime he could only be employed on a monthly basis. In fact he was all right for money, because his salary while on leave was paid by the Government in recognition of his services to the CID.

The terms of employment offered to him by the Museum trustees were not exactly munificent: he was to be given a curator's salary of £750 per annum for three years and a free house. In November, before going on leave, Louis accepted the conditions with the proviso that they would not 'preclude my being placed on more generous terms later.' He agreed to the terms, he said, not because he considered them satisfactory 'or commensurate with my qualifications. Nor do I consider that the terms are commensurate with the work and responsibility of the post.'[7]

Louis gave three reasons for acceptance (in fact he had no alternative, as he had no prospect of any other job in view.) He had to continue the work at Olorgesailie; he had begun to make arrangements for a Pan African Congress on Prehistory to be held in Nairobi early in 1947; and he was anxious to be there when a decision was reached on a scheme to make extensions to the Museum. For these reasons, he said, he had turned down other prospects of employment elsewhere; but the trustees merely regretted that the funds available to them would not permit the payment of a higher salary to the curator. In fact they were probably embarrassed at the little they were able to do for Louis in return for the time he had spent as honorary curator throughout the war. In 1943 the Secretary had informed him that the trustees offered an honorarium of £150 'as an appreciation of the very valuable services rendered by you to the Museum during the year 1942, but in no way representing the value of such services.' Certainly the trustees would have liked to offer him a better salary in the terms of his new contract if they had been able to do so, but their hands were tied by financial restrictions.

During his leave Louis got his affairs at Steen Cottage settled and, as usual, much of his time was spent as a busman's holiday, working on his material at the Natural History Museum. He was getting more and more frustrated by Hopwood's delays and was forced to take on a lot of the work himself. Most of this work had to be done at the Museum, since the comparative material he needed was housed there. Louis gained many advantages from his long-standing association with the BM – members of the geology department always afforded him every facility for study, put a room at his disposal whenever he came to London, and provided secretarial help. The benefits outweighed the delays caused by Hopwood, of whom Louis expected too much; but at times he was sorely tried by the sluggish pace of civil service channels.

After Louis returned to Nairobi in 1946 he became the full-time curator of the Coryndon Museum and, for the first time in his life, had a regular job with a certain amount of security. He augmented his income by taking on handwriting cases for the police, charging a minimum fee of £25. He also did voluntary work in connection with conservation and the formation of Kenya's National Parks.

Before the war he had served on a committee of enquiry to work out the future policy of game reserves. The game department had made efforts to control poaching and restrict hunting licences, but it was understaffed and the odds against it were overwhelming. African pastoralists protested that their stock was being killed by lions and clamoured for the reduction of the reserves. As long ago as 1933 a Royal Commission had supported the idea of proclaiming the Nairobi Commonage a National Park, but there were difficulties with the Somalis who grazed their cattle there and the matter was dropped. In the face of government and public apathy the case was taken up by an accountant, Colonel Mervyn Cowie, who was within an inch of success when war broke out and the question was shelved for another six years. Cowie's story was told in the film *Where No Vultures Fly*, first shown in 1951, and in his book *Fly Vulture* (1961). Credit for the formation of Kenya's National Parks, of which he became the first director, was entirely due to him.

When the Government was at last empowered to establish National Parks at the end of 1945, Louis became one of the founder trustees. The Nairobi National Park was proclaimed in 1946, followed by the huge Tsavo National Park in 1948. Two years later twelve National Parks and Reserves were afforded varying degrees of protection under the care of the trustees, who continued to battle against lack of money and the depredations of poachers. It took up a lot of time, but it was for a cause in which Louis was passionately interested.

At this time Louis was much preoccupied with plans for the prehistory congress, and during his leave he had sounded out the reactions of his colleagues to such a proposal. As soon as he took over curatorship of the Museum he got down to work in earnest, for the success of the congress would depend on the most detailed planning and organization. The idea was to give African prehistorians the opportunity to meet one another and discuss their work, as well as to open the eyes of the rest of the world to what was being done by these pioneers. Most were underpaid, many were amateurs who excavated in their spare time with no official standing or financial support. They had little time to read about what others were doing, still less time to write reports of their own. Inevitably their outlook was parochial, and it was not surprising that African prehistory was in a state of confusion.

Nowadays collaboration between scientists of different disciplines is so taken for granted that it is hard to realize that in the 1940s this was extremely rare. The congress Louis was planning was not only the first to deal exclusively with African prehistory, it was also the first to mix archaeologists with geologists and human anatomists. Of the 55 official delegates, nearly half were not prehistorians: there were 15 geologists specializing in the Quaternary period (Pleistocene and Recent), five palaeontologists and five anatomists.

African prehistoric research had started a generation later than in western Europe, but the parallels between the advance of knowledge in the two continents are close. Finds could neither be dated nor properly classified for lack of comparative material, and in each case there was a long time-lag between the discoveries and a framework on which to hang them. The first stone age implements from South Africa had been recognized in 1855, and the first handaxes were found in 1873; yet it was not until the 1920s that Goodwin and van Riet Lowe proposed a separate terminology for the African stone age, having found that European terms just would not work. A. J. (John) Goodwin and Professor C. (Peter) van Riet Lowe, both of whom were at the Nairobi congress and have since died, laid the foundations of African prehistory shortly before Louis set out on his first expedition to East Africa.

There were parallels, too, in the reception given to fossil skulls in Africa and Europe. The first Neanderthal skull, found at Gibraltar in 1848, was ignored; the second, from Neanderthal itself (1856), was regarded by a professor from Bonn as the remains of a Mongolian cossack suffering from rickets who had died while in pursuit of Napoleon's army. Java Man (1891) was dismissed by some as an idiot, and even its discoverer, Dubois, at first thought it was an extinct gibbon. Rhodesian Man was similarly regarded as a pathological freak at the time of its discovery in 1921. The first australopithecine, found at Taung in 1924, was something entirely new, so perhaps it was only to be expected that its true status and significance was not recognized. The leading anatomists of the day brushed it aside as being a mere chimpanzee, and Professor Raymond Dart's voice proclaiming it a hominid cried in the wilderness for twelve years before anyone would listen. Then, from 1936 onwards, Dr Robert Broom began finding adult australopiths in the Transvaal. Few of the experts had the courage to admit that they had been wrong over 'Dart's baby' so they maintained a lofty silence.

Incredibly, this was still the situation at the time of the Nairobi congress in 1947 – ten years after Broom began to blast australopiths out of the hard limestone and bribed a schoolboy to part with the precious teeth hidden in his pocket. One leading anatomist, probably *the* leading anatomist, at least kept an open mind: this was Professor W. E. (later Sir Wilfrid) Le Gros Clark of Oxford. Just before the congress he travelled to South Africa to see the original fossils himself, instead of judging by casts as others had done. He came back convinced, and he backed the hominid status of the australopiths up to the hilt.

Louis induced the Governments of Kenya and Tanganyika to contribute to the costs of the congress, and the Companhia de Diamantes de Angola also made a donation. It had not been easy to persuade the various governments to part with money to send delegates to Nairobi. An exception was South Africa, for Field Marshal Smuts took a great personal interest in Broom's work; he went to the lengths of providing a military plane to transport the large contingent from South Africa to Nairobi, and on the way it picked up delegates from Southern and Northern Rhodesia, Angola and Mozambique.

Participants converged from 26 different countries: from Great Britain, France, Sweden, Spain, the USA, India and Ceylon, as well as from all parts of Africa. In those days there were only a few hotels in Nairobi, and none would accept coloured guests; the few delegates who were not white were accommodated privately – including the late Paul Deraniyagala from Ceylon who had the distinction of being a Cambridge Blue. As Organizing Secretary, Louis had to arrange these delicate matters.

Abbé H. Breuil, doyen of prehistoric art, was elected president of the first Pan African Congress on Prehistory; and Dr Broom, palaeontologist extraordinary, was vice-president. The congress opened on 14 January 1947 with a formal ceremony; flags of the countries represented fluttered proudly from the Town Hall – except for those of Portugal and Egypt, which were unobtainable in Nairobi. The Portuguese and Egyptian delegates protested, so *all* the flags were hauled down. After this slight contretemps the Governor, Sir Philip Mitchell, made a welcoming speech, which was followed by replies from Abbé Breuil representing France, van Riet Lowe (South Africa), Le Gros Clark (Great Britain). Others who spoke included Dr F. Cabu (Belgian Congo), resplendent in medals; and Wendell Phillips (USA), the baby of the congress. ('What a lad,' whispered Dr Broom, 'he talks as though he were Uncle Sam.')

Ladies had to parade in hats and gloves for this interminable ceremony, which continued throughout the heat of the afternoon. There was then a cocktail party at Government House, where delegates got to know each other. Sir Philip Mitchell soon disappeared: 'He's gone to have his bath', said an indiscreet ADC.

'Do you know what worries me most about Nairobi?' said Dr Broom. 'The cocktail habit. Why strong, healthy young men and women need stimulants is beyond me. It makes me despair of Kenya. It's a greater menace than the Indian problem.'

Robert Broom was in his eightieth year but was far more energetic than many people half his age. He had much to discuss with the youngest delegate, Wendell Phillips, who was in his twenties. On behalf of the University of California, Wendell was about to lead a fossil-hunting expedition to South Africa. One of his supreme talents was to extract money from people – later he was to collect oil wells in three continents and became a millionaire many times over. He had got together planes, boats and land vehicles, as well as all manner of other expensive equipment, for his forthcoming onslaught on the australopithecine caves. And he had received the blessing of Field Marshal Smuts. Long ago Smuts had relieved Broom of the burden of medical practice and obtained a post for him at the Transvaal Museum so that he could concentrate on fossils; Broom therefore had no alternative but to co-operate with the University of California expedition.

The australopiths are embedded in extremely hard breccias, and the only way to extract them is to blast them out with dynamite and pneumatic drills. The Monuments Commission had laid down that no specimen found *in situ* might be removed without their consent, and Wendell asked how this hurdle was to be overcome. 'Well, you can soon make them loose, can't you? Then they will be on the surface' replied the incorrigible Broom, whose favourite maxim was 'Laws are made to be broken.' Wendell also asked whether he should bring a geologist with him. 'Bring a Wesleyan minister if you like,' replied Broom, 'he would be as much good as a geologist in those caves.'

The big guns of the Nairobi congress were undoubtedly Broom and Le Gros Clark. As Fellows of the Royal Society, and the most distinguished of the delegates, they had no reason to give themselves airs and they were the simplest and most delightful people to talk to. Le Gros, as he was called by his friends, qualified during the first world war and served in the RAMC. After three years in Sarawak, he became Professor of Anatomy at St Bartholomew's Hospital and then at St Thomas's in London. He was appointed Professor of Anatomy at Oxford in 1934, where he remained until his retirement in 1962. Somewhat portly in figure and ponderous in speech, he was a complete contrast to Broom, who was slight and staccato; but both were brilliant lecturers. As a result of the Nairobi congress, Le Gros Clark developed a great interest in palaeo-anthropology and became closely associated with Louis's research, as told in the next chapter. He also did much behind the scenes to help Louis in his career. Louis respected his judgement and confided in him perhaps more than in any other scientific colleague.

Louis was in his element at the congress, discussing, arguing, and often exercising great tact. Some of the sessions were not altogether harmonious, since national pride was involved over questions of priority. For example there was the 'Tumbian' culture, first described from the Congo and then found to be similar to Wayland's 'Sangoan' from Uganda. Dr François Cabu representing the Belgian Congo was eventually persuaded to abandon the term 'Tumbian', though not without emotion. Tears streamed down his cheeks and everyone felt so unhappy that they would gladly have sacrificed the Sangoan, despite the presence of old Wayland himself in all his solidity. After the Tumbian was erased from the vocabulary Cabu threw his arms round Louis and said he quite understood, and everyone breathed again.

The week in Nairobi was strenuous enough with its packed programme of papers, formal receptions and informal parties, but the excursions were even more demanding for Louis and Mary. They had to arrange transport, accommodation and catering for a mixed bag of men and women ranging in age from 25 to 80 in a country where hotels were almost non-existent outside the main towns.

The formal opening of Olorgesailie was a simple matter as it could be done in a day. After the Chief Secretary, Sir Gilbert Rennie, declared it open to the public, the Abbé Breuil replied at considerable length, although it was far too hot for speeches. He was wearing his safari outfit – khaki shirt, knickerbockers and outsize braces which broke under the post-prandial strain; the dignity of his address was completely spoilt by his efforts to hold up the knickerbockers, and by the attempts of his audience to control their laughter.

There was also an excursion to the Rift Valley sites including Kariandusi, where new trenches had been opened and which, like Olorgesailie, had been made into a 'museum on the spot'. The showpiece, however, was Gamble's Cave, type site of the Kenya Capsian and, one might say, type site of Louis himself. A section of the floor of the shelter had been cleared and, as the tools were so abundant, delegates were allowed to keep any they found; there was keen competition. The Abbé Breuil, clad this time in a voluminous black cloak, scrambled energetically up the steep slope to the rock shelter, pausing occasionally to describe the glories of Lascaux which had recently been found. As he talked he traced the outlines of bisons, cattle and horses in the dust with his stick.

The most ambitious excursion, and by far the most difficult to organize, was to Tanganyika; it covered nearly a thousand miles and involved taking tents. It took place after the formal sessions were over, so everyone was in holiday mood and did not mind that almost everything that could possibly go wrong did. Cars taking the party up the precipitous road to Ngorongoro Crater boiled furiously, and lorries preceding the convoy with food and equipment took the wrong turning and failed to turn up. An unforgettable memory is of Dr Broom perched on the rim of the Crater at sundown, swiping bats with a rolled newspaper and, as they fell stupefied, stuffing them into his pockets. At last he paused to examine his finds and most of them he rejected, but a few he replaced, still alive, into his pocket. One he studied very closely for some time: 'Ah, a species new to science, I fancy,' he pronounced with satisfaction. Like Louis, he was interested in everything.

Next day came the moment for which everyone had been waiting: Olduvai. There had been rain, almost unheard of in January, and some of the more adventurous members of the party took the opportunity to cool off in a pool beneath a waterfall in the gorge. This was immediately below the spot where Louis and Reck had camped in 1931. After a quick explanation of the main features of the various beds and a rapid look at the artifacts and fossils, the delegates were dragged away almost by force, as they had to proceed to the cave-painting sites at Kisese and Cheke. Louis had had to cut tracks through the bush to enable the elderly members of the party to get up to the shelters, and once again the Abbé Breuil was in his element, comparing the paintings with those of South Africa and of France and Spain.

On the return journey, near Namanga on the Kenya border, there had been a flash flood, and a brown river in full spate had made mincemeat of the road. Heeling over at a sharp angle on the brink of a waterfall was a bus, heavily loaded with Indian passengers, which completely blocked the convoy. Louis managed to persuade the passengers to stop twittering and get out and lend a hand, and their combined efforts with those of the prehistorians eventually got the bus on its four wheels again. While this was going on Dr Broom, dressed as always in stiff collar and blue suit, rolled his trousers up to the knees and paddled happily through the torrent.

For the younger delegates, the congress had been a wonderful opportunity to meet the giants, with whom they were able to discuss their problems informally. As the numbers were relatively small, everyone got to know each other well and many friendships were formed which continued later in correspondence. People in lonely outposts no longer worked in a vacuum, and for the first time there was a sense of togetherness among African prehistorians. Probably this was the most valuable result of the congress, although of course there were many of a more technical nature.

The final session was devoted to formulating a number of resolutions, which were subsequently published,[8] urging the various governments to get a move on. After saying how 'deeply impressed' the congress had been at the work already being done, the resolutions 'respectfully requested' the heads of state to do far more: to grant recognition and financial assistance to prehistorians; to provide for the establishment of a Pleistocene geologist; and to set up an Archaeological Survey. Louis had begun to agitate about an Archaeological Survey in Kenya in the late 1930s, and just before the 1947 congress he had again bombarded the Colonial Office, via the Chief Secretary in Nairobi, with plans and estimates.[9] He suggested, of course, that he himself should be director of the Survey, at a salary somewhat larger than he was getting as curator – but nothing came of it. Some of the resolutions made at the congress did bear fruit – in time; but a good many, like the one about the Archaeological Survey, fell on stony ground.

In inaugurating this Pan African Congress on Prehistory, Louis hoped that it would be the first of many, which would meet at regular intervals in different parts of Africa. His optimism was fully justified and the congresses went from strength to strength. In the words of the constitution, the Pan African Congress on Prehistory was to meet 'every four years or at such other interval as circumstances shall direct'. As time went on, the 'circumstances' became complicated by politics and it became increasingly difficult to find a suitable venue. Field Marshal Smuts had issued a warm invitation for the second congress to be held in South Africa in 1951, but he died in September 1950, and the next Government insisted that non-Whites would be unacceptable, so all arrangements were cancelled. It was by then too late to find an alternative location for 1951, and the second congress was held in the autumn of 1952 in Algiers. Louis attended it, as he did them all except the fifth: Nairobi 1947, Algiers 1952, Livingstone 1956, Leopoldville (now Kinshasa) 1959, Teneriffe – the one he missed – 1963, Dakar 1967, and the seventh congress, Louis's last, at Addis Ababa in 1971.

Robert Broom had promised to live for the second Pan African Congress, but sadly he died in April 1951, the year in which it should have taken place in the adopted country of this fighting Scot who had lived in South Africa ever since 1897. So much in his obituary in the *Pretoria News* reminds one of Louis: it referred to his penetrating mind, almost intuitive, which enabled him to take short cuts, and to the fact that he always worked at a great pace, 'moving along the corridors of the Museum at a jog trot.' Always eager to help the real seeker after knowledge, he was at his best with young people, 'whose unquenchable curiosity he took the greatest pains to satisfy'. Also like Louis he was 'always a fighter, nothing gave him more delight than to provoke controversy'. The writer of this obituary refers, too, to Broom's generosity in 'communicating his magnificent finds by personal letter practically as soon as they came out of the rock and publishing them with a minimum of delay.'[10] Some might have wished that Louis had delayed before rushing into print with some of his more controversial conclusions: but how much better to stimulate discussion rather than withhold publication for fear of criticism, as some of Broom's and Louis's more timid colleagues were apt to do.

Everyone who had been at the First Pan African Congress on Prehistory agreed that it had been an unqualified success and that the organization had been superb. Dr Alex du Toit, the prominent South African geologist, in his vote of thanks, paid tribute not only to Louis but also to his 'not less willing, though self-effacing partner'. This sums up Mary, yet it gives a misleading impression; no one is more self-effacing, yet beneath is a very strong personality. She preferred to work quietly and efficiently behind the scenes, leaving the public fireworks to her husband.

By far the most important result of the Pan African Congress from Louis's point of view was the initiation of research into the Miocene, as described in the next chapter. Another most unexpected outcome was an invitation to the Leakeys by the Portuguese to come to Angola to sort out problems encountered in the exploitation of diamond mines. This must have been one of the very few, if not the only, occasions when prehistory came to the aid of mining geologists, with all their sophisticated equipment, in determining the economic potential of mineral deposits.

The chief geologist of the Companhia Diamantes de Angola at Dundo, Ing. Jean Janmart, took an interest in prehistory and had been one of the delegates to the Nairobi congress. His difficulty was to assess the age of alluvial gravels found in test pits which were overlain by thick deposits of red sands. Some of these gravels were Miocene, others dated from different periods in the Pleistocene; some contained diamonds, others did not. Obviously it was essential to establish their age and likely content before embarking on large-scale excavation. Owing to the chemical composition of the deposits none contained any fossils, which would have helped with the dating; but Janmart hoped it might be possible to establish the ages of the gravels on the basis of the stone tools contained in some of them. He persuaded his Company to invite Louis and Mary to sort out the cultural sequence, for a fee and with all expenses paid.

Louis took unpaid leave from the Museum, and the two of them had an enjoyable break with full VIP treatment. As Louis relates in his memoirs, *By the Evidence*, Mary was usually referred to as 'Mr Leakey' since she smoked, drove a car and wore trousers; the wives of the Portuguese working at the mine led a most boring life, hardly ever going out at all, and certainly never doing anything so unfeminine. The African miners, Louis was shocked to find, were nearly all illiterate and were treated almost like slaves. When it was too wet for archaeology Louis used to amuse himself by recording their string figures ('cat's cradles') which were new to him – one was called 'the fowl's anus'. He afterwards published them in a short paper. Louis and Mary also produced a more serious paper on the cultural sequence, published in 1949 in the annals of the Dundo Museum;[11] this was the first detailed account of the stone age in Angola, and the mining company was well pleased.

The Angolan visit had important repercussions for Louis personally. One of his dreams was to extend the space in the Coryndon

Museum, and he had been so impressed with the Dundo Museum that he was even more determined to bring pressure to bear on his trustees. Their answer to his glowing accounts of the splendours of Dundo was that alas in Kenya there were no diamonds. However, with typical cunning, Louis deliberately overcrowded the exhibits in the Coryndon and eventually the trustees agreed that something must be done. The Government was persuaded to help financially towards the extensions, and a multi-racial committee was formed to set about fund-raising among the three richest communities: the British, the Ismailis and the Hindus. Louis's plan was to build a new wing with three main halls, to be named after Churchill, the Aga Khan and Gandhi. The Churchill Gallery was to house marine exhibits and reptiles; as the Aga Khan took a great interest in prehistory and history, the Hall of Man was to be named after him; and the Gandhi Hall was to contain minerals and fossils because, as Hindus do not approve of the taking of life, their Hall could contain no examples of the taxidermist's art. There was also to be a room for botany, panelled with local timbers; and an upstairs gallery for insects, including Kenya's glorious butterflies. The ground floor of the old building would be confined to mammals, mostly in habitat groups.

It had been proposed that the Kenya War Memorial should take the form of extensions to the Museum, but African opinion, rather naturally, was in favour of technical education rather than culture and a technical college was built instead. However, in pressing the Museum's claims to government support, Louis had pointed out that, in addition to its educational services, it was doing a great deal free of charge for a number of government departments. For the agricultural department it undertook the identification of plants; for the forest department the identification of insect pests and of rodents causing damage in nurseries. For the medical department, it identified snakes, insects, spiders and the hosts of human parasites; for the veterinary department, it identified plants in cases of cattle poisoning, as well as venomous snakes. The geological department called on the Museum to help in the naming of fossils; the game department obtained from it information on the breeding habits of animals and birds; and the desert locust survey obtained field assistance from its staff, as well as help in identifying plants.

Even the Museum's educational programme was not confined to conducting children round the exhibits, for it also made loans of teaching material to the educational department. Perhaps the Kenya Government was surprised at the amount the Museum was actually doing in all these fields; at any rate it decided to donate a lump sum of £5,000 and a pound for every £3 collected by public subscription.

The appeal was launched on 1 February 1949, and by the time the Leakeys returned from leave in England the following year the fund stood at £54,000. This was enough to get on with the building, although another £10,000 was still needed for additional facilities and decoration. The trustees appointed a building committee and an architect, both of whom disagreed with some of Louis's strongly held views: they were concerned with appearance, he, as curator, with the most suitable setting for the exhibits. In some matters he was overruled, notably in the provision of windows which caused distracting reflections on the show-cases. Louis simply blacked them out.

The new wing was opened by the Governor, Sir Evelyn Baring, on 25 February 1953. Two hundred people attended the ceremony, including a party of Kikuyu elders from Kiambu who had helped to raise funds. Unfortunately the man who had done the most for the project, Louis himself, was unable to be there, and the assistant curator, Donald MacInnes, had to do the honours: this was four months after the Mau Mau emergency came into the open, and Louis was acting as interpreter at the trial of Jomo Kenyatta.

7 Island of Apes

One of the immediate results of the Pan African Congress had nothing to do with prehistory in the strict sense of the word, that is, as applied to man. The congress had not been confined to prehistory, nor even to Quaternary geology, but had stretched back to include man's possible ancestors in the Lower Miocene, twenty million years ago. Ever since 1932 Louis had been finding fossil mammals, including apes, in deposits of this age in western Kenya; and at the 1947 congress many of the delegates saw these specimens for the first time. Professor Le Gros Clark was much impressed, and soon after he persuaded the Royal Society to contribute £1,500 for a British-Kenya Miocene Expedition to investigate the deposits.

The earliest known ape remains – which at that time consisted of a solitary bit of broken jaw – came from Oligocene beds of the Fayum, Egypt, dating to about 30 million years ago. After that, apart from the East African finds, the evolution of the apes was unknown until the late Miocene of Europe and India, some 12 million years ago. The Lower Miocene apes of Kenya bridged that long gap; they provided possible ancestors of the gorilla and chimpanzee, even perhaps of the hominids, and obviously it was important to find more of them.

The first Miocene fossils from East Africa were discovered in 1909 at Karungu, on the eastern shores of Lake Victoria. The Provincial Commissioner of Nyanza Province, Mr C. W. Hobley, took a great interest in such things – he had been with Professor Gregory when the first handaxes were spotted at Olorgesailie – and he promptly despatched one of his officers to investigate. This young man was eaten by a crocodile, but before his untimely end he collected some fossils which were sent on to Hobley. Eventually they found their way to the British Museum (Natural History).

Two years later the BM sent one of their palaeontologists, Dr Felix Oswald, to the area to add to the collections.

There was then a lull until 1926, when a former government medical officer named Dr H. L. Gordon found fossils on his farm at Koru, east of Kisumu. These he sent to Wayland, who forwarded them to Hopwood at the BM. To his great excitement Hopwood found that they included part of the upper jaw of an ape – the first ever Miocene ape from East Africa.

In that same year Louis first set eyes on the island which was to produce so many of his most spectacular discoveries, Rusinga Island at the mouth of the Kavirondo Gulf. He was on his way to Entebbe to visit Wayland and, by a stroke of that famous luck, the steamer passed the island in daylight instead of by night as it usually did. Through his fieldglasses Louis looked longingly at the whitish beds and made up his mind to land on Rusinga as soon as he got a chance. Hopwood was equally determined to go to Koru to follow up Gordon's finds, and they both got their opportunity during Louis's 1931–1932 expedition.

Hopwood spent five weeks at Koru and succeeded beyond his wildest dreams. For once he was not slow in describing the finds, and in 1933 he published three new genera of Miocene apes.[1] One he thought must be close to the chimpanzee stock, so with a nice touch of humour he named it *Proconsul africanus* after 'Consul', a well-known captive chimp in the USA.

While Louis was working at Kanam and Kanjera early in 1932 he was lent a boat by the District Commissioner at Kisumu, and at weekends he and Donald MacInnes would go to Rusinga. On their very first trip, within a few hours of first setting foot on the island, Louis found part of a lower jaw of *Proconsul.* The journey took six hours, so there was not much time to explore; nevertheless, by the end of the season they had found eight promising sites and fragments of at least six fossil apes, as well as many other kinds of animals.

Louis took up the search again during his fourth expedition in 1934–35 (the occasion of Boswell's visit to Kanam). Peter Kent spent a month mapping on Rusinga and working out the main sequence, but the geology is incredibly complicated and it was many years before it was elucidated. Kent had with him the surveyor, Sam White, and a number of Louis's trained African assistants. (Kent reported that Heselon was a treasure, 'but Juma slack, and had ten women in his hut.') They made some excavations and collected a good many fossils, including more ape fragments, and Louis and Kent transported five crates of bones by canoe from the island to Homa Bay on the mainland. They were caught in a storm and were terribly tossed about, but finally made the shore with their precious cargo.

Louis and his team were not the only ones who were showing an interest in the Miocene at that time: Archdeacon Owen, his old friend and sometimes rival, was particularly active. At Ombo, north of the eastern end of the Kavirondo Gulf, he found a fossil rhino. Next he hurried off to Maboko, a small island one mile from the northern shore of the Gulf, where a party doing tsetse control research had reported fossils. The Archdeacon began excavating – the one thing that Louis had begged him not to do – and had immediate success. He entrusted one of his finds to his son Tony, who was going to London, and this is how he received news of its reception at the BM: 'Hopwood looked at it', wrote Owen's son, 'said it was a complete puzzle, and that he thought it was like a piece of tooth Leakey had brought back from Kanam. After much head-scratching he said it looked as if it might not be a true elephant. He handled it with something akin to reverence and said he wished he had found it. He said it was definitely something new.'[2]

It was, in fact, the tooth of a type of mastodon with a very long lower jaw. The Archdeacon then proceeded to excavate part of the skull of this beast, and in December 1933 Louis thought it was time he sent MacInnes along to keep an eye on things. After MacInnes departed, Owen continued alone. He unearthed some ape teeth and limb bones, including an almost complete femur of *Proconsul*. He sold these fossils with many others to the British Museum, and Hopwood only discovered them and realized their significance many years later: they were the first limb bones of a Miocene ape ever found.

Louis himself began to work at yet another Miocene site, which turned out to be exceptionally important. It was a small area on the farm of Mr Sam Evans at Songhor, north-east of Koru, which was amazingly rich in ape remains: from one small exposure alone, no less than ninety ape fossils have been collected.

For some time after this Louis could not get back to the Miocene, but he snatched a few days' leave to revisit Rusinga in 1940 and again in 1942. He was well rewarded, for at the site known as R1 he found the most complete jaw of any Miocene ape yet known, with the chin region intact and the full dentition on one side. It was of a larger species, later to be named *Proconsul nyanzae*. Louis reported the find briefly in *Nature* in 1943,[3] but left MacInnes to describe it more fully elsewhere, along with other specimens from Rusinga and Songhor.[4]

After the war was over Louis was able to publicize his finds, and the jaw made a big splash in the *Illustrated London News* of 24 August 1946, with photographs on the front page. He also made his first television appearance, and once again the *Illustrated London News* (7 September) reported the event, with a full-page drawing showing him facing the cameras: 'Dr Leakey was seen on the television screen of thousands of British receiving sets' said the caption:

> showing and describing the *Proconsul* and comparative jaws. . . . Our drawing, made in the BBC studio at Alexandra Palace . . . shows Dr Leakey . . . in the brilliant glare of the footlights, speaking into a microphone seen hung in front of him from an overhead boom, and holding up the *Proconsul* jaw.

Television was news in the mid '40s!

Apart from the fact that it was the most complete jaw of a fossil ape of such antiquity yet known, there were other reasons for the excitement. Louis favoured the idea that it was less chimp-like than Hopwood had supposed when he named it *Proconsul*, and that it was close to the form of the ancestral hominids. One reason was that it lacked a 'simian shelf', a ridge of bone which unites the two sides of the lower jaw in modern apes. Louis was apt to get worked up about the significance of this feature: because it was never found in man, he argued – rightly as it turned out – that the presence of one in the Piltdown jaw proved that it could not possibly be human. There were a number of other features in the

Proconsul jaw which also differed from those of modern apes: the shape and size of the cheek teeth, and in particular the shape of the dental arcade. (The answer was that the apes did not specialize until after Miocene times: *Proconsul* retained a number of monkey-like characters which we humans have stuck to; in some ways we are more primitive than the apes.)

This fine jaw was the last important find made in the long exploratory period of Miocene research. It was the fossil which, more than any other, excited Le Gros Clark and led up to the first British-Kenya Miocene Expedition.

Immediately after the congress Louis and Mary took three of the delegates to see Rusinga Island. When the boat got stuck on a rock Louis mobilized the local football team, but their efforts to push it off were in vain. One of the passengers was Miss Dorothea Bate of the BM, an elderly lady of Victorian outlook who, to her intense embarrassment, was carried ashore on the shoulders of a muscular Luo.

Six months later, in July 1947, Louis and Mary, with five-year-old Jonathan and two-year-old Richard, embarked on the British-Kenya Miocene Expedition. With the Royal Society grant and a contribution from the late Aga Khan, the expedition was well equipped; Louis was able to hire a motor launch, the *Maji Moto* (Swahili for 'hot water'), to transport the party from Kisumu to Rusinga instead of borrowing an unreliable boat as he usually did. Camp was pitched a few hundred feet above the lake shore, where the mosquitoes were less of a menace, and Louis engaged twenty local labourers to work with his trained African staff.

Rusinga is about nine miles long by five miles wide. Its coastline is very irregular and in shape it resembles Cyprus – looking something like a camel lying down, with a hump in the middle and a long, neck-like peninsula projecting towards the north. The island is thickly populated by the Nilotic Luo people – its most famous son was Tom Mboya, Minister of Economic Planning and Development, whose promising career ended by assassination in 1969. Rusinga is intensely cultivated, but fortunately for palaeontologists – although not for the local agriculturalists – the soil has been eroded into numerous gullies which cut into the underlying Miocene deposits. These are composed mainly of lake silts and tuffs and other materials ejected from Kisingiri volcano on the mainland. In Lower Miocene times this mountain must have been as large as Kilimanjaro is today; it is the most westerly of a chain of volcanoes extending along the Kavirondo Rift Valley, and the mineral content of its ash was responsible for the beautiful preservation of the Miocene fossils.

When Louis began work in 1947 about 45 fragments of apes had already been found. He went first to the site where the 1942 *Proconsul* jaw was discovered and immediately spotted a tooth of the same species. It seemed a good omen. Next one of the workmen found a rhino jaw and, on following this up, Louis saw that there was a skull embedded in the side of the gully. It had been damaged by exposure, but almost the whole skeleton was lying buried beyond the skull. This rhino became *the* major operation of the expedition. Some of the bones had to be encased in plaster-of-Paris; to prevent the plaster from hardening too quickly in the sun, Louis posted a man to stand statue-like beside him, holding aloft an outsize umbrella to form a patch of shade. Apart from their costume, which was anything but exotic, they looked like some eastern potentate and attendant slave.

The rhino was found to be a new species of *Dicerorhinus*, the same genus as the rapidly disappearing Sumatran rhino of the present time; it was named *leakeyi* in honour of its discoverer. Three genera of Miocene rhinos were found on Rusinga and, by an extraordinary coincidence, two of them were represented at this site, R1, their skeletons intermingled.

Spotting a rhino skull is not difficult, even when only a small part of it is exposed on the surface; but the only way to find an ape tooth or a tiny rodent jaw is to crawl on hands and knees. The white deposits are dazzling, and the eye is constantly distracted by an ubiquitous scattering of fossil crocodile vertebrae and tortoise scutes. Each exposure must be covered systematically with a fine tooth comb; the work is back-breaking.

For every ape tooth found on the surface at least ten are recovered by riddling the soil. For this you have to know where to look, following up clues provided by surface finds. As an example of persistence we may cite Donald MacInnes's discovery of the jaw of a new species of the gibbon-sized ape *Limnopithecus*, which was named *macinnesi*. Most of the teeth had broken off, and he searched the surface for them in vain. Next day he riddled the surrounding area but recovered only a few fragments. He spent yet another whole day riddling; in the bag was one piece of molar which fitted on to some other scraps, plus an even smaller fragment from the base of a canine tooth. A palaeontologist would consider the time well spent.

The fossil localities are widely scattered, and well over a hundred are known; but the main concentrations are in three areas. One is near the 1947 camp at Hiwegi Hill, below the 'camel's neck' peninsula. Another is on the opposite side of the island at Kathwanga; and the third is a little further south at Kiahera. The variety of fauna at these various sites is truly amazing: at least sixty species of mammals, of which nearly half were first recorded from Rusinga. There are ancestral elephants, rhinos, pigs and hippo-like anthracotheres; primitive ruminants allied to giraffids; a giant hyrax, rather horse-like and occupying the same ecological niche as modern zebras; tragulids, of which the modern chevrotain is an example, ranging in size from a rabbit to a sheep. Rodents were found in embarrassing variety and profusion; MacInnes worked on them for several years but gave up palaeontology before they were finished, and by the 1970s more than 10,000 rodent specimens had been amassed from the Lower Miocene of East Africa.

Interesting but also irritating from the palaeontologist's point of view were the primitive carnivores known as creodonts, some of which played the part of modern hyenas and crunched up many a good bone that would otherwise have been preserved for posterity. Many of these creatures were unique: no less than six new genera and fifteen new species were eventually named from the East African Miocene sites. They range in size from a stoat-like animal to one as large as a grizzly bear. One which must have been leopard-sized, judging by its upper jaw and two teeth which are the only parts known, was named *Leakitherium hiwegi* – Leakey's beast from Hiwegi.

As well as the mammals and the almost too plentiful reptiles, there are numerous fossil fish and shellfish from sites which must once have been in the lake. Other sites which were obviously on land produce fruits, seeds and leaf impressions; these botanical fossils are particularly valuable in reconstructing the ecology of Miocene times. The general picture is of wooded volcanic slopes, with gallery forest bordering streams and open savanna country in between. There were also swamps and shallow lakes which dried up periodically. The fossil fauna supports conclusions drawn from the flora: there were creatures suited to many different habitats. 'Flying squirrels', which glide from tree to tree, lived in the gallery forest; apes and bush-babies emerged from the trees to drink at lakes and streams, where they would have been vulnerable to crocodiles and other carnivores. Ruminants would have grazed and browsed on the savanna, and a large species of spring hare also implies grassland. *Deinotherium*, described by Wayland as 'that elepho-walrus of the swamps', and the hippo-like anthracotheres would have disported themselves in the shallow lakes. There was something for everybody on Rusinga, hence the tremendous variety of species.

The bones of all these animals were soon covered over by lake sediments or volcanic ash, hence their preservation. But the deposits and their relative ages are extremely complex, and even now after several geologists have had a go at them various problems remain. Peter Kent did a preliminary survey in 1934–35. For the 1947 expedition Louis engaged a young man called Ian Higginbottom – invariably referred to by the Indian storekeeper on Rusinga as 'Mr Bottomhiggin' – and later in the year he was joined by a very experienced geologist, Dr (now Professor) Robert Shackleton. There was little doubt that most of the sediments were Lower Miocene, but some of the fauna seemed to be slightly later than others. Some of the problems were solved after potassium/argon became established in the 1960s: most of the dates for the Rusinga deposits fell between 20 and 16 million years.

While the geologists were mapping and Donald MacInnes was plastering the rhino skeleton Louis was all over the island looking for new sites. He had with him, of course, Heselon; and another stalwart was an eagle-eyed Luo called Zadok who had a new species of carnivore named after him: *Metapterodon zadoki*. Mary was tied to Jonathan and Richard for most of the time, but the boys amused themselves by fishing or sailing the ingenious reed boats made by the Luo children. The housekeeping was simple as there was little choice: tough goat or skinny chicken, made more interesting by the addition of a particularly virulent curry powder from the local store, with paw paw and bananas for dessert. The hours of darkness were spent cataloguing and marking specimens by the light of hurricane lamps suspended from the trees.

Most of the party used to swim regularly in the lake; but there were crocodiles, and Louis took the precaution of firing a discouraging shot before entering the water. Nobody bothered much about bilharzia, which is endemic in shallow water near human habitation. (The parasites develop in water-snails and penetrate the skin of an imprudent human bather; the eggs pass into either the bladder or the rectum, and pass out in the urine or faeces. If they reach water they hatch out into swimming forms, which seek out water-snails and the life cycle begins again.) The low-lying islands of Lake Victoria are notoriously unhealthy, and it was most unwise not to take precautions against bilharzia. The whole Leakey family got this unpleasant disease in 1954 as a result of wading through a swamp; Louis, Jonathan and Richard spent some time in hospital, while Mary was treated at home with the customary cure in those days, antimony tartrate. Her pulse got so low that the treatment had to be stopped, and it was a long time before she fully recovered. Louis got bilharzia at least three times in his life, and the painful treatment left him very thin for a year afterwards. In 1948 he was stricken with gall bladder trouble on Rusinga; he was extracting a *Proconsul* jaw when he first felt the symptoms and insisted on finishing the plastering himself, although he was vomiting all the time. The cause was not diagnosed until much later, when the whole gall bladder was removed. For the rest of his life Louis was unable to digest greasy foods and was violently ill every time he ate cold mutton fat, which he could never resist. At other times he suffered from kidney stones and glandular fever; he invariably tried to ignore his ailments which were often brought on by sheer neglect. No doubt it was a coincidence, but both Mary and Donald MacInnes developed acute appendicitis on Rusinga; they had to be rushed by boat to Kisumu hospital – 'rushed' being a relative term as in each case the boat was delayed by mechanical faults. MacInnes nearly died and was out of action for months.

During the 1947 expedition, however, the hired boat *Maji Moto* behaved well, and the Leakeys were able to save much time and energy in getting to distant parts of the island by lake rather than by walking. They were also able to explore other Miocene localities, including Karungu on the mainland where the first fossils were found in 1909. They had planned to spend the night in the District Commissioner's hut, which was used only on the rare occasions when he or one of his officers visited this remote area to settle disputes. Unfortunately he happened to pick that very evening to arrive, and must have been most disconcerted to find his hut occupied by four adults and a couple of children – Louis and Mary, Ian Higginbottom, myself, Jonathan and Richard. We turned out at once and fixed our mosquito nets to trees, spending a most disturbed night, with hippos snorting on the shore immediately below and hyenas overturning all the basins, buckets and tins. There was also a most peculiar selection of fauna in the little house known in East Africa as the *choo* (pronounced as in 'show'). As well as bats and every form of insect there were creatures as large as mice scuttling over the floor and seat: but these were no mice, they were soliflugids or 'pseudo scorpions'. In this particular environment their long antennae are extremely ticklish.

By the end of the 1947 season 64 more primate specimens had been found – mostly, but not entirely, from Rusinga. Songhor was also producing exciting results. In 1932 Louis had found there part of a large canine tooth similar to that of a gorilla, and in 1947 he got a lower jaw fragment containing part of that same tooth. In the following year its tip was recovered, but even that was not the end of the story. In 1962 Jonathan happened to be in the area and heard that a schoolboy had found part of the jaw of a large fossil ape at Songhor. Louis hastened to Kisumu and was shown it by the boy's father, the Provincial Surgeon; it fitted perfectly on to the original piece found in 1947. This mandible became the type specimen of *Proconsul major*, the largest of the three species of *Proconsul* which must have been the size of a gorilla.

Louis, with his flair for publicity, wrote a letter to *The Times* about the season's work, and this brought rich rewards. It was read by Mr Charles Boise, a London businessman who had worked for the Union Minière in Katanga as a young man and become interested in prehistory. Louis's account of the difficulties and expense of working on such a remote island as Rusinga inspired Mr Boise to send a cheque to the enterprising leader of the expedition. It arrived completely out of the blue, and Louis's amazement can be imagined: never before had he been given money without having to beg for it!

With this gift of £1,000 he bought a Commer truck fitted luxuriously as a caravan. No longer did he have to hire lorries to transport his gear to Kisumu or to the scene of any of his other operations, and he and his family could sleep comfortably in it instead of having to pitch tents.

Soon afterwards Mr Boise came to the rescue of the second British-Kenya Miocene expedition. The Royal Society had not renewed their grant and Louis was getting desperate. A report in *The Times* of 30 December 1947 may have been prompted by him as a subtle piece of propaganda to stir the conscience of the British public: 'A well equipped and richly endowed expedition from the University of California is now in Africa to explore these sites discovered by British scientists. . . .' The expedition ('with half a million dollars backing' wrote Louis to Mr Boise) was led by none other than that enterprising young man Wendell Phillips, whom we met at the Nairobi congress. He was steered well away from western Kenya and instead went to Losodok, west of Lake Rudolf. The party had some success, finding the first fragments of fossil apes from that area. Louis went there himself in 1948 and again in 1951, but concluded that the limited results did not justify the cost of a large-scale expedition to that remote and waterless country.

Mr Boise had meant to contribute £500 for the 1948 expedition to western Kenya and a further £500 for 1949, but because of the threatened competition by the University of California he sent the whole £1,000 to Louis straight away. Then, with national pride at stake, the Kenya Government also made the first of their many contributions towards the British-Kenya Miocene expeditions; later on they must have wondered why they ever established such a precedent, for Louis's finds were so important that he was able to press his claims relentlessly and successfully for many years to come.

On 11 February 1948 Louis's mother died at the age of 82. Towards the end she had been a great anxiety to her family. Gladys Beecher and her husband, who had lived close by, had to move from Limuru, and Mrs Leakey could not be left alone. Louis had asked the Town Clerk of Nairobi for permission to move her little house, lock stock and barrel, to the plot beside his own house near the Museum; but she died before these plans could be implemented.

In June Louis went to Songhor, where he spent six weeks and collected more than sixty primate specimens as well as plenty of other material. The family then joined him at Rusinga, camping this time at Kathwanga on the west coast, on the opposite side of the island to the 1947 camp. The mosquitoes were even worse, but the Leakeys had the advantage of being within walking distance of many new fossil localities. The men were set to work digging trial trenches at the most promising site, R106. On that memorable day, 2 October, the Leakeys went exploring to the west of the excavations on the borders of the adjoining site, R107. This was by no means the first time they had combed this particular gully, but it is only too easy to miss something and they were taking no chances. Mary's keen eye spotted some fragments of bone on the surface, and in looking up she noticed a tooth in the side of the cliff above her. She called to Louis and they cut a platform on which to stand, after which Mary delicately uncovered the area surrounding the projecting tooth. In the words of Louis's journal of the following day:

'Returned to the ape skull with Mary, Heselon, Nderitu and Zadok and got it out. It is very broken up and large parts are missing, but we have the whole jaw, most of the face, including the orbit on one side, a large part of one side of the frontal and bits of parietal. . . . The form of frontal in an adult is almost infantile, as I fully expected it would be if, as I have argued so often, modern apes are very specialized in respect of supra-orbitals.' (i.e., brow-ridges.) On the following day he notes: 'Mary and I worked all day on the skull with Durofix. There is more of it than we thought, but it is most terribly warped.'

This skull of *Proconsul africanus* was the first skull of a fossil ape, of any age, ever to be found. Even today, twenty-five years later, only three others are known, including another more fragmentary one from Rusinga.

At this time the Leakeys were still dependent on the Kisumu Fisheries boat and had to curb their impatience until its return. As soon as they got to Kisumu they sent a cable to Professor Le Gros Clark in Oxford; he was godfather of the first Miocene expedition and was studying all Louis's primate material, so he had to be the first to hear of the great discovery. They then hurried back to Nairobi, where they decided that Mary, as the finder, should be the one to take the skull back to England in person. As Louis said in his following letter to Le Gros Clark: 'I simply could not bear it if this specimen got lost or damaged in transit, for our chances of another within any reasonable time are small. After all, we've been hunting a long time.'[5]

The VIP treatment began at once, with BOAC arranging a free flight for Mary and her precious load, which was insured for £4,000 and travelled in a box on her lap. At each stop – and there were several in those days – she was escorted by police to the airport buildings and the box was locked in a safe while in transit. On arrival at London airport she was photographed by the Press and had to pose on the gangway and again in the VIP lounge. She cabled to Louis: 'Both arrived safely. Overwhelming reception airport.' To Mary, who hates the limelight, it must have been an ordeal. There was another police escort from airport to terminal and she then took a train to Oxford, where she unpacked the skull in Le Gros Clark's laboratory.

The day before Mary arrived in England a short report and photograph appeared in *Nature*; it drew attention to the extreme fragility of the skull, adding that 'it must have required consummate skill for its successful removal from the deposits.'[6] It also required consummate skill to reconstruct it: one square inch of the jaw, for example, was in no less than thirty-six fragments. 'Mary has got it together perfectly,' wrote Louis proudly to Le Gros Clark, 'although many of the pieces were about the size of a match-head.'[7] The parietal bones, which were eggshell thin, took nearly a month to piece together. Although Mary's intention had been to glue the pieces together fairly quickly in order to give a general impression of the skull's appearance, in fact only one piece needed to be readjusted. This is even more remarkable considering the amount of distortion caused while the skull was still embedded in the rock.

After only ten days study of the fossil Le Gros Clark made a preliminary report to the Colonial Office. He emphasized not only the skull's hominid-like characters, such as the absence of brow-ridges, but also several monkey-like features. These included the narrow nose opening and the shape of the convolutions of the brain, as shown by markings on the inside of the skull. Le Gros was the foremost authority of his time on the anatomy of the brain, so he knew what he was talking about. Louis thought of *Proconsul* as a member of the pool from which the hominids developed, and he played down the ancestral chimp aspect as advanced originally by Hopwood when he named the genus after 'Consul'. This was good business from the point of view of publicity and fund raising; but apart from that, Louis was convinced that *Proconsul* was distinct from the apes since it had no simian shelf reinforcing the jaw. Later on he created a separate family, the Proconsulidae, as distinct from the ape family, the Pongidae; but he got little support from his colleagues for this view.

Soon after showing the skull to Le Gros Clark, Mary arranged a private view for Mr Charles Boise, who was so delighted with the result of his support for the expedition that he produced yet another generous cheque. With the money, Louis bought the *Miocene Lady*, a 42 ft twin-engined motor launch which had formerly been used for deep sea fishing off Mombasa. He was now independent of hired transport on water as well as on land, with a tremendous saving in costs. The hire of a motor boat between Kisumu and Rusinga was £20 per trip, and it had usually been necessary to go about once a week to the mainland to collect stores and mail. The *Miocene Lady* also earned her keep by being hired out to government officials and others when the Leakeys were not using her.

In April 1949, after the gaps had been filled in with plaster, the skull was exhibited in the central hall of the Natural History Museum, and crowds flocked to see it. The Secretariat in Nairobi had agreed that, because of its great scientific importance, the skull could be housed in London on an indefinite loan on the clear understanding that the Kenya Government should retain the ownership.

Naturally the skull overshadowed all the other finds made on the 1948 expedition, but these were even more numerous and varied than those of the previous season. To mention just one, near the old camp at Hiwegi Louis found a block of limestone containing the jaws and associated limb bones of *Limnopithecus macinnesi*. The humerus showed that the arms were much shorter than those of the modern gibbons; like *Proconsul*, *Limnopithecus* had not yet specialized. He must have progressed through the trees on all fours rather than by arm-swinging in the manner of the modern gibbons.

Louis had good reason to be pleased with the results so far. By the end of the second season the total bag of hominoid fossils from all the East African sites totalled two hundred and twenty-six specimens. Five years later, the number had doubled; judging by the distribution of the bones and teeth, it was estimated that more than 450 individual apes were represented in this collection. They came from quite small areas exposed by the hazards of erosion and must represent but a minute fraction of the total ape population, which must have been enormous in Lower Miocene times in parts of East Africa. Louis realized that he had an almost unlimited field for research which was unique in the world.

Mary's providential find of the *Proconsul* skull had come at a most opportune moment to stimulate support for future expeditions. In a letter to Le Gros Clark written on 15 October 1948, about a fortnight before Mary took the skull to England, Louis said:

13. The skull of *Proconsul africanus*, a Miocene ape nearly twenty million years old, found by Mary Leakey on Rusinga Island in 1948. The smooth contour of the forehead is in marked contrast to the heavy brow-ridges of modern apes

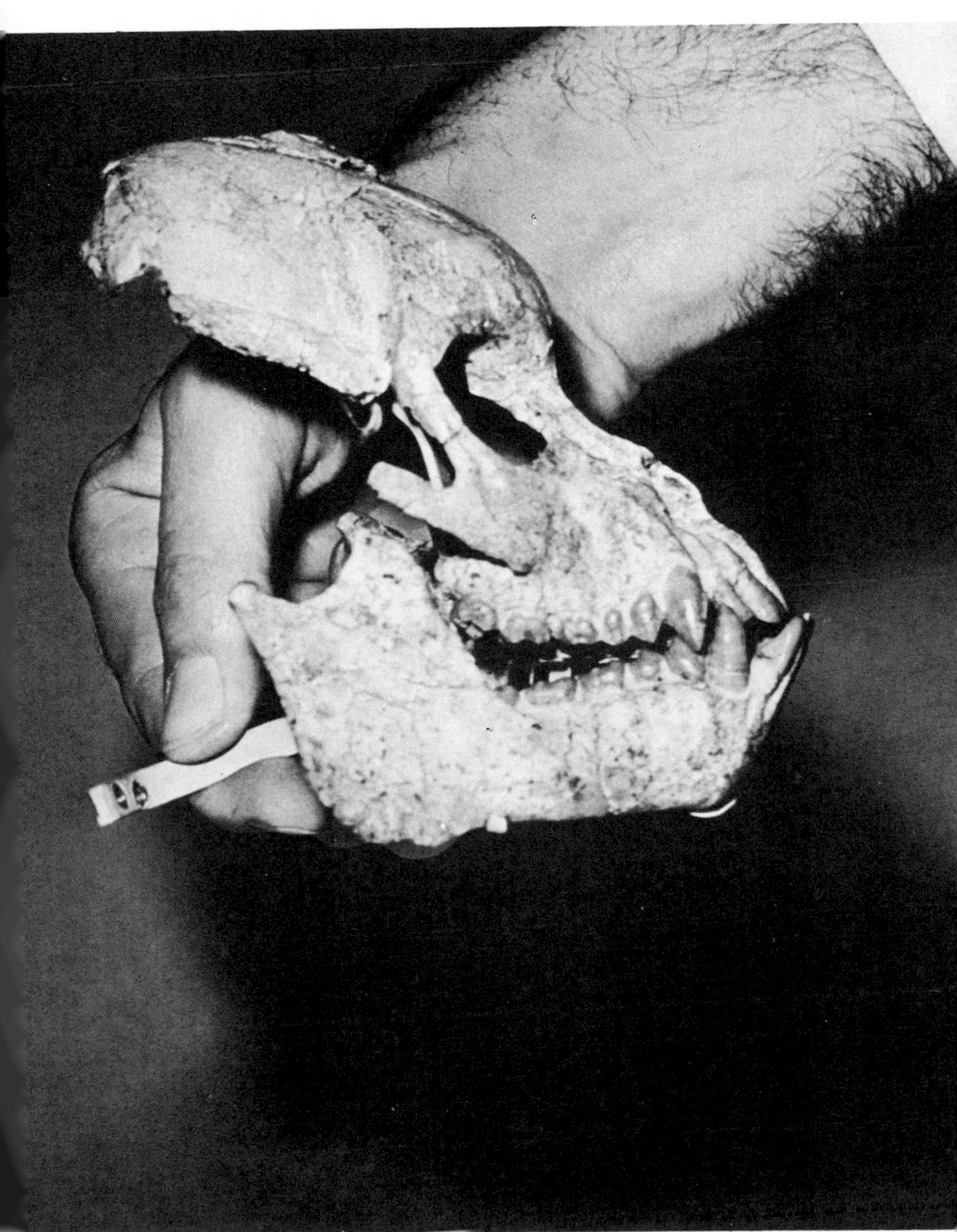

14. On an expedition to a remote area of northern Kenya in 1949 Louis used a new truck given to him by his benefactor Mr Charles Boise. Intrigued by all the paraphernalia is a local Samburu guide, whose spear got badly in the way when he sat in the truck

15. *Below* While the equipment is being loaded Louis and the author enjoy breakfast before setting off on a day's fossil-hunting

> I do very much feel that we have got to make fullest use of publicity in connection with this skull, for the raising of funds for further work. . . . As you know, plans are before the Kenya Government for money for a five-year research scheme. This new discovery has already fired the imagination of a number of members of Government and, as the new five-year plan is to be discussed in the near future, and as the Government is very much influenced by what it calls the publicity value for the Colony of this sort of work, I think that anything you can do in the near future would prove very beneficial. Quite apart from this, by stressing the importance of this work to the public press, other sources of funds might become available, just as reports two years ago led Mr Boise to give us funds.

Louis was often accused of being a publicity-seeker; here, in his own words, is the answer to his critics.

Le Gros Clark did not have Louis's flair for publicity, but as an eminent Fellow of the Royal Society his opinion meant much to the Kenya Government; he left them in no doubt as to the importance of Louis's work.

When Louis applied for support for 1949 he was able to enclose press cuttings about the *Proconsul* skull. The Chief Secretary noted: 'It would seem that this sort of scientific inquiry probably gathers impetus and work can be found as long as money is available.'[8] In that statement he was absolutely correct. Three years later Louis was asked to confirm that 1952 would be the last year for which he would be applying for a grant,[9] to which he replied: 'I am afraid it is not possible to confirm *positively* that 1952 will be the last year in respect of which I shall be applying for a grant for Miocene research.' And later in the year he added: 'On the whole I think it likely that I *shall* want a further grant.' Not only did he ask for a further grant, but he asked for an increase from £1,500 to £1,750 – and got it. Five years later the Chief Secretary finally put his foot down and insisted that the contribution for 1958/59 was to be the last one.[10]

When Louis applied to the Kenya Government for his usual permit to excavate in 1949 he asked for an extension of the licence to include Heselon. 'He is as fully qualified to take charge of the excavations as I am,' he wrote. 'I want Heselon Mukiri to be ranked as a member of the Kenya Miocene expedition, thereby excluding him from the paragraph . . . which says "Other excavation by natives in the absence of the permit holder is not covered by this permit".'[11] The concession was granted – probably the first time such a permit had ever been given to a 'native'.

Louis never neglected to follow up clues to possible fossil localities however tenuous. One such had been reported by Dr Robert Shackleton during the course of a geological survey in 1942-44 to the country around Maralal in northern Kenya. He had covered this inaccessible area by camel, so the number of fossils he could collect was strictly limited; but the ones he did bring back appeared to be Miocene, and this was good enough for Louis. Early in 1949 he set out to have a look for himself, with a friend from England, Hilary Stokes, and myself as passengers. The three of us sat in the front of Charles Boise's splendid Commer truck, which was still a relatively new toy, while perched at the back on top of all the gear was Heselon and a Luo named Agustin who had acted as cook at Rusinga. A natural clown, his antics kept even the somewhat dour Heselon amused, and his culinary talents were first class. He always wore a green pork-pie hat, and I never saw him without a pipe in his mouth – the Luo, both men and women, are compulsive pipe smokers.

Maralal, for which we were heading, was on the borders of some eight thousand square miles of semi-desert country presided over by the Samburu, wild looking people who are closely related to the Masai. It was a closed area to everyone except administrative officers, game wardens and members of Livestock Control, and we had to obtain a special permit to enter it. The District Commissioner at Rumuruti insisted that we should take with us a policeman to act as guide, but we soon found that this languid young man did not know the country at all and he would not even condescend to help push our cumbersome vehicle when it got stuck: beautiful as the Commer was, she proved equally difficult to extricate from mud or sand.

After leaving the Wamba road south of Maralal we climbed an escarpment along a faint track; presently it petered out and we were completely lost. Then suddenly we spotted a tent in the middle of nowhere; it belonged to an officer of the Meat Marketing Board who was buying Samburu cattle, and fortunately his staff were able to direct us to Kirimun springs. We then set off on foot, following Robert Shackleton's geological map in the general direction of his supposed Miocene sediments. After walking a few miles through thick bush, with 'wait-a-bit' thorns tearing our clothes and pepper-ticks covering our legs, we spotted two small patches of white deposits; but the fossils were disappointing, consisting mostly of fish, crocodile and tortoise. We decided there was not much future at Kirimun, and that next day we would push on to Palagalagi, another spot marked on Shackleton's map.

At dawn we filled all available receptacles at the springs, a very slow business as the top layer had to be carefully ladled off with saucepans to avoid scooping up the muddy sediment. We were soon surrounded by a giggling audience of Samburu women and children, to whom we gave some empty tins; these were just about the only toys the toddlers had ever owned and they were soon happily making mud pies and throwing water over each other like any child at the seaside. Presently an enormous Samburu with an eight-foot spear asked if he could join our staff; he told us he was a former game scout and knew the country well, so we were delighted to take him on. Just as we were ready to leave, there were cries of '*Faru, faru*!' and a huge rhino lumbered past. The Samburu had volunteered to walk ahead of the truck and guide us through the lava boulders and pig-holes, and the rhino happened to be going in exactly the same direction; but our new assistant was quite unmoved and trod almost on the animal's heels, apparently driving it along with his spear.

Churning along in bottom gear, it took over an hour to cover the five miles to Palagalagi. We then left the truck on the edge of an escarpment with a magnificent view of the Uaso Nyiro River below and proceeded for about three miles on foot. Sure enough, our excellent guide knew exactly where to find the 'white earth' we were seeking and we explored the deposits slowly. There were crocodile and tortoise remains in profusion, as there had been at Kirimun, and I was beginning to feel depressed; when I saw a semi-cylindrical object protruding for about an inch from the side of a gully I could not believe it could be anything but the back of a tortoise. So far there had been only small bits of these animals, so I shouted across to Louis 'Do you want a *whole* tortoise?' He took one look at it and said 'I think that is a mastodon tusk.' We got to work with picks in the side of the cliff and after a few hours we had uncovered a fossil tusk five feet long. The ivory was in a fragile condition and could not be removed without plaster-of-Paris, which entailed carrying gallons of water in kerosene tins for three miles through the bush. By the time we had got the tusk encased a few days later, there was about 100 lbs of plastered ivory, strapped to a stout branch, to be carted back to the truck. I was not very popular. Louis alone was pleased with what inevitably became known as 'Sonia's tortoise'.

However, I was not the only one to be misled by tortoises. Soon after Olorgesailie was discovered there was great excitement over some supposed fragments of human skull which turned out to be tortoise scutes. Again, when Louis found the skull of *Homo erectus* at Olduvai in 1960 he at first thought the pieces were from the carapace of a fossil tortoise. In her book *Valley of the Wild Sisal*, Mary said that the resemblance had deceived both her and Louis on many occasions, so I am in good company. The moral is 'always check your tortoises', and of course the Leakeys always did.

Our Samburu guide was most upset that we should devote so much time and energy to extracting this crumbling and worthless ivory, and told us repeatedly that he could lead us to plenty of good live tuskers if we would only follow him. He was rather solemn and perhaps his responsibility weighed heavily on him, for we had nothing except his long spear to protect us from elephant and rhinos.

Apart from the 'tortoise', I made another peculiar discovery at Palagalagi, although I had no idea what it was. Undoubtedly it was a tooth, about the size of a thumbnail, and its bumps reminded me of something. After gazing at it for some time through a lens, Louis got quite excited; he pronounced it to be the unerupted molar of a foetal mastodon, something he had never seen before. Later we found two adult mastodon molars close by, with identical cusps but each tooth about nine inches long, which must have belonged to the unborn baby's mother. There were other finds – even the Samburu joined in the search – but the only sign of a primate was one tooth of a bush-baby, and we decided to call it a day.

On the return journey to Kirimun we happened to notice a black object which proved to be part of the truck's spring, broken off on our outward trip. Louis spent two hours on his back experimenting with ingenious makeshifts and put his thumb out of joint. Later that evening he had an acute attack of shivering and retired to bed with a large dose of quinine: effective prophylactics had not yet been developed, so that Louis suffered constantly from malaria.

On expeditions such as this, Louis was a good companion. He was always enthusiastic about finds, however insignificant, and made one feel one had made important contributions to the sum of knowledgc. All told, we had collected about a hundred fossils sufficiently diagnostic to be worth keeping. If the safari had not paid large dividends from the scientific angle, it had at least served a purpose in eliminating the area from the need for a full-scale investigation. Also, once the fauna had been studied, it was possible to add 'Upper' to the word 'Miocene' on the geological map.

Year after year, work went on at the Miocene sites of western Kenya and only a few of the highlights can be mentioned here. In 1951 Dr Thomas Whitworth of the University of Durham studied the geology of Rusinga and the neighbouring island of Mfanganu and made some spectacular discoveries on the Gumba peninsula in the south-eastern corner of Rusinga. Inside a pothole about six feet wide and six feet deep he found some blocks of limestone stuffed as full of fossils as a plum pudding with currants. The material was extremely hard and it took years of patient work to extract the bones, which included the remains of pigs, ruminants, rodents, and large lizards. One block was particularly exciting as it contained parts of the skull, jaws, arm, hand and foot bones of *Proconsul africanus* – and the fragmentary skull included the occipital and temporal bones, which had been missing in Mary's 1948 skull. The arm and hand bones were the first relatively complete specimens from any fossil ape yet known, and they were studied exhaustively. Gradually it was becoming possible to build up an Identikit picture of *Proconsul* and his habits. The animal, it appeared, showed many characters of the quadrupedal monkeys, but was also an incipient brachiator; in other words, he was learning to swing by his arms, although he normally progressed on all fours.

The next excitement was something far removed from apes: fossil insects. Early in 1952, the chance discovery of a well-preserved fossil beetle led to an intensive search, with amazing results. A letter from Louis to Kenneth Oakley of the British Museum (Natural History), written in January 1952, tells of how it happened: 'Mary and I have just come back from Rusinga, where at long last we have found fossil insects and other invertebrates, including spiders. The reason why we have not found these before, I think, is due to the fact that we were looking for the wrong sort of thing. I can only recollect having seen fossil insects and spiders (other than in amber) in a compressed form in fine stratified beds, so you can imagine my surprise when we suddenly started to find complete insects wholly uncompressed and undeformed and looking as though they were alive.'

There were insects of many different kinds, completely mineralized, yet with every detail chiselled as though by a sculptor: eyes, wrinkles, even the vanation of the wings had been preserved. After such success on Rusinga, Louis and Mary began to search also on Mfanganu Island, where they worked out a way of panning and got hundreds of tiny ants. Mary also found a complete fossil ants' nest; Professor E. O. Wilson of Harvard, who studied it, said it was undoubtedly the first known fossil insect colony preserved as a unit. Many of the ants were stuck on to fossil leaves, so evidently they were tree-ants; presumably the branch to which the nest was attached had broken off and fallen into the water, where it was engulfed in mud and so preserved.

Louis sent an exhibit of fossil insects from the two islands to a meeting of the Geological Society in London, where they caused a good deal of interest. An extract from the Society's *Proceedings* reports:

> The preservation is unusual: solid calcitic casts of the exact original form, often preserving with some perfection features such as eyes and

> mouth parts. . . . The specimens exhibited included lepidopterous larvae and pupae, beetles, a cicada, an egg mass of *Mantis*, and a tick.[12]

The Leakeys had also found grasshoppers, a worm, and a caterpillar which must have been in the process of changing its skin when it died. It would have been covered over with silt immediately, for under tropical conditions a caterpillar goes squashy within a few hours of death.

Eventually Louis amassed about three hundred fossil insects, which he tried to clean by hand under a binocular microscope; the Natural History Museum recommended hexametaphosphate of sodium to dissolve the matrix, which probably saved his eyesight.

There were some even more curious finds. At the site known as R107 on Rusinga, close to where Mary found the *Proconsul* skull, part of a small fossil bird had some of the flesh and muscles preserved. And there was the head of a large fossil lizard with the flesh replaced by mineral and the tongue hanging out of the side of its mouth. Louis sent it to the man who had encouraged him so much as a boy, Arthur Loveridge, who by then was Professor of Herpetology at Harvard; he pronounced it to be a new species of *Gerrhosaurus*.

Louis, of course, had dreams of finding fossil mammals, even apes, 'in the flesh', but sadly none have turned up – with one possible and intriguing exception. In 1943, Major G. Grundy had written to Louis:

> About 1932, I was prospecting and the locals on Mfanganu brought us some fossils. The one in question was about the size of a hand, was obviously part of a skull, and was remarkable for the fact that parts of the brain had been preserved. On our return to Kisumu . . . a number of people saw the skull (portion) and we had intended to hand it over to Archdeacon Owen. Then someone unknown lifted it and that's all there is to it.[13]

Could it have been a skull, with brain, of *Proconsul*? Louis would have given his entire, if meagre, fortune to know.

While on such subjects, there was another possible skull that vanished, this time at the hands of Owen himself. In 1949 Louis went to Maboko to continue excavations where the Archdeacon left off; he was told by the workmen that, although most of the fossils were of elephants, there had been a skull which they said was 'rather like that of a human'. Louis mentioned this in a letter to Owen's son John, saying: 'Certainly I never heard from your father of any discovery of such a skull on Maboko, but then I never heard of the discovery of the limb bones either, and their presence in London came as a complete surprise to all of us.'[14] (These were the *Proconsul* limb bones that the Archdeacon had sold to the British Museum (Natural History) which have already been mentioned.) John Owen could throw no light on the matter of the skull, but his mother said in a letter to Louis: 'I feel sure that Walter packed up a skull which interested him very much and sent it to the British Museum. . . . My impression is that it had a low forehead and large eye sockets. . . . I think it was in 1944 or 1945.'[15]

Louis himself believed that 'this missing skull is probably buried somewhere around Maseno', as he wrote in a letter to Mr Eric Firth of Fort Ternan in 1959. This, however, seems unlikely, as the Archdeacon always believed in selling his fossils wherever possible and anything as interesting as this he would almost certainly have sent to the British Museum, as his widow suggested in her letter. In 1934 Owen had offered Louis his whole collection of fossils from 'Mariwa, Ombo, Kiboko' [*sic:* Maboko] 'and a few things from Kanjera' for £145; needless to say, Louis had no hope of raising this sum. The Archdeacon suffered from collectomania, but he certainly did not ignore the commercial aspect of his finds. When I was doing research for this book in the National Archives in Nairobi, I came across a faded photograph of Archdeacon Owen with a skull on a table beside him; it was impossible to make out whether the skull was human or anthropoid, but it looked more like the latter. It just might have been a picture of that mysterious skull from Maboko.

Sir Wilfrid Le Gros Clark – he was knighted in 1955 – and Louis sent a joint report to *Nature* in 1955 outlining the past seven years' work on the Miocene of western Kenya.[16] Between 1947 (when the first British-Kenya expedition was launched) and 1955, the number of fossils collected from all the various sites amounted to 15,000, of which more than 11,000 had come from Rusinga. Louis had had to find specialists to describe not only all the many groups of mammals, but also the reptiles, fish, insects, mollusca and botanical remains.

The mammals were described in a new series published by the British Museum (Natural History) under the title 'Fossil Mammals of Africa', of which the first volume was by Le Gros Clark and Louis on *The Miocene Hominoidea of East Africa.* It included all the Miocene ape fossils found up till 1948, including some which MacInnes had described in a preliminary report published during the war. The *Proconsul* skull appeared just in time to form the *pièce de resistance*, and the monograph was finished in 1949. It then suffered a gestation period of more than two years before appearing in print towards the end of 1951.

This was the first of 22 volumes by specialists on Miocene and Pleistocene groups of African animals, of which 17 were on the Miocene. Four of the volumes were written by Donald MacInnes, but gradually he lost his interest in fossils and became absorbed in the study of icons and architecture. In 1954 he left the Coryndon Museum to take up a three year research fellowship at the School of Dental Surgery Medical School in Birmingham – among the teeth he studied were those of sea urchins! Louis owed a great deal to this loyal and unassuming friend who had taken so much of the palaeontological work off his shoulders.

The Fossil Mammals of Africa series formed an invaluable source of reference for specialists all over the world; but in 1967 the BM decided it could no longer finance it, to the great regret of many people and especially Louis himself. The reasons were partly economic; but also the Museum felt that its publications should be concerned only with its own collections, and it was no longer receiving fossils from Africa. When the Royal Society supported the first British-Kenya Miocene expedition it had stipulated that all type specimens of hominoids should go to the BM, but all other types were to go to the Coryndon Museum; after 1948, when the work was financed mainly by the Kenya Government, all finds became their property.

Louis had to find an alternative means of publishing his finds, so he started a new series edited by himself under the imprint of the Academic Press. The title was changed to 'Fossil Vertebrates of Africa' to accommodate reptiles, fish and birds as well as mammals, and the first volume appeared in 1969.

In initiating Miocene research in East Africa, Louis started a snowball which is still gathering momentum. Today at least thirty main fossil localities of this period are known, stretching from west of Lake Albert in Zaire to Karamoja in eastern Uganda, and from the Kavirondo Gulf in Kenya to Lake Rudolf in the north. Louis always regarded the Miocene as his personal property, perhaps with justification considering the amount of work he had put into it; when others applied for permits to work these deposits, he adopted a 'hands off' attitude. As he had the ear of the Government, rival expeditions were kept in check until the middle 1960s, by which time Louis was unable to do the field work himself.

8 Towards Uhuru

The 1950s should have been the most rewarding decade of Louis's career, and in many ways it was; but it was overshadowed by the Mau Mau uprising which destroyed the old Kenya and ultimately brought about the new. Just as Louis's scientific work had been interrupted by intelligence duties during the war, so once again he was to get involved in politics.

Otherwise everything was going well. Louis was in his prime: an *Observer* 'Profile' entitled 'The White Kikuyu' described him in July 1954 as a 'lean and boyish figure, active, provocative and intensely lively.' (Twelve years later the same paper was to call him 'a tireless old scholar in a boiler suit'.)[1] He had proved himself to be a most able curator, and in 1953 the Museum's extensions, for which he had fought so hard, were opened. The Pan African Congresses on Prehistory which he had initiated attracted ever increasing numbers of participants, and no less than three congresses were held during the 1950s. Miocene research proceeded at a pace which exceeded even Louis's expectations; and at long last excavations got under way at Olduvai, with dramatic results in 1959.

The decade started with a much-needed break: the Leakeys had not been on leave for five years, and in June 1950 they took their sons to England. Jonathan was now eight, Richard five, and Philip was just one year old – for Mary had had a third boy on 21 June 1949. With their usual need for economy the family was planning to go by sea; but BOAC offered them a free flight in return for allowing their pictures to be taken for advertising purposes. Needless to say they accepted with alacrity.

The Leakeys rented a cottage at Ewhurst in Surrey and spent a good part of their leave excavating a mesolithic pit dwelling at Abinger nearby; their report on the finds was published by the Surrey Archaeological Society, and the site is still open to visitors today. Louis and Mary also took their benefactor Charles Boise to see the cave paintings of the Dordogne, including Lascaux, and of Altamira in Spain. Mr Boise was getting on in years, but they found him a good travelling companion; small and spare, with a lively intelligence, he was fascinated by all they showed him and, as Mary put it, 'he never fussed'. Jonathan went with them, but the other two boys were parked with Mary's aunts, who found young Philip rather a handful.

Louis's work was beginning to reap rewards in the form of academic honours, and Oxford University, where he had once been known as 'the senior wangler', bestowed on him an honorary doctorate of science for his contributions to physical anthropology. The convocation was held on 25 July 1950, on the occasion of a meeting of the Fifth International Anatomical Congress, of which Professor Le Gros Clark was president, and no doubt he had not a little to do with Louis's doctorate.

Another memorable event during Louis's leave was a meeting with his daughter Priscilla, whom he had last seen when she was five. She was now eighteen, and the conditions made by Frida at the time of the divorce allowed the children freedom of choice as to whether they wanted to see their father once they were grown up. Priscilla did want to, very much indeed; she had been dreaming about their reunion all through her schooldays. Colin, as the man in the family, felt more resentment that Louis had done practically nothing to support Frida and her children; he was not particularly keen to see his father, and they did not meet on this occasion.

Priscilla and Colin's education had been paid for mainly through the sale of the house at Boscombe, which Canon Harry Leakey had left to Frida. Louis's parents had always remained on friendly terms with her and used to visit her and their grandchildren whenever they came to England. It was a good thing that Frida had some money of her own, as Louis was barely able to support one family, certainly not two. She augmented her income by occasional radio talks and writing, but mainly she threw herself into good works on a voluntary basis. She was a leading light of the Women's Institute, ran a welfare centre, and, during the war, became emergency food officer and billeting officer, taking in evacuees at The Close. When Girton lagged behind other villages in their efforts at bone salvage (for the manufacture of glue), Frida stuck a notice on each dustbin collecting point which read 'Women of Girton, lay your bones here.' Needless to say, the figures shot up immediately. After the war, Frida became voluntary county organizer for the Women's Institutes, and she is now a County Councillor. Priscilla and Colin were taught at home by governesses until 1942, after which they both boarded at a co-educational school at Keswick. Colin went on to a prep school in Warwickshire when he was eleven, and then to Gresham's School at Holt in Norfolk. Priscilla, like her aunt Gladys Beecher, finished her education at Cheltenham Ladies' College.

Priscilla sometimes heard of her father's doings through a friend of her mother's, a contemporary of Frida's at Newnham, and through Donald MacInnes, who was Priscilla's godfather and who remained a friend of Frida's after she parted from Louis. Priscilla would also pore over her father's entry in *Who's Who*, from which she learned of the existence of her half-brothers. During that 1950 leave she saw Louis on his own and did not meet Mary and the boys until the family were next in England four years later, by which time Priscilla was married.

Louis picked her up in the village of Girton; he did not even know what she looked like, but she recognized him at once from photographs. They spent the day watching birds on the Breck and – typically – Louis took her to see the flint knappers at Brandon. He laid himself out to charm his teenage daughter, but both found the occasion rather a strain and the thaw came only on the way home after they had given a lift to a soldier. Priscilla sat in the front of the car practising the string figures that Louis had taught her, which was his invariable way of breaking the ice, whether with children, teenagers or unknown African tribesmen. From time to time he would stop to demonstrate new ones, or dart into a quarry to collect flint and make a stone tool. The soldier obviously thought he was being driven by a lunatic, and his discomfiture made them both laugh. Father and daughter established a rapport just before it was time to part for several years.

Colin's first meeting with Louis happened about two years later, shortly before he left school at the age of nineteen and during one of Louis's brief trips to London on some scientific mission. Priscilla by then was training as a physiotherapist, and she arranged for them to see each other in Holland Park, where they sat awkwardly on a bench getting acquainted. Colin says he felt no sense of relationship whatever, and he was not at all interested in bones and stones. However, he was bold enough to dispute Louis's claim that man originated in Africa; why, he said, should there not be fossils equally old elsewhere, which had not yet been discovered? He sensed a conflict in Louis's mind: he was put out that a member of his family should question his authority, yet at the same time he seemed to be pleased that his son should have independent views.

Apart from his Museum work, Louis was much occupied at this time with problems connected with Kenya's National Parks. Not only did up-country archaeological sites, such as Olorgesailie, come under the protection of the National Parks, but also coastal ruins. Louis began to agitate about the great Portuguese fort at Mombasa, Fort Jesus, which was being used as a prison. After many years of prodding, the Prisons Department moved, the Calouste Gulbenkian Foundation of Lisbon put up some money, and Dr James Kirkman undertook the restoration.

Louis was also involved in another conservation struggle which concerned a threat to Mzima Springs in Tsavo National Park. This lush oasis in semi-desert country was famed for its hippos and other aquatic life, and in 1953 there was a proposal to tap Mzima's 'Long Pool' for Mombasa's water supply. This would entail the building of a weir to raise its level by about eight feet, which would have meant the end of the hippos' nursery, for the vegetation would have been submerged and the bank would have been too steep for the animals to climb out. It was the first real challenge to the security of Kenya's National Parks, and the trustees employed a firm of consulting engineers to draw up alternative plans. The director of the Parks, Colonel Mervyn Cowie, visited the site with Louis and the engineers, and their report was sent to the Member for Agriculture and Natural Resources, who was in the uncomfortable position of being responsible both for the National Parks and for Mombasa's water supply.

No action was taken, so the trustees tried to present their case to the Governor.[2] Unfortunately the application got clogged in administrative channels, so Colonel Cowie launched a massive Press campaign. There was a tremendous response, and the ripples of Mzima Springs reached out across the world. When the Governor, Sir Evelyn Baring, read all the angry letters, he demanded an explanation as to why he had not been informed of these matters, only to be told that an interview had not been granted. Sir Evelyn promptly went to Mzima Springs, and one glance at the hippos was enough to convince him that something must be done. In the crystal clear water, the hippos can be seen tiptoeing along the bottom, their huge bulk floating as gracefully as a weightless astronaut in a space capsule.

The Government arranged for a re-examination of the proposals, and an alternative solution was accepted; the water was drawn off before it emerged at the spring, and the hippos were saved. Some people thought it was a lot of fuss to make about a few hippos, mostly those who had not actually seen them in this unique setting. Any damage to the place would have been a tragedy to the world as a whole. In addition, an important question of principle had been involved and the trustees of the National Parks breathed more easily after they had won their case. It had seemed at one moment that legislation could override the National Parks Ordinance, which was thought to be inviolate. Also, the machinery for meeting such a crisis had appeared to be ineffective: the trustees had been unable to state their case at the highest level until a Press campaign had forced the issue. It had been a valuable lesson all round.

As far as prehistory was concerned, one of the Leakeys' main tasks in the early 1950s was to study the rock paintings in Tanganyika, some of which Mary had copied in 1935. Louis had obtained a grant for this purpose from the Wenner-Gren Foundation for Anthropological Research, which came to his aid on many future occasions and did a great deal to stimulate prehistoric research in general throughout Africa. The Foundation's headquarters is in New York but it also owns a magnificent castle in Austria, Burg

Wartenstein, where conferences are arranged each summer; many were concerned with African prehistory, and Louis attended them on several occasions. Like the Pan African Congresses on Prehistory these symposia helped to keep scientists involved in the study of man in touch with one another, and provided a platform for thrashing out ideas.

Unfortunately the grant for the study of the rock paintings at Cheke, Kisese and other nearby shelters lasted for only one season, and for the next two years Louis struggled to find money to complete the work. It was most important to do so, for Mary had developed an entirely new technique whereby the actual contours and texture of the rock were reproduced as a realistic background to the life-sized paintings. The results of her work were a great draw to the public when they were displayed in the new Hall of Man at the Coryndon Museum, and the method was so much admired that Mary got orders from other museums as well for her reproductions of the rock paintings.

In 1952, the second Pan African Congress was held in Algiers from 29 September to 4 October; it was for ever associated in Louis's mind with the fact that while he was there he heard that Mau Mau had been forced into the open. His thoughts, therefore, were not entirely on the congress, which in any case was North Africa-orientated and French-orientated and for the most part was of little direct concern to him. Its main value lay in the renewal of contacts with fellow prehistorians and geologists, and in enabling Louis to meet those who had made their mark since the 1947 congress in Nairobi.

In the excursion to Tunisia which preceded the working sessions in Algiers the delegates got involved in floods near Tebessa which were even worse than those encountered on the way back from the Tanganyika excursion in 1947. The party was also inundated by hospitality, and orgies of whole roast sheep left little time or inclination to linger over archaeological sites, some of which had to be inspected after dark by the light of matches. At the congress, Louis gave papers on his old favourite the climatic sequence during the Pleistocene in East Africa; on the environment of the Miocene apes in western Kenya; and on the survey of

16. *Above* Louis and Mary take Jonathan and Richard to the Tower of London during their 1950 leave; five-year-old Richard looks apprehensive, having been told that Beefeaters also eat little boys

17. *Right* Louis was awarded an honorary DSc by the University of Oxford on 25 July 1950; with him is Professor W. E. Le Gros Clark, who supported his research and described many of his finds

Overleaf

18. Louis gives a demonstration of butchering a buck with a stone tool to delegates of the 3rd Pan African Congress on Prehistory at Livingstone in 1955

prehistoric art in Tanganyika which he had recently made with Mary. After the formal business ended, Louis skipped the excursion to Morocco which followed and flew back to Nairobi. Almost as soon as he arrived, he heard of the murder by Mau Mau of one of his oldest friends, Chief Waruhiu.

Even before going on leave in 1950, Louis had heard of sinister rumblings in Kenya, and while he was away they became even louder. At a meeting held beneath the sacred fig tree at old Chief Koinange's headquarters at Kiambaa, mass oathing ceremonies were held to unify the Kikuyu. Then in March 1950 Nairobi became a city, and the East African Trades Union Congress called for a boycott of the celebrations: there were rumours that the occasion was to be the signal for more thefts of land by Europeans, and that part of Kiambu district was to be incorporated within the city boundaries. There was no foundation for such rumours, which had been started by political agitators to stir up nationalist feelings.

It is thought that the words 'Mau Mau' were first used in 1948, but Louis did not hear them until after his return from leave when some Kikuyu elders told him of a secret society calling itself by that name. His warnings to government officials about this society, as well as the significance of the oathing ceremony at Kiambaa, were not taken seriously. Louis was known to be something of a fanatic where the Kikuyu were concerned, and this, they thought, was just one more example of Leakey hysteria. The Government did not show any real concern for at least another year, but in the circumstances this was perhaps understandable.

The secret nature of the society made proof of its existence impossible to obtain. After the state of emergency was declared, all documents found at the headquarters of the alleged leaders of the movement were examined carefully, but the words 'Mau Mau' were not found; and at their trial the defendants all said 'We don't know Mau Mau.'

As Louis was so closely concerned with the political happenings of 1952–55 it is impossible to ignore those unhappy years. He was involved in intelligence work and in the trial of Mzee* Jomo Kenyatta; and he also wrote two important books about the causes and manifestations of the Mau Mau movements. The summary which follows is taken partly from the first of these books, *Mau Mau and the Kikuyu*, published at the end of 1952 within two months of the declaration of the state of emergency.[3]

The roots of Mau Mau went back to the proscribed Kikuyu Central Association, which found outlets for the spreading of nationalist propaganda in independent churches and schools. Some of these schools taught anti-European and anti-Christian doctrines and were even used as centres for oath-taking; most of them were closed by the Government after the emergency was declared. The main training ground for nationalist politicians was the Kenya Teachers' Training College at Githunguri, founded in 1939 by Mbiyu Koinange after his return to Kenya from Cambridge. In spite of a degree from Columbia University and a diploma from St John's, he soon found that there were no suitable openings for a Kikuyu with his qualifications under the colonial regime. He was offered a post as an educational officer Grade III and, as a great concession, he was to enjoy the salary scale of an Asian of equivalent rank – £182 per annum, rising to £300. Not unnaturally, he became embittered and thereafter spent much of his time abroad; and when he left Kenya in 1951 he was not allowed to return for another ten years.

After the Kikuyu Central Association was proscribed, it reappeared under the *nom-de-plume* of the Kenya African Union, which was open to all tribes. Any connections between the KCA and the KAU were hotly denied, but former KCA leaders dominated the new organization. The Kenya African Union was founded while Jomo Kenyatta was in Europe, but in 1947, soon after his return to his native land after fifteen years' absence, he was elected its president. In the meantime Kenyatta had acquired political sophistication in the heady atmosphere of the London School of Economics and Moscow, and with his compelling gift of

*The Swahili word *mzee* means old, but as a prefix to a man's name it is a term of respect, implying wisdom.

oratory and his burning desire to 'set my people free', he quickly gained an immense following.

Many of his associates came from the district of the government-appointed chief Koinange, who was now in his eighties, and Kenyatta married as his third wife one of Koinange's daughters, thus reinforcing the alliance. He also took over the running of the Teachers' Training College at Githunguri, which had been founded by Koinange's son Mbiyu. In order to achieve his aim of self-government, Kenyatta had to have *all* the Kikuyu behind him, not merely those of the Kiambu district; and eventually he would need the support of all the other tribes as well – hence their nominal inclusion in the Kenya African Union. However, the KAU was dominated by Kikuyu, who cut themselves off from the rest, and eventually the younger, more militant members got the upper hand. Kenyatta's hopes of an inter-tribal onslaught towards self-government faded, and with them his hopes of avoiding violence.

Why, apart from the influence of powerful and intelligent leaders, was the Mau Mau movement confined almost entirely to the Kikuyu? For one thing, they were the most numerous: there were well over a million of them, one-fifth of the entire African population of Kenya. They occupied some of the most fertile land in the country, they were overcrowded, and they coveted more; but land hunger was only one of the many complex factors that led to Mau Mau. Paradoxically, the basic cause must probably be laid squarely at the feet of such well loved and saintly people as Canon Harry Leakey, whom the Loyal Kikuyu Patriots of Kiambu had called 'a successful bridge between black and white' on the occasion of his retirement in 1933. The missionaries had caused the disintegration of tribal structure and beliefs and, although this happened to other tribes besides the Kikuyu, the Kikuyu were nearest to Nairobi, were more intensively missionized, and were given more educational opportunities than the others.

In spite of their education the Kikuyu were fundamentally superstitious, and no amount of mission training could eradicate their fear of supernatural reprisals to anyone breaking an oath administered with the age-old ritual. Oathing to bind them to a common cause began to get under way early in 1952, and those suspected of giving away information about what was going on were promptly despatched; officially, they 'disappeared'. The KAU also began to produce parodies of Christian hymns, set to well-known tunes (and even to the tune of the national anthem) but with new words; the main theme was 'get rid of the white man', but very few Europeans understood Kikuyu and were amazed at the apparent religious fervour and patriotism displayed at mass meetings. At a KAU meeting at Nyeri in July 1952 Kenyatta spoke to an audience estimated to number more than twenty thousand. At another meeting at Kiambu in August he denounced Mau Mau and reiterated the aims of the KAU: self-government and the end of racial discrimination. This did not satisfy the militants, who emphasized their point by assassinating Senior Chief Waruhiu: as a staunch Christian he was utterly opposed to the secret oathing and plans that were being made for an armed rebellion, and he had had the courage to voice these opinions. Louis dedicated his book *Mau Mau and the Kikuyu* to Waruhiu's memory.

The Secretary of State for the Colonies at the time, Mr Oliver Lyttelton (afterwards Lord Chandos), described Mau Mau as 'an unholy union between ancient witchcraft and modern gangsterism'. In fact, as Louis made clear in his second book *Defeating Mau Mau*, a third, more insidious and infinitely more dangerous element was involved: Christianity.[4] Unlikely as it may seem, Mau Mau drew its strength from religion. Leaders of the movement let it be known that in order to be a true Kikuyu and to enjoy all the benefits that were to come people must undergo a spiritual reawakening in the form of a new initiation ceremony. They were not told what was involved, merely that it was in the cause of freedom. The 'service', which accompanied the taking of the oath, was led by a 'priest' of one of the independent churches, and the solemn nature of the ceremony was strongly emphasized. It involved a mixture of themes drawn from the Old Testament and ancient Kikuyu – distorted – and Louis described the effects thus:

> When to this religious aspect of the movement is added the great power exercised by the magical and mystical acts that accompany the actual oath-taking, it is not difficult to see how it became possible to make so many normally peace-loving Kikuyu into the fanatical, murdering maniacs that they have become under Mau Mau.[5]

Little or nothing was known about this religious aspect at the time (1952) when Louis wrote *Mau Mau and the Kikuyu*, and in his second book, published nearly two years later, he owns that this involvement with Christianity came as a complete surprise to him.

Many of these first oathings took place in the huts of squatters on European farms, where there was much discontent. The areas most affected were in the Rift Valley and on land between the Aberdares range and Mount Kenya, where most of the labour for farms and public works was Kikuyu. Squatters worked for reduced wages in return for a small piece of land on which they could grow just enough to support their family and graze a limited number of stock. But families grew and herds multiplied, and only the more fortunate squatters, or their fathers, owned a plot of land in a native land unit where the surplus could be accommodated and the old retire. Under such circumstances the Mau Mau promise to restore European land to its 'rightful' owners met with a most favourable response.

By Kikuyu custom, an oath had to be made voluntarily, in public, in the open and by daylight; Mau Mau oaths were administered forcibly, in secret, in huts and at night. Because the ritual bore a superficial resemblance to that used in genuine oath-taking ceremonies, the victims dared not break their oath or report what had happened.

Louis began writing *Mau Mau and the Kikuyu* in October, and the manuscript reached Methuen's in London on 5 November, only two weeks after the state of emergency was declared. It was published on 11 December, nearly a month ahead of schedule. Within the space of 114 short pages, Louis managed to condense the most important factors of the grievances which led up to Mau Mau. In spite of its incredibly rapid production, it was an excellent piece of work, which opened the eyes of thousands of readers who were totally ignorant of the causes of the rebellion.

As Elspeth Huxley put it in *Time and Tide:*

> There is not likely to be a fairer or more accurate account of the origins of Mau Mau and of its relationship to the Kikuyu than Dr Leakey provides in his short book. It is a measure of the ignorance of the British Parliament and people about a situation they are sup-

posed to control that so much will come as a surprise to so many.[6]

The *Times Literary Supplement* went further:

> It is not too much to say that if this book had been written thirty years ago and policy shaped accordingly by administrators and settlers, the present discontents in Kenya might never have arisen.[7]

In September, a new Governor took over: the late Sir Evelyn Baring, afterwards Lord Howick of Glendale. He was immediately plunged into dealing with the worst crisis that any colonial governor had yet had to face. On 20 October, 1952, he signed the proclamation of the state of emergency, after which the Government had power to act – and it did so swiftly. More than a hundred leaders of the KAU were arrested and Jomo Kenyatta, with five others, was charged with the management of Mau Mau. He was apprehended at his house at Githunguri and was flown to Lokitaung, the remotest place in the Colony. There, in the desert country west of Lake Rudolf, he was to remain for the next seven years. After the detention of the alleged leaders, the more fanatical element gained power and at least five higher grades of oaths were administered. Both those who administered them and those who took them were unclean, outcasts who would go to any lengths because they were already doomed.

Kenyatta's trial, together with four other executives of the Kenya African Union and the chairman of one of its regional branches, began on 24 November, was adjourned until 3 December, and then lasted for fifty-eight days. It was held at Kapenguria, near Mount Elgon and the Uganda border, an administrative post in a restricted area where no one could enter without a permit; the location was chosen in order to prevent huge crowds from attending the trial, but nevertheless a good many people somehow managed to wangle permits. The courtroom was an unused building destined to become an agricultural school, apart from which there was a Distict Commissioner's house and a couple of prisons: Kapenguria, in fact, lacked any charm and all amenities. The nearest hotel and telephone – even the nearest drinking water – was at Kitale, nearly thirty miles away along a dusty track.

The charge was that Mau Mau was a part of KAU and that the

accused, who managed KAU, *ipso facto* managed Mau Mau. The magistrate was Mr Ransley Thacker, QC, who had recently retired, and the prosecution was led by the Deputy Public Prosecutor, Mr Anthony Somerhaugh. Leading the defence was Mr Denis Nowell Pritt, QC, well-known for his anti-imperialist sentiments. In the words of a reporter at the trial: 'So completely is the Court dominated by the personality of Mr Pritt that it is difficult to feel that it is the accused Africans and not the Crown witnesses who are on trial.'[8] The police officer in charge of the case was Superintendent Ian Henderson of Special Branch, who spoke Kikuyu fluently and who won two George Medals for his work during the emergency; his best-selling book *The Hunt for Kimathi* (1958) is a revelation of the courage of the hunters and the fanaticism of the hunted. And the court interpreter was L. S. B. Leakey.

The trial was a legal farce, rigged from the start for reasons of security. The very first witness, who testified to having had the Mau Mau oath administered to him by Kenyatta, later admitted bribery and perjury. Then Pritt was charged with contempt of court for sending a cable to four British Members of Parliament protesting at holding the trial in such a remote place and in a closed district; some of the counsel for the defence, he said, were excluded and this amounted to a denial of justice. The case was adjourned for more than a fortnight, but the charge failed. Next Pritt protested against Louis's interpreting: 'I keep getting notes from my clients that translations are wrong and that other things are interpolated,' objected Pritt. 'I must insist that only what I ask be translated to the witness and that only the witness's answer be translated. There ought not to be a lot of conversation between the translator and the witness in Kikuyu.'

One of Pritt's objections, and Somerhaugh's quick riposte, caused some merriment. 'It is impossible to read Dr Leakey's book, which was published in the middle of this trial,' said Pritt, 'without being convinced that he was making as plain as possible an innuendo that my clients, or some of them, are the people who are dominating and leading Mau Mau.' To this Somerhaugh replied: 'It is certainly a book against Mau Mau. If his clients like to wear the hat, it will fit.' 'A grossly improper observation,' was Pritt's comment.

Pritt protested altogether five times against Louis's interpreting. On the fifth occasion, a Muslim woman stated that she had been at a certain place for seven months before the holding of a meeting at which Kenyatta had spoken. 'She probably means seven Islamic months,' interposed Louis. This interjection was the last straw for Pritt, and also for Louis, who withdrew. In the words of the *Daily Herald* of 8 January, 1953, 'Dr Leakey walked out of the Court, his face drawn and ashen grey with anger, after asking the magistrate's permission to go'. He was replaced as interpreter first by a Scottish missionary, then by a Kikuyu court interpreter – to whom objections were also made – and finally by a coffee farmer. In fact, Louis was probably within his rights to elucidate witnesses' statements, for the interpreter's oath reads as follows: 'I swear by Almighty God that I will well and truly interpret *and explanation make* to the court and the witnesses of all such matters and things as shall be required of me to the best of my skill, knowledge and belief' (my italics). Louis had said that it was difficult if not impossible to translate the actual words, as the speakers sometimes used allegorical phrases which would have been meaningless in English, and he therefore had to substitute equivalents as best he could. The magistrate had said himself that there was 'no other man in the Colony better qualified than Dr Leakey to act as interpreter', and certainly Pritt did not appear to be better pleased by the ones who took over after Louis's withdrawal.

Mr Somerhaugh wrote to Louis soon afterwards:

> First let me say that nothing disturbs or shall disturb our friendship. But I think (while admitting that I may be wrong) that you should have stood up to Pritt in the witness box. I think the public who were on your side throughout would have liked to have seen you vindicate yourself. . . . When I told Pritt I was not calling you he said at once 'Why? Is Leakey running away?' However, I used my instructions and said that you could not be called because of the allegations made against you . . . I hope you will be satisfied that I put the case in the proper light and that you have been vindicated to the extent that Pritt's accusations have been publicly shown to be baseless.[9]

Of course Louis was prejudiced, as was the magistrate himself; but the allegation that he sometimes interpreted what he thought witnesses *meant* to say rather than what they actally did say must be unfounded: there were enough people present who knew both Kikuyu and English well enough to prevent this happening, including Kenyatta himself.

In the same letter, Somerhaugh continued:

> With regard to your sitting with me in Court, I have told the AG that I think it would be unwise. It would give ground to Pritt's assertion that you were biased and *ergo* 'prosecution minded'. Could you not bring up the mass of untranslated material and work on it here, so that I could have the benefit of consulting you?

And that is what Louis did. He returned as a witness on document translations on 26 January 1953, and in the evenings he worked at Kitale with the help of a typist. There was a great deal to do, for he translated not only the documents taken from Kenyatta's house, but also such things as Kikuyu 'hymn' books. (These were the subject of another protest by Pritt, who said they should be called 'songs' rather than 'hymns'). Kenyatta's cross-examination began on 28 January and Louis did not miss a word of it, for he was extremely interested to hear what Kenyatta had to say. For a month Louis commuted between Kitale and Kapenguria, returning to Nairobi at weekends to make sure his family was all right.

Just before the beginning of the trial the Leakeys had moved into a new house at Langata, about twelve miles outside Nairobi. The curator's house in the Museum grounds was becoming far too small for their growing family and they bought a five-acre plot at Langata, building the house with the aid of African workmen and an Indian foreman. The rooms formed four sides of a square round a courtyard and were designed so that the dogs could be let out at night without going outside the house: the garden was surrounded by thick bush and there was danger from the occasional leopard as well as from Mau Mau. As Louis had to be away so much, he was very worried about security, and from Kitale he sent a wire to the Superintendent of Police in Nairobi: 'Urgently request increase guard my house and family from present single elderly constable who quite unable remain awake all night every night alone. Consider extra guarding essential as increasing number defence witnesses return from Kapenguria telling how my assistance prosecution breaking down defence witnesses.'

For his work as interpreter and translator of documents, Louis was given a mileage allowance and living expenses plus an honorarium of £250. A letter signed on behalf of the Attorney General thanked him for:

> your splendid work on behalf of the Crown in the case of R v. Kenyatta and others . . . I know, and probably no one knows better, how much the Crown owes to you for your invaluable advice and help in the preparation and presentation of that case and although I know you put in countless hours of work and study with no other thought than that of assisting the cause in which you so sincerely believed, nevertheless the Government of Kenya thinks it right that it should make some acknowledgement of its indebtedness to you by paying you this honorarium.[10]

There was never any doubt in Louis's mind that Kenyatta could have used his influence to stop Mau Mau, but he was equally certain that he was in no way to blame for its later manifestations. Louis had a good deal of sympathy with the nationalist cause, but he was deeply shocked by 'his' tribe's way of going about it and their complete break with custom and tradition. After Independence, Louis shared with most citizens of Kenya a profound respect for Mzee Kenyatta's wisdom and tolerance. In a curious way the two men had a good deal in common. Kenyatta has been described as devious, cunning, gregarious yet secretive, with a belief in the supernatural,[11] all of which could apply also to Louis. Each was a showman, both loved children, they even shared a delight in cooking (which was Kenyatta's job during the years he spent at Lokitaung). Their characters, for all the veneer of Western sophistication, were very African, very Kikuyu.

The result of the trial was a foregone conclusion; one of the accused, a Luo, was acquitted, but the others got the maximum sentence of seven years' hard labour. Pritt appealed twice to the Privy Council in London, but on each occasion the petition was dismissed without any reason being given. The reasons were obvious enough; but the authorities had underestimated the strength of the movement, and the detention of its leaders may have had the opposite of the desired effect.

The work done by Louis for the CID during the emergency was basically the same as his war work – making vernacular broadcasts, building up a network of informants, transmitting messages received over the bush telegraph. One of his most reliable sources of information was a well-known figure who is now dead; a courageous opponent of Mau Mau, he used to send Louis long letters in Kikuyu giving details of meetings and those who addressed them. Other correspondents would give names of those known to have committed murders and sometimes reveal their hiding places, or would give information about those who were supplying food to gangs in the forests.

Louis also worked closely with the administrative officers. As an example, to one Provincial Commissioner he wrote that in a certain area there was a strong Mau Mau group led by four men, whom he named. He also said that a certain clerk who pretended to be anti-Mau Mau used his position of trust to provide cover for Mau Mau people, and that he laid supposed information against loyal KPA (Kikuyu Provincial Association) members in the hope of having them repatriated to the Reserve.[12] Some weeks later, the PC told Louis that this information had been investigated and found correct, and that the clerk and the four Mau Mau leaders had been arrested. He expressed his gratitude and asked Louis to keep him informed of any other evidence he came across.[13]

Not all administrative officers, however, were so grateful to Louis for teaching them their business. He wrote to one DC to inform him that some KPA members had received a government order telling them that they must be cleansed from oath-taking and pay a sum of sixty shillings each. Louis pointed out that loyalists should not be penalised, and suggested that action had been taken by some person who was not aware of what the KPA stood for. The DC replied testily that these people had not been forced to be cleansed, and that others at the ceremony had paid the money voluntarily to help the loyalist cause. 'Your friends did not contribute,' wrote the DC, 'and I do feel that these persons have been unduly touchy. I would so much rather they had brought their troubles to me on the spot rather than retail them to you with, I suspect, elaborations.' It was not easy to work for both sides, Kikuyu and European, as Louis appeared to be doing, and perhaps it was only natural than neither side should really trust him.

Because of his intelligence work, Louis was guarded wherever he went by a Meru tribesman, who today works as a driver in the workshops of a well-known garage in Nairobi. The Mau Mau put a price of £500 on Louis's head, a very large sum in their financial state – and one which no doubt would never have been met – and grimly flattering. There were a number of Kikuyu working at the Museum, and one of them was suspected of having been involved in an incident which might have cost Louis his life: driving to Kisumu one day, he found that the U-bolts on his vehicle had been deliberately loosened.

Louis's old friend Charles Boise was particularly worried for his safety. In November 1953 he wrote:

> I have no doubt that you could continue to be of assistance to the authorities in dealing with Mau Mau, but I think the preservation of your life so that you may continue your researches into the antiquity of man are easily of predominant importance. Surely you could usefully occupy yourself in your research work elsewhere in areas which would remove you from the imminent danger to your life. Please write me fully and frankly on this subject. I have no doubt I could arrange for you to visit the Forminière area in the Belgian Congo. Then there are new and very interesting discoveries in South Africa which would well repay a prolonged visit.[14]

There were many times when Louis might have welcomed such suggestions, but this was not one of them. At times he had thought of leaving Kenya because of the lack of opportunities and funds, but he was not one to run away from danger, particularly when he felt that the Kikuyu needed him. Throughout the emergency he remained optimistic about the country's future and he was determined to do all he could to help in the rehabilitation of his people.

Gradually the efforts of the security forces and the home guard began to take effect and, as the hard core of the Mau Mau took to the forests, the Kikuyu gained confidence. A major turning point in the campaign came with Operation Anvil on 24 April 1954 when the entire population of Nairobi was screened and some 30,000 suspects were packed off to detention camps.

Compared with the many thousands of Kikuyu who died at the hands of their fellow tribesmen, European casualties were relatively light. The official figures for those who were killed during the emergency are 32 European civilians and 63 members of the security forces; 26 Asian civilians and three members of the security forces; 11,503 African 'terrorists', 1,819 'loyalists', and 101 members of the security forces.

Among the Europeans who were murdered were Louis's cousin Gray Leakey and his third wife, Mary, on their farm near Nyeri at the foot of Mount Kenya. (Gray had married two of the governesses who had taught Louis and his sisters at Kabete, both of whom had died: first Elizabeth Laing and then Bessie Bull. By his first wife he had had four children, including Nigel, the VC.) After the first world war, Gray had obtained 2,000 acres under the Government's soldier settler scheme, but eventually a severe drought forced him to sell out and for a time he managed the White Rhino Hotel in Nyeri, after which he bought another farm. He was well known for his sympathy for African aspirations and was well liked by his employees. In 1954, Gray was seventy years old, a diabetic and very deaf, yet he always refused to carry firearms; a few weeks before his death he had been held up by two armed terrorists, but when he told them he was unarmed they let him go. On 13 October he and his wife Mary and his step-daughter Mrs Diana Hartley were having dinner when a large gang broke into the room, after killing the Kikuyu servant. Mary Leakey was strangled and Gray was dragged outside, but Mrs Hartley managed to escape into the loft and afterwards raised the alarm by firing a rocket.

There was no trace of Gray, but two days later the security forces killed three terrorists in the forest and found some of his clothes in their hideout, as well as a letter which said: 'We are making arrangements to the sacrifice. We completed well that one European.' It was signed 'General Kabui' and addressed to 'Dear Sir Kaleba'. A note from 'Field Marshal Kaleba' also came into the hands of the police asking for the names of the men who caught the European named 'Murungaru' ('the upright one'). Over the next few weeks a most intensive search was made and tracker dogs followed the scent to the forest near the Sagana Royal Lodge, Kenya's wedding present to Queen Elizabeth, but they then lost the trail.

After five weeks, acting on information given by captured terrorists, the police found the remains of Gray's body in a hole disturbed by hyenas within five miles of his house. He had been buried head downwards, possibly while still alive; but as he was a diabetic he may well have been unconscious. Nearby, a sheep had been sacrificed. It was a ritual murder, believed to have been instigated by a Kikuyu prophetess who had been told in a vision that the killing of 'a really good European' would provide useful magic, causing the fortunes of the Mau Mau to turn for the better.

Gray Leakey had served in the Carrier Corps during the First World War and in prisoner-of-war camps in the second, so he was given a military funeral in Nyeri. The service was conducted by the Bishop of Mombasa, Dr Leonard Beecher, and was attended by the Governor, Sir Evelyn Baring, and by the GOC East Africa, Lieutenant General Sir George Erskine. Louis, who of course also went to the funeral, was badly shaken by his cousin's horrible death and immediately broadcast to the people of Kenya warning them to be constantly on the alert. 'Although it grieves me deeply to have to speak of my family's mistakes,' he said, 'I feel that I must do so if I can help to prevent similar tragedies for others.' He listed six lessons that were to be learnt. The Mau Mau were on the lookout for those who did not take full precautions. The Mau Mau would cut through the telephone line (they had). Everyone should have more than one switch to fire rockets (Gray's switch was out of reach in the bedroom, and the rocket could not be fired until Mrs Hartley was able to come down from the loft). Arms should be attached to you with a lanyard (Gray's weapons were locked in a safe). It was unwise to count on servants to help, however loyal. Doors should not be left unlocked. (Gray trusted his servants implicitly and never locked the doors.)[15]

Already in the early months of 1954 there had been talk of how to restore peace, and at a meeting at Government House prominent Kikuyu and other African leaders met to discuss ways of bringing this about. They included government-appointed chiefs, two members of Legislative Council, ministers of religion and moderate politicians. A joint statement was prepared calling on the Kikuyu to have nothing to do with Mau Mau. These leaders then asked the Governor to arrange a conference between representatives of the three main communities, African, Asian and European, to work out details of how to end the emergency. This was probably the first time that the three communities had collaborated in this way for a purpose that affected them all so deeply; Louis played his customary role as interpreter.

Louis's own policy for winning the peace was set out in his book *Defeating Mau Mau*, published in 1954. Since the time when *Mau Mau and the Kikuyu* appeared in 1952 he had learnt a good deal: he had the facts brought out at the Kapenguria trial, the experiences of his intelligence work, and above all the knowledge amassed by the screening teams. As a reviewer in *The Times* said: 'Dr Leakey has the modesty to re-examine some of his conclusions in the first [book].'[16] Nearly all the notices, however, pointed out that some of the policies he advocated were bound to meet with opposition. Many of his constructive proposals, remarked a reviewer in the *Economist*, went much further than the rehabilitation plans of the Kenya Government and were bound to be keenly criticized 'because they ask a very great deal. It is fair to observe, however, that they ask a great deal equally from all races and from all sections of the community. . . . From the Church leaders Dr Leakey asks virtually the impossible.'[17]

As he had done twenty years earlier with his book *Kenya: Contrasts and Problems*, Louis managed to upset just about everybody: churchmen, politicians, educationists, agricultural experts, farmers, employers of African labour of all kinds. However, as the reviewer in the *Economist* concludes, his proposals 'constitute perhaps the first imaginative effort to show the sort of mental adjustments that are required from all races in a multi-racial society if it is to succeed'. Today most of these proposals seem obvious; twenty years ago they were far from obvious to any but the most enlightened.

Perhaps the most important and the most obvious point that Louis made was that the maintenance of the White Highlands for exclusive European occupation was no longer feasible. In fact by now most of the settlers had seen the writing on the wall, and all but the staunchest reactionaries had braced themselves for the inevitable; but it was ironic that in the years to come they were to be bought out by the Kenya Government on loans from the British Government. Louis also advocated the abolition of the squatter system, which was gradually replaced by African re-settlement schemes within the former White Highlands. More controversial at that time was his contention that there must be improvement of wages and conditions, with equal pay for equal work, irrespective of race and colour.

Louis put particular emphasis on education, and the following passage from *Defeating Mau Mau* could apply equally well to other societies many years after the words were written:

> The salary scales of teachers were also very low, and in consequence the people who were attracted to this profession were not always the best, but quite often those who could not obtain better paid employment elsewhere. Many boys and girls grew up into young men and women having some little book learning but without any real training in how to behave as adults in the life of the community. Dishonesty of all kinds became common and sexual morals degenerated. The old sexual laws were no longer obeyed (they were not even known), but there were no others that had been inculcated in the young. Drunkenness and disrespect for authority became widespread.[18]

Perhaps the most controversial of all Louis's commandments for winning the peace concerned the role of the Church and, as his reviewer in the *Economist* had said, perhaps he was asking the impossible of the leaders of the Church (including his own brother-in-law, the Bishop of Mombasa). He pointed out that if these leaders failed to win the masses to Christianity, they would turn to other 'religions', like Mau Mau or Communism; and he suggested that new independent churches should be formed which allowed both polygamy and female circumcision (so long as it was done skilfully). This was really asking too much; but although Louis might find few supporters for female circumcision, many people, if they were to be completely honest with themselves, might find a good deal to be said for polygamy.

Other points in *Defeating Mau Mau* concerned improved agricultural methods and control of water resources; a campaign to teach methods of birth control; the adoption of English rather than Swahili as a *lingua franca*; help for vernacular newspapers; and the formation of a new political organization to replace KAU and embrace all tribes. Most of these reforms came to pass, although some took longer than others.

Louis ended his book on a note of optimism, expressing his faith that wisdom and common sense would prevail and that 'the peoples of Kenya will jointly show that it is possible to work together in harmony for the common good and progress of all'. His optimism has been justified.

Once the emergency began to draw to a close in the summer of 1954, the Leakeys were able to go to England on leave; but it was not much of a holiday for Louis, as he spent a good part of it in London writing a paper on fossil pigs. He always had a penchant for pigs, both fossil and living – and incidentally, he had a very plausible explanation for 'why the warthog got his warts', which sounds rather like the subject of one of Kipling's *Just So Stories*. During periods of drought, a warthog can eat grass underneath low thorn bushes which other animals cannot reach because of the prickles; he grazes supported on his elbows and the warts act as pincushions for the thorns, protecting the eyes.

Louis's first ever purely palaeontological paper had been on pigs: the 'Fossil Suidae from Olduvai', published in the *Journal of the East Africa and Uganda Natural History Society* in 1942. As the years went by, he collected so much new material, especially from Olduvai, that he realized that it would be necessary to describe the pigs in far more detail; and the obvious medium for publication was the British Museum's *Fossil Mammals of Africa* series. Miss Dorothea Bate was to have tackled it, but she died in January 1951, long before the task was anywhere near completed. It was then suggested that the late Sir Gavin de Beer should do the job in co-operation with Hopwood, to whom it was hoped he would act as a spur. Unfortunately – for Louis – Sir Gavin became Director of the Natural History Museum and the project fell through. 'It is doubtful if he will ever tackle them', wrote one of his colleagues to Louis. 'He not only gets immersed in general administrative affairs but does not take kindly to the hard grind of detailed work. He took a short and rapid flight with *Archaeopteryx*, and when he crash landed he tossed the whole affair over to Swinton. To change the metaphor, he will only suck a very juicy orange and soon throws the skin away to pluck another.'[19]

In the end Louis lost patience and did the job himself. During his 1954 leave he shut himself up for two months in a cubbyhole off the fossil mammal gallery of the Natural History Museum, surrounded by pig bones and teeth. 'There was always a space for Louis' said one of the staff. 'He was like a breath of fresh air.' (Or perhaps a hurricane?) He would be let in at 8.30 every morning, an unprecedented privilege: visiting research workers, like the general public, normally have to wait until ten. Louis had the benefit of Dorothea Bate's notes, and within a few months he sent a draft to Dr W. N. Edwards, the Keeper of Palaeontology. 'I have now got Hopwood thoroughly interested' wrote Edwards to Louis in March 1955, 'and at the moment he is at his critical best.... The whole paper gives the impression of having been dictated at speed and not subsequently pulled together.... I have therefore told Hopwood to rearrange or rewrite as may seem necessary.'

This did not please Louis at all, but as it was to be published by the BM there was little he could do about it. The proofs did not appear until 1958, by which time both Edwards and Hopwood had retired. Louis was very angry about certain errors and sent an outburst to Edward's successor as Keeper of Palaeontology, Dr Errol White, FRS, who replied: 'You have, I fear, indulged your little weakness of rushing to conclusions without being aware of the facts.'[20] How often might that have been said about Louis!

'Some East African Pleistocene Suidae' appeared in 1958 as No. 14 of the *Fossil Mammals of Africa* series; in it Louis described not only the pigs from Olduvai but also from Eyasi, Olorgesailie, Kanam, Kanjera and a few other sites. Always an incorrigible splitter, he named eleven genera and twenty-seven species, of which eight were new. Some of the names were later revised – but then it is always easier to criticize than to start from scratch. Most palaeontologists who tackle a job of this magnitude are specialists with fairly narrow horizons, whereas Louis was a jack-of-all-trades; he completed in a few months a task that would have taken most people years and most of his conclusions are still valid. Louis was never afraid of tackling anything.

Apart from the pig paper, the main event of the Leakeys' 1954 leave was a meeting between the Kenya contingent and part, at least, of the English family. Earlier that year, Priscilla was married from her mother's house at Girton to Justin Davies, a schoolmaster and the younger son of Vernon Davies, founder of Davies Tutors. A tea party was arranged at the London house of Mr and Mrs Vernon Davies, where Justin and Priscilla were introduced to their Kenya relations. This was the first time that Mary and Priscilla had met and they eyed each other warily, while Jonathan, Richard and Philip were on their best behaviour.

Colin at that time was doing his National Service as an RNVR officer in the Mediterranean, so Louis was unable to see him; but in the following year, 1955, Louis asked him to do him a service, and Colin was flattered and pleased. The Geological Association awarded their Henry Stopes medal jointly to Louis and Mary, and, as they could not be there to receive it personally, Louis asked Colin to act on his behalf. It was the first time the medal had been given for work done outside the British Isles and was quite an occasion; Colin acquitted himself well, read a letter of gratitude from Louis, and made a short speech himself. If Colin showed courage in acting on behalf of his somewhat controversial father whom he hardly knew – and for his stepmother whom he did not know at all – so too perhaps did Louis in appointing an untested deputy. This was not the first 'gong' that Louis had collected but it was only the second in England, so it was important to make a good impression. His first had been the Swedish Geographical Society's Andrée plaquette awarded to him in 1933 for having spotted a skull in an air photograph published in a newspaper. S. A. Andrée and two companions set out from Spitzbergen in 1896 to fly over the North Pole in a balloon and were never seen again. Their remains were found 35 years later by a Norwegian expedition, following the clue in the photograph: it appears that after the balloon came down they may have died as a result of eating tainted polar bear meat.

In the summer of 1955 the third Pan African Congress on Prehistory took place at Livingstone, Northern Rhodesia (Zambia). The time schedule had got out of step owing to the non-co-operation of the South African Government over the second congress so, in order to get back into line, this one was held three years after the 1952 Algiers congress rather than at the usual interval of four years. During this period great strides had been made in the study of African prehistory; there were still a good many amateurs struggling with inadequate funds, but at last the impact of an increasing number of whole-time professionals was being felt. Also, during the early 1950s radiocarbon dating was getting into its stride, and with the advent of 'absolute' dates, 'relative' dating by means of the climatic sequence was beginning to outlive its usefulness.

The congress coincided with the David Livingstone centenary celebrations in July 1955, and the accommodation available in the small town was stretched to its limits. There were seventy representatives from African countries, of whom nearly a quarter came from the Union of South Africa: their Government had boycotted official delegates to the previous congress in Algiers, but this time they turned up in full force.

Perhaps the paper which caused the most stir was one by Professor Raymond Dart on 'The australopithecine osteodontokeratic culture'. Dart had an incorrigible liking for long words, but, as any classical scholar will appreciate, this tongue-twister simply means 'bone, tooth and horn'. This is what Dart wrote in the summary of his paper:

> The Australopithecinae had discovered in mammalian skeletons an adequate predaceous armamentarium and thereby were laying the foundations of that particulate anatomical and physiological experience which, in my opinion, was an essential apprenticeship for the ultimate acquisition by man of speech.

In other words, the australopiths used bones to bludgeon one another – laying the foundations for Robert Ardrey's *African Genesis* and the concept of 'man the killer'.

If anyone should conclude from this verbosity that Dart lacked a sense of humour, they would be wrong; naturally his statement was greeted with a good deal of hilarity, in which he himself joined, but he was dead serious about the hypothesis itself. His evidence had been collected by the painstaking analysis of the contents of five thousand tons of dumps at the Makapan Limeworks near Potgietersrust. The bone fragments in these dumps, which ran into hundreds of thousands, included many which Dart maintained showed signs of use – other people said signs of chewing by carnivores – and comprised his 'predaceous armamentarium'. All this was heady stuff for prehistorians, who are notoriously suspicious of any new theory of this calibre, and Dart was hurt by the reception he got. Not for the first time he found himself crying in the wilderness.

There was, however, at least one man at the congress who was fascinated by Dart's hypothesis. Himself a 'tool-maker' par excellence, this was Mr Leighton A. Wilkie, senior partner of Wilkie Brothers, inventors of cutting tools, machines and processes. Wilkie Brothers were the founders of great manufacturing corporations in the USA and Canada and owners of a huge distributing organization, with a network of chain stores selling their products all over the North American continent. In 1951 the brothers formed the Wilkie Foundation for charitable purposes, and in its brochure is a quotation from Carlyle's *Sartor Resartus:* 'Man is a tool-using animal . . . without tools he is nothing, with tools he is all.' Naturally Mr Leighton Wilkie was thrilled to hear about the world's first possible tool-makers, and in the years to come he supported Dart up to the hilt. He was also to make many grants to Louis for his projects in the future, including the launching of Jane Goodall on her studies of chimpanzees as told in Chapter 12.

Louis was president of this third Pan African Congress, and he took particular pains to get to know the younger delegates whom he had not met before; he was pleased with them and optimistic about the future work of the new generation of African prehistorians. Jealousy of possible successors was not one of Louis's faults, at least so long as they did not impinge too closely on his own personal field. Organizing Secretary of the congress was Dr J. Desmond Clark, now professor of anthropology at the University of California at Berkeley, who at that time was curator of the excellent little Rhodes Livingstone Museum in Livingstone. He had built it up almost from scratch, and for this work, as well as for organizing the third Pan African Congress on Prehistory, he was awarded the CBE. Louis, who had built up the Coryndon Museum in Nairobi and had initiated and organized the first congress – as well as doing intelligence work in the war and during the Mau Mau emergency – was never mentioned in the honours list. Presumably he was too controversial.

Some of the delegates at Livingstone persuaded Louis to demonstrate the skinning of an animal with stone tools he had made himself, and he agreed to do so if a suitable carcase were produced. The price of local goats was rather high, so Lolly Sussons, who organized the transport for the congress, volunteered to scour the countryside for a buck. This was not so easy, as nearly all the game had been wiped out in the anti-tsetse campaign – a tragic and ineffectual operation.

The first night Lolly Sussons drove many miles, returning empty-handed in the early hours of the morning; but on the following night he managed to shoot a duiker, which he deposited on the kitchen floor before going to bed. When his wife went in to see about breakfast next morning, she was transfixed with horror: there was a neatly skinned duiker, lying on its back with its pink legs pointing rigidly in the air. 'I'll try once more,' said her patient husband, 'but tell that cook that if he so much as lays a finger on anything I bring back I'll skin *him*, alive.'

The following night he was again successful, and this time the buck was deposited in the office of the Museum, where a guard was mounted over it until the hour appointed for Louis's demonstration. The animal was then placed under a tree, and blocks of flint were collected from the fountain in the courtyard where they had been soaked to make them more workable – flint is hard to quarter when it is dry. Louis first made a crude chopper, similar to an Oldowan tool, with which he began the skinning. Next he made a most convincing looking cleaver, with which he deftly and rapidly removed the rest of the skin. Finally he produced a neat backed-blade, such as the Kenya Capsians might have used, and dismembered the buck into joints. 'Now what about eating a bit,' someone called out; and without flinching, Louis seized a leg and chewed off a piece of the raw meat. By this time he was covered in blood both from the animal and from his own finger, which he had cut on a bit of flint.

It is difficult to appreciate the efficacy of stone tools until one has actually seen them being used, and Louis's audience was amazed at how quickly it was possible to make the necessary equipment and butcher an animal. Many of them thought that this had been one of the most valuable lessons they had learnt during the entire congress.

For relaxation during the emergency, and as a change from the weightier matters discussed in his two Mau Mau books, Louis dipped into his almost unlimited store of animal knowledge to write the text of *Animals in Africa* (1953) to accompany photographs taken by the incomparable Ylla – the pen name of Ylla Koffler.[21] Even today, when so many lavishly illustrated coffee-table books on animals are produced, few can rival her art with the camera of twenty years ago. Ylla of the bright eyes and infectious laugh will long be remembered by those who knew her all over the world, for she was truly international. Ylla had a bird-like quality, perching briefly in New York, Paris or London before flying off on photographic safaris to East Africa or India, where she was killed falling out of a jeep. It seems strange now to read in Louis's introduction to that book that he found it necessary to explain the purpose of the East African National Parks, which in those pre-package-tour days had been seen by very few visitors from Europe or the USA. Louis also put in a plea for more detailed studies of animals in the wild, which today are commonplace but in the 1950s were rare; in the years to come he himself initiated several research projects on apes in their natural surroundings (Chapter 12) and he planned to do this long before most other scientists had thought of it.

Animals in Africa, as well as a second book on wildlife which Louis wrote many years later, *Animals of East Africa* (1969), dealt mainly with the more spectacular animals.[22] He also planned to write about the smaller creatures, but publishers were not interested; the public, they said, demands the 'big five' – lion, elephant, rhino, buffalo and giraffe, with leopards and hippos thrown in for good measure. What an opportunity was missed by not encouraging Louis to write also about the little creatures known as 'slow game', especially in connection with African folk lore and methods of hunting, about which he knew so much. As an example, he told in one of his lectures about how Bushmen catch a certain species of rodent which makes its home in disused birds' nests. When a nest is deserted, you can see light through the holes; but when a fat mouse is curled up inside, the nest appears opaque. The Bushman, therefore, has no need to investigate every nest; he merely goes up quietly to the opaque ones and squeezes the animal inside.

Louis was always interested in African animal lore and also native remedies, particularly one which concerned the use of zebra fat as a cure for tuberculosis. During his first expedition to Olduvai in 1931, he found his Kikuyu staff collecting zebra fat from a lion kill, which they later sold to the Luo in western Kenya. The price was high – ten shillings for two to three ounces – and later he heard that in the old days the Kikuyu would pay a whole goat or a sheep for a small lump of zebra fat; they, as well as the Masai and Wakamba, believed it was a cure for tuberculosis in its early stages. Louis mentioned this in his book *Kenya: Contrasts and Problems* and was delighted when a reviewer in *Discovery* (June 1936) pointed out that the Pasteur Institute had found that a fatty diet promotes the secretion of lipase, by which the system can break down the protective envelope of the tubercle germ. Now, one of the facts of zebra life is that they are always plump, even after a drought which has reduced every other animal to a skeleton; Louis thought there must certainly be something very peculiar about the yellow fat and he did his best to find out what. For years he tried to interest various research laboratories in investigating the properties of this fat, and one did agree to make some tests. They reported that the sample was inactive against the TB organism and left it at that; with streptomycin available, no one was likely to work up much enthusiasm for zebra fat as a cure for TB. This story illustrates the lengths to which he would go to satisfy his enquiring mind; he was never satisfied until he had got an answer and, although he never did get the answer about zebra fat, he plugged away at the problem at intervals over some forty years.

Louis's insatiable curiosity and his gift for imparting knowledge made him an ideal father for growing boys and his sons probably learnt far more from him than they ever did at school. All three went to the Duke of York School near their home at Langata, Jonathan as a boarder and the other two by day. Jonathan, who took after Mary, was much quieter than his rather obstreperous brothers and was quite studious, but the others did as little work as possible. 'All my sons are late starters,' Louis once wrote to a prospective headmaster in England, 'and I fear Philip may be an even later starter.' Philip apparently spent most of his schooldays catching hyraxes in the trees, while Richard preferred riding and had a great way with horses. Louis himself took an active interest in the Langata Pony Club, where he regularly watched his sons performing. With Mary, he founded a Dalmatian Club in Nairobi in 1949; and he also became vice-president and later president (1959–1961) of the Kennel Club.

In the holidays the boys usually went to one of the sites where their parents were working and, although at times they got fed up with bones and stones, there were many compensations. They were always encouraged to do their own thing; Louis believed in letting them make their own decisions and learn by experience, even when Jonathan developed a potentially lethal interest in snakes. Louis was invariably stimulating, always knew the answers to their questions, and produced fascinating bits of information about nearly everything they came across. He taught them bushcraft, just as he himself had been taught by Joshua as a boy at Kabete. The boys learnt to recognize the calls and tracks of animals and birds, which plants were edible and which poisonous.

No Leakey would ever have starved in the bush. They could catch a hare or small antelope in their hands and skin it with a stone tool sharpened in a few seconds. In his book *Animals of East Africa* Louis tells of how hares escape from a pursuer by suddenly 'jinking' to one side and then doubling back on their tracks; as a boy, he had noticed that just before the 'jink' the animal lays its ears down and, by side-stepping at that moment, he had a 50–50 chance that the hare would run straight into his hands. Another means of survival in the wilds is by scavenging, and Louis put this to practical test with the assistance of Richard. Naked, and armed like Samson with the jawbone of an ass – or more probably a zebra – they approached a kill, brandishing their weapons to drive off the hyenas. If one of them did this alone, the hyenas would not budge; but if both did it at the same time, the animals retreated. They also found that if they were both in a vulnerable position bending down to cut off meat from the carcase, the hyenas would come in to attack; but if one stood up and threatened while the other got on with the job, it was possible to fend them off. One of Louis's theories was that the hominids took to scavenging because of competition for vegetable foods with the giant baboons that existed in Pleistocene times; by scavenging, early men learnt the advantages of co-operation and, in practising self-defence, they learnt also to be aggressive. Louis's experiments with a jawbone at least proved Dart's point that an osteodontokeratic 'predaceous armamentarium' would have been effective against predators. But as for lions, Louis maintained there was nothing to be afraid of: man smells nasty to a carnivore and a lion, unless he is old and toothless, doesn't eat people. In a place like Olduvai, this must have been reassuring.

Louis's beloved pluvial hypothesis, which had stood him and many others in good stead for some thirty years, had been seriously challenged for the first time at the 1955 Pan African Congress on Prehistory at Livingstone by Dr H. B. S. (Basil) Cooke, then of the University of the Witwatersrand. Three years later Cooke published a paper[23] in which he argued that some of the evidence for 'pluvials' in East Africa was not very convincing, and then a very senior geologist, Professor Richard F. Flint of Yale, took up the cudgels. In 1957, Flint embarked on an extended tour of East Africa under the auspices of the Wenner-Gren Foundation to see the evidence for himself. He went to the Congo (Zaire) and Uganda, and afterwards Louis took him to Kanam and Kanjera, Gamble's Cave, Kariandusi, Olorgesailie and Olduvai. Louis found him difficult, which is not surprising as the two men could not have been more different: Louis full of enthusiasm, bursting with theories; Flint the typical professor of popular imagination, plodding and rather pedantic, noting down details rather than embracing the whole magnificent spectrum which Louis laid at his feet.

They started the tour on the *Miocene Lady*, for Flint was particularly anxious to see Kanam and Kanjera which are difficult to get to except by lake. Apart from Louis and Dick Flint and his wife, the party included Professor Phillip Tobias, a physical anthropologist from South Africa who features much in the next chapter, and also the geologist Dr W. W. (Bill) Bishop and his wife, who had recently shown the Flints round Uganda. They all settled down for the first night on board, the two women inside the cabin, Tobias and Bishop outside on 'hot seats' above the engines, with Dick Flint extending his great length in the well between them and Louis lying at his feet athwart the stern. 'It never rains at this time of the year,' said Louis confidently; whereupon they were lashed by a tropical storm of exceptional ferocity and the *Miocene Lady* spun round in circles. Lightning streaked across the sky and torrents of rain descended on Louis and on Flint's feet. Louis retreated on to the floor of the cabin between the ladies and spent most of the night noisily inflating his leaking air mattress. For breakfast he fried some lake fish which he had bought from the Luo fishermen and handed each member of the party a cupful of cornflakes to crumble in lieu of breadcrumbs. They then proceeded ashore and Louis washed himself among the bilharzia-infested reeds: 'I have had it so often it doesn't matter any more,' he told the horrified Americans. After his ablutions, he led Flint to one of the geological exposures at Kanjera and was about to whisk him off to the next when the professor sat down to draw the section and take copious notes on each minute detail of the lithology. Louis got more and more impatient, darting here and there and unsuccessfully trying to persuade Flint to come and look at better exposures. Later he suggested a trip to Rusinga, but Flint declined the invitation; he had got his grant to study the Pleistocene, not the Miocene, and to the Pleistocene he would stick. Louis, for once, was speechless; probably never before had anyone turned down an opportunity to see Rusinga.

Louis had protested that any conclusions made on such a rapid tour would be worthless; but conclusions Flint made, and in 1959 he published them.[24] From the evidence he had seen, he thought there was no proof of any pluvials or interpluvials earlier than Louis's Gamblian in the Upper Pleistocene except at one place, Olorgesailie. From then on, reliance was to be placed on absolute dates obtained by radiocarbon, and later by potassium/argon for the earlier periods; the physicists took over, and the criticisms by geologists such as Cooke and Flint sounded the death knell of the pioneer days of relative dating. By then Louis was too set in his ways to adapt to the new regime, and in some cases he continued to cling obstinately to his original climatic framework, which had served him so well for so long.

In theory, after the end of the emergency in Kenya Louis should have had plenty of time to devote to Museum work and research, but he abhorred even a partial vacuum and he found plenty to fill the space left by his intelligence duties. Long after these had officially ended he went on visiting his Kikuyu contacts to pick up gossip, and he was constantly warning the police that so-and-so still had firearms and ammunition, that somebody else was sheltering a terrorist, or that a certain person was trying to get Mau Mau reorganized. He also served on the Appeals Tribunal under the Forfeiture of Lands Ordinance, which empowered the Government to seize land belonging to terrorists. He continued to serve as handwriting expert in criminal cases; and he gave lectures, broadcasts and Kikuyu lessons. He tried to encourage people to learn this difficult language so that they would gain a better understanding of the Kikuyu and their problems; similarly, he urged the adoption of English rather than Swahili in order to avoid the misunderstandings that arose through each party trying to communicate in a language foreign to both. Louis was constantly in demand to lecture on the social revolution that was taking place in Kenya, and he spoke at schools all over the country, to teacher training colleges, to CID recruits, the Kenya Regiment, clubs, societies and study circles. His main theme was the rehabilitation problems of those who had been released from detention camps, sometimes after being held there for years; they would have to be accepted back into the life of the community and be given the right to express their views. Louis was perturbed by the division of the Kikuyu into goats and sheep – 'loyalists' and 'rebels' – and urged that such epithets be dropped. If the division were to become a barrier, reconciliation would be impossible; and, after all, their aims were the same, even if their methods differed.

Louis also set out to determine reactions about the continued detention of Jomo Kenyatta, which he did by picking up a random sample along the road between Nairobi and Kisumu. Of the Africans to whom he gave lifts, he noted that 'thirty-four had either never heard of Jomo Kenyatta, or showed no interest in his return'. His notes do not record the total number of passengers he picked up, nor the proportion represented by the thirty-four. However, he concluded that 'the suggestion that the vast majority of Africans support Kenyatta will not stand up to critical examination'; that 'most are wholly indifferent'; and that 'the vocal nationalists do not represent the majority'. He duly forwarded his impressions to higher authority, who must have been amazed that such sweeping statements should be made on the basis of such a small sample. With his scientific training, even though not as a statistician, Louis should have known better. This story may serve to show why he was not always taken as seriously as he would have wished.

So often Louis had the right ideas but put them over in the wrong way, or antagonized people by his dogmatism. Perhaps this is one of the reasons why he never achieved his greatest ambition, which was to be elected to the Royal Society. Among other things the Kanam controversy died hard, and Louis had several enemies within the Royal, as well as allies such as Sir Wilfrid Le Gros Clark and Sir Julian Huxley who did their best to get him elected. In December 1957, Dr Kenneth Oakley, who was a Fellow of the British Academy, wrote to Louis:

> A number of people have been saying lately 'Shouldn't L.S.B.L. be an FRS? The answer of course is yes, but in fact the Royal no longer seems to admit anyone whose work is mainly in prehistory or anthropology. It seems agreed that the appropriate honour for those scientists whose work fringes on the humanities is FBA. The competition to be elected FBA is pretty severe, because there are only about two hundred (compared with five hundred FRS) and all the Arts as well as borderline subjects are covered. Elections are once a year and in some years no one in prehistory or anthropology gets elected. Nominations have to be made on 8 January for July elections and I have reason to know that your name is likely to be put up unless you have any strong objection.[25]

In his reply Louis said:

> If I accept the suggestion, will it remove or lessen my chances for FRS? I feel that my Miocene discoveries since 1940, my Pleistocene work at Olduvai and elsewhere, and my work on pluvials is much more appropriate to FRS than FBA, and that is what I would like to aim at. If accepting your proposal would ruin my chances for FRS later on, then I'd rather wait.

Louis also consulted Sir Wilfrid Le Gros Clark, who said: 'I am most disappointed about the other thing [FRS] but I have not been able to get adequate support. I don't feel prospects are good, as competition for other branches of science is becoming very fierce. So I do feel that you should go ahead with FBA.'[26] This is what he did, and was elected a Fellow of the British Academy in 1958. (Mary also became an FBA in 1973, after Louis's death.)

From time to time the Royal Society would invite Louis to demonstrate his latest finds at their conversaziones and soirées and he would make great efforts to be present, sometimes to the extent of coming specially from Nairobi to London if he could fit it in with other commitments and get his fare paid for some other purpose. If he was unable to be there himself, he always arranged for colleagues to demonstrate his material. But for all the good it did him he might as well have saved his time.

By the end of the 1950s Jomo Kenyatta's sentence to seven years' hard labour was drawing to a close, and Louis was worried about the effect his release might have. Former detainees were joining an illegal organization called the Land Freedom Army which, in Louis's opinion, had strong links with Mau Mau; as before, he felt that the Kenya Government was not treating the matter seriously enough, and he tried to draw attention to the situation in the British Press. In May 1961, under the title of 'Time for a firm hand in Kenya', he wrote an article in the *Sunday Telegraph* urging immediate action; then, he said, 'the subsequent release of people like Jomo Kenyatta would be seen in its proper light as an act of grace by a strong Government and not as an act of weakness by one which is unable to control an illegal organization'. The situation, he continued, was too much like what it had been in 1951–52 to be looked at with complacency, and he concluded 'Kenya today is on the edge of an abyss'.

The abyss, as we now know, was rather less yawning than Louis had feared, and others besides himself had learnt their lesson and taken appropriate action. Perhaps it would have been even less menacing if Jomo Kenyatta had been released earlier, but it was not until April 1961 that he was sent from Lodwar to Maralal, from where he at last returned to his home in triumph in August of that year. Thereafter the wind of change blew all too gently for nationalists, but it seemed like a hurricane for diehards of the old colonial regime. In October 1961 Jomo Kenyatta was elected president of KANU, the Kenya African National Union; less than two months later Tanganyika gained her independence, and Uganda followed within a year. But Kenya had to wait for *uhuru* – freedom – until 12 December, 1963, when, with the theme of *harambee* – togetherness – Jomo Kenyatta became Prime Minister.

9 Olduvai, Valley of Bones

Louis, like Ezekiel, was 'set down in the midst of the valley which was full of bones . . . they were very many in the valley, and lo, they were very dry'. The comparison was made by the orator in requesting the Chancellor of the University of Guelph to confer the degree of Doctor of Laws *honoris causa* on L.S.B. Leakey in 1969, ten years after Louis made his name in the Valley of Bones.

Ever since his first expedition to Olduvai in 1931, Louis had patiently anticipated the treasures which he knew were there for the taking when he had the time and money to dig for them. Twenty years later the exploratory period ended, and the results were to be as spectacular as even Louis had dreamed. Yet paradoxically it was the exploratory period which he most enjoyed; once the detailed, methodical excavations of the 1960s got under way he began to get bored.

After frustrating delays his book *Olduvai Gorge* was at last published in 1951.[1] Cambridge University Press needed a subsidy of £500, and Louis had an inspiration as to how he might get it. He approached the late Dr John T. Williamson, the Canadian geologist who discovered the Madui diamond mines in Tanzania in 1940 – the mines that produced the fabulous 54-carat pink diamond presented to Queen Elizabeth on her marriage. Dr Williamson was renowned for his reluctance to give interviews and for his phobia against publicity, but Louis got his money.

It was a most unfortunate moment for the book to appear, since the excavations which began in that very year, 1951, made a good deal of it out of date. The geological foundations laid down by Reck stood the test of time pretty well for another decade; however, major revisions had to be made to Hopwood's chapter on the fauna. The fossil mammals of Bed I and the lower part of Bed II proved to be quite distinctive from those of the upper part of Bed II through Bed IV, making nonsense of Hopwood's 'single faunal stage'. In the end Louis had to re-examine all the fauna; by the time the first volume of a new series on Olduvai appeared in 1965, he concluded that only six of the 24 species named by Hopwood from Bed I could be certainly identified.[2] This was not entirely Hopwood's fault; he had had only scraps to go on, and when more complete remains turned up it was not surprising that many of his identifications proved to be wrong. Also, during the ten years following publication of the 1951 book the 51 species listed in it were increased by more than a hundred.

The main part of that book, however, was concerned with artifacts. For the first time Louis described the Oldowan culture of Bed I, and traced the evolution of the handaxe culture from Bed II through Bed IV. This scheme, too, became partly obsolete after Mary's excavations, which were to show that a Developed Oldowan existed side by side with the early Acheulian handaxe culture. She concluded that the variations which Louis attributed to an evolutionary sequence were more likely to be local trends or fashions, perhaps even family traditions among the toolmakers.

None of this was known when the Leakeys began their excavations early in 1951. In order to tackle Olduvai seriously they needed money; as Louis would be working in a foreign country he could not expect the Kenya Government to pay his curator's salary, and he had to take unpaid leave while in Tanganyika. During the exploratory period they had been able to get by with only a small staff, but now it was necessary to engage a large labour force. This meant not only money for wages, but also money to pay for petrol to bring water at more frequent intervals for the enlarged staff. Once again Charles Boise came to the rescue, making a seven year covenant to take care of recurrent expenditure at Olduvai; later he set up the Boise Fund in Oxford, administered by trustees, to aid research on African prehistory in general. For capital expenditure – needed for equipment such as new tents and a water tank – Louis obtained grants from the Wenner-Gren Foundation and the Wilkie Brothers Foundation, and he even got a little money from the Tanganyika Government.

Ever since 1935 the Leakeys' camp had been on the north side of the main gorge, which involved walking several miles to reach some of the sites in the side gorge. They now intended to work at these sites, so Louis was determined to get the vehicles as near as possible. He managed to find a way up the escarpment from the Balbal Depression, and they pitched camp part of the way down the slope above BK. Here they were sheltered from the howling winds which had made life so unpleasant at their previous camp. The plan of campaign was to concentrate on excavations in Bed II, particularly at BK and SHK. As it turned out they found so much material that they were kept busy in Bed II for seven years. Only then were they able to turn their attention to the oldest bed, Bed I, and began to find hominids.

When Louis and Mary located the BK site in 1935 they had decided it must be given top priority, and it more than came up to expectations. It was to produce more than 11,000 artifacts of the type which Mary later called Developed Oldowan. The excavations of the '50s also yielded enormous quantities of fossil mammals both at BK and SHK. They came from the upper part of Bed II, which at that time was thought to be Middle Pleistocene. But as the result of new dating techniques the boundary between Lower and Middle Pleistocene has now been pushed right up into the lower part of *Bed IV* and dates from about 700,000 years ago. The fossils found by the Leakeys throughout most of the 1950s were in fact nearly all Lower Pleistocene.

Many of the genera and species were entirely new, and the fossils were in a marvellous state of preservation. At most sites a collector gets quite excited if he finds a broken piece of fossil jaw, or a horn core; at Olduvai there are whole skulls, sometimes even almost entire skeletons. By now the cream has been skimmed from the surface over the whole length of the Gorge, but in the 1950s important finds could be picked up without even digging.

The Lower Pleistocene, especially during the time represented by the upper part of Bed II, was the age of giants. Perhaps due to the onset of faulting which changed the drainage pattern, open grasslands began to spread and an incredible variety of gigantic herbivores flourished. Their size can be accounted for by the ideal feeding conditions, perhaps also connected with the abundance of minerals in the volcanic soil.

One of the most spectatular of all the Olduvai giants is *Pelorovis oldowayensis*, whose name tells a tale. For one thing, the spelling of the specific name indicates that it was discovered a long time ago, when 'Oldoway' was used rather than Olduvai.* Reck, in fact, collected the first fragmentary skull of this animal in 1913. The '*ovis*' part of the generic name shows that it was taken to be some kind of sheep, and for the next forty years *Pelorovis* remained in that family: imaginative reconstructions in the *Illustrated London News* invariably showed it towering over a Merino ram for comparison.[3] Nothing like it was known anywhere in the world, but when the Leakeys began their intensive work at Olduvai in the 1950s they found many more remains of this puzzling beast, including a complete skull with teeth which Reck's find had lacked. From these there was no doubt that *Pelorovis* was no sheep, but was related to the buffaloes.[4] This story illustrates the kind of problems faced by palaeontologists working with incomplete material, and how the magnificent finds from Olduvai cleared up such difficulties. Perhaps it was remarkable that Hopwood got so much right in his chapter in the 1951 Olduvai book, and hardly surprising that he got some wrong.

The largest horn cores of *Pelorovis* have a span of two metres, and the horns themselves must have been considerably longer than the cores. This animal must surely have been awe-inspiring, but it does not seem to have daunted the hominids: the Leakeys found a 'slaughter-house' at BK containing the bones of *Pelorovis* and other large beasts. Evidently a whole herd of *Pelorovis* had been driven into a swamp, but although the hunters were able to

*Regarding the spelling of Olduvai, the Secretary of the Royal Geographical Society wrote to Louis in 1936: 'We have looked up the question of Olduvai or Oldoway . . . The name appears in the map belonging to Oscar Baumann's book of 1894 as Duvai (the Masai name for wild sisal). The War Office 1/million of 1917 gives Olduvai . . . I should judge that Olduvai is the spelling to be used, and it makes quite a good adjective as Olduvaian, which may be useful to you.' The adjective, however, is invariably Oldowan, as in the culture of that name, being easier to spell and to pronounce.

drag out the smaller animals they had been defeated by the larger ones. One complete skeleton was found in an upright position; evidently the creature had met a lingering death in the bog. The immature animals had been pulled to the edge and cut up on the spot: the whole area was littered with stone tools and flakes.

Most amazing of all in the profusion of species during the Lower Pleistocene were the pigs; sadly, they suffered a rapid decline, and today the African pigs are represented only by that comedian the warthog, the bushpig, and the magnificent forest hog. As with so many other groups of herbivores, 'there were giants in those days'. The Lower Pleistocene *Afrochoerus nicoli* had tusks nearly a yard long: small wonder that Hopwood, when first confronted with a broken piece of tusk, confused it with that of a mastodon. The body of this pig must have been as massive as a hippo, and when Louis named it after Mary (née Nicol) she regarded it as a doubtful compliment. That champion fossil collector Heselon Mukiri also had two fossil pigs named after him: *Mesochoerus heseloni* and the earlier *Promesochoerus mukiri*.

If the first exploratory phase of research at Olduvai had ended in 1950, the year 1958 may be said to mark the end of the second phase. The excavations made in Bed II during those seven years were a remarkable achievement, and not only for the wealth of fauna and artifacts that they produced. For the very first time, the actual living floors of early hominids had been uncovered; and also for the first time detailed excavation techniques had been used on sites of such an early age. Mary had been responsible for much of this work and already she had become 'hooked' on Olduvai.

Remains of the hominids themselves were disappointingly elusive; the total bag was one milk molar and a canine tooth, found at BK in 1955. The Olduvai hominids were given numbers prefixed by 'H': thus Reck's skeleton was H1, the 1935 skull fragments were H2, and these teeth were H3. Meagre though these remains might be, the molar caused some stir among those known to the trade as 'dental cuspologists'; it was very large, and it had a complex cusp pattern and one extra cusp. The arguments about its status went on for some time in scientific journals, for the child who had shed those teeth was as yet unknown – he was a

'*Zinjanthropus*', whose discovery was to mark the beginning of the third and most intensive phase of work at Olduvai.

When the Leakeys decided to turn their attention to Bed I in 1959 it was a problem to know where to begin, as they had so many sites lined up for investigation. Heselon seemed to decide it for them when he found a fragment of lower jaw containing one molar, obviously hominid, at MK (MacInnes Korongo), one of the lowest sites in Bed I. Two other isolated teeth were found by sieving and the Leakeys were all set to begin excavations there when certain events put a stop to it; these events led to the discovery of the most famous fossil ever to come out of Olduvai. The story of its find has become a part of history.

The late Armand Denis and his wife Michaela were neighbours of the Leakeys at Langata, and Louis had arranged for their partner, Des Bartlett, to come to Olduvai to film the excavations. As they wanted him to be in at the start, they spent a couple of days exploring while they waited for his arrival. On 17 July Louis was not feeling well and stayed in camp while Mary and the Dalmatians, Sally and Victoria, nosed over the slopes of Bed I at FLK (Frida Leakey Korongo), near the junction of the main and side gorge. About twenty-two feet below the top of the bed Mary spotted some bone eroding out. As she describes it in her book *Valley of the Wild Sisal:*

> I was doubtful at first whether it was hominid, since the mastoid region that was exposed was quite different from any I had seen in human skulls. Instead of being solid bone it was permeated with air cells, such as are found in skulls of particularly heavy animals, to compensate for excessive weight. However, after brushing away a little of the covering soil I saw two teeth that were unquestionably hominid. They were so large that I mistook them for molars, although they were in fact premolars.

In a high state of excitement she rushed back to camp to fetch Louis, whose illness was immediately forgotten. His reaction must have been like a cold shower: 'When he saw the teeth,' writes Mary, 'he was disappointed, since he had hoped we would find *Homo* and not *Australopithecus*.' Louis was always obsessed by the need to find independent proof of the existence of a true *Homo* in the Lower Pleistocene to vindicate the Kanam jaw; as yet, apart from that controversial specimen, there was no reason to suspect the presence of *Homo* at such an early age except in Louis's mind.

Leakey's luck really worked overtime that day; not only did it lead Mary to H5, but it also arranged for a first class photographer to be on the spot soon after its discovery. The Leakeys only had to curb their impatience for two days and then, filmed by Des Bartlett, they began to collect the many fragments of bone surrounding the original find, which they had not moved. The unearthing of 'Zinj' was to appear in one of Armand and Michaela Denis's well-known 'On Safari' programmes on BBC television.

The surrounding soil, and tons of scree below the find, was sieved and washed; the greater part of the skull was there in about four hundred fragments. In camp Mary began to fit the pieces together, as she had done eleven years earlier with the *Proconsul* skull; in all she was to spend about eighteen months on the jigsaw. The Leakeys made a preliminary excavation on the spot, but had to stop by 6 August as their overdraft was reaching alarming proportions. This excavation, however, was enough to show that the skull had come from a living floor which contained many broken bones and Oldowan tools.

Louis lost no time in sending a note to *Nature*, and it appeared in the issue dated 15 August, less than a month after the find; but publication was delayed by a printer's strike, and the issue was not available until some weeks later.[5] After pointing out the skull's resemblance to the robust australopithecines of South Africa, Louis proceeded to create a new genus for it. 'I am not in favour of creating too many new generic names among the Hominidae' he wrote (to which the sceptics might have had something to say), 'but I believe that it is desirable to place the new find in a separate and distinct genus. I therefore propose to name the new skull *Zinjanthropus boisei*.'

'*Zinj*' comes from the Persian word for African – the ancient Persians referred to the coast of East Africa as 'land of the Blacks' – and '*anthropus*' is of course Greek for 'man'. In bestowing the specific name *boisei*, Louis paid the greatest compliment he could offer to Charles Boise, who had supported his work at Olduvai before he – and it – became world famous. 'Zinj', H5, was known affectionately within the Leakey family as 'Dear Boy'; but because of his huge cheek teeth he was also called 'Nutcracker Man', and it was this name that caught on among the public.

Disappointed though he might be that Dear Boy was not a *Homo*, Louis had no doubts that he was the maker of the tools found at the living site at FLK, which at the time certainly seemed a reasonable supposition to make. Unfortunately, though, he could not resist overstating his case. In the report in *Nature* he said: 'There is no reason whatever, in this case, to believe that the skull represents the victim of a cannibalistic feast by some hypothetical more advanced type of man.' This was the very argument that he so often used himself to explain the presence of human remains which did not fit in with his theory of what they *ought* to be like.

The delay of the publication of *Nature* until the first week in September caused some embarrassment, for the Leakeys were due at the Fourth Pan African Congress on Prehistory at Leopoldville (Kinshasa) at the end of August and Louis was bursting to show the skull to his colleagues. The name *Zinjanthropus boisei* could not be mentioned until the specimen had been described formally, and it was also essential that the news about the find should not leak outside scientific circles until the East African Press had been informed. The story is told that Sir Mortimer Wheeler, who was in Nairobi soon after the discovery, asked Louis whether he could see the precious specimen, but Louis said that it was in the bank vaults and unobtainable; in fact, at that very moment Sir Mortimer was leaning against the safe in which Zinj was lodged!

On the way to the congress at Kinshasa the Leakeys stopped overnight at Johannesburg, and for the second time in her life Mary flew with a unique skull she had found in a box on her lap. She wrote later: 'One can only regard this as quite irresponsible behaviour. We had no right to subject an irreplaceable fossil to the hazards of air travel.'[6] In Johannesburg they showed Zinj to Professor Raymond Dart and to Phillip Tobias, who had recently taken over the chair of anatomy at the University of the Witwatersrand from Dart. Tobias reported later that Dart was dewy-eyed with emotion and said to Louis and Mary 'I am so glad that this has happened to you of all people'.[7]

Tobias's professional involvement with Leakey discoveries had come about in 1955 when he had taken a new look at the Kanam jaw in the BM. In his subsequent report to *Nature* he stressed that the distortion of the chin had been caused by a swelling over the lesion on the interior surface, which had exaggerated the jaw's modern appearance. He was convinced that it was not *Homo sapiens* which had 'gravitated into the wrong layer', but that it represented a more archaic type of man. He also had this to say of the Boswell episode: 'It is difficult to avoid asking whether too much was not expected of the 1934–35 expedition and too much read into Boswell's report.'[8] Altogether, Louis was well pleased; and at the congress he asked if Tobias would undertake the definitive study of Zinj. 'I was dumbfounded,' said Tobias. From that moment he switched his interests from the physical anthropology of living peoples to palaeo-anthropology. His monograph on Zinj was to be the most detailed study of a single fossil skull ever made.

Working as he did in South Africa, Tobias was in a particularly good position to make comparisons with other australopiths. More than three hundred individual specimens had been found by Dart, Broom and his assistant Dr John Robinson in the cave breccias of the Transvaal. They ranged from a single tooth to almost complete crania and lower jaws – which Zinj lacked – and included both the 'robust' Zinj-like form and the smaller 'gracile' form. Why then such excitement over the Olduvai find?

It was more complete than most; it was rather different; it came from a new area; and it was subjected to the full glare of publicity at a time when the general public was becoming more interested in such things. Also, although it was not known at the time of the discovery, Zinj could be dated, whereas the South African australopithecines could not.

Louis announced Zinj in his presidential address at the opening session of the Pan African Congress on Prehistory on 22 August, and the news was released to the Press ten days later after the formal description had appeared in *Nature*. 'Nutcracker Man' –

19. A quarter of a century after his 1931 expedition to Olduvai, Louis gazes nostalgically over the site where he found the first stone tool

Louis thoroughly enjoyed a challenge: 20. *Above* skinning a ram for his staff with a stone tool; 21. *Below* negotiating the road to Olduvai after the rains; 22. *Opposite* demonstrating the use of bolas stones – and getting tangled in the process

23. *Pelorovis* had horn-cores with a span of two metres; those of a modern ram are shown for comparison. 24. *Below* Admiring the skeleton of *Deinotherium*, a primitive relation of the elephants, at Olduvai in 1960: with Louis and Mary are Professor C. Arambourg (wearing topee), Professor Raymond Dart (stooping), and Dr Desmond Clark (taking notes)

it was Phillip Tobias who had called him this – was still in bits, but he was the star turn of the congress. He held a series of receptions in the room Louis and Mary were occupying at the Jesuit University of Louvanium, granting an audience to a privileged few each evening.

Mary need not have had retrospective qualms about subjecting Zinj to the hazards of air travel on the way to Johannesburg and Kinshasa, for at least parts of him were to go many thousands of miles later on. In October Louis was due in Chicago to take part in the Darwin centenary celebrations, and on the way he arranged to give a talk at the British Academy in London, of which he had been made a Fellow in the previous year. In the words of the *News Chronicle* of 8 October 1959:

> The doctor walked into the lecture room carrying a wooden box secured by a strap. From it he pulled three plastic bags each containing part of the skull. He put the parts together, covered the lot with the glass sides of an old aquarium and told his audience about Mr Nutcracker.

Another newspaper reported that the audience was so large that 'television stars like Sir Mortimer Wheeler had to stand against the wall'.[9]

Louis and Zinj stayed the night with Justin and Priscilla Davies at their school at Brackley in Northamptonshire, where the boys were among the first non-scientists to see the skull. By this time the Davieses had two children: Alison, born in 1955, and Andrew, born in 1957. (Louis had met his grandchildren in the spring of 1958 when he went to England on leave by himself – Mary had stayed at Langata to look after her sons and an elderly aunt who was living with the family.) In a house full of schoolboys and toddlers the presence of a VIP such as Zinj was a great responsibility. Prescilla spent a sleepless night worrying that someone might knock over his box, or that the house would be burgled or set on fire. Next morning Zinj signed his name in the visitor's book, giving his address as 'Upper Villafranchian', the palaeontologist's term for the later part of the Lower Pleistocene.

On this occasion, Louis renewed his brief acquaintance with his eldest son Colin, who was then twenty-five and whom he had not seen for some years. Justin and Priscilla were amused at the extraordinary likeness, not only in looks but in gestures and manner of speaking; the words poured out, neither listening to the other and each becoming more incoherent as he got excited. After their first rather sticky meeting in Holland Park, they had lunched together some time later and Colin lost his awe of his father; he remembers the occasion well because it was the first meal he had ever had in a Chinese restaurant, and they stayed talking far into the afternoon until they were swept out with the crumbs.

After finishing his National Service, Colin went to King's College, Cambridge, where he got his degree in the natural sciences, specializing in botany. He then won a Colonial Office studentship to Exeter University for one year, followed by a year at the University of the West Indies in Trinidad where he spent his vacation hitch-hiking in small planes with diamond millionaires to collect fungi. In 1957 he had been to Ethiopia to study plants and the snails which transmit bilharzia, and Louis had been most interested in his adventures. In his reply to Colin's letter describing them he said: 'I am having this letter typed as you find my writing even harder to read than I do yours.' Their illegible handwriting was yet another thing they had in common: both were in too much of a hurry to waste time sitting at a desk. Colin inherited from his father a great catholicism of interests but, unlike Louis, they were not confined to science. He loved music, and later collected eighteenth and nineteenth century watercolours; he was also a vintage car enthusiast and the proud owner of a 1934 Rolls Royce. Louis was much taken with his eldest son and regretted that their paths did not cross more often; but after Colin began work in Uganda in 1961 they were able to meet more easily.

Louis did not stay long in England, but he resisted the temptation to take Zinj with him to the USA; he left him safely locked up in London and merely took a cast of his palate in his baggage. Louis's fare had been paid by the University of Chicago to enable him to give a talk at the Darwin centennial in November. It was providential that the celebrations should happen to fall at that particular moment: Louis had come armed with the perfect example of a 'missing link', and proof that old Darwin had been right when he prophesied that Africa would turn out to be the original home of man. The newspapers had a bonanza: 'Nut-cracking African skull "missing link" says expert.'[10] It was a big occasion, with Sir Charles Darwin, grandson of the great man, as guest of honour; Louis's old friend Sir Julian Huxley was VIP number two, and Louis and Zinj tied for third place. The cameras of Encyclopaedia Britannica Films whirred as Louis gave his talk – and so began the treatment he was to get from that moment on whenever he appeared in the United States.

This was Louis's first visit to America. He had nearly got there in 1952 and, although the trip was cancelled, it is an amusing story. He had been asked to advise on the making of a film about East Africa in the 1890s, for which he was to get a fee of $1,000 plus expenses. Louis sent to the film's director in California various items of Masai warriors' fighting equipment, but stipulated that he must advise in person on the way the *moran* moved and wielded their weapons. The actors playing the part of the warriors, he said, must remove all body hair; the little fingernail of the right hand must be long and all the others short; spears must never be leaned against anything; noses must be blown in the correct manner; perspiration must be wiped off only from the face and with a bunch of leaves; the actors must learn to quiver properly in frenzied excitement. . . . 'I cannot describe it all,' wrote Louis, 'I could only demonstrate.' The trip was cancelled because Louis refused to allow his name to be associated with the film unless *all* his demands were met – and in view of the extent of the demands it is hardly surprising that the director shied off. Louis had told him that he had to cut out 73 'impossibles' in the script for King Solomon's Mines before they started shooting the film. One of these 'impossibles' had been a huge tarantula which found its way into Deborah Kerr's skirt; when Louis protested that there were no tarantulas in Africa the director insisted that, as they had had a mechanical one made at great expense, it must be used.

Soon after the Darwin celebrations in Chicago, Louis paid the first of many visits to Salt Lake City, where he gave two public lectures and a couple of seminars at the University of Utah. There could be no better testimonial to Louis's power of persuasion than his conversion of the Mormons – or at least some of them – to the doctrine of evolution. This, he always maintained, could be reconciled with the story of the Creation of Genesis simply by interpreting a 'day' as so many million years. Notices announcing his talk declared 'Brethren may attend but must not believe'. But many of them did come to believe, and Louis was to return several times at the Mormons' request to lecture and appear on television; in 1971 the University of Utah gave him an honorary degree.

Louis always believed in killing as many birds as possible with one stone, and he certainly accounted for a good many during that epic voyage in the autumn of 1959. Profiting from his free trip, he lectured at 17 universities and various scientific institutions – a grand total of 66 talks. This was the first of his marathon lecture tours which thereafter were to become an annual event.

The providential grant which took him to Chicago also enabled him to proceed with the prime object he had in mind, which was to raise funds for really large-scale excavations at Olduvai. Soon after Zinj was found Louis had written to the National Geographic Society in Washington suggesting they might like an article on the discovery for their magazine, the *National Geographic*; but they turned it down. He then got an introduction from Armand Denis to Dr Melville Bell Grosvenor, who was then president of the Society, and went to see him. Dr Grosvenor has a good nose for a story; he arranged for Louis to put his case at a meeting of the NGS research and exploration committee, and they too were inspired by Louis's eloquence for the potential of Olduvai.

In the words of the minutes recording that historic meeting on 9 November:

> It was voted that the Committee recommend a grant to Dr Leakey of $20,200. . . . Further, that the Society shall have exclusive American publication rights for its official journal, and the Society shall further have the right to send a writer and photographer to cover the project.

From that moment the Leakeys never looked back; the National

Geographic Society, and its journal, made their name a household word in America and has supported their work ever since.

Louis did not know how much money he would get as a result of that first visit to Washington, nor when the grant – if there was to be one – would come through; in the meantime the Wenner-Gren Foundation and the Wilkie Brothers Foundation tided him over so that he could pay off his overdraft and resume excavations at the Zinj site, FLK, in December 1959. Early in 1960 he heard the great news: the NGS grant was a very substantial one, and he could engage a large labour force and really get to grips with Olduvai. In that year the Leakeys put in 92,000 man-hours, more than twice the number of hours spent there during the past thirty years: no wonder they got results.

A good many of those hours were woman-hours rather than man-hours, for Mary spent a whole year at Olduvai, with only short breaks. Louis would appear at fairly frequent but never very long intervals, as he was tied to the Museum in Nairobi. With the prospect of many months of work at FLK, the Leakeys transferred their camp from the side gorge back to the north of the main gorge, close to the site of the old 1935 camp. They needed working space larger and more substantial than a tent, and Jonathan helped the African staff to build a fine thatched house; they also installed one much-needed luxury, a refrigerator. Jonathan was now nineteen and had just left school; he was planning to start up a snake park near the Museum in Nairobi, but in the meantime he was a great help to Mary, organizing the supplies, maintaining the vehicles – and making some important discoveries.

The men were put to work removing the deposits above the Zinj living floor. This proved to be thick with bones and tools, and Mary plotted the position of each piece before it was removed. Eventually she produced plans unrivalled in their exactitude and in the amount of information they gave. Within an area of about six-and-a-half by four-and-a-half metres, and surrounded by chips of quartz, were bones which had been smashed into tiny fragments: evidently this was the kitchen of gourmet hominids who appreciated marrow and brains. To the windward side was a strip almost devoid of debris where, presumably, they had erected a brush fence. Outside this bare patch was another concentration of rubbish, but here the bones were more complete and the tools larger than in the central area.

Louis was proud of the excavations and wanted some of his scientific colleagues to see them; but naturally he had to get permission from the National Geographic Society who were financing the operations. Perhaps he had a hunch that something exciting was going to turn up, for in his letter to Dr Melvin Payne, then Vice-President of the NGS, he said he would like to invite them 'so that if controversies arise, as they are certain to do, there will be several people who can speak from personal knowledge' (of the site).[11]

He invited an anatomist, a palaeontologist and an archaeologist: the veteran Professors Raymond Dart and Camille Arambourg, and Dr Desmond Clark. The NGS also sent the archaeological representative of their research committee, Dr Matthew Stirling, who was the first of many NGS visitors to Olduvai. All were most favourably impressed by the care Mary was putting into the excavations at the Zinj site.

Louis also put on a piece of showmanship for them by disjointing the leg of a cow with stone tools. Oldowan choppers were found to be not altogether satisfactory as the edges were too thick, but small flakes of quartzite, such as were found on the Zinj living floor, did the job perfectly. Louis repeated the performance at Christmas that year for the benefit of his staff; he was filmed skinning a ram with a stone tool by the NGS star photographer, Bob Sisson.

The only disappointment about FLK was that the hoped-for lower jaw of Zinj did not turn up. However, a hominid tibia and fibula were found on the living floor; they seemed very slender to go with the massive Zinj skull, but their significance was not appreciated until after Jonathan had made his great find.

While all the activity was going on at FLK, Jonathan would often wander off to hunt for fossils. About 300 yards to the north of the excavations he found the jaw of a sabre-tooth cat, which was something very rare at Olduvai. The men were put on to sieving the surrounding soil, but instead of getting any more of the sabre-tooth they recovered the tooth of a hominid. The excitement switched from FLK to 'Jonny's site', known as FLK NN ('North North') to distinguish it from yet another site called FLK N. Then, on 2 November 1960, Jonathan found at FLK NN a hominid mandible and two pieces of parietals – the bones from the side of the skull. Although the teeth were from the lower jaw whereas Zinj only had uppers, they were obviously quite different; the incisors and canines were relatively large compared with the cheek teeth, but in Zinj there was a tremendous contrast in size between the front teeth and the huge nutcracker premolars and molars. From the state of eruption of the teeth, this new individual, H7, would have been about twelve years old by modern standards, while Zinj was probably in his late teens; making allowances for this difference in age, the parietal bones were relatively bigger than those of Zinj. For want of a better name, this precocious child was referred to as 'pre-*Zinjanthropus*', since he came from a slightly lower level than Zinj.

Altogether, FLK NN produced parts of four individuals – two adults and one juvenile, as well as a premolar and a collar bone now attributed to '*Zinjanthropus*'. The two adults were each represented by some bones of the left foot – one said to be that of an arthritic old woman – while the juvenile also left behind most of the bones of his hand; these finds were of particular importance, since the limb bones of the early hominids were completely unknown apart from the tibia and fibula from FLK.

In September 1960, just two months before Jonathan made his sensational finds, Louis wrote in an article in the *National Geographic*:[12]

> In some respects this new Stone Age skull [i.e., Zinj] more closely resembles that of present day man than it does the skulls of the gorilla or of the South African near-men . . . *Zinjanthropus* represents a stage of evolution nearer to man as we know him today than to the near-men of South Africa.

He must have wished he could have eaten his words, for now, within a year of his discovery, Zinj had had his nose put out of joint by a far more man-like newcomer, 'pre-Zinj'. Granted that Louis had to persuade the National Geographic Society that in

Zinj he had a likely candidate for 'the first man' in order to ensure their continued support – but need he have stuck out his neck quite so far? Even a layman looking at the skull could not be fooled: Zinj, with his gorilla-like crest on the top of the cranium and his low brow, was quite obviously far more like the robust australopithecines of South Africa than he was like modern man – to whom, quite frankly, he bears no resemblance at all.

Just a month after Jonathan's discovery of the pre-Zinj child, Louis made an equally spectacular find himself. Near the junction of the main and side gorge he noticed a small gully which he thought had not been explored; it is an uninspiring looking place, a small patch of grey soil in the middle of an expanse of brownish soil covered with coarse grass, and probably few people would have given it a second glance. Louis walked over to it and there on the surface was a small heap of bones, which at first he took to be the broken carapace of a fossil tortoise. It proved to be a large and massive human skull, and in great excitement he rushed back to FLK to tell Mary that he had at last found 'Chellean Man'.

At that time the handaxe culture was divided into an earlier 'Chellean' and a later Acheulian stage, each named after sites in France. In Europe the Chellean is now known as the Abbevillean, and in Africa it proved to be an illusion – the whole handaxe sequence is now called Acheulian. Although the skull was lying on the floor of the gully, there was no doubt that it had eroded out of the upper part of Bed II which contains *early* stages of the handaxe culture: hence the reason for Louis speaking of 'Chellean Man' rather than 'Acheulian Man'. No remains of the early handaxe-makers were yet known; jaws found by Professor Arambourg at Ternifine in Algeria were associated with rather advanced handaxes, and so too was the Swanscombe skull from Kent. The Olduvai skull seemed to fill a large gap and justified Louis's excitement. But just as Louis had been disappointed that Zinj was not a *Homo*, so now he was disappointed in the nature of this particular *Homo*.

In his book *Olduvai Gorge* he had prophesied that when remains of handaxe man were found at Olduvai they would be 'of *Homo sapiens* type, but primitive'.[13] This skull was no *sapiens* – it had the most massive brow-ridges yet known, far more massive than those of Java Man or Peking Man. There could be no doubt that it was a form of *Homo erectus* like its Asian cousins. A reconstruction of the unfortunately named 'Chellean Man' appeared on the front page of the *Illustrated London News* on 4 March 1961, and a more horrific, pugilistic-looking character could not have been dreamt up for an illustration to science fiction. In having a more man-like and less hirsute face, he was even more terrifying than the reconstruction of Zinj which had appeared in the same periodical the previous year.[14]

As there was already a site at Olduvai known as LK, Leakey's Korongo, the gully where the skull was found became LLK, Louis Leakey's Korongo. Unfortunately there were no tools at that small exposure, and Mary's work had shown that elsewhere two cultures were present in the upper part of Bed II: the Developed Oldowan and the Acheulian. Of the two, it seemed more likely that Louis's man was associated with the Acheulian: the tools are large and heavy and must have been shaped by someone strong, and the size and ruggedness of the skull certainly suggest that it had belonged to a powerful individual.

Louis reported the leg bones from FLK and the foot and hand bones from FLK NN in *Nature* in December;[15] but he sat on the other finds in order to be able to announce them at a Press conference arranged by the NGS in Washington in February 1961. His formal descriptions of the pre-Zinj child's jaw and parietals, as well as H9 – the 'Chellean' skull – appeared in *Nature* on the following day, 25 February.[16] By coincidence another member of the Leakey family was in the news that day: Colin announced his engagement to Susan Marshall, a physical training instructress at Perse School, Cambridge; they were married from her parents' home at Truro, Cornwall, on 12 August that year.

For once Louis refrained from giving 'pre-Zinj' a scientific name: he only went so far as to say 'It seems that we are dealing with a quite distinct type of hominid'. But at the Press conference he made a sensational disclosure. One of the parietal bones had fracture lines radiating from a central point, and a sharp-witted reporter asked if the child had died as the result of violence. Louis is said to have replied that pre-Zinj *might* have received a blow on the head from a blunt instrument. This was enough for the Press: 'Murder Most Foul,' they cried; 'Earliest Human Killed by a Blunt Instrument.' Louis later hotly denied that he had used the word 'murder'. Nevertheless, in an article in the *National Geographic* he wrote: 'I think it is reasonable to say that the child received and probably died from what in modern parlance is known as "a blow from a blunt instrument".'[17] Some years later, at a conference on aggression at the University of California at Los Angeles, he indignantly repudiated the sensational reports which had appeared at the time: 'Without knowing whether the hole was caused by an accident or falling out of a tree, it became murder,' he said. The fracture lines, in fact, might equally well have been caused by the expansion and contraction of the clay in which the fossil was embedded.

The National Geographic Society paid not only Louis's return fare to Washington and his hotel accommodation, as they were to do every year from then on, but also an honorarium of $650 for two lectures he gave on Olduvai at Constitution Hall. This was also the occasion for showing the film made by Des Bartlett, which had been assembled by the NGS. In January the Society's president, Dr Melville Grosvenor, had written to Armand Denis: 'I hear from the staff from time to time of your wonderful cooperation with the Leakey film and that whole project. We are so grateful to you for first bringing him to our attention. He was, and is, an *extraordinary* find.'[18] Louis tried to make quite sure that the film was being assembled as *he* wanted, and six months before the première he wrote to ask the NGS:

> Will you please let me know a bit more about how the time is divided between speaking and film support? I have lectured more than a thousand times to popular audiences since 1924 and would like, if possible, to plan my own presentation. . . . I should also like to have a large say in what shots should be used for the supporting film.[19]

Perhaps the NGS were a bit apprehensive about the reception that would be accorded to a man who made such demands, but they need not have feared. Afterwards Miss Joanne Hess, organizer of the National Geographic Society's lecture programmes, wrote to Armand Denis:

> I have never seen such an overwhelming response to a lecture and congratulations are still pouring in. . . . The whole lecture was superb. There were many, many rounds of applause for the photography. Dr Leakey's narration was excellent. He was extremely tired by the time the evening lecture rolled around, because of meetings, Press conferences, etc., and I don't think he realised how well he was doing. But the whole thing was tops and we all hope this will not be his last appearance on our platform.[20]

It certainly was not his last appearance on their platform: the National Geographic Society had got themselves a star who was to reappear regularly by popular demand.

Louis gave two other lectures in Washington a few days later, one organized by the Smithsonian Institution, the other to the National Academy of Sciences. He also gave a number in England, both before and after his visit to the USA. The two most important were the Herbert Spencer lecture in Oxford, on 10 February, and the Thomas Huxley lecture in Birmingham on 3 March. This last was the date of the Wenner-Gren Foundation's annual banquet in New York, but Louis turned down an invitation to attend this function of the Foundation which had supported him so often in favour of the Birmingham lecture for which he was to be paid the princely sum of £25! The reason was prestige: the lecture was to be published.

A shoemaker, according to the proverb, should stick to his last; Louis had a good many lasts, and he was better when he stuck to those connected in some way with prehistory; but his missionary streak sometimes tempted him to try to put the world to rights. In the Herbert Spencer lecture at Oxford, at which he appeared resplendent in the robe and cap of an honorary DSc of that University, he tackled the thorny question of racial superiority. He rightly argued that there were fundamental mental and psychological differences between Africans and Europeans, but he also implied that the former were superior in certain aspects of their social structure, customs, law, justice and religion. Before cultural contact with Western civilization, he said, Africans had no death penalty except for persistent murderers; women had greater freedom, including sexual freedom, and had their own methods of birth control; there were no destitute widows and orphans, lonely spinsters, unmarried mothers or prostitutes. One reviewer called the lecture 'a rather discursive rebuttal of the brasher and more irrational allegations of African "racial inferiority" '.[21]

Louis's other big lecture, the Thomas Huxley in Birmingham, was very different; addressed to specialists, it concerned his proposed reclassification of the Hominoidea. The two talks made unhappy companions when they were published together in a short book entitled *The progress and evolution of man in Africa* (1961).[22]

Although Louis – as always – was a big success in America, in the United Kingdom his reception was definitely more reserved. The notices of this book were by no means good, and the unfortunate episode of the pre-Zinj child's 'murder' had made a bad impression. This was the year of the first space flights and of the reading of the first word in the genetic code; readers were becoming ever more sophisticated and more enlightened and they liked to be able to treat their scientists seriously. A brilliant skit by B. A. Young in *Punch* (8 March 1961), reproduced here by kind permission, just about summed up the reactions of the 'man in the street' to the latest Olduvai discoveries and their discoverer:

More secrets from the past: Oboyoboi Gorge

What may well prove to be the oldest crown cork known to man has been found here by Dr C. J. M. Crikey, the anthropologist. It is thought to be at least 500,000 years old. 'I cannot yet give an exact estimate of its age,' Dr Crikey said, 'but I am sending it back to the museum for radio-cola tests, and these should establish definitely how old it is.'

The finding of the crown cork throws an entirely new light on the use of crown corks by prehistoric man. Until quite recently it was assumed that crown corks had come into use only in comparatively recent times. If the radio-cola tests confirm Dr Crikey's estimates, all previous theories about the use of crown corks will have to be revised.

The cork lining layer had disappeared completely, leaving only the circular metal disc with the characteristic corrugated rim. There is no trace of any inscription having appeared on the crown cork, but X-ray pictures may reveal some kind of prehistoric trade mark under the layer of oxidisation which encrusts the metal at present.

Our Scientific Correspondent writes: The Oboyoboi Gorge, where the prehistoric crown cork was found, is a 300-foot cleft carved out of the surrounding countryside of Tanganyika by the seasonal waters of the Oboyoboi River. The age of any remains found in the bank can be accurately assessed from their height above the level of the river bed, the recently discovered pre-Zinj man, calculated to be 700,000 years old, being at the bottom and Mr Julius Nyerere at the top.

It seems possible that the remote ancestor of man who inhabited the area at the epoch to which the crown cork has been assigned – we may conveniently refer to him as the 'post-Zinj man' – used rudimentary stone tools to fashion crown corks for his crude bottles, probably by cutting a rough circle from a sheet of tin and then laboriously turning up the edges and pressing in the corrugations one at a time. The cork lining would then have been cut from the bark of the giant cork trees that may have flourished there at the time and shaped to fit with the aid of a primitive stone knife.

The radio-cola tests to be applied to the crown cork provide a peculiarly elegant method of measuring the age of any prehistoric object. Cola exists in the form of a number of isotopes. One of these is the radio-active isotope radio-cola. This decays at a rate which is accurately known, throwing off an electron to become stable bitter lemon. By comparing the amount of free radio-cola present in a bottle of cola with the amount theoretically present before the bottle was opened, it is possible to calculate how long the sample has been decaying and so arrive at an accurate estimate of its age.

If the radio-cola tests confirm Dr Crikey's estimate that the crown cork is 500,000 years old, it will be at least 499,950 years older than any other crown cork known to exist.

STOP PRESS: A message from Dr Crikey's camp at Oboyoboi Gorge states that the crown cork found there last week is not prehistoric but was dropped by Armand and Michaela Denis during their visit to the site a year ago. 'The whole thing was a laughable mistake,' Dr Crikey said, 'but it emphasises more than ever the tremendous importance of checking and double-checking all one's calculations.'

Louis returned to Nairobi in March 1961 and soon began working at an important new Upper Miocene site in western Kenya. It was to be dated by potassium/argon to about 14 million years – some four million years later than Rusinga and the other Lower Miocene sites.

In April 1959 an orange farmer called Fred Wicker had sent Louis a large fossil bone, telling him there were plenty more on his property at Fort Ternan, forty miles east of Kisumu. This is within a few miles of Koru, where Hopwood had worked in 1932. At that time Louis had noticed an extension of the Lower Miocene beds in the direction of Fort Ternan, but they were covered by a series of deposits nearly 600 feet thick. He spent some days searching for fossils in these beds, but the vegetation was dense and he failed to find any. He was therefore particularly interested in Wicker's bone, and a few weeks after receiving it he and Mary went to Fort Ternan to look around. There were certainly fossils, and Louis suspected that they were Upper Miocene or early Pliocene – a period which was completely unrepresented in East Africa at that time.

For the next two years the Leakeys were absorbed in Olduvai, and it was not until April 1961 that Louis was able to begin excavations at Fort Ternan, with a grant from the NGS. The work was left mostly in the hands of Heselon and his assistants, with Louis paying frequent visits. On 23 June he called there on his way to Rusinga with a distinguished palaeontologist, Professor George Gaylord Simpson of the American Museum of Natural History. Heselon proudly displayed the fossils found since Louis's visit ten days previously and finally, with a smile on his face, produced a small tin. Louis shouted 'We've got it!' and rushed over to show Simpson the contents of the tin: two pieces of the upper jaw of a primate and loose lower molar.

Louis described them not in *Nature*, as was his usual custom, but in the *Annals and Magazine of Natural History*.[23] It is not a man, he admitted, but 'heading very strongly in that direction'. True to form, he created a new genus and species, *Kenyapithecus wickeri*. After concluding that the creature 'shows a greater or lesser approach towards the structures we associate with the Hominidae', Louis left the question open as to the family in which it should be placed. Among the diagnostic features he listed the small canine tooth and a well-defined 'canine fossa'. This hollow in the cheek bone below the eye sockets is found in man but not in apes; Louis set great store by its presence or absence, just as he did by the presence of a simian shelf in distinguishing the apes. As was not unusual with Leakey discoveries, a heated controversy was to ensue over the new genus; but meanwhile there was plenty of action at Olduvai.

Mary had packed up at Olduvai in February and did not begin again until October 1961. As a result of the success of the previous season's work the NGS increased their grant and she was able to continue the excavations for a full year. Almost immediately she had to contend with floods which, if not actually unprecedented, were exceptional. During the so-called 'short' rains, beginning in November, the river in the Gorge was in spate for nearly two months, and for days at a time it was impossible to cross it. Ropes were tied to trees on either side, but even with their aid a man was swept away and was rescued only with great difficulty.

Although the floods made excavation very difficult, work was put in hand at two sites in 1961–62. One was at the base of Bed I at DK, Donald's Korongo, and the other was at the top of this bed at FLK N, situated between the Zinj site at FLK and Jonathan's 'pre-Zinj' site at FLK NN. The year before a geologist seconded by the Tanganyika Geological Survey had dug a test pit at FLK N and come across fossil bones and tools which were obviously lying on a living floor. When Mary began excavations she found there were five of these floors at different levels. At two of them there was an almost complete skeleton of our old friend *Deinotherium*, and the cutting tools which lay all around showed that scavenging hominids had made the most of this feast. There were also a great many remains of small animals on the living floors including lizards, frogs, chameleons and – incredibly – more than fourteen thousand rodents!

The only trace of a hominid at FLK N consisted of a single toe-bone; but in fact it was of great interest, since this particular bone had been missing in the foot from FLK NN. It was given the full treatment by Dr Michael Day, who used the University of London's computer to do a multivariate analysis of its features;

this was a pilot study of the uses of such methods for bones other than skulls, and it confirmed the human, bipedal character of the foot from FLK NN.

Also at FLK N were bones of fish and, above all, birds. Olduvai as a whole has produced the largest collection of fossil birds from Africa. There were geese, ducks, pelicans, flamingoes, waders of all kinds – the soda lake which existed at Olduvai in Bed I times must have been quite as spectacular as the bird sanctuary at Lake Nakuru today. Evidently birds featured quite largely in the diet of the hominids – but how did they catch them? Presumably after dark, when the birds were roosting. No doubt early man should be credited with far more ingenuity than he is generally allowed.

One indication of this was obtained at DK, the other site dug during 1961–62 and the earliest of all the living floors at Olduvai. After getting through a great thickness of consolidated tuff, Mary came upon an unexpected concentration of lumps of rock; it was not until she had removed some of them that she began to suspect there was a pattern in their distribution. In her usual methodical way she had already plotted their position, so there was no problem in putting them back. Sure enough, the rocks formed a rough circle about four metres in diameter: presumably they had served to anchor branches to form a windbreak, and in view of the howling winds which tear across the plains this seems a reasonable supposition. People living in the desert country of northern Kenya, such as the Turkana, make just such crude shelters today for the same reason.

In March 1962 Louis and Mary left the excavations in the hands of assistants and, accompanied by Jonathan, went to Washington. Louis had already paid two triumphant visits to the National Geographic Society, but this was the first time that Mary had been to the United States; the reason for the journey was that they had been awarded jointly the Society's highest honour, the gold Hubbard Medal. Since its inauguration in 1906 this medal had been awarded only 19 times, and never before had it been conferred on a couple. The inscription reads that it was bestowed on the Leakeys for 'revolutionizing knowledge of prehistory by unearthing fossils of earliest man and giant animals in East Africa'. Mary recalls that she was almost speechless with fright when she had to express her thanks to such a distinguished audience.

As usual, Louis also held a Press conference after reporting to the NGS. By now reporters expected him to announce something spectacular every year, nor were they disappointed: he was able to tell them about the world's earliest hominid, *Kenyapithecus wickeri* from Fort Ternan.

Soon after Louis received yet another medal: the Wenner-Gren Foundation's Viking Medal, the highest honour in the field of anthropology (and also the biggest – four inches in diameter). For the first time the selection of the medallists had been left to associates of the Wenner-Gren's journal *Current Anthropology*, representing anthropologists all over the world. They were invited to vote for 'the scientist who has impressed the greatest number of colleagues with the importance of his contributions' and were asked to give their reasons. Here are extracts from the letters of some who chose Louis: 'While his major contributions have been in the field of human palaeontology, his broad range of scholarly accomplishment has added a richness to his observations and a depth to his interpretation of prehistory.'... 'Because of his contribution in recovering the *Zinjanthropus* skull, his excellent writings about early African beginnings, his knowledge of the native peoples of East Africa, his aid to the Government in solving problems of East African natives.'... 'An anthropologist who practices "participation" in living African cultures as well as in the prehistoric cultures, reaffirming the principle of human brotherhood.'[24]

Nearly all those who voted for Louis emphasized the broadness of his interests and contributions to anthropology; and yet it has been suggested that one factor prejudicing his chances of election to the Royal Society was that he was not specialized *enough*!

The four top names in the postal ballot had only a few votes to choose between them, so all four got the Viking Medal; but the prize money was increased so that each received $2,500. Louis and the other British anthropologist, Professor E. E. Evans-Pritchard, received their medals at a dinner in London arranged by the Royal Anthropological Institute on 24 May 1962. As Mary had already returned to East Africa, Louis took Priscilla as his guest to the dinner; in his speech he said that he would use some of the prize money to pay for her and her husband to visit Kenya.

Louis kept his promise, and the Davieses came out to spend Christmas that year at Langata. Colin and his wife Susan also joined them, so for the first time the entire family was together. By then Colin was a lecturer at Makerere College (now University): he had told the Colonial Office that the one place he did not want to be sent to was East Africa as he had no wish to fly under the family colours, whereupon he was promptly posted to Uganda. Towards the end of 1961, he and his bride had driven up from Mombasa and spent two nights at Langata, where they had met Mary and the boys for the first time; but Colin did not really get to know his half-brothers until that Christmas visit a year later. One indelible memory is being asked by Jonathan to hold one end of a large python; another is climbing Ol Doinyo Lengai, an active volcano near the southern end of Lake Natron. Susan also recalls her trepidation at Olduvai when Louis advised them to leave their tent flaps open so that the lions could walk through.

With all the exciting finds coming from Olduvai in the early '60s one would have thought that Louis would have devoted his energies to the Gorge with renewed vigour, but it did not work out like that. The professionals took over, and Louis, because of that very lack of specialization that had so impressed the associates of *Current Anthropology*, lost control of the site he had put on the map.

Mary was fully qualified to develop the archaeological side and needed no help other than manual labour. The fauna and the hominids were parcelled out for study by specialists, group by group and almost bone by bone. And the geology and dating were receiving expert attention, which meant that Louis could no longer indulge in the speculations that he so much enjoyed. He was extraordinarily suspicious of the new-fangled 'absolute' dating by potassium/argon and other methods which had superseded his climatic correlations. It was, of course, pure coincidence that Flint's paper criticizing the climatic evidence in East Africa appeared in 1959, the year of the discovery of Zinj; but the two events were contributory causes to Louis's bowing out in favour of the professionals.

The advent of radiocarbon dating in the 1940s was the most significant step ever made in the study of archaeology, but its time span of a mere 50,000 years was of limited value in a place like Olduvai. Pottassium/argon dating, developed in the late '50s, could extend back over almost boundless horizons of time, but it too had its limitations: it could be used only on rocks containing potassium – and some of the volcanic rocks at Olduvai were ideal. The results of dating by this technique at Olduvai gave unexpected significance not only to the hominids found there but to the whole question of the age of the Pleistocene. These dates made history by being the very first ever obtained from hominid living sites, and indeed the first from archaeological contexts of any kind anywhere.

The potassium/argon method was pioneered by Dr Jack Evernden of the University of California, Berkeley, and Louis first took him to Olduvai to collect samples of tuffs and basalt in 1958. There were teething troubles, just as there had been in the early days of C14 dating; but gradually the hazards of collecting samples free from contamination came to be understood, and Evernden got a consistent cluster of dates around 1.75 million years for the lower part of Bed I. Such an age for the *upper* part of the Lower Pleistocene seemed incredible at the time; although nowadays it is generally accepted that the Pleistocene began more than two million years ago, the usual estimates then were of the order of 600,000 years. When Louis, Evernden and his co-worker announced the 1.75 million year date in *Nature* in 1961 it caused a sensation.[25] There were the inevitable arguments, and other dating laboratories produced conflicting results; but Evernden and Curtis's dates have stood the test of time and have been confirmed by independent methods, such as fission-track dating and palaeomagnetism.[26]

In 1961 Dr Garniss Curtis went to Olduvai to collect more samples for dating from different parts of the Gorge and from various levels. While he was there the Leakeys asked if he knew of a competent geologist who could come and sort out their problems. The result was the introduction of Dr Richard Hay of Berkeley, who first came to Olduvai in 1962 and has returned there each summer ever since. His work has provided a complete picture of the dramatic events that shaped the Olduvai area – volcanic outpourings and earth movements, waxing and waning lakes, the formation of sand dunes, the forces of erosion carving out gullies. It was then possible to establish for the first time the relative position of sites in the main gorge and side gorge, as well as the sources of raw materials used by the tool-makers. Apart from his merits as a geologist Dick Hay had one very important attribute: he was one of the few men who managed to work amicably with Louis for any length of time. Louis occasionally lost his temper when Hay disproved one of his cherished theories, but Louis respected his competence and enjoyed his company.

As well as having the benefit of a geologist, in 1962 the Leakeys had for the first time plenty of other helpers; as a result the finds came thick and fast, so that only the highlights can be mentioned here. A young friend of the family named Margaret Cropper distinguished herself by finding part of a human skull, H12; small and thick-walled, it was named 'Pinhead'. The skull had eroded out of Bed IV and been trampled to bits by Masai cattle, but it could be reconstructed. It seemed to be a late example of *Homo erectus*, possibly a descendant of the people represented by the massive skull found by Louis in Bed II in 1960.

Now that there was no shortage of labour, men could be spared to scour the gullies; the result was a good crop of fossils, including hominids. The two most exciting, both from Bed II, were found in 1963. The first came from MNK in the side gorge, where the Leakeys were building a shelter to protect the living floor. A workman collecting stones to put into a cement mixer spotted a single hominid tooth which led to the recovery of the faceless 'Cinderella', H13. After clearing the surrounding grass, several pieces of skull were picked up, while others turned up as a result of sieving. Eventually it appeared that there were parts of three individuals: 'Cindy' herself, parts of the skull of a child, and some teeth of an older person ('Cindy's Grandma').

The second important person to emerge in 1963 was 'George', H16, who came from the base of Bed II, quite close to the Zinj site. Like Pinhead, poor George was in a shocking state after having been trampled into thousands of tiny fragments by the feet of Masai cattle; but although only the vault of his skull could be reconstructed his teeth were well preserved. Neither George nor Cinderella were at all like Zinj, but apparently they could be linked with the fragmentary remains of Jonathan's pre-Zinj child. So far, with uncharacteristic patience, Louis had refrained from naming this child; but now, armed with these new finds, he was in a position to do so.

All this time he had been waiting to see what the anatomists could make of the limb bones from FLK and FLK NN. The study of these bones had been entrusted to Dr John Napier of the Royal Free Hospital, to whom Le Gros Clark had sent the arm bone of *Proconsul* from Rusinga found in 1951. At that time Napier was not concerned with either primates or fossils; but during the war he had specialized in hand surgery, and Le Gros Clark respected his skill as an anatomist. After Napier agreed to study the hominid limb bones from Olduvai, Louis used to post specimens to him in tobacco tins. Each bone was carefully wrapped in lavatory paper – Louis always kept a large supply of this commodity, which he used to prevent plaster of Paris from sticking to fossil bones. Napier would then parcel out the specimens among his colleagues at the Royal Free; he himself kept the hand bones, Dr Peter Davies studied the tibia and fibula from FLK, and Dr Michael Day got the foot bones, including the toe from FLK N.

Napier's conclusions on the hand bones from FLK NN pleased Louis very much indeed: they were, said Napier, 'strikingly human in one revealing and . . . critical character. The tips of the fingers and thumb were surmounted by broad, stout, flat, nail-bearing terminal phalanges, a condition that, as far as we know, is found only in man.'[27] Such a hand with its spatulate thumb, he thought, would have been quite capable of constructing simple tools of the Oldowan type.

Meanwhile Michael Day had unwrapped twelve foot bones from the tobacco tins he had been given and fitted them together after setting them up in plasticine. 'My hair stood on end,' he told me. 'The foot was completely human.' It was a great moment of truth. There could be no possible doubt that the owner of that foot had walked upright, not only occasionally but habitually. It all added up: a small, slender creature about four-and-a-half feet tall, who walked upright, had hands capable of making tools, human-looking teeth, and a relatively large brain. Here at last was Louis's Lower Pleistocene *Homo* – for there was no doubt in his mind that 'pre-Zinj' was a *Homo*, even if a very primitive one.

While the anatomists were busy on the limb bones, Phillip Tobias had to switch from his study of the Zinj skull and turn his attention to the cranial remains of the pre-Zinj child and also to Cinderella and George. The result of their joint efforts was a paper in *Nature* of 4 April 1964 in which Leakey, Tobias and Napier announced nothing less than 'A new species of the genus *Homo* from Olduvai Gorge'.[28]

The new species was named *habilis*, meaning 'able, handy, mentally skilful, vigorous' according to the inventor of the name, Professor Raymond Dart, who never lacked inspiration on such occasions. Not only did Leakey, Tobias and Napier create a new species of man, they actually had the temerity to revise the diagnosis of the genus *Homo* itself in order to accommodate the new species. The fat was truly in the fire, and Louis came in for a barrage of criticism that has not abated to this day. However, as though to make some concession, in the same issue of *Nature* Louis allowed Zinj to be demoted from generic to sub-generic rank: the name was now confined to brackets as *Australopithecus* (*Zinjanthropus*) *boisei*.

Even Louis's old ally Sir Wilfrid Le Gros Clark turned against him over the naming of *Homo habilis*, maintaining to his dying day that it was an australopithecine. He and Louis fired salvos at each other in the columns of *Discovery* in 1964,[29] and three years later Le Gros Clark repeated his views in his book *Man apes or ape man*? 'It is really very sad,' commented Louis to a colleague, 'that he should have written such a book as his swan song.'[30] It was somewhat premature to talk about a 'swan song'; Le Gros Clark did, in fact, die in 1971, but even Louis could not have known this at the time.

While attacking *Homo habilis* in *Discovery* in 1964 Le Gros Clark took the opportunity to pitch in to *Kenyapithecus wickeri*. An American palaeontologist, Dr Elwyn Simons, had taken a new

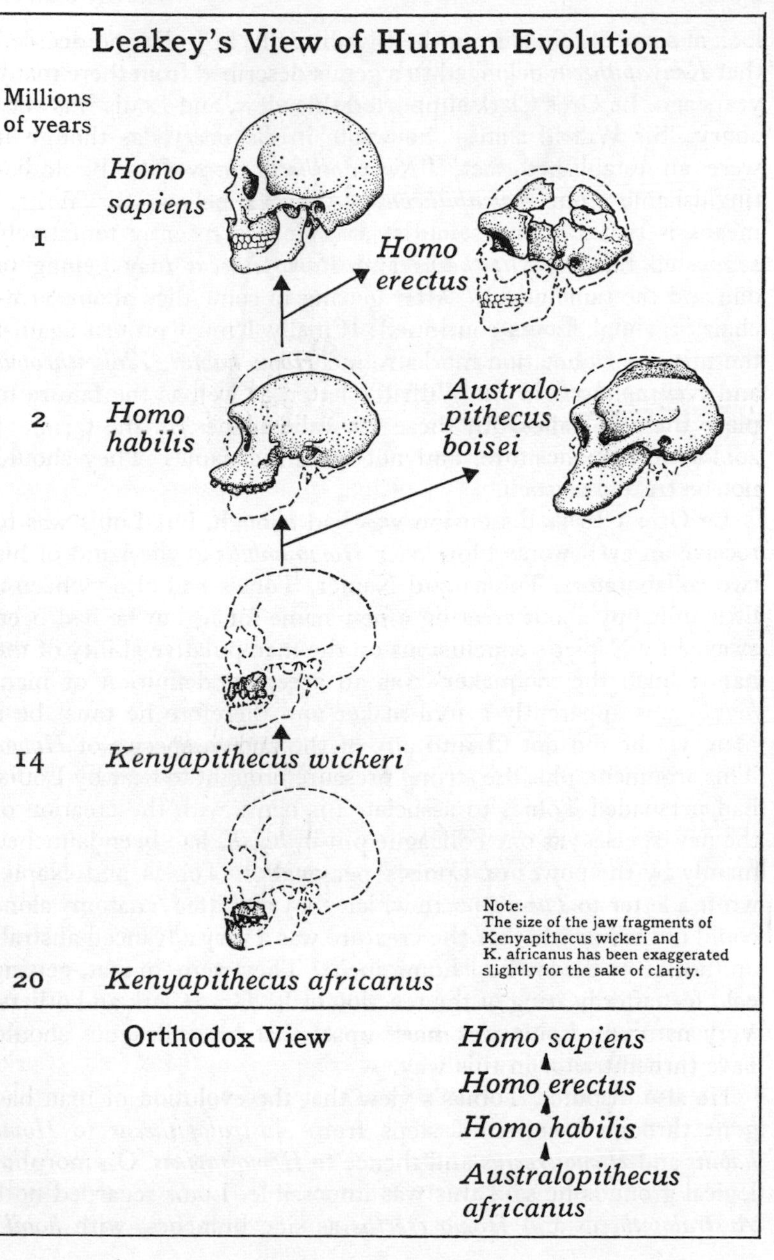
Leakey's View of Human Evolution
Millions of years
Homo sapiens
1
Homo erectus
2
Homo habilis
Australopithecus boisei
14
Kenyapithecus wickeri
20
Kenyapithecus africanus
Note: The size of the jaw fragments of Kenyapithecus wickeri and K. africanus has been exaggerated slightly for the sake of clarity.
Orthodox View
Homo sapiens
Homo erectus
Homo habilis
Australopithecus africanus

look at some old finds from the Siwalik Hills in India and decided that *Kenyapithecus* belonged to a genus described from there many years ago. Le Gros Clark supported this view, and Louis was very angry. 'Sir Wilfrid states,' he wrote in *Discovery*, 'as though it were an established fact, "*Kenyapithecus* proves to be indistinguishable from *Ramapithecus*". What I believe Sir Wilfrid means is that a young scientist at Yale has recently tentatively suggested that *Kenyapithecus* and *Ramapithecus* may belong to one and the same genus.' After getting in some digs about 'armchair juggling', Louis continued: 'Finally I must protest against the misuse of quotation marks round *Homo habilis*, *Zinjanthropus* and *Kenyapithecus* in Sir Wilfrid's letter, as well as the failure to place them in italics. All these are valid names, in the terms of zoological nomenclature, and not mere nicknames. They should not be treated as such.'

Le Gros Clark's dissension was bad enough, but Louis was to receive an even worse blow over *Homo habilis* at the hand of his two collaborators, Tobias and Napier. Tobias had always been a little unhappy about creating a new name for it, but he had been swayed by Napier's conclusions on the manipulative ability of the hand: 'man the toolmaker' was an accepted definition of man, *habilis* was apparently a tool-maker and therefore he must be a man, yet he did not fit into any of the known species of *Homo*. This argument, plus the strong pressure brought to bear by Louis, had persuaded Tobias to associate his name with the creation of the new species; as one colleague put it, *habilis* had been launched mainly by the power of Louis's personality. Tobias and Napier wrote a letter to *The Times* in which they admitted 'anatomy alone could not tell us whether the creature was a very advanced australopithecine or the lowliest hominine'.[31] They were, in fact, getting cold feet after hearing of the reaction of Le Gros Clark and others. Very naturally Louis was most upset that his colleagues should have turned traitor in this way.

He also disputed Tobias's view that the evolution of man had gone through a series of steps from *Australopithecus* to *Homo habilis* and *Homo erectus* and thence to *Homo sapiens*. On morphological grounds he said this was impossible. Louis regarded both *Australopithecus* and *Homo erectus* as side branches, with *habilis* alone on the main stem leading to modern man; and he also believed that at Olduvai he had evidence of all three living contemporaneously.[32] One argument in favour of this theory was 'George', H16; after reconstruction had been completed, Louis decided that 'George' might not be a *habilis* after all, but a possible ancestor for the massive *Homo erectus* skull, H9 ('Chellean Man').

In a Press release handed out in April 1965 Louis 'urged his colleagues to review all their previous ideas about human origins and to substitute for those theories new ones which were more in keeping with the facts that were now known.' Louis certainly asked a good deal of his colleagues! So often he was one jump ahead of them; but his evidence was insufficient to convince others, who could hardly be expected to follow his intuitive reasoning.

The controversies in scientific journals were nothing new, but the publicity resulting from the Olduvai discoveries was certainly unprecedented in Louis's career. Millions of people read about his exploits in the *National Geographic*, and the implications of this sudden fame are discussed in a later chapter. The first of these articles, on the discovery of Zinj, appeared in 1960; others followed in 1961 and 1963. In January 1963 the NGS sent a television crew to Olduvai to make a film of the Leakeys at work. Members of the Society flocked to see the site they were supporting: Dr Melvin Payne came for the first time in 1963 while the camera crew were there, Dr Melville Grosvenor and his son came a year later; and in 1965 a party of 19 from the NGS visited the Gorge.

The publicity engendered by the NGS had repercussions in the popular Press all over the world, and Louis received innumerable requests for autographs and photographs, as well as letters asking for jobs. For example, from a student in Seattle: 'I am willing to do anything for the privilege of working with the Leakeys in Africa.' And, following one of Louis's lectures: 'Some young people get excited over a rock concert, but I got excited over your lecture. Thank you for answering my letter and giving me some hope of having my dream come true.'

One specimen from his fan mail read as follows: '*Dear Sir*, from unreliable sources I have heard of the fame of your museum and I would like to ask you to send me some pictures of the following findings: (1) Findings from Zinj anthopus boisei (Leakey);

(2) Findings from Proe Zinj anthopus; (3) Findings from homo nobilis (a gentle man).' *Homo habilis* was called a good many things in his time, but this was certainly an original contribution.

The year 1964 marked the end of the third and most intensive phase at Olduvai; after that, excavations were closed down and were not resumed until 1968. Mary needed time to write up the archaeological results from Beds I and II, while various specialists were studying the fauna. Louis described some of the new material – and redescribed some of the old – in the first volume of a new series, *Olduvai Gorge 1951–1961: Fauna and Background* (1965), with special emphasis on the Bovidae (the family which includes antelopes).

By the time excavations ceased in 1964 about twenty hominid specimens had been collected. Olduvai had become famous, and with improved roads it was no longer inaccessible. It could not be left unprotected from souvenir-hunters, so a few men were left to look after the camp while the Leakeys were away. Also, because of the damage done to 'George' and 'Pinhead' by the hooves of Masai cattle it was essential to fence in some of the most important sites.

After some controversial boundary changes – which Louis had actively but unsuccessfully opposed – Olduvai had been excised from Serengeti National Park and included in the Ngorongoro Conservation Unit. In an area of this category the needs of man and domestic animals have equal rights with wildlife and scientific interests, and the Masai could wander over the Gorge at will. Normally they had no wish to do so, but for a few weeks after the rains they brought their cattle right down into it to graze and water. This is the season when wildebeest are calving on the plains and are apt to be infected with malignant catarrh – known poetically in Afrikaans as *snotsiekte*. The Masai therefore take avoiding action to prevent the disease from spreading to their stock and drive them into the gorge. Generally they move down along well-marked paths; but after watering, the cattle spread out on their way back to the plains, grazing and trampling all over the Leakeys' sites. One of their favourite routes is at the junction of the main and side gorge, just where the fossils are thickest.

After consultation with the Tanzania Government, Louis arranged a conference at Olduvai to discuss ways of protecting the sites. It was attended by government representatives, the Regional Commissioner, staff of the Serengeti National Park and the Ngorongoro Conservation Unit, the Masai representative in the Legislative Assembly and – most important of all – thirteen of the local Masai elders. The talks went on all day, and eventually the Masai agreed to exclude their cattle completely from two small areas with a corridor between. And the Government agreed to contribute towards the cost of fencing.

As compensation to the Masai for losing some of their grazing grounds Louis promised to construct two dams. The NGS put up most of the money, and in 1965 the dams were built – with considerable difficulty. Cement had to be brought from Arusha, 137 miles away, and water for mixing it had to be transported nearly thirty miles from Ngorongoro. Unfortunately after a few years the dams no longer held water; and the Masai elders failed to control some of their warriors, who had a meat feast right in the middle of the stone circle at DK in spite of the shelter which was supposed to protect it.

Louis was always interested in Masai customs and remedies, just as he was in those of the Kikuyu or for that matter any other people. When the Masai cut or scratch themselves, they rub into the wound the juice of the wild sisal, *ol duvai*; it contains a neurotoxin which stops pain as well as acting as an antiseptic, and the Leakeys also found it very effective. One day in 1963 Louis lost all feeling in one hand and leprosy was suspected. At University College Hospital in London he had a miogram to record his nervous responses, and was asked if he had been using any unusual remedy; he remembered the *ol duvai* juice and that, apparently, was the cause of the trouble. He happened to be particularly sensitive to it, whereas Mary still uses it constantly without any ill effects. One man's meat is another man's poison, and perhaps this story symbolizes the relationship between Louis, Mary and the Gorge. During the last ten years of his life Louis played little part at Olduvai, whereas Mary obviously has affinity with the place. However, it was Louis's efforts at fund-raising that enabled her to go on digging and slowly digesting what she found.

He could not have gone on getting money without publicity, and he never underestimated the importance of this aspect of his work. The 1961 piece from *Punch* already quoted illustrates how Olduvai – and Louis – caught the public imagination; another, published in the same periodical on 10 June 1964, shows that the interest was sustained:

"When God at first –"

When the first men were fashioned in the good Lord's forge,
He sent them, it seems, to the Olduvai Gorge,
There to be tested and kept an eye on
With the proto-lizard and proto-lion.
This hyphen-pithecus and Homo-that,
With the archaeo-elephant and palaeo-cat,
Lived there, and died, and were hidden away
Under layer on layer of African clay
Till countless millions of years should run
And Leakey discover them, one by one . . .
While, back in the heavenly forge, the Lord
Went back again to the drawing board.
I sometimes wonder: suppose that I
Were digging out there, at Olduvai,
And I brought to light a significant bone
Of a kind I could positively call my own;
And under the bone, when I'd worked it free,
I found (let us say) an ignition key –
Should I declare it, as of course I ought,
Or should I just pocket it? Perish the thought!

10 Leakey and Son

Men who are absorbed in their career sometimes neglect their wife and children; but Louis led the sort of life that his family could share. There are both advantages and disadvantages in an unorthodox upbringing in the bush, as Louis himself had experienced and as his sons were to find out as well.

When the boys were young Louis had hoped that they would follow in his footsteps; when one of them actually did so, he had mixed feelings. In a way he resented Richard's intrusion into his preserves, yet at the same time he was immensely proud of his achievements. Richard could never have got where he is today without Louis, but equally he could not have remained there if he had lacked ability. And when sons follow the same path as their father, it is even more likely to end in tears if the son is efficient. When Richard began to take a turn in the driving seat, there was a clash of personalities, resentment, at times even anguish – but there was also mutual affection and respect. The relationship between Louis and Richard, and between Louis and Mary – who also impinged directly on his professional career – was naturally more complicated than with non-competing members of the family.

Leakey and Sons had always been a family business: Jonathan found the first *habilis*, Richard erected the buildings for the present camp at Olduvai, Philip had beaten tracks over some of the most difficult terrain in the Gorge. All three were moulded by their parents' unconventional way of life and by the surroundings in which they were brought up. Even Colin, who never had the chance to be inspired personally by Louis as the others were, gravitated to East Africa – albeit unwillingly at first. Here, too, there must have been something in the genes that led him to the natural sciences and adventure.

Jonathan did all his schooling in Kenya – there was never

enough money to send him anywhere else. Richard went to a London crammer for a few months to work at chemistry, physics and biology, and succeeded in getting two A levels; Louis made tentative enquiries as to whether there would be any hope of getting him in to St John's, but Richard found life in England intolerable and the idea was abandoned. While Richard was there he was sent by Louis to interview the headmaster of Leighton Park School, near Reading, on behalf of his younger brother; and Philip was duly pushed off to school in an alien country at the age of sixteen, just as his father had been at the same age. Philip found GCE chemistry particularly hard going and, like Louis and Richard before him, hated the lack of freedom; one term was as much as he could stand. (One can hardly imagine Canon Harry allowing Louis to leave school because he was homesick.)

Jonathan, Richard and Philip inherited their love of wildlife from both parents. They were always surrounded by animals – wild, feral and domestic, but never in cages. A description in the *National Geographic* gives a vivid, but not entirely accurate, account of the camp at Olduvai: '. . . a raucous menagerie of orphaned wildebeest calves, abandoned antelopes, dogs, monkeys, fowls, cats, baboons, jackals and field mice – all living in harmony.'[1] The Leakeys never had all these creatures at the same time, and Mary indignantly denies that she would ever keep fowls. Nevertheless it is true that there are always 'pets' at Olduvai, even if they themselves are not always aware that they are regarded as such; every morning at breakfast, Mary scatters cheese for the field-mice, lizards and birds, and her favourites among the regular callers are a pair of ravens, who summon her impatiently if she is a moment late in appearing. Oliver, the wildebeest calf, was perhaps the most endearing and intelligent member of the 'extended family' – to use a favourite term of social anthropologists. Then there was Simon, the Sykes monkey, who was appreciated by few outside the Leakey family. As Louis has described, nothing was safe from Simon's insatiable curiosity, particularly the drinks cupboard; one day he was found very much under the influence, sitting in a pool of alcohol and surrounded by broken bottles.[2]

With their heads filled with Louis's stories about animals, and their lungs filled with the wide open spaces, it is not surprising that his three sons should take up work connected with animals and plants. The idea of working within four walls, or in any place other than East Africa, would have been unthinkable.

Jonathan's special love had always been snakes, although he also had a way with amphibians: his Kenyan jumping frogs won a cup in Johannesburg and went on to compete in the California 'Olympics' – the annual contest at Calaveras initiated as a result of Mark Twain's story 'The celebrated jumping frog of Calaveras County.' The snake park which Jonathan started near the Museum in Nairobi is still going strong. It includes facilities for the milking of venom, which he supplied to research and medical institutes all over the world. Soon after the snake park was opened he was bitten by a carpet viper, three years later by a green mamba, and finally by a black mamba. Miraculously he survived: all these snakes are deadly unless the right antidote is given immediately. As a result, Jonathan is now allergic to antivenene and thinks twice before handling a venomous snake. This did not stop him from going to Thailand with 'Iodine', that world famous snake-man C. J. P. Ionides; they collected sixteen king cobras in the jungle and Jonathan – as his family feared he might – brought back hundreds of cobra eggs to Kenya.

In December 1963 Jonathan married a girl from South Africa, Mollie Knights-Rayson, and leased some land on the shores of Lake Baringo in Kenya. There he has a snake farm and also grows melons; irrigated by an elaborate method devised in Israel, the fruit is exported mainly to Swiss and German markets. Jonathan, like his brothers, also profited from the safari boom: in partnership with two others he opened a luxurious camp for tourists on an idyllic island in Lake Baringo.

Richard, from the age of seventeen, ran a successful safari business at first by himself and later in partnership with Alan Root, the gifted wildlife photographer. Philip in due course set up Phil Leakey Safaris; but he is more of an idealist and is less practical than his brothers, and he soon became involved in other ventures. Inspired by his half-brother Colin he collected orchids enthusiastically while still a schoolboy, after which he became a mineral prospector, specializing in vermiculite. Philip had a short-lived marriage to a Californian girl, Lynn Bailey, and then had an ambition to develop the Nguruman Hills – a wild and beautiful stretch of country between Lake Magadi and Lake Natron – for the ultimate benefit of the Masai.

Although their philosophies are very different, physically Richard and Philip are much alike and both take after Louis. Richard has dark eyes like his father, Philip's are blue like his mother's, but both are tall and lean and even better looking than Louis as a young man. They have also inherited his charm: an American friend of Louis's described Richard when he met him for the first time as 'bright and witty, and indeed can turn it on just like his old man.'

Jonathan, who is temperamentally more like his mother, has quite separate interests and has kept out of the family arguments. The issues between Richard and Philip do not have a direct bearing on this story; but those between Louis and Mary, and between Louis and Richard, cannot be ignored. Much is explained by the fact that during the 1960s Louis's hip joint gradually became completely ossified as a result of osteoarthritis. He bore the pain with great stoicism, limping when he thought nobody was looking but immediately straightening if he knew someone was watching. He was no longer able to do the active fieldwork for which he had such a flair, and it was very hard to have to take a back seat while Mary and Richard did the driving.

As his family became more and more absorbed in their own careers Louis began to feel lonely. Because of his perennial charm plenty of women were ready to give him the sympathy and appreciation he needed, and so he began to intensify old relationships and form new ones. Usually the partner was completely uncritical; adoration, though comforting, can also be cloying, and Mary's occasional acerbity must have been refreshing. He was jealous of her increasing independence, just as she was jealous of his women friends; but although they had their ups and downs, there can be no doubt that Mary meant more to Louis than anyone else in his life.

Once the continuation of the work at Olduvai was assured under the benevolent aegis of the National Geographic Society there were three alternatives open to Louis. He could continue his curatorship of the Museum in Nairobi and leave the fieldwork at Olduvai entirely to Mary; he could resign as curator and work there himself; or he could obtain leave of absence from the Museum and get his salary from other sources. Louis had been curator for the past twenty years, fifteen of them in a full-time capacity, and he was getting tired of administrative duties which kept him tied to his desk when he might be getting on with research. He therefore put certain proposals up to the National Geographic Society.

Early in 1961 the NGS had agreed that they would pay his salary for one year if he could take unpaid leave from the Museum. However, as Louis pointed out, this would put the trustees in a spot. They could not hope to find someone of the right calibre to take over the curatorship on such a short-term basis, and Louis pressed the NGS to guarantee his salary for three years. In April 1961 he wrote to the chairman of the Museum trustees, Sir Ferdinand Cavendish-Bentinck, to tell him about the proposition. He said he would like to retain his association with the Museum in an honorary capacity and continue to be responsible for the palaeontological and archaeological collections, but he did not wish to cut the anchor chain irrevocably. His resignation was accepted and on 30 June 1961 Mr R. H. (Bob) Carcasson, an entomologist, was appointed acting director of the Museum.

In taking this step Louis had an ambitious plan in mind. He aimed to establish an entirely new organization, affiliated with the Museum, to cope with the palaeontological and archaeological material from Olduvai and the Miocene sites.

The actual finding of fossils is relatively simple compared with the amount of work that has to be done on them afterwards – cleaning and reconstruction, study and description. By now the collections had become so large it was impossible to house them, let alone study them, within the Museum. Fossils and artifacts were battened down in packing cases, piled up in outhouses and the basement, lining the passages.

The Kenya Government had no money to spare for research, and the sum allocated to the Museum trustees was inadequate even for day to day expenses. Although they could give no financial support, the trustees agreed to the formation of the Coryndon Museum Centre for Prehistory and Palaeontology, 'as part of the overall organization of the Museum services, but as a separate entity.' Louis, as honorary director of the Centre, would be responsible directly to the board of trustees and not to the director of the Museum. The Centre was to be fully autonomous in respect of administration as well as finance, and Louis undertook to raise the money to pay the staff and keep it going.

The Centre began its life in July 1962. All the study collections of prehistoric and archaeological material were moved into buildings adjoining the Museum formerly occupied by the Desert Locust Control. Louis persuaded the Ford Foundation of New York to provide £2,000 per annum for three years, and the National Geographic Society gave £350 per annum towards laboratory expenses connected with the work on material from Olduvai. It was little enough; but Louis was fortunate in his staff, who were prepared to work for a pittance in order to gain experience.

The post of deputy director of the Centre was filled neatly by means of an administrative manoeuvre. In October 1961 a young and able archaeologist, Glynn Isaac, had been appointed warden of Olorgesailie. The mechanism for the protection of prehistoric sites open to the public was complicated and apparently somewhat haphazard. Under the Ancient Monuments Ordinance of 1934 they came under the jurisdiction of the regional commissioner of the province in which they were situated, and the amount of protection they were afforded depended on the interest and enthusiasm of the officer concerned. Under the National Parks Ordinance of 1949 the trustees of that body became responsible for the maintenance of these sites, but in practice they were controlled by the Museum trustees as agents for the National Parks. Finally in 1963 the new Centre for Prehistory and Palaeontology took over the administration on behalf of the Museum trustees. Glynn Isaac was thus able to serve two masters: for six months he looked after the sites in an honorary capacity while finishing his research on Olorgesailie for his doctoral thesis; and at the same time he was deputy director of the Centre.

Like Dick Hay, the geologist who worked at Olduvai, Isaac was one of the few men who managed to hit it off with Louis for any length of time. When asked to account for his success, he gave what he called a 'recruit's eye view of the general' in these words:

> Louis, I think deliberately, stayed away while I got established at Olorgesailie and I was grateful for this, as it enabled us to avoid conflicts of approach. When I was taken on as his deputy at the Centre, an explicit box and cox policy was established, with me at the desk when he was away and me in the field when he was in Nairobi.

The other person who helped enormously during the early days of the Centre was Shirley Coryndon, now Mrs Robert Savage. Her first husband, Roger, was the son of Sir Robert Coryndon, after whom the Museum was named. In 1950 she had been taken on as voluntary assistant to Donald MacInnes, with whom she worked at Rusinga and other Miocene sites and from whom she learnt much about palaeontology. Today she is the acknowledged expert on fossil hippos.

In addition to the small salary that Louis paid to Shirley Coryndon, he had to provide an assistant for Mary on the archaeological side, as well as wages for technicians and other African staff. Before the end of the first year of its existence the Centre was already in the red. But Louis was always confident that one of the foundations he had been importuning would come to the rescue; and sure enough, in June 1963, the National Science Foundation made a grant of £17,228 to be spread over a period of five years. Louis promptly engaged a technical officer, Ron Clarke, who was to prove his worth in making casts and doing reconstructions of the Olduvai hominids. He also took on a new palaeontological assistant to replace Shirley Coryndon, who had moved to London and got a job at the Natural History Museum.

Meanwhile Louis became a visiting professor for the first, but not the last, time: in April–May 1963, as Regent's professor at the University of California's Riverside campus, he gave a series of six lectures. The theme was 'The evolution of tool-making and tool use and its effect upon human physical and mental evolution', which gave him plenty of scope for his ever-popular demonstrations of tool-making. Regarding man's mental evolution, he concluded that the greatest danger today was lethargy – of which he himself could never be accused. He also collected from the University of California his second honorary doctorate, this time of law. In thanking him for his lectures the chancellor wrote: 'You were a great stimulus, not only to the campus but the entire western half of the United States.'[3]

When Richard was eighteen he used some of the money he had made out of his safari business to learn to fly; he did this from Wilson Airport, just outside Nairobi, while his parents were away. Although Louis was not always enamoured of new-fangled ideas, like isotopic dating, he would certainly have seen the advantages of his son becoming a pilot; Mary, on the other hand, might well have tried to stop him. Richard could not have put his money to better use: by flying his own plane he was to become just as much of a pioneer in prehistory as his father had been from the ground a generation earlier. It is impossible to overrate the importance of aerial surveys in a territory like East Africa, where so many fossil localities are in inaccessible, trackless country. Beginning in the mid 1960s, many new sites of the greatest significance were first discovered from the air; all that remained was for someone to get to them by land and prepare a rough airstrip, after which it was comparatively easy to exploit them.

Richard's first major involvement with prehistory, and his first big responsibility, came as the result of a flight over Lake Natron in 1963. When he told his parents about the sediments he had spotted around the mouth of the Peninj River, on the north-western shore of the lake, he found they already knew about them: Mary had once driven past in a Land-Rover, but there had never been time or money to explore further. Richard persuaded them to take another look from his plane, which took some courage on their part as he still was a very inexperienced pilot, and Mary admits she was terrified.

Richard and Glynn Isaac next did a land reconnaissance, which was not quite so easy. From Olduvai there is a track with an unspeakably awful surface as far as the southern – and unfossiliferous – end of Lake Natron, after which there is nothing. Their

Land-Rover got stuck when they tried to proceed along the shore, but eventually they managed to reach the Peninj delta and collected a few fossils. On the next occasion they tried the alternative and much longer route from Nairobi via Lake Magadi – a vision of inferno, with dark satanic mills and weird pieces of industrial archaeology used in the extraction of soda. Like Natron, the surface of the lake has a thick crust, part white, part lurid pink; and across the apparently treacherous surface runs a road from shore to shore.

After completing the last fourteen miles across Lake Natron by boat, Richard and Glynn Isaac arrived at the Peninj River and lost no time in enlisting the help of the local inhabitants, the Sonjo, to clear the ground for an airstrip. Richard had thought of an ingenious method of getting Land-Rovers to the site without having to drive them there: he persuaded the RAF to airlift the vehicles in the course of a training exercise. By that time the Sonjo were quite blasé about the sight of his light plane coming and going, so they were not particularly concerned at the appearance of a heavy, four-engined machine. The Swahili word *ndege* means both 'bird' and 'plane', so when this pregnant-looking bird disgorged a couple of vehicles the Sonjo merely thought it was laying eggs.

Isaac organized a systematic search of the deeply eroded gullies and, within a week of their arrival, a member of the Olduvai staff named Kamoya Kimeu made a find which made all the difficulties and discomfort worth while. Embedded in a block of sandstone at the top of an almost vertical slope he spotted a massive jaw. Richard was in Nairobi, but Isaac hurried to the nearest telephone at Magadi, and next day Louis and Mary flew to Peninj to inspect the jaw before it was moved. There was no possible doubt: here was Zinj Mark II and, providentially, the very part that was missing in the Zinj Mark I skull.

Louis published a brief note about it in *Nature*,[4] and with such success coming within a few days of the exploration of a new site he had no difficulty in raising money for excavations from the National Geographic Society. An expedition was launched in June 1964, with the scientific work directed by Glynn Isaac and the organization done by Richard. Philip also went along, as well as Margaret Cropper – said by Mary to be the best assistant she had ever had at Olduvai.

Isaac immediately began excavations at the jaw site; but although ten men scraped and sieved for nearly three months, not another fragment ever turned up. Richard meanwhile pioneered a track up the escarpment so that they could explore the plateau by Land-Rover – in the heat of Natron one does not walk more than is absolutely necessary. They found many fossils, but no more hominids, and Richard and Margaret discovered handaxes and other stone tools. Louis and Mary came to inspect the artifacts, crossing the lake by scow and looking for all the world like Anthony and Cleopatra on the Royal barge, gliding through the purple water surrounded by a cloud of pink flamingos.

In anticipation of more newsworthy hominids the National Geographic Society commissioned a Kenya cameraman, Bob Campbell, to make a film of the operations. There was no lack of colourful background, but there are limits to the amount of footage that can be expended on flamingos, or, for that matter, on prehistorians tramping around looking for fossils. The Sonjo were therefore roped in as extras and were filmed going about their daily business: herding goats, cultivating maize, millet and sweet potatoes with irrigation from the Peninj River, retiring for the night into their huts built on stilts. The resulting film, *Land of the Sonjo*, was to stand Louis in good stead during his American lecture tours.

On 12 December 1964, the first anniversary of Uhuru, Kenya became a Republic. At the wish of the President, Mzee Jomo Kenyatta, the name of the Coryndon Museum was changed to the National Museum, and the Centre became the National Museum Centre for Prehistory and Palaeontology. President Kenyatta became a patron of the Museum, and two vice-patrons were elected: Mr C. J. P. Ionides, the 'snake man'; and the Rt. Hon. Malcolm MacDonald, OM, formerly Governor of Kenya, then Governor General, and finally British High Commissioner.

No better man than Mr MacDonald could have been found to guide Kenya during the first years of independence. He had an open mind, mixed well, and was a personal friend of President Kenyatta. He was also a good friend to Louis and took a great interest in his work, visiting Olduvai and other sites when he could manage to get away from his official duties. Mr MacDonald did Louis three very good turns: by bringing him together with President Kenyatta for the first time since their confrontation at the Kapenguria trial; by arranging for him to meet the Emperor of Ethiopia, with results that are described later; and by helping him over problems connected with obtaining his Kenya citizenship.

One day Louis was telling Mr MacDonald about the Fort Ternan finds and the latter asked if the Prime Minister, as Mr Kenyatta then was, knew about them. Louis replied that he did not, and that he hesitated to ask for an interview as they had not met since the trial and he did not know what sort of reception he would get. When Mr MacDonald next saw the Prime Minister he asked if he would like to come to lunch at State House to meet Louis and hear about his latest finds. Mr Kenyatta said he would be delighted, adding that he was a great admirer of Louis's work. On the appointed day Louis arrived a few minutes early and was obviously nervous; but when Mr Kenyatta entered the room, he greeted Louis with a beaming smile and outstretched arms. They had an animated conversation in Kikuyu before remembering their host and reverting to English. There is no doubt that Mzee forgave and forgot anything that Louis had done during the emergency; he was too big a man to bear a grudge.

Like many other members of the British community who wanted to stay on, Louis was anxious to get his Kenya citizenship through before the country became a Republic. Although the President personally bore him no grudge, it was impossible at that stage to know what sort of attitude his successor or his other ministers might take in the future. Under the British Nationality Act of 1964 people of UK origin were given a right to resume British citizenship if things should ever go wrong in Kenya. Louis wanted to make sure that he had that right, but unfortunately he could not prove that he was of UK origin.

He had been born in Kenya at a time when the country was not even a Colony but a Protectorate; his father was born in France, and he was unable to trace the place of birth of his paternal grandfather, James Shirley Leakey. James Shirley's father James Leakey, RA (1775–1865), known as 'the Devon artist', had lived in Exeter for most of his life, but the local clergy were unable to find any entry in the parish records concerning the birth of his son in 1824. Louis then wrote to the Librarian and Town Clerk of Exeter, who discovered that James had been away between 1821 and 1825. It appeared that during at least part of that time he had been painting in France, so it seemed likely that his son had been born there.

Louis then appealed for help to Mr Malcolm MacDonald, who wrote a personal letter to the Home Secretary, Sir Frank Soskice. Mr MacDonald has kindly allowed me to quote from it:[5]

> I venture to trouble you to give your personal attention to a Kenya citizenship question which arises in the case of Dr Louis Leakey, the very distinguished archaeologist who lives in Nairobi and works throughout East Africa. I presume to write to you personally because I believe this is a matter of great importance not only to Dr Leakey, but to the whole British community in Kenya. Dr Leakey, like a considerable number of other prominent members of the British community here, wishes to become a Kenya citizen before Kenya becomes a Republic on December 12th. It is to be hoped that his example will be followed by a large number of Europeans and Asians who have their homes and futures here. This I believe to be very important for the future of Kenya and for good relations between all races in the country.
>
> The right which has been given by the British Nationality Act 1964 to persons of United Kingdom origin to resume citizenship of the United Kingdom, if unhappily anything goes badly wrong here, has played a large part in persuading leading members of the British community to take the step of becoming Kenya citizens. Unfortunately, although Dr Leakey and his forebears are as English as anyone, he does not qualify under that Act, by reason of the accident that neither he, his father nor his father's father was born in the United Kingdom. . . .
>
> Under Section 1 of the Act you, as the Secretary of State concerned, have a discretion to permit resumption of United Kingdom citizenship in the case of a person who does not qualify as of right. Were it not for the rather special circumstances of his case, Dr Leakey

25. *Above* The Leakeys' work was a family business – and that included the Dalmatians. Eleven-year-old Philip watches his parents excavate the 'pre-Zinj' living site at Olduvai, discovered by Jonathan in 1960

26. *Below* Mary with Simon, the Sykes monkey, whose tricks made him appreciated by few outside the Leakey family

27. The Sonjo, who live in the country round Lake Natron, watch the RAF's big bird laying 'eggs' – Land Rovers for Richard's expedition

28. *Below* The Peninj jaw – 'Zinj' Mark II — was found among these formidable gullies above Lake Natron in 1964

would be quite content to take his chance that, if subsequently he had to apply for resumption of United Kingdom citizenship, a future Secretary of State would regard his case as one which came within the spirit if not the precise letter of the Act. But Dr Leakey, by reason of his highly specialized knowledge of the Kikuyu tribe, played a very important part in the security operations during the Emergency in Kenya before Independence. This was a duty which was thrust upon him as a patriotic subject, and one which he performed with distinction. In consequence of this he has an apprehension, which I believe to be reasonably well founded, that if in due course extremist political leaders were to gain control in this country, he might be seriously victimized. . . .

If you were satisfied that Dr Leakey is a person who would be likely to be given the benefit of your discretion, if he ever applied for resumption of United Kingdom citizenship, would it be possible for him now to be given some official assurance on those lines, and also an assurance that his application would be considered and decided quickly if the need arose? . . . I have referred above to the possibility of 'extremist' political leaders gaining control of this country at some time in the future. They are the only people who might feel some stored-up animosity against Dr Leakey for the reasons that I have given. Mr Jomo Kenyatta and his principal Ministers in the present Government feel no such unfriendliness towards him. On the contrary, they like and admire him greatly as a person, and for his outstanding and world-famous work in East Africa; and they will be very pleased if he can become a Kenya citizen.

In his reply the Home Secretary stated that, while he could not commit himself as to the way in which discretion might be exercised in the future, a fairly clear indication had been given by Lord Derwent to the House of Lords.[6] The relevant extract from the official report of 12 March 1964 read as follows:

It is impossible to say in advance in what types of case resumption of nationality will be allowed. The essential thing is that applicants must have a strong connection with the United Kingdom. . . . It may well be that a man's great-grandfather or great-great-grandfather was born in this country, but not his father or his grandfather, and he may still have strong connections with this country – business connections, or children at school here – and such a case would undoubtedly be viewed sympathetically.

Louis could claim no such connections; but the situation was saved by his brother Douglas, who by now had left the Forestry Department in Kenya and, with his wife Beryl, had retired to Devon, the land of his forefathers. Douglas discovered that their grandfather James Shirley was buried at Le Havre and that the gravestone bore the following inscription: '*Enterré ici repose le corps de James Shirley Leakey, homme de lettres anglais né à Exeter, Angleterre, le 9 Octobre 1824, mort au Havre le 31 Aout 1871.*' There it was, indelibly engraved, 'born in Exeter'! Mr MacDonald forwarded these particulars and an officer in the Commonwealth Relations Office replied: 'The new evidence contained in Dr Leakey's letter may be accepted as establishing that he will be entitled to resume United Kingdom citizenship if he so chooses and that the register in which you recorded his renunciation of citizenship may be endorsed accordingly.'[7] Happily the need never did arise, and Louis held a Kenya passport for the rest of his life.

Perhaps it would be an exaggeration to suggest that Louis thought of England as 'home' like so many expatriates; yet curiously enough considering his upbringing and his love of Kenya he had strong emotional ties with the mother country. The years at Cambridge and the British scientists with whom he had worked during the early part of his career had made a lasting impression. Although he was all in favour of independence for Kenya, when it actually happened he found it quite difficult to adjust to *harambee* (togetherness); for example, he would never have considered taking on an African secretary so long as he could get work permits for Europeans.

If Louis had reservations, his sons, who had never known any home other than Kenya, had no such divided loyalties; they were delighted with their new citizenship and, unlike Louis, wanted no safeguards about resuming British nationality if the need ever arose. Richard in particular is far more of a 'White African' than Louis ever was; after he had made his name he was featured in *Life* (12 September 1969) and was reported as saying: 'People say that the white man has no future in Kenya. That's rubbish. But if he has a white face, he must have a black mind.' More than thirty years earlier his father had expressed the view (in his book *Kenya:*

Contrasts and Problems) that there was no future for white men in Kenya, and had got into trouble over it.

Tanzania had gained her independence in December 1961, two years before Kenya, and at first the Government had plenty of weightier matters than fossils to occupy their attention; but by 1964 the new National Museum in Dar es Salaam had come into existence, and there was need for material to fill it. An observer said in April of that year: 'The new museum is unbelievable. For the past week it has been exhibiting one monitor lizard. Nothing else!' However, progress was rapid, and a special strongroom was being constructed to house the star turn, Zinj, and other fossils from Olduvai.

As a result of Louis's recommendations Olduvai had been declared a scientific reserve as long ago as 1932. At that time there were no restrictions on the ultimate disposal of the finds, and Louis had given fossils to the BM, to museums in Cambridge, Oxford and Paris, and of course to the Coryndon Museum. After 1945 the permit to excavate stipulated that a proportion of the finds was to be sent to the museum in Dar es Salaam as soon as it was in a position to exhibit them and care for them properly.

Under British administration no one had been particularly concerned about where the fossils were housed, but after independence the Government tried to insist that material should not be taken out of the country at all. Louis, however, had no difficulty in producing good reasons for stalling: the necessary comparative material and literature were not available in Dar es Salaam, nor were there any trained laboratory technicians, and all these he had at the Centre in Nairobi. Then, under the Antiquities Act of 1964, regulations were tightened; permits stated that finds might be taken out of Tanzania for study only for such periods as the minister concerned might specify. How could a non-scientist be expected to understand that it was impossible to specify a definite period? It was hard enough to find an appropriate palaeontologist to study each particular group of fossils; to impose a time limit was completely unrealistic, since each specialist had to fit the work in with his other commitments.

Phillip Tobias's monumental study of Zinj had taken nearly four years to complete, as he had had to do it in the intervals of his administrative and teaching duties at the University of the Witwatersrand. By the end of 1964 it was finished, and Zinj could at last return to the land of his birth. The air conditioned strong-room was ready to receive him, and Louis was well pleased with it: it would be the envy of most curators in America, he said. For Zinj was not to be on show to the public, who had to be content with a cast. This is by no means unusual with type specimens – those named as new species; but imagine the outcry if the most valuable pictures in the National Gallery were kept in vaults and only copies were on view!

A formal ceremony for the handing over was proposed which, Louis hoped, would impress upon the Government the fact that the skull was of international importance and must be treated with respect. President Nyerere agreed to receive it in person on 26 January 1965; and Zinj was insured for £30,000 to cover the period of his travels. A number of big names representing top scientific institutions were invited: the Royal Society of London, the National Academy of Sciences in Washington, the Académie des Sciences of Paris, the Academia Sinica of Peking, the Soviet Academy of Sciences. The National Geographic Society, Zinj's godfathers, was represented by Dr Melvin Payne.

One person whom Louis was particularly anxious to invite was Phillip Tobias, who had spent so much time on the final reconstruction of the skull. The Tanzanian Government was not on speaking terms with the Government of South Africa, but they agreed that, although he might not represent the University of the Witwatersrand or any other organization, he might come as a private individual. Science, in this case, rose above politics.

No less than three hundred and fifty guests were invited, and the arrangements were handled most skilfully by Hamo Sassoon, Conservator of Antiquities for Tanzania. Mary, as the finder, actually presented Zinj to President Nyerere; but she managed to avoid making a speech, which Louis did on behalf of both of them. Nor did the President make a speech, leaving this to his Minister of Community Development and National Culture. There were congratulatory orations by the representatives of the various foreign scientific institutions, a tour of the Museum for the VIPs, a cocktail party, and finally a public lecture by Louis. It was quite a day.

After Dr Payne and two other members of the NGS who attended the ceremony returned to Nairobi, they were joined by the entire research committee. Richard organized a safari, taking them to various National Parks as well as Olduvai, Olorgesailie and Fort Ternan. Louis and Mary accompanied them, as well as Jonathan and his wife Mollie, and in the words of the Society's notes on the inspection tour 'they were not only most knowledgeable about all phases of East Africa but also extremely co-operative, helpful and congenial'. The research committee was obviously impressed by the people, as well as the work, that they were supporting.

Not long after the Zinj ceremony the University of East Africa conferred upon Louis an honorary doctorate – one of the first to be bestowed by the new University. Louis received it in Dar es Salaam in August from the chancellor, Dr Julius Nyerere.

On 9 December Zinj came back into the limelight by appearing on a Tanzanian postage stamp. The background to the skull was based on a photograph taken the previous year of the excavations at MNK at Olduvai; it includes the unmistakable figure of Louis in his boiler suit, as well as Mary, Heselon, and Dr and Mrs Melville Grosvenor of the National Geographic Society who were visiting Olduvai at the time. First day covers were much in demand by collectors, and by mailing them the Leakeys made a small profit which was put into the research funds.

By the end of June 1965 the annual grant from the Ford Foundation for the running of the Centre came to an end. Louis was particularly worried about the staff, who had been given provisional notice from time to time because of the uncertainty of the financial position. Always in the nick of time he had managed to prevent the complete collapse of the Centre, but there was now an urgent need to increase the staff's salaries.

Also, the place was bursting at the seams with all the material pouring in from the Miocene sites, from Olduvai and from

Olorgesailie. In 1964 the Wenner-Gren Foundation had given money to build a new laboratory to be called the Fejos Memorial Laboratory in memory of the Foundation's director of research, Dr Paul Fejos, who had signed the recommendation for the grant just before he died. The building was put up quickly, and before the end of the year it was opened by his attractive and extremely competent widow Lita (now Mrs Osmundsen) who succeeded him as director of research.

When Dr Payne and other members of the NGS research committee visited the Centre a few weeks later, they were horrified to see Mary trying to cope with huge numbers of stone tools in 'a couple of closets'. They therefore recommended the erection of yet another new laboratory especially for the study of material from Olduvai. By the end of the year this building, adjoining the Fejos Laboratory, was opened by Dr Payne in the presence of Kenya's Minister for Education – Louis's old friend Mr Mbiyu Koinange.

Two new laboratories did not satisfy Louis, and he planned to expand even further by setting up an entirely new department of comparative osteology. Nowhere in Africa was there a truly representative collection of skeletons of modern animals, without which it was impossible to make studies of the fossil forms. Louis had been brooding over the idea of building up such a collection for some time; and in the summer of 1965 he brought it to the attention of an international gathering in Austria, where the Wenner-Gren Foundation held a symposium.

When Lita Fejos invited him to attend she had asked him to prepare a complete inventory of the Miocene and Pleistocene fauna of East Africa. Louis was horrified: he was in the middle of excavations at Fort Ternan, and said in reply: 'I am preparing very lengthy papers dealing with some 40 genera and species, the vast majority new to science and only two of them so far described in print.' (These finds are described later.) He added that it was 'wholly premature to ask for such an inventory at the present time. . . . It was for these and other reasons that I most urgently suggested that this year was too early for this particular conference'.[8] Although it was inconvenient for Louis, it suited about forty other scientists; not unnaturally the conference went ahead.

It took all Lita Fejos's tact and charm to induce Louis to get the lists done. When he had a particularly time-consuming job like this he would throw it at Shirley Coryndon at the BM; he did so now, and the inventory of faunas was duly completed in time for the conference, while Louis himself produced some brief notes. He then changed his mind several times as to whether he would attend in person; but in the end he did go for the first week, which concerned palaeontology, while Mary went only for the third week and contributed an important paper on Olduvai to the archaeological section. There were some tricky moments in some of the sessions when Louis disagreed with other delegates, but tact was exercised and Louis's prickles were smoothed.

With anyone else such behaviour both before and during the conference would have been intolerable; but because of Louis's personality, and the fact that he was the grand old man of African prehistory, his *prima donna* conduct was forgiven. In the idyllic surroundings and comfort of the Wenner-Gren Foundation's Austrian castle, Burg Wartenstein, it would be difficult not to thaw; off duty, Louis was the life and soul of the party, performing conjuring tricks and thoroughly enjoying himself.

Pushed hard by Louis, one of the resolutions made at the symposium was to establish one or more centres containing study collections of skeletons of modern animals to assist palaeontological research: 'It has been noted that Dr Leakey is already developing plans for one such comparative anatomy centre . . . and it is recommended that every possible support and encouragement be given to this Centre.'[9]

The Wenner-Gren Foundation lost little time in giving support and encouragement – to the tune of $20,000. This was enough to erect and equip a laboratory attached to the Centre in Nairobi; and the balance covered the initial costs of staffing and starting a collection. But the Wenner-Gren people made it quite clear that they were not committed to further funding; like the Centre itself the Department of Osteology was to be Louis's direct responsibility, and was to cause him just as much worry and effort to keep it solvent. Meanwhile, after the Ford Foundation grant for the Centre came to an end, Louis raised at different times money from the National Science Foundation, the Rockefeller

Foundation and the Royal Little Foundation; the last two helped also with grants for the Department of Osteology, and Louis also got funds for it from the Vincent Astor Foundation.

No time was lost over building the new department, which was opened in June 1966. The Game Department was asked to send in any carcasses they came across or report their whereabouts so that they could be collected. Rather naturally the Nairobi City Council insisted that the animals should be boiled outside the City boundaries, so a building was acquired for this purpose at Tigoni, near Limuru. Tanks big enough to boil an elephant were installed, and four men were engaged as skinners and boilers.

The aim was to acquire complete skeletons of every vertebrate species in East Africa – not just one of each but fifteen, in order to show age and sex differences and individual variations. By the end of the first year a thousand skeletons had been boiled, cleaned and stored. Hippo skeletons poured in from Murchison Falls National Park in Uganda, crocodiles were collected from Lakes Victoria, Baringo and Rudolf; Louis even got the senior game warden at Addis Ababa to arrange for the collection of rare Ethiopian species such as the mountain nyala.

As had happened with the Centre, within a year of its formation the Department of Osteology was thoroughly overcrowded. Once again Louis expanded, getting a grant from the Rockefeller Foundation for yet another new building.

In the summer of 1966 Richard and Margaret Cropper got married. They had fallen for each other in the romantic setting of Lake Natron and shared the same interests; they seemed to have everything in common except, as it turned out, temperament. But for the moment it seemed the perfect match.

Soon after their marriage they embarked on a palaeontological expedition to Lake Baringo, quite close to Jonathan's home at Kampi ya Samaki (Fish Camp). In the course of mapping the area John Martyn, a young geologist from Bedford College, London, had found fossils which included an almost complete skeleton of a primitive kind of elephant, and Richard and Margaret were summoned to remove this giant relative of the 'woolly mammoth'. They did an excellent job, encasing the bones in plaster of Paris and transporting the huge block back to Nairobi for exhibition in the Museum. Other fossils included a new species of Colobus monkey and a large extinct baboon; Richard described these in his first scientific paper, published in the first volume of a new series edited by Louis, *Fossil Vertebrates of Africa.*[10]

After their return to Nairobi Richard and Margaret worked voluntarily at the Centre, where Richard took charge of the administrative work during Louis's frequent absences abroad. As he had already shown in his safari business, Richard proved to have a flair for administration; perhaps for the first time Louis began to realize that he had an obvious successor.

Meanwhile Louis's ego received a tremendous boost by a most unexpected letter which gave him enormous pleasure. In October 1966 the Master of St John's asked if he would accept an honorary fellowship.[11] Louis said in reply:

> Your letter was a delightful surprise and I feel very honoured that my College wants me as an Honorary Fellow. I readily and gratefully accept. I have always been very grateful indeed to St John's College for the wonderful support I was given, both as a student, then as a research student, and finally as a research fellow, when few people believed that East Africa could be expected to make any contribution to the study of human evolution.[12]

Intellectually and for reasons of prestige Louis would have got more satisfaction if he had been elected to the Royal Society, but emotionally he was even prouder of this gesture from the college which had nurtured him and later spurned him: the wheel had turned full circle since the days of Kanam and the divorce.

While Richard was making his name in wildest Africa, Louis travelled further afield in the concrete jungles of America. There, for the first time in his life, he found abundant support, both moral and financial. Every year the NGS paid his fare to Washington where he held a Press conference to announce the latest discoveries. After that he travelled all round the States giving as many lectures as he could fit in; sometimes he gave them for absurdly small fees, but each appearance helped to build up the public image. Medals, honorary degrees and visiting professorships fell like autumn leaves as his work at last obtained wide recognition, largely through the NGS's brilliant publicity in the post-Zinj era.

In the magnificently illustrated pages of the *National Geographic* millions of readers got to know about 'Finding the world's earliest man' (*sic:* Zinj) in 1960; 'Exploring 1,750,000 years into man's past' (1961); 'Adventures in the search for man' (1963); 'The Leakeys of Africa' (1965). Above all there was the film 'Dr Leakey and the dawn of man' about Olduvai, the discoveries and the discoverers. Quote, from a scene showing Louis bumping along in a Land-Rover: 'Committed to a lonely quest in a savage land, Dr Louis Leakey has thrived on a diet of dust and heat and hardship.' People expect their heroes to endure hardship, and it was this aspect in particular that caught on. Also, the quest for man's origins had a tremendous appeal at that time as a form of escapism from the troubles of the present. This hour-long TV spectacular, put on by the Columbia Broadcasting System, was seen by an estimated 26 million Americans in November 1966. Louis's benefactor Mr Leighton Wilkie wrote: 'It was a smash hit and was the most talked about program that has been on the air for a long time.' As another correspondent put it, Louis became 'very big in this country' overnight.

As an example of the sort of itinerary that he undertook in the USA we may cite his lecture tour in January–March 1967; it was the most strenuous yet, and as a result he had a warning that he was asking the impossible of his long-suffering constitution. In the middle of January he went to Israel in connection with a dig for which he was helping to raise funds. On 21 January he dined in hall at St John's to say thank you for his honorary fellowship. He lectured in London on 23 January, and next day went to Paris for a meeting, returning to London the same evening. A few days later he was in America, speaking at Duke University on January 29, at the Virginia Polytechnic Institute next day, and at the Academy of Natural Sciences, Philadelphia, the day after. The following evening he spoke at a gala dinner in New York sponsored by the Tanzania Community Development Committee and the World Wild Life Fund; the $15,000 raised was divided equally between the World Wild Life Fund and Louis's monkey research centre at Tigoni (Chapter 12). The next night he lectured at a Wenner-Gren Foundation supper conference; on February 5 he was in Chicago, two days later at the University of Colorado, Boulder.

All this was but a prelude to the main tour. Between February 8 and 28 he lectured at fifteen different Junior State Colleges in California under the auspices of CAPES (College Association for Public Events), for a fee of $500 per lecture. CAPES wrote to Louis afterwards to say that their community service directors had been unanimous in their reports that 'you were the finest speaker they have ever had and that you drew the largest audiences ever'.[13] Students flocked to hear him, queued for tickets, stood or sat on the floor. Louis was the elder statesman and they hung on his every word, even if they could not always understand his English pronunciation; he had a message for youth, and he generally ended his talk on an optimistic note for the future.

After this marathon tour Louis lectured at Riverside on March 3 and on the following day, when he was due to speak at the Chicago Academy of Sciences, he collapsed on arrival at O'Hare airport. Even for a younger man such an itinerary would have been too much; Louis was sixty-three. The first newspaper reports were alarmist and suggested a heart attack, others said it was an embolism, both of which Louis indignantly denied: 'I collapsed from fatigue,' he said. In fact, sheer exhaustion may have brought on one of his epileptic fits. Then, in lifting him on to a stretcher, the ambulance men injured his back; Louis was far more upset about this than about his collapse.

About this time Richard's powers of diplomacy were revealed in negotiations with the Tanzania Government over the return of Olduvai fossils. Having got Zinj they were now agitating to get everything else to which they were entitled under the 1964 Antiquities Act. Louis was in an absolute frenzy at the idea of parting with 'his' precious collections; but he had sat on them for a very long time and could not go on indefinitely making the excuse that the material was being studied. Some, at least, of the Tanzania Government's claims were fully justified, and it was important to show willing and meet some of the demands, as otherwise permission to excavate might be withheld.

For reasons of prestige the Government was particularly concerned about type specimens. So far they only had one 'type' besides Zinj. The British Museum had fifteen type fossils from Olduvai, including most of the pigs; and from pre-war collections there were four types in Munich and six in Berlin, notably *Elephas recki*, *Pelorovis oldowayensis*, *Equus oldowayensis* and *Hippopotamus gorgops*. No wonder that Tanzania was feeling left out in the cold – it was almost as bad as the rape of the Elgin marbles or the Benin bronzes.

To go into the whole question a meeting was arranged in Dar es Salaam on 31 March 1967; and Louis, perhaps realizing that he might find it difficult to be dispassionate, actually agreed to letting Richard go in his place. The meeting was held in the office of the Principal Secretary of the Ministry of Community Development and National Culture; and those present included the Commissioner for Culture, a representative from the Treasury, the Conservator for Antiquities, the chairman of the trustees and the curator of the National Museum of Tanzania. Against such a battery of big guns Richard managed to hold his own very successfully.

He was asked to provide lists of *all* material from Olduvai: cultural collections, fauna and hominids. Richard pointed out that a good many had already been sent, but apparently they had been 'mislaid'. Not only did the Tanzanians require the names of every specimen, but also catalogue number, provenance, year excavated, present whereabouts, by whom studied, and date of publication (if any). Richard said what an admirable idea: he would be delighted to compile a card index if only he had the staff to do so. However, he agreed to provide as much information as possible.

For their part the government representatives said that every effort would be made to improve the facilities of the Museum so that in future the Olduvai material could be studied within the country. Louis must have groaned when he heard this: where in Tanzania would they find specialists to study the pigs, hippos or any other group of fossils? Where would they find a Tobias to study the hominids?

Less than a fortnight after the meeting the Principal Secretary, Mr F. J. Mchauru, acknowledged receipt of the first lists sent by Richard: 'I must congratulate you on your speedy attention to this matter,' he wrote, adding that he was searching for the missing lists which had been sent to his predecessor.[14] It was not in the least surprising that they had got lost in view of the administrative tangles and rapid changes of responsibility with which Louis had had to contend in his dealings with the Government over Olduvai. At one moment he would be in communication with the Ministry of National Culture and Youth, the next with the Ministry of Community Development and National Culture, not to mention the Ministry of Agriculture, Forests and Wildlife, the curator of the National Museum, the conservator of Ngorongoro, and the Regional Commissioner. Many of these officials were exceedingly helpful and fully sympathized with his problems: one 'Permanent' (*sic*) Secretary, when he was moved on to another Ministry, wrote: 'Well, Louis, I must say I thoroughly enjoyed working with – or is it for – you, while it lasted.'[15]

On the whole Louis was not too unhappy about the outcome of the meeting in Dar, and admitted to Dr Melvin Payne that the attitude of the Tanzanians did not seem to be quite so fixed as he had feared.

As the National Geographic Society was so intimately connected with Olduvai, Louis would have liked Dr Payne, their vice-president, to have been present at the meeting. However, it might not have been altogether tactful for him to go to Dar: although the Tanzania Government was not in a position to contribute towards the excavations, there was no need to underline the fact that Olduvai was an American-sponsored project worked by Kenyans. Instead Dr Payne attended a follow-up meeting in Nairobi two months later, at which Louis and Mary were present as well as Richard. The Tanzanian team was much as before, except that in the meantime there had been a ministerial reshuffle.

Louis made an impassioned speech: *all* museums, he said, have to send their collections all over the world for study by specialists. The Tanzanian Government might feel that the return of material had been slow, but perhaps they did not quite realize the quantities involved: the artifacts from Beds I and II amounted to more than 32,000, and the fauna to over 50,000 specimens. It would be quite impossible to study all this material in Dar; it would require a lot of space and a lot of time, and Mary could not do the work without abandoning her home and family for years.

The Tanzanians were also concerned by the fact that the guides at Olduvai were Kenyans. The whole question of access of visitors had presented unbelievable difficulties. In 1966 the Tanzanian Government had agreed that entrance fees might be charged; but until Olduvai was declared a National Monument later in that year, guards and guides were not government servants and so could not collect fees on behalf of the Government. Months of revenue was lost beneath a tangle of red tape. The actual collecting of the money, however, was nothing compared with the complications of disposing of it. Fees had to be remitted to the Conservator of Ngorongoro, who then forwarded them to the appropriate Ministry in Dar es Salaam, who – eventually – reimbursed the Olduvai Protection account in the bank at Arusha. Louis was constantly having to pay guides' salaries out of his research account, or even out of his own pocket, and it took years of correspondence before the long loop via Dar was short-circuited.

Until the mid 1960s only the most intrepid visited Olduvai; but after the construction of the all-weather road between the tourist lodges at Ngorongoro and Seronera, which passes within a few miles of the Gorge, members of organized safaris began to call in increasing numbers. By 1966 there were nearly 5,500 visitors of 44 different nationalities. The large majority came from the USA, so the guides had to be English-speaking and their services were therefore more costly.

The high spot on the visitors' itinerary was, of course, FLK, where Zinj was found. The sites of all the other hominids are marked with a small concrete slab with their number, H1 etc; but Zinj has one the size of a tombstone inscribed 'The skull of

Australopithecus boisei (Zinjanthropus) was found here by M. D. Leakey July 17th, 1959.'

After doing his apprenticeship at Natron and Baringo, Richard got his toughest assignment yet in the Omo valley, north of Lake Rudolf in Ethiopia, in the summer of 1967. This marked the turning point in his career: after Omo he left the safari business to his partner and became a full-time anthropologist.

Fossils had been collected in the Omo valley as long ago as 1902 by a French expedition, and again in 1934 by Professor Camille Arambourg of Paris. Louis himself had been there briefly in the course of his gun-running in the Second World War, when he picked up a few fossils on the side. Then in 1959 Professor Clark Howell of the University of Chicago reached the Omo by Land-Rover from Kenya and spent a month there. He had a permit to collect fossils, but this information was not passed on to the nearest police post at Kalam – the radio operator had been unable to make contact; Howell therefore had to kick his heels for ten days before he was allowed to make a start. When he was ready to leave he was told that he could take no specimens out of the country without permission from Addis Ababa, so, having had experience of the delays likely to ensue, Howell got out. He left his boxes of fossils in charge of the governor of the province, but when he wrote asking to have them forwarded he got no reply.

Louis came into the story in 1966 when the Emperor of Ethiopia made a state visit to Nairobi. President Kenyatta gave a luncheon party for him at State House and, at the suggestion of Mr Malcolm MacDonald, Louis was invited. He chatted to the Emperor about his finds, and His Imperial Highness asked if anything comparable had been found in his country. Louis assured him that the material was there, but that it was very difficult to get permission to work it. Haile Selassie promised that if Louis would organize an international expedition to the Omo, he would give him every help by instructing his ministers and provincial governors to co-operate. Because of the previous interest of the French and Americans, he wanted them to take part in such an expedition, as well as a team from Kenya and representatives from Ethiopia. Louis later followed up this invitation by going personally to Addis Ababa, where he was received by the Emperor and held discussions with two of his ministers. Everything was arranged for the expedition to go to the Omo in June 1967 for three months. Louis sent a cable 'Omo OK' to Clark Howell, who had long ago given up hope of being able to return; he persuaded the National Geographic Society to sponsor the Kenya party; and he then went to Paris to tie up everything with Arambourg, the doyen of the expedition.

They agreed that the three teams should work in separate areas: eighty-two-year-old Arambourg naturally chose the southern portion where he had worked before; the Americans under Howell would be immediately to the north of the French; and Richard, who was to lead the Kenya team, was allocated a completely unknown area. This was to the north of the great bend in the Omo, on the opposite – eastern – side of the river to the French and Americans. It consisted of a long, winding strip about two miles wide – some hundred square miles of badlands, part heavily eroded sediments, part thick bush. It was by far the most difficult of the three sectors, but Richard had considerable experience of those sort of conditions. It took him two days to cover the last forty miles, but there were other things to contend with besides the terrain: bandits were notoriously trigger-happy on the eastern side of the river. The Kalam police made him take on ten armed guards, but he promptly unloaded five on to the French party and two on to the Americans. A worse problem was the river itself; Richard had hoped to tow the equipment on a raft behind a small motor boat, but the engine could not cope against the strong current and everything had to be ferried across in small loads.

Soon after their arrival they had their first adventure with the enormous crocodiles which haunt the Omo. Richard wrote to tell his parents about one which thrashed against the current straight at their small boat: 'We turned the boat and managed to glance it, but even so it shot straight out of the water and snapped at the side of the boat. Less than a mile upstream another giant started towards us at fantastic speed.'[16] The answer, obviously, was a boat

29. At the Centre in Nairobi, Richard shows the Peninj jaw to his parents and Dr Melvin Payne, then vice-president of the National Geographic Society which financed his expedition

30. *Top left* 'Zinj' featured on a Tanzanian postage stamp issued in December 1965; in the background, based on a photograph taken at Olduvai, are Louis, Mary, Heselon, and Dr and Mrs Melville Grosvenor of the National Geographic Society 31. *Top right* A picture in *New Scientist* of 6 April 1967 reflects the interest in Leakey discoveries – and Louis's incorrigible tendency to create new species for his finds. 32. *Directly above* On 26 January 1965 'Zinj' was handed over to the National Museum at Dar es Salaam; with Louis and Mary is Professor Phillip Tobias

that could move faster than the crocs, and the NGS promptly provided one. As soon as he heard about this incident Dr Payne cabled that a boat with more powerful engines was on its way: he was concerned about their lives. Richard had Margaret with him, as well as Bob Campbell; another member of the party was Allen O'Brien, future founder of the Leakey Foundation in Los Angeles, but to his everlasting regret he was not with the others when they were attacked. He has an affinity with crocs and is an expert on rivers; he had provided the rubber boats in which the equipment was ferried across.

Thanks to the new boat Richard was able to explore places impossible to reach by land. On 29 June Louis wrote to tell Dr Payne that Richard had reported on the radio telephone that he had reached some new exposures where they had found a fossil human skull and parts of a skeleton; the discoverer was Kamoya Kimeu, who had spotted the Zinj jaw at Lake Natron. A few weeks later Dr Paul Abell, an American chemist from Rhode Island University who was working with the Kenya team, found part of a second human skull, Omo II, on the opposite side of the river. The two specimens were very different, especially when viewed from the back; Omo I looks just like the skull of a robust modern man, whereas Omo II is broad-based, giving it a somewhat 'bull-necked' appearance. The first has rather prominent brow-ridges and a smooth curve at the back of the skull; the second is much longer, and has thicker walls, a lower vault, receding forehead, and a thick ridge at the back. The bones were beyond the range of carbon 14 dating, but oyster shells from just above the horizon containing the skulls gave an age of about 130,000 years when dated by the uranium/thorium method. Louis was absolutely delighted: he saw a *sapiens* line running from *Homo habilis* right through to Omo I, and what he called 'a more *erectus*-like sapient group' extending from 'George' of Olduvai Bed II through to Omo II.

Just before Omo II was found Louis flew up to have a look round himself. He landed at the strip near the American camp and then went on to the Kenya camp, across and up the river against the current. 'I amused myself by counting the crocodiles,' he wrote to Dr Payne.[17] 'I could see only the larger ones since the river is in many places more than a hundred yards wide. I counted 598 crocs, none of them less than seven or eight feet long and some nearly twenty feet.' Richard's camp, he explained, was on top of a cliff about 130 feet above the river; looking down, it was usually possible to see up to thirty crocs basking on the bank below. The next morning Louis looked at some of Richard's sites, in the afternoon they visited the Americans, and on the following day they flew by helicopter to the French camp, thirty-five miles away. Louis certainly saw the advantages of modern methods of transport: 'The helicopter', he said in the same letter to Dr Payne, 'used mainly by the US group, is paid for by the number of hours used. However, Richard and I are also paying for certain parts of the use of this helicopter and frankly the last ten days would have been almost impossible if it had not been available. I think we shall have to consider seriously having a helicopter next season, shared between the three groups'. Next season, in fact, there were to be only two groups: as a result of what Richard saw from the helicopter he went to East Rudolf instead.

By the end of that first season both the French and American teams had collected several australopithecine teeth, as well as abundant fossil mammals; and in the years to come the Omo expeditions were to go from strength to strength, opening a new era in palaeontological studies. But in the Kenyan sector, most of the deposits were considerably younger, and fossils were disappointingly sparse.

After the end of the 1967 season Richard went back to the Centre and rose in the hierarchy to the position of assistant director. The Centre was a hive of activity: the French and American contingents of the Omo expedition used it to study their collections; a number of visiting scientists were doing research on fossil mammals on Louis's behalf; and Mary, assisted by Margaret, was working flat out on the artifacts from the Bed I and Bed II living floors for her volume in the new Olduvai series.

Louis had summarized the state of knowledge on the Olduvai fauna in his book *Olduvai Gorge 1951–1961*, but by the time it was published in 1965 the new studies going on at the Centre already made some of it out of date. Tobias's monumental study of Zinj appeared in 1967 as the second volume in this series: *The cranium of Australopithecus (Zinjanthropus) boisei*. As editor, Louis had warned Tobias:

> I shall disagree *politely* with your theory that the common ancestor of *Homo habilis* and *Australopithecus* was an australopithecine rather than a hominine and shall also not agree with the concept of *Homo erectus* being derived from *Homo habilis*. . . . Otherwise I shall have nothing but praise for a truly magnificent job.[18]

When Mary saw the draft of Louis's editorial note for the volume she did not think he had disagreed politely enough; she persuaded him to modify the wording so that the question of a common ancestor was left open.

The 'hominine' ancestor referred to by Louis in his letter was, of course, *Kenyapithecus wickeri* from Fort Ternan; and, what is more, by this time he had produced what he regarded as an even earlier hominid.

Ever since the discovery of *Kenyanpithecus wickeri* in 1961 Heselon had carried on excavations at Fort Ternan year after year. The total number of specimens soared to nearly ten thousand, including many entirely new to science. Most fascinating were various kinds of peculiar animals on a miniature scale, for example a fully grown rhino no taller than a donkey. On one occasion Heselon wired to Louis that he had found an animal with horns like the branches of a tree: it turned out to be a relation of the giraffe, with antler-like appendages. There were also a great many fossil antelopes, the earliest known south of the Sahara.

Some of the bones were disjointed and scattered, but there were also curious concentrations of almost complete skeletons. Louis's ingenious explanation was that the animals had been overcome by sudden escapes of poisonous gases emanating from tectonic springs, and that at times so many had died that scavengers were unable to cope with them. In the Albert National Park in Zaire there were grassy depressions containing clear water known as *masuku*; usually the water was innocuous, but periodically it had disastrous effects. Louis went to see these *masuku* and was thrilled when, just as he was clicking his camera to photograph a hyena drinking, the animal dropped dead.

The man for whom *Kenyapithecus wickeri* was named, Fred Wicker, was intensely interested in what was going on on his farm and, inspired by all that Louis told him, decided that he must further his education. Although past forty years of age, he won a scholarship to Cambridge and Louis helped to get him into St John's. Wicker was toying with the idea of reading prehistory and palaeontology, but Louis dissuaded him: 'Of course the curriculum has changed a great deal since I was there,' he wrote:

> but I don't think you fully appreciate what I did in order to do the work that I am now doing. There is, of course, no single course of study which could fit a person to do what I am doing. I did a tripos in modern languages, then a tripos in archaeology and anthropology, and thereafter a post-graduate course in vertebrate zoology and geology, and then a year in anatomy at the Royal College of Surgeons which I combined with a course in meteorology.[19]

Wicker decided to stick to agriculture, botany and zoology, and the senior science tutor was so impressed by his exceptional ability that he proposed that he should go straight into research for an MSc without first taking an ordinary degree.

Wicker had engaged a manager to look after his farm while he was away, but things soon got out of control. Cattle were stolen, the house was broken into, and there never seemed to be enough money to pay the wages in spite of the fact that the orange trees were yielding good crops. On several occasions Louis helped out by lending money, but he could not go on subsidizing the farm indefinitely.

Wicker was determined to go through with his degree, even at the price of financial ruin. He tried unsuccessfully to sell his farm, which was eventually taken over by the Central Agricultural Board. By the time he got his PhD in 1968 and wanted to go back it was too late; he could only get a visitor's permit for Kenya, so he emigrated to South America. On Louis's recommendation the Government agreed to excise twenty-six acres containing the fossil site and hand them over to the trustees of the National Museum for protection as a scientific reserve.

Apart from its effect on the life of Fred Wicker the discovery of *Kenyapithecus wickeri* provoked renewed activity at the Lower Miocene sites of Rusinga and Songhor, where Louis hoped to find additional evidence of the hominid's ancestry. Apart from brief visits work had been discontinued there between 1954 and 1966 because all hands were concentrated at Olduvai and Fort Ternan; Louis now used money from the Boise Fund and the William H. Donner Foundation to resume the search. An American geologist, Dr John van Couvering, began mapping on Rusinga; and his wife Judy discovered a mandible of what Louis and Le Gros Clark had named '*Sivapithecus africanus*'. As early as 1948 they had noted that there was something curiously hominid-like about its upper jaw; now that Louis had the first known lower dentition of this creature, his impressions were immeasurably strengthened. At the Centre he began to search for overlooked or wrongly described specimens from the old collections, and from time to time he would pounce on a fragment of jaw or isolated tooth which he would allocate to '*Sivapithecus*'. In 1967, he renamed it *Kenyapithecus africanus:* not only was it a perfect ancestor for *Kenyapithecus wickeri*, but he could now claim to have found the earliest hominid in the world.[20]

That year a great deal of excavation was done at Fort Ternan. Among the finds were bones which had apparently been broken open deliberately, and an antelope's skull showing a depressed fracture; the damage, according to Louis, was of the type associated with the use of a blunt instrument. What is more he claimed to have found the actual weapon. In the middle of a fine-grained ancient soil, where the only large objects were fossils, lay a lump of lava with a battered edge. Louis sent off to *Nature* a paper entitled 'Bone smashing by late Miocene Hominidae' in which he said that the discoveries strongly suggested that *Kenyapithecus wickeri* 'was already making use of stones to break up animal skulls in order to get at the brain, and bones to get at the marrow'.[21] Here was more ammunition for the sceptics, but by now Louis was becoming fairly impervious to their onslaughts.

Dr Elwyn Simons, as already mentioned, had cast aspersions on the legitimacy of *Kenyapithecus*, and he then proceeded to demolish Louis's Lower Miocene apes one by one. *Proconsul* he regarded as a sub-genus of *Dryopithecus*, and the gibbon-like *Limnopithecus* he said was a species of *Pliopithecus*. Possibly Simons might be accused of excessive lumping, but Louis was certainly the arch-splitter: by 1968, he had distinguished at Fort Ternan representatives of no less than six different *families* – not merely genera – of higher primates![22] It was a bit much for primatologists to swallow.

In December 1967 the 6th Pan African Congress on Prehistory was held at Dakar; it was exactly twenty years since Louis had organized the first congress in Nairobi, and he had very much hoped that this one would also have been held there. 'I am not as young as I was,' he admitted to the reigning Secretary of the congress, 'and whereas I could reasonably hope to guide visiting colleagues to many important sites in 1967, it may be otherwise in 1971.'[23] Louis had been unable to get an official invitation from the Kenya Government for 1967, but it was not for want of trying. Up till the very last moment before he boarded the plane for Dakar he was hoping to get a favourable reply to his many enquiries so that he could announce the invitation at the congress; he also got Richard to do some diplomatic prodding while he was away, but without result. Louis still did not entirely give up hope and persuaded the standing committee of the congress to wait another two months before accepting an alternative invitation; but Nairobi stayed silent, and arrangements were made to hold the 1971 congress in Addis Ababa. No doubt the Kenya Government did not wish to commit themselves to a lot of expense in four years' time, any more than they did in 1967.

Louis did not like to be thwarted; he had usually been successful in twisting the arm of the colonial government, as when he had got money out of them year after year to support his Miocene research; but with the new regime things were very different. Perhaps this is one of the reasons why he turned his back on Kenya so often to cross the Atlantic. He was used to getting his own way and up till now he had usually got it, but even he could not have it both ways. As Louis spent so much time out of the country, Richard played an ever increasing part in the administration of the Centre. Thus a vicious circle developed, with Louis wanting to keep control in his own hands, yet at the same time having to absent himself to keep the Centre going by his fund-raising tours. He was also involved in all sorts of other enterprises at this time which needed even more money. Hc simply had to keep in the public eye, and he could not do this by sitting in Nairobi.

11 The Leakey Foundation

If the discovery of Zinj had been a turning point, several inter-related developments which took place in 1968 had an equally profound effect on the remaining four years of Louis's life. This was the year in which a hip operation put a brake on his physical activities; the year in which Richard became director of the National Museum and led his first expedition to East Rudolf; the year in which the Leakey Foundation was set up in Los Angeles. These events were inter-related because the operation made fieldwork impossible and Louis had to leave this to Mary and Richard, with the result that he became increasingly absorbed in the affairs of his foundation.

In January he went as usual to Washington to report to the NGS, but this time he was accompanied by Richard, who was very much involved in connection with Omo. At a meeting of the research committee Louis held forth for some time about plans for the coming season; the areas in which the American and Kenya parties had worked, he said, were not worth further effort, so in future all three would concentrate in the French area to the south. While this was going on Richard kept very quiet; he had no intention of being junior boy to the French and American professors or, as he put it, 'turning over the goodies to the PhDs.' At last Dr Grosvenor asked if he had anything to say. 'Yes,' said Richard, 'I don't want to go to Omo at all. I would like the money to work my own area at East Rudolf.' There was an appalled silence and then Louis muttered something about the impatience of youth. After recovering himself he pointed out that before committing the NGS to all that expenditure it would be as well to find out if there was anything worth working at East Rudolf. Richard had landed briefly by helicopter and said that the deposits looked hopeful, but they were a completely unknown quantity. The research committee retired to consider their verdict and found in favour of Richard. 'You can have the money,' Dr Grosvenor told him, 'but if you find nothing you are never to come begging at our door again.'

While this was going on in America, back in Africa Louis was being crossed by his wife. The incident in Washington may have been the beginning of the rift between father and son, but in the case of Mary one had been widening for some years, keeping pace with her growing independence and fame. The University of the Witwatersrand, prompted no doubt by Phillip Tobias, proposed to confer honorary doctorates of science on both Louis and Mary; it was probably unique, said the Vice-Chancellor, for a husband and wife to receive honorary degrees at the same time.[1]

Louis refused the honour and used all his powers of persuasion to try to make Mary do the same. Phillip Tobias was bitterly disappointed, but Louis wrote to him:

> I am afraid that you do not even faintly understand the situation as it affects me here. Whereas my own President and one or two of the other Ministers would be entirely favourable to my accepting such an honour from the University of the Witwatersrand, the effect on popular and public opinion would be very grave indeed here, and even more so in Tanzania. . . . Clearly if I accept I would become very closely associated (in the minds of some people) with that University which, in spite of the wishes of its governing body and authorities generally, does in fact practise apartheid.[2]

(In his speech when he had received an honorary doctorate from the University of East Africa in 1965 Louis had said: 'People frequently ask me why I devote so much time to seeking out facts about man's past. . . . The past shows clearly that we all of us have a common origin and that our differences in race and colour and creed are only superficial.')

Mary was not concerned with politics and went ahead, receiving her degree in Johannesburg on 30 March. Louis was deeply hurt at this breach of family loyalty and unity. It is symbolic of Mary's detachment from Louis's new life that she should have been in South Africa when he was about to go to London for an operation.

For years he had suffered from osteo-arthritis in his hip, but he would never take the time to do anything about it until forced to by the agony he was enduring. At last he agreed to have a plastic joint, which was put in at the Catholic Nursing Home in south London on 4 April. Three weeks later the traction was taken off, and by the middle of May he was out of hospital, hobbling on crutches. He recuperated in London for one week, after which he flew to Washington for physiotherapy. For several hours a day he did exercises, with long sessions lying on his back; but after ten days of this routine he insisted on keeping dates with the Leakey Foundation people in Los Angeles. He should have had physiotherapy for much longer, and he should have kept up his exercises conscientiously, which he did not do. To reduce the strain on the hip he was put on to a strict diet, which was hard to bear as he loved good food, but he did make heroic efforts to lose weight. This was about the only concession he made to his disability.

He did not manage to get away from the United States until the end of July, after which he spent ten days in England and finally got back to Kenya by the middle of August. He had been away for four months.

A good deal had been going on in his absence. Louis was particularly sad to miss the retirement ceremony of his age-group contemporary Heselon Mukiri, who was presented with a diploma and $1,000 on behalf of the National Geographic Society. Heselon made a moving speech, saying how much his friendship and lifelong association with the Leakey family had meant to him.

After a dormant period of four years Mary had resumed excavations at Olduvai. With the advent of tourists *en masse* she moved her camp away from the guides' huts on the north side of the main gorge to its present position on the opposite side, well off the beaten track. The research, as mentioned earlier, had gone through three periods: the exploratory phase, which lasted for twenty years; the excavations, beginning in 1951 and culminating in the discovery of Zinj in 1959; and the four years of intensive work which were the result of having adequate funds for the first time. The year 1968 opened the fourth and current phase, which began with the discovery of the last important skull to come to light at Olduvai so far. This was 'Twiggy', H24, the earliest hominid of all, coming from the base of Bed I and dated by potassium/argon to 1.9 million years. About 300 yards from the stone circle at DK a workman picked up a lime concretion containing bones. At first Louis thought it was a baboon skull – he likened its appearance to a broken egg, with bits of eggshell sticking out in all directions. It took six months to extract Twiggy from her shell, and another year to reconstruct her to presentable shape. She got her name because she was squashed flat, not because of her decidedly retroussé profile – but it is undeniable that this also gave her a distinct resemblance to the reigning fashion model of the day.

When Louis defined the new species *Homo habilis* in 1964, one of the criteria had been that 'the facial skeleton is not concave or dished as is common in members of the Australopithecinae.' Now if anyone was concave or dished it was Twiggy; and yet Mary described her as a *habilis* in a paper in *Nature* in 1969[3], and two years later in a joint paper she and Louis said she was 'clearly not an australopithecine.'[4]

The cause of the trouble was the super-masculine Zinj in all his robustness; if in 1959 Mary had happened to find a Mrs Zinj, the differences between australopiths and 'habilines' would have been much less apparent. Richard's finds at East Rudolf, as well as those from the Omo valley, were to support the evidence from Olduvai that two different types of hominid co-existed in the Lower Pleistocene, as Louis always maintained. But one man's *Homo* is another man's *Australopithecus*, and in Richard's publications he used the latter name exclusively for the robust, Zinj-like type and his more delicately built female counterparts. The Leakeys did not recognize a distinct 'gracile' species of australopith in East Africa, the type which is known in South Africa as *Australopithecus africanus*.

During those four months while Louis was away in the summer of 1968 Richard was officially appointed administrative director of the National Museum. For some time Louis had been putting forward a persuasive case for such an appointment before the trustees, but the main difficulty had been to find a suitable title. There was already an acting director in the form of Bob Carcasson, and, as Richard was only twenty-three, it may be imagined that Carcasson was not too happy about his position vis-à-vis a prospective co-director. However, the problem was solved by his decision to leave Kenya, and Richard's appointment was duly announced at a trustees' meeting on 17 May. Louis was delighted; the running of the Centre was still in his own hands, so there was no question of competition.

Within a few weeks the new administrative director was off on his first historic expedition to East Rudolf. In addition to Richard and Margaret, the party included Dr Paul Abell, the photographer Bob Campbell, a palaeontologist named John Harris, two African assistants and a cook. The security situation was bad, with well-armed bands of raiders roaming the area, so the expedition was accompanied by a 34-man escort with machine guns, sandbags and other war-like equipment.

Lake Rudolf was discovered in 1888 by the Hungarian Count Teleki, who named it after Prince Rudolf of Austria. The lake is shaped rather like a boomerang, with Allia Bay forming the waist on the eastern side. To the north of this bay is a sharp point called Koobi Fora, a name known to only a handful of people before Richard put it on the map by making it the centre of his operations and eventually establishing his permanent camp there. During the Second World War the District Commissioner at Marsabit, the nearest administrative post, sent Louis a sketch map of the area north-east of Lake Rudolf which included the name 'Kubi Fur'.[5] Louis asked if he could send 'a native collector who has worked at Omo' to look for fossils there, but the answer was 'no', as it was unadministered country. After the war he never managed to pursue the matter, as the logistics of mounting an expedition would have been too difficult and costly.

Few prehistorians are blessed, like Richard, with a camp situated beside miles and miles of sand, populated only by a magnificent variety of water birds and basking, harmless, fish-eating crocodiles. The water feels slightly slimey, but it is not at all unpleasant for swimming. Huge herds of zebra wade right out into the lake up to their necks to cool off, but the even more numerous topi are landlubbers and watch from the shore. It is very hot, but the temperature is made bearable by a strong wind – often too strong for comfort.

One form of transport well suited to negotiate the sand is a camel, although Richard denies that it is the best. He used camels for reconnaissance in 1969, and a picture of him mounted on one of these beasts, pipe firmly gripped between the teeth and looking somewhat apprehensive, was to become a favourite with magazine editors. In an article in *Life*, it appeared under the apparently incongruous heading 'On safari with a man called Ostrich', which is Richard's native name because he is so tall and angular.[6] However, scientists are usually in too much of a hurry to adapt to the leisurely pace of a camel, preferring to churn through the sand in a Land-Rover.

Koobi Fora is nearly six hundred miles from Nairobi, and the party took five days to get there; they were lucky if they did more than sixty miles a day, but recently the last part of the road has been much improved and the journey can be done in one long and exhausting twenty-four hours.

After six weeks, half way through the season, Richard wrote an interim report to the National Geographic Society. His team had discovered fossil-bearing sediments covering an area of well over two thousand square miles, with fauna as old as, and apparently some of it even older than, that of Olduvai and Omo. They had found two fragmentary australopithecine jaws, as well as some bits of skull of a different kind of hominid. Already the National Geographic Society's faith in Richard was fully justified. Louis, on receiving a copy of the report, merely commented in a brief note to Richard 'It is most interesting'; but when he actually saw the fossils he was really excited.

Louis overlapped with Richard in Nairobi for two months and then he was off again, leaving a letter which read: 'This is to inform anyone concerned that I, L. S. B. Leakey, authorize my son, Richard E. Leakey, to act on my behalf in all urgent administrative and scientific matters at the Centre for Prehistory and Palaeontology where a decision must be taken quickly. He will, in fact, have the position of Acting Honorary Director for the Centre during my absence.'

Louis's first port of call was a London hospital for manipulation of his hip. He was very stiff and could hardly hobble; in spite of his dieting the joint had had to bear far too much weight and, in addition, Louis had abused it in a series of mishaps. Only ten weeks after the operation he had had a nightmare and thought the room was on fire; in jumping out of bed he gave the unhealed joint a nasty jolt, which caused him a good deal of pain. Then, a few months later, when he was beginning to walk reasonably well, he slipped on a wet London street and in saving himself from being run down by a bus he again damaged his hip. The third accident took place after his return to Nairobi: a student telephoned at night to say that an African assistant was unconscious and had been taken to hospital, and when Louis hurried out of the house at Langata to go to see him one of his metal sticks snapped. He fell hard on to the concrete, further delaying the recovery of the maltreated joint.

Louis had incredible courage; he never let up, walking at maximum possible speed with his two sticks. He even stumped over the gullies at Olduvai and clambered about at Fort Ternan, still with that eager look in his eye as though he expected to fall over a hominid at any moment. He was absolutely determined not to be beaten by his disability and kept going through sheer will power. He even insisted on driving a car, to the terror of some of his passengers. Michael Day, the anatomist who studied the *habilis* foot bones and subsequently many of Richard's finds, tells of an incident one night on the outskirts of Nairobi when Louis was showing off his new Volvo. They were flagged down at a road block by police armed with rifles, but Louis merely greeted them volubly in Kikuyu and drove off at high speed, his head still sticking out of the window. Sweeping down the middle of the road, he knocked down several red lights and thought it a huge joke.

After manipulation of his hip in London, in that crowded year Louis put in a month as 'professor at large' at Cornell University, Ithaca. Only the title was a novelty; the duties were the same as those he had performed with such success at Riverside in 1963, and again as visiting professor at the University of Illinois for six weeks in 1965. The post of professor at large at Cornell had been inaugurated in 1865 – the first incumbent was the great geologist Louis Agassiz – and was revived in 1965 to celebrate the University's centenary. Visiting professors, 'scholars of the very highest international distinction', were elected for a period of six years and were expected to stay on the campus for not less than two weeks every three years. There were never more than eighteen professors at large at any one time, six being appointed at two-yearly intervals.

After the election of the first batch in 1965 Louis's name came up for the second list two years later. He was appointed in these glowing terms:

> Be it known that the Board of Trustees of Cornell University elects Louis S. B. Leakey, an explorer of the distant past, probing with large learning the quiet depths of Africa's space which to the anthropologist is also time, who has indeed discovered the ancestors of Adam, ordered and named them, giving us and our posterity new progenitors.

In addition to prestige, from Louis's point of view there were several obvious advantages in accepting, not least the stipend of $3,500 for each month of residence, plus travel expenses and free board and lodging. He had hoped that he would be able to take off from this comfortable 'hotel' and fit in some additional lectures on the side, but he found that this was precluded by the regulations. However, he thoroughly enjoyed university life – it was a pity he could not have had more of it, for he was ideally suited to it, at least for short spells: his restless spirit could never have been anchored indefinitely at any seat of learning.

Louis imposed his own conditions when he accepted; the proposal to house him in a club on the campus did not suit him at all. 'I must be independent.' he wrote to the professor of anthropology and archaeology. 'When I am on a job of this nature I like to be able to housekeep and cook for myself. Sometimes I start work before 5 a.m. and want to make myself breakfast around 6.30; sometimes I work very late and want hot soup or even a whole meal at 11 p.m.'[7] Needless to say, he was given his own apartment.

The duties of a professor at large were not very onerous and Louis performed them to perfection. He gave a public lecture, and another to graduates and members of the faculty, as well as holding seminars for undergraduates and being available for consultation. He would hold the floor with small groups of students in his apartment, roving over every possible subject, demonstrating how to make stone tools or bake bread. Louis enjoyed himself just as much as the students. He paid a second visit to Cornell only a few months before he died and wrote: 'I am looking forward to coming again to the campus, as the last time I enjoyed myself very much indeed.' And the resident professor replied: 'Knowing the general appeal of your lectures, I have taken the precaution of reserving our largest auditorium.'[8]

One of the reasons why Louis was so popular with young people was that even as an old man he kept his youthful enthusiasms – for instance, baking bread. When he visited the National Geographic Society he always stayed at the nearby Jefferson Hotel, where he was an institution; he would sometimes take over the kitchen while the staff stood round to watch him demonstrate his bread-making, and on the rare occasions when the loaf failed to rise he was really upset. Not only did he keep up his old interests, but he was continually taking up new hobbies – and with notable success, as with his triumphs with the Fancy Guppy Association. Louis had always been interested in tropical fish, and on one of his visits to the USA he had been given a pair of very fancy delta-tails. Soon the house at Langata was lined with tanks, and Louis got much enjoyment out of producing exotic varieties from the inmates. By careful selective breeding, crossing the progeny of the delta-tails with wild guppies, he was able to exhibit at international shows in England. In 1967 he entered in seven classes and won a first prize as well as a fourth and a fifth place.

Although Louis and his work received wider recognition in America than elsewhere, he was not without honour in his own continent. The year 1968 brought in a bumper harvest of African decorations. The Royal African Society awarded him their Wellcome Medal for 'distinguished service to Africa' – past recipients had included Dr Schweitzer and Dame Margery Perham. The President of Senegal, who had met Louis at the Pan African Congress at Dakar, appointed him a Commander of the National Order of the Republic in recognition of his services to Africa as a

33. Heselon Mukiri, a member of Louis's Kikuyu age-group and leader of his scientific staff, retired in 1968 after 42 years' service

34. Allen O'Brien flies a kite in California – and most people thought the idea of forming the Leakey Foundation without an endowment fund was just as frivolous

whole; as this was a political order, not a scientific one, Louis obtained permission from President Kenyatta before accepting. Finally, towards the end of the year the Emperor of Ethiopa presented him with the Haile Selassie I Award for African Research, a gold medal and diploma plus 40,000 Ethiopian dollars.

Mary went with Louis for the ceremony in Addis Ababa, after which she returned to Kenya to look after Jonathan and Mollie's first baby, Julia, while they were in America. This was Mary's first grandchild and Louis's sixth. (Priscilla had two children; and Colin and Susan had three daughters, Emma, Tess and Tamsin, born in 1963, 1965 and 1966.) Mary's appearance with Louis at Addis Ababa was something of an event, for they were seldom away together nowadays. Her interests kept her either at Olduvai or at the Centre, and she disapproved of many of the activities in which Louis had become involved; nor did she care for some of his new friends in England and the USA. Mary was pleased when Louis was appreciated as a scientist, but she did not like the personal adoration he so often provoked.

Louis's hip operation had prevented him from being present at the birthday in Los Angeles of The L.S.B. Leakey Foundation for Research Related to Man's Origin, affectionately and more conveniently known as the Leakey Foundation. It was born on 26 March 1968 after a long and rather troublesome pregnancy. The last part of its cumbersome title was frankly secondary to the first, for its prime object was to help and hence promote L. S. B. Leakey personally. The idea was to ease Louis's financial burdens, first by arranging more realistic fees for his lectures and then, once there was some money in the bank, by supporting his projects.

In order to whip up potential contributors to the Foundation Louis was expected to put in appearances at social functions, which added considerably to the amount of engagements he had to fit in to his Californian tours. Almost certainly the strain hastened his end; but the blame cannot be attached entirely to the Foundation's devoted members, who worked their fingers to the bone to help him. It was equally the fault of Louis himself, who invariably tried to do too much. He also expected too much, acting like a spoilt child demanding ever more expensive toys and getting worked up if they did not arrive by the next post. His frenzied drive to raise money for research, and his impatience at the slowness of doing so, increased distressingly as his physical condition deteriorated.

The man who started it all was Allen O'Brien, whom we met briefly in connection with Richard's 1967 Omo expedition. Allen loves adventure and has a passion for rivers, and it was on the Nile in 1964 that he first heard the name Leakey. As he boarded Irving and Electra Johnson's ketch *Yankee* at Aswan two passengers got off: they were Mr Gilbert Grosvenor, son of the president of the NGS, and his wife Donna, who were on their way to visit Olduvai. They told Allen about the object of their journey, and as soon as he got home he looked up articles about Louis's exploits in the *National Geographic*. From one of these he learnt that Richard was organizing safaris and, with typical impetuosity, he promptly put through a call to Nairobi from his home at Newport Beach, near Los Angeles. The telephone was answered by 'Mrs Leakey' and, assuming that she was Richard's wife, Allen outlined his wishes for a tour of East Africa for himself and his wife Helen. In fact he was speaking to Mary: Richard was not yet married and was at his London crammers, so his parents were taking care of his safari business while he was away, and plans for the O'Briens' trip were soon arranged.

Allen and Helen had dreams of high adventure on the lines of what they had seen in the movies: days in the bush, watching white hunters locked in mortal combat with rogue elephants, nights under the stars, surrounded by roaring lions and Masai warriors brandishing spears. Such a picture was rudely shattered on arrival in Nairobi, where innumerable posters and brochures offered them every comfort in tourist lodges. Allen tried to telephone Richard to tell him that was not at all what they wanted, and once again was answered by Mary, who suggested he should call Louis. Hesitating to trouble the great man, Allen did so, and was told to jump into a taxi and come round and see him. As Richard was not there to arrange the sort of safari they had in mind Louis perhaps felt responsible; in any case he suggested they should accompany him to Olduvai next day.

They left before dawn, and for the next eight hours Louis kept up a running commentary on the animals, birds, plants and people that they passed on the way. By the time they reached Olduvai they were breathless, but not so Louis; hardly giving them time to eat or wash, he subjected them to three days' intensive exploration of the Gorge and an introductory course on prehistory. But they loved it: this was the real Africa they had come so far to see, and this was the ideal man to show it to them.

Allen O'Brien's background is a success story. He graduated from high school in 1933, one of the worst years of the depression, and worked in a gas station and as a parking lot attendant before he discovered his talent as a door-to-door salesman. So good was he at persuading housewives to buy pots and pans that he made enough money to feel secure for the first time in his life. Then came the war, when he made use of one of his other talents: cooking. As chief cook in the Merchant Marines he got to know and enjoy the rugged life of the waterfronts, which increased his natural restlessness and distaste for office work. After the war he sold electrical apparatus to industry on behalf of a wholesale firm and eventually started his own business in San Bernardino, near Los Angeles. He worked very hard at it for ten years, after which he decided there was no more need to be a slave to dollars. He made a deal with his right hand man, giving him 25% of the business and continuing to draw a salary himself without being tied to day-to-day affairs; the business thrived, and Allen was at last free to indulge in his taste for adventuring. He explored Mexican rivers, ballooned over the Alps, dived for treasure, made expeditions to the New Hebrides, New Guinea, and the Okavongo Swamp in Botswana; he trudged thousands of miles through Indonesia, carrying only a duffle bag and an attaché case. With such a background it is hardly surprising that Allen was so fascinated by Louis, or that Louis appreciated Allen's qualities.

They next met in February 1966, when Louis was lecturing in California and stayed with the O'Briens at Newport Beach. Louis found the freeways far more alarming than any hazardous African bush track, so Allen acted as his chauffeur, driving him to business appointments, lectures, student gatherings and parties. In his fund-raising campaigns Louis never turned down an invitation, however obscure the host might be – one never knew what might come of it. He was much in demand, for a hostess's ascendancy on the social ladder was accelerated by capturing such a prize.

But Louis's talks were given not only for the financial rewards they might bring; he would travel just as eagerly to address a high school at the request of one of his young admirers. His urge to inspire students was genuine and deeply felt, and they responded accordingly. The '60s was a time of profound unrest, of demonstrations against the Vietnam war, of the Kennedy and Martin Luther King assassinations; it was a time of groping for something beyond the present, and Louis provided inspiration. Young people wanted to know where they had come from, and he told them; they also wanted to know where they were going, and he gave them hope. After reviewing the fossil evidence for human origins, he would point out the lessons to be learnt from the past on the dangers of over-specialization, and express his faith that man would manage to avoid extinction by using his specialized brain.

The peak of Louis's popularity on university campuses and college halls came before the advent of the Jesus people, but already hippies, flower people and others had set the scene for a revival of interest in religion. When Louis stressed its compatability with science he always got a big ovation. He would go back to his old theme, which had often distressed his parents, that faith should not be disguised by the doctrines of formalized religions.

On the occasion when Louis stayed with the O'Briens in February 1966 he filled Caltech's Beckman auditorium, a beautiful new building roofed inside by a sparkling golden dome. The elite of Los Angeles came to hear his talk on 'New light on the evolution of man', and many came from much further afield. Several of those whom Louis inspired that evening were to become the backbone of the Leakey Foundation.

In spite of his desperate need to raise money Louis was still hopelessly naïve about fees – in fact he sometimes forgot to mention them at all when negotiations were being made. When he accepted Caltech's invitation to speak he is supposed to have said that his fee would be $100. Dr Edwin Munger of Caltech said some years later: 'Caltech refused to play a part in having one of the authentic geniuses of the world exhaust his energy by talking at $100 a time when we felt he could easily ask for and receive $1,000 for one talk. And this was the offer we made him.'

Allen O'Brien took the matter in hand and acted as agent, ensuring that the minimum payment would be $500 a lecture. This is what Louis got in the following year, 1967, when he did his marathon tour for CAPES which resulted in his collapse at the airport in Chicago; and it was this collapse that caused his friends in southern California to think seriously about what they could do to help him. Allen, who never believed in doing things by halves, went much further than mere thinking and devoted all his energy into setting up a foundation in honour of the man he so admired. He was completely undeterred by the fact that probably never before in history had a foundation been formed without one vital asset: an endowment fund. But before pursuing the fortunes of the Leakey Foundation it is necessary to outline one of Louis's far-flung ventures which brought him in close touch with two people who might be described as the Foundation's godfather and godmother. The first was Mr Robert Beck, who put most into it in terms of money; and the second was Mrs Arnold Travis, who probably put most into it by way of work and drive.

As though Louis had not got enough on his hands in Africa and America, he had to take on Israel as well. At Ubeidiya, south of the Sea of Galilee, an early Pleistocene site had been discovered in 1959 as a result of commercial earth-moving operations; parts of a hominid skull turned up, and there was great excitement when it was thought to be an australopith. (Eventually it appeared that it was probably no older than bronze age.) Every season from 1960 onwards the site was excavated by Professor G. Haas, zoologist and palaeontologist, and the late Professor Moshe Stekelis, archaeologist, both of the Hebrew University at Jerusalem, with very limited funds from the Israel Academy of Sciences. Mary visited Ubeidiya in 1963 and was struck by the likeness of the fossils and artifacts – Developed Oldowan and Acheulian – to those of Bed II at Olduvai. Both Haas and Stekelis, as well as their palaeontological colleague Dr Eitan Tchernov and the archaeologist Dr Ofer Bar Yosef, subsequently visited Olduvai and other East African sites.

Louis was particularly interested in Ubeidiya since it had a bearing on the migration routes presumably taken by early man up the Rift Valley from Africa to Israel, so that when he heard of the difficulties Haas and Stekelis were having in raising funds he promised to help them. Since the whole focus in that part of the world was on biblical archaeology, no government support was forthcoming for early man excavations. Also the operations were extremely costly, as it was necessary to remove a great thickness of overlying deposits.

In 1964 Louis wrote to a rich engineer he knew in California, Mr Herschel C. Smith, to ask if he would help. Back in the 1920s 'Hersh' had worked with the US Geological Survey in Jordan; he was also interested in archaeology, and was a specialist in earth-moving machinery. It would be difficult to think of anyone more likely to be interested in the Ubeidiya project; but it was a bad moment to approach him as he was suffering from ulcers, and he said he must postpone a decision until he had seen the site for himself. This he did in the following year, and he then agreed to make a substantial grant towards the Ubeidiya excavations provided that they should be the joint responsibility of the Israel Academy of Sciences, UCLA, and the Isotope Foundation.

This last was concerned with isotopes only very indirectly, insofar as its founder was Dr Willard F. Libby, pioneer of radiocarbon dating, Nobel prize-winner in 1960, and professor of chemistry at UCLA; and that his object had been to provide relatively cheap shelters for Americans in the event of nuclear warfare. The Foundation also supported scientific, including archaeological, projects of various kinds. Mr Herschel Smith was a friend of Libby's and, by making his contribution through the Isotope Foundation, he would be able to get tax benefits. At the same time Smith proposed that Louis should be given a chair at UCLA, and that he should be 'titular head' of the Ubeidiya project; however, Louis replied that he had too many other commitments – as indeed he had – but that he would be willing to act as 'official adviser'.

No sooner was it launched than the operation foundered: UCLA insisted on taking part in the field research, but the Israelis were equally determined not to have a joint expedition, as they had their own highly competent team of specialists. In the middle of these delicate negotiations, in September 1966, Herschel Smith died – and the money with him, as he had not put anything in his will about the contribution he proposed to make to Ubeidiya. There seemed to be a complete impasse, and Professor Stekelis was getting very worried. Early in 1967 Louis paid a flying visit to Jerusalem to sort things out before going on to California, where Dr Libby introduced him to his friend Mr Robert Beck. A former executive vice-president of Scientific Data Systems of Santa Monica, Mr Beck was a millionaire many times over. He was looking for a cause to support, and almost immediately agreed to contribute a large sum towards Ubeidiya, to be paid through the Isotope Foundation. UCLA's part was to be restricted to 'collaboration' rather than active participation; and both Louis and Mary were to be 'overall directors', which meant that they should visit the excavations occasionally to advise.

Ironically, just when the money was assured and the Israelis were all set to begin really large-scale operations, on 12 March 1967 Professor Stekelis died; he was in his laboratory, discussing plans with Haas, when he collapsed from heart failure. This was only six months after the death of Herschel Smith, and the project now received yet a third blow: the Isotope Foundation said that they would have to reconsider the allocation of funds, since the personal leadership of Stekelis had been a major consideration. They were unimpressed by assurances that the elderly and ailing professor had had a most competent archaeological assistant in Dr Ofer Bar Yosef. Louis wrote both to the Isotope Foundation and to Robert Beck saying that he was 'staggered' at their hesitation, and Dr Libby then asked Louis to come to California to go into the whole matter yet again.

Libby's letter was written only three weeks after Louis's collapse at Chicago after his CAPES tour; the obvious inference is that Libby was concerned not only about the competence of Stekelis's successor but also about Louis's own ability to supervise the excavations personally. Having only just returned to Nairobi the very last thing Louis wanted to do was to have to go back to California, particularly as his back was still painful after having been ricked by the stretcher-bearers. At this point the role of entrepreneur was assumed by Joan Travis, future secretary of the Leakey Foundation, who went to see Libby to explain the difficulty; Libby admitted that he was suspicious about Louis's true state of health. Three months later Robert Beck paid a visit to East Africa to assess the situation. Louis took him to Olduvai, Olorgesailie, Fort Ternan and Peninj (Lake Natron), and in a letter to Joan Travis Louis said: 'He [Beck] expressed himself as exceedingly happy at the state of my health. I walked him off his feet up and down cliffs in spite of my hip and back.'[9]

At this point it is necessary to make a slight diversion to explain how Joan Travis had come into the Leakey orbit. Her husband Arnold's father, Mr Marion M. Travis, had made a fortune out of oil and was an ardent Zionist. He was also a lifelong friend of Colonel John Patterson, constructor of the railway from Mombasa to Lake Victoria and author of *The man-eaters of Tsavo.* During the First World War Colonel Patterson had fought in Palestine with Allenby, afterwards retiring to the USA on a small pension. Mr Travis helped with money, later taking Patterson into his own home, where the Colonel lived for the last ten years of his life. Patterson's son Bryan was a Harvard palaeontologist who had led an expedition to northern Kenya; he suggested that Louis should look up Mr Travis when he was in California, thinking that he might be interested in supporting the Ubeidiya excavations. Mr Travis went to one of Louis's lectures, became fascinated by the man and his work, and introduced Louis to his son Arnold and daughter-in-law Joan. They were equally captivated, as was their 15-year-old daughter 'Cyndie', who asked Louis if he would speak at her University High School in West Los Angeles; he immediately agreed, with the result that she was awarded a certificate of excellence for her 'contribution to the entire student body in having arranged the outstanding Dr Leakey assembly'. So it was that Louis became adopted into the Travis family, and hence the part played by Joan in the Ubeidiya negotiations.

The excavations there seemed to be doomed: the next disaster was the six days' war in June 1967. Ubeidiya was close to the border and there was a good deal of sniping, but by August it was possible to resume the work and Louis called there on his way to London and America. There was still considerable tension, it was almost impossible to obtain manual labour, and Drs Tchernov and Bar Yosef were struggling with the help of four foreign girl students and what Louis described as 'three young illiterates of rather low calibre'. It was on that occasion that Louis got his only war wound, having never been anywhere near the firing lines in either of the two world wars. He was driving along with Tchernov, talking no doubt about fossils, when they went straight past a check point without even noticing it, and a spent bullet struck Louis on the forehead. The only damage was a bruise and a slight scar, but he was very proud of his war wound and always kept the bullet as a souvenir.

The earliest artifacts and associated fauna at Ubeidiya probably date from about 700,000 years and the site is possibly the earliest known locality with human culture outside of Africa, certainly one of the earliest. Year after year the excavations were to continue, and without Louis's struggles they might well have ground to a halt. Eventually, in 1970, the Isotope Foundation transferred the funds designated for Ubeidiya to the Leakey Foundation, and after this money ran out Louis once more fought to keep the project going. One donation was due to Louis's never-failing response to young people and is worth recording: some fourteen-year-old Californian boys had made a film in which they enacted excavations at 'Olduvai', and when Louis heard about it he gave them a talk and showed them slides, with the result that the father of one of them gave $5,000 for Ubeidiya through the Leakey Foundation.

The Ubeidiya story refutes allegations made by some of Louis's critics that he sponsored research mainly for the glorification of Leakey, for in this case, apart from the actual fund-raising, all the credit went to the Israelis.

Allen O'Brien's motive in setting up the Leakey Foundation was to spare Louis exhaustion; the support of scientific research was secondary, but of course this aspect had to be put over to potential contributors. Allen discussed ways to go about it with his cousin Dr John D. Roberts, head of the department of chemistry at Caltech, since that Institute had recently engaged professional fund-raisers in connection with the provision of new facilities. Dr Roberts put him on to Dr Edwin S. Munger, professor of geography and specialist in African politics, who had recently joined Caltech to add what Allen calls 'pizzaz', or sparkle. A meeting was arranged at Dr Munger's house, to which Allen brought his friends Mr Robert N. Moodey, a banker, and Mr James A. Smith, an attorney; and that same day they all called on the head of a professional fund-raising organization in Los Angeles. He was not at all optimistic about the chances of launching a foundation without any money, nor of its appeal to contributors; but he agreed to undertake a feasibility study for $10,000, and Mr Moodey said he would try to arrange a loan for this amount from his bank.

The plan was to interview about twenty experts in the field of prehistory, mostly colleagues who knew Louis personally, to test their reactions and find out what measure of success such a foundation might be expected to have. Dominated as it was bound to be by Louis's emphatic views and his own projects and prejudices how much would it be likely to appeal to the public and motivate them to subscribe? On the face of it success seemed unlikely. One of the professional researchers employed by the fund-raising organization predicted that the odds were so heavily against the project getting off the ground that he declined to serve; another, an ex-preacher, regarded Louis as a fraud, made his excuses and also retired. The rest went ahead, but by the time their air fares and other expenses had been accounted for the $10,000 feasibility study had soared to $25,000. Not only was there nothing with which to pay the bill, but at the end of all this effort the collective opinion of the researchers was unfavourable.

Allen O'Brien, however, was not one to be put off so easily. Together with Louis and two of the fund-raisers he went to see Dr Melvin Payne, who had just become president of the National Geographic Society. Dr Payne had loyally supported the Leakeys' work at Olduvai for the past six years, and he might well have frowned upon the idea of a foundation to steal some of the thunder; but in fact he welcomed it generously. Putting his arm round Louis's shoulder he said 'Anything O'Brien wants to do is fine with me, so long as it's good for my friend Louis.' He was invited then and there to serve on the board of the Foundation, which Allen was determined would go ahead despite the gloomy prognostications of the experts.

When the name was being considered Allen had suggested 'The L. S. B. Leakey Foundation for Prehistory and Palaeontology', on the model of the Centre in Nairobi. That, however, would have been too restricted for some of the purposes that Louis had in mind, notably research on living monkeys and apes; he therefore insisted on inserting the all-important word 'related' into the title, which became The L. S. B. Leakey Foundation for Research Related to Man's Origin. The objects, as laid down in the articles of incorporation, were the following (with some later additions): (1) To explore and excavate sites having an important bearing on the physical and cultural evolution of early man; (2) To carry out laboratory studies of the materials resulting from exploration and excavation; (3) To conduct taxonomic and behavioural studies of living primates as a necessary corollary to the archeological and palaeontological findings, and to provide an insight into contemporary man's behaviour. Other objectives were to provide educational training both in the field and in the laboratory through fellowships, scholarships and travel grants; to broaden the education of students and the general public by means of lectures, film strips and slides; and to publish scientific reports of field observations and laboratory findings. The most vital and immediate objective, on which all the others would depend, was to 'solicit, collect, receive, acquire, hold and invest money'.

According to that expensive feasibility report, the board had three main tasks to perform, all of which seemed fairly obvious even to such novices at the game as Allen and his supporters. Having prepared a case statement of the Foundation's aims and purposes, they must build up a 'constituency' of people to help financially, and the members of the board must dive deep into their own pockets. These two last considerations were to prove an almost insurmountable stumbling block except in the case of Allen himself, who dived deeply and repeatedly.

The board was to be composed of a science and grants committee to advise on the worth of projects, and an executive committee to manage fund-raising; obviously the last came first, and the science and grants committee could not function until there was some money to allocate. Although the Foundation officially came into being in March 1968, its first grant was not made until December of that year.

A number of influential people were invited to serve on the executive committee, each one of whom had different ideas on how to go about raising money (but none of whom appeared to be over-anxious to put up the money themselves). Allen realized that it would be impossible to get started with such a mixed bunch pulling in various directions; he therefore proposed that three of the committee should first try to get the Foundation on its feet – himself, the attorney Jim Smith, and the banker Bob Moodey – and that the others should join later when the worst of the teething troubles were over. Moodey arranged a bank loan, guaranteed by O'Brien; Smith drew up a constitution; and negotiations were made with the Internal Revenue Service to secure tax-free status for the Foundation. Having sorted all this out, the three original trustees were joined by some half dozen others on the executive committee.

The two who did most of the work were the 'Leakey ladies', the secretary, Joan Travis, and the treasurer, Mrs Hugh Caldwell. Tita Caldwell's main function was to arrange parties to entice potential contributors and, as so often happened with Louis, she had been enrolled via the younger generation. The Caldwells' daughter Penny had written to him from the University of California at Berkeley saying that she was interested in his work and would like a job in Africa, with the result that she later worked at the primate research centre which Louis founded near Nairobi and her mother became a Leakey fan. Another member of the original committee was Mr Ed N. Harrison. In his 'backyard', as he puts it, he has his own Foundation, a museum in which he houses the world's biggest private collection of birds' eggs. Some fifteen years before the formation of the Leakey Foundation he visited Nairobi and found that he and Louis shared a common interest in ornithology. Mr Harrison was also president of the board of governors of the Los Angeles County Museum, as well as owning a large office block in the City, and he was an obvious choice for membership of the board of the Leakey Foundation.

Most of the members of the executive committee had little, if any, knowledge of prehistory; their interest – and it was a great one – centred on Louis himself. With commendable vigour the ladies threw themselves into organizing brunches, lunches, cocktail parties and dinners, often with famous film stars as guests, nearly always with millionaires. As Tita Caldwell put it, these functions provided them with 'stimulating intellectual and social involvement as well as very real opportunities for individual cultivation and solicitation of funds.'[10] Such gatherings would have sent most scientists home screaming – Mary's reactions may be imagined – and Louis's presence was the essential bait to lure the guests. The opportunities for soliciting funds were there at these parties, but there was seldom a positive answer to Allen's repeated question 'How does it translate into money?'

At first it seemed that the only result of the Foundation was to add considerably to Louis's commitments in his already hectic schedule. Critics of the Leakey Foundation who assert that the pressures it generated had an adverse effect on Louis's health, which almost certainly it did, ignore two factors. One is that his energy and restlessness at this time were such that he had to fill every moment of the day; if the Foundation had not packed his programme for him, he would have done so himself. The second aspect is that Louis positively *enjoyed* the functions, the dramas and the clash of personalities, the plans and the gossip. Above all, he adored being the centre of attention.

Joan Travis in particular was a very good friend on whom Louis came to rely more and more. In her he always found a sympathetic ear, and over a period of years she kept in touch with faithful regularity, informing him at great length of everything that went on in the Foundation. Joan is extremely energetic and purposeful, yet at the same time paradoxically soft-voiced and restful; like many Jewish people, she and her husband are warm-hearted and hospitable and they tried to take the utmost care of

Louis when he stayed with them. The Travises live at Westwood, near Beverly Hills and very close to UCLA, and they also own a ranch at Blythe, on the Colorado River, where Arnold and his partner run California's biggest processing plant for cattle food and other agricultural produce. After a couple of years when he stayed with the O'Briens at Newport Beach, Louis took root at the Travises and visited them regularly every year for the rest of his life. Not only was their house nearer to his lecture venues and to business and social appointments, but it had the added advantage of a heated swimming pool in which he loved to relax and exercise his back and hip. Louis was thoroughly spoilt, as he had been also with the O'Briens, but perhaps after a life of hardship such comfort was deserved.

Joan Travis and Tita Caldwell were devoted to Louis and to the Foundation's cause – which, in fact, were one and the same in their eyes. Being such hard workers themselves they perhaps did not realize that what they took in their stride might be too much for an elderly man with a poor record of health. Certainly Louis never gave the impression that it was too much, and he accepted cheerfully whatever they arranged. As an example of the sort of programme the ladies prepared for Louis, here is an extract from one of Joan's letters to him referring to his forthcoming visit in 1969:

> We have attempted to be very selective in the number and contributor potential of people invited to get together with you – no mass meetings or impersonal dinner parties. A few meetings with individuals who want to see you and whom you will want to see privately; a few brunches with mixed old-new men; a dinner party at the Darts, to which three or four important friends of theirs have been invited on Sunday; a Monday night affair at Tita's with a handful of important guests. . . .[11]

(The 'handful' was a mere twenty.) Louis embarked on this daunting programme with his ears still ringing to the stirring rendering of 'O Canada' at the convocation of the University of Guelph, where he had just received yet another honorary degree. After the hectic week in Los Angeles had ended, Joan Travis summed up what the executive committee got out of Louis's appearances: 'You have added a new dimension to our lives – a fascinating glimpse of another world. . . .'[12]

Allen O'Brien put it this way: 'All we had constituted was a new group which gained personal satisfaction from having Louis (principally) and other prominent scientists (secondarily) as guests at social affairs.' The trouble was that the members of the committee were tightly connected socially with the guests they invited to the parties, and they found it highly embarrassing to solicit them for money. When it became painfully clear to Louis that social aspects far outweighed hard cash, he suggested that prominent and wealthy citizens should be circularized with an invitation to become Fellows of the Foundation. For this privilege they were expected to contribute a thousand dollars, and in return they would be invited to 'intimate parties' at which they could enjoy a tête-à-tête with the great man. The scheme caught on and gradually the desired 'constituency' was built up, although not on a scale large enough to satisfy either Allen or Louis.

Without one man, who became a trustee in July 1969, the whole operation might have foundered: this was Robert Beck, the rescuer of Ubeidiya. An industrialist from the Middle West, Beck had sold his electronics business to Xerox and suddenly found himself with great wealth and a growing standing in the community of southern California where he now lived. At the same time he began to spread his wings in other directions: he emerged from a semi-fundamentalist religious background and, as a shy and retiring bachelor in his early forties, he got married soon after he became involved in the Leakey Foundation. He started to worry about the way the world was going and what he personally could do to alleviate the situation, particularly in connection with conservation and pollution. Although the origins of man were not exactly what he had in mind Louis gave him plenty of other ideas. Never before had Bob Beck come across anyone with such an all-embracing mind, and he came to regard his new friend as a father-figure. Louis, for his part, liked nothing better than a disciple who was prepared to listen, and he became extremely fond of this endearing character who was undergoing a sort of spiritual awakening.

Bob Beck could have supported all the activities of the Leakey

Foundation on one finger without feeling it, but very sensibly he worked it so that others should also have to make an effort. In August 1969 he promised to hand over $40,050 worth of securities by the following January on condition that the other trustees raised an equal amount, and within three months the challenge had been met. A year later, in September 1970, Mr Beck gave the Foundation what it had so sorely needed from the beginning: an endowment fund. He pledged up to one million dollars, to be matched within five years; in other words, for every donation received from others, whether for general funds or for specific projects, he would pay an equal amount into the endowment fund. In making this magnificent gesture he described his motives as follows: 'The purpose of the challenge donation I am making is not simply to finance specific research. It is, more than anything else, to encourage other people to make funds available for intelligent and imaginative use of the scientific community. There is no question that we must urgently take action for our own preservation and that of our environment. The thrust to this end must come from the concern of the private individual and the scientist together.'[13]

The capital was not to be touched – except in a case of dire need with the unanimous approval of the trustees – and at first there was very little in the way of matching donations, and hence very little income. Louis, who was deeply committed in all directions, began to get extremely impatient at the lack of ready cash. Even before the Foundation was a year old he was expecting manna to fall from heaven and complained vociferously when it did not. To Allen O'Brien, whose aim was to get a hundred Fellows to provide a thousand dollars each, he wrote ungratefully: 'I think your suggested figures are much too conservative. I cannot believe that you will not get more by the end of the year. If you don't, you might as well pack up the Foundation and let me go on raising money myself. After all, I am going to need more than twice that amount for the next year for current expenditure.'[14]

Louis could, of course, have gone on raising money himself without 'packing up' the Foundation; but he was worried that other foundations and individuals might assume he could now get all the money he needed through his own foundation and would not give him any more.

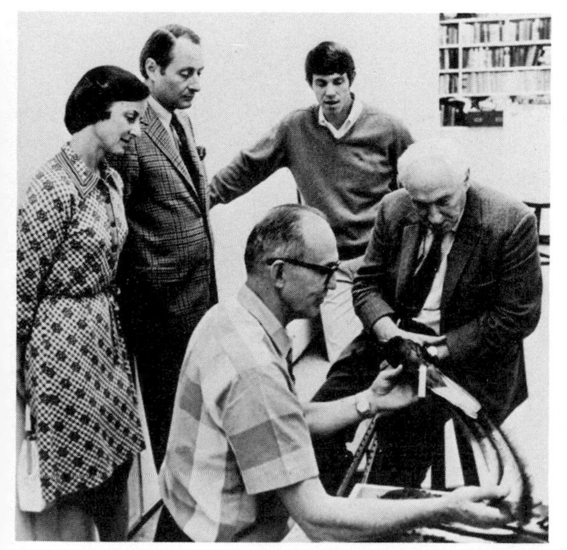

35. Ed Harrison, president of the Leakey Foundation, shows Louis a bird skin in his private museum in Los Angeles, the Western Foundation of Vertebrate Zoology. With them is Joan Travis, hard-working secretary of the Leakey Foundation

6. Robert Beck (right) presents a portrait of Louis by Alvin Gittins to the Leakey Foundation office

37. Louis, on crutches after his hip operation, outside the Fejos Laboratory at the Centre in Nairobi; it was named after the late Paul Fejos, director of research of the Wenner-Gren Foundation, New York, who paid for the building

38. *Below* Louis shows visitors round the Fejos Laboratory in 1969

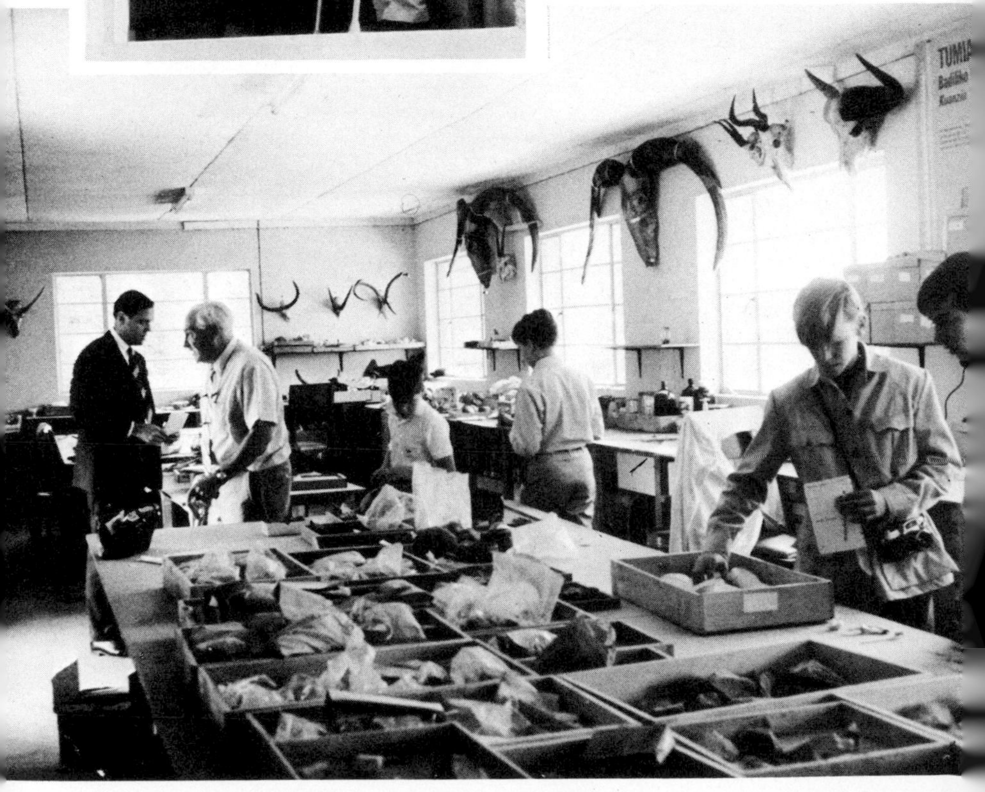

As anyone who has tried to interest big foundations will know, it is not easy to convince them that one's own particular project is more worthy of support than the hundreds of other appeals they receive. Selling one's wares takes up a lot of time and demands dogged persistence, involving personal visits, innumerable letters, form-filling and account rendering. Having built up a long list of sponsors by his own efforts it is understandable that Louis did not wish to lose their support for the sake of what he might get out of the Leakey Foundation some time in the distant future.

In another letter to Allen O'Brien he wrote:

> There is too much talk, too little action, too many grandiose ideas for future development while present needs are not being met. This makes potential donors afraid their money won't be spent on carrying out the objectives they wish to support. I am forced to say that if my proposed October visit does not produce more concrete results I shall simply have to suggest the abandonment of the whole Foundation idea and return to my own more simple and less time-consuming fund raising efforts.[15]

Allen, who knew Louis well, was not at all put out, as most people would be; he merely rebuked him very gently: 'Throwing cold water on enthusiastic friends serves no purpose. You have a lot of fine people working very hard for you here and I implore you not to discourage them.'[16]

Fortunately the Foundation had few overheads. It had free office accommodation, at first at Robert Moodey's house at Newport Beach, which soon became known as 'Nairobi West', and then in the building owned by Ed Harrison in Los Angeles. The only paid employee was one executive director, and Allen paid the salaries of the first two to hold this post out of his own pocket. The third incumbent was the extremely competent Gary Phillips, who helped to persuade Robert Beck to make his munificent gift.

As soon as there was some money in the bank the science and grants committee could operate, even if only on a small scale. Among its first members were Dr Melvin Payne; Dr Edwin Munger of Caltech; Dr Clark Howell, leader of the American team in the Omo expeditions; and Dr Sherwood Washburn, anthropologist of Berkeley who was particularly interested in the study of living primates. Others who joined the committee later included Mr Harold Coolidge of the National Academy of Sciences of Washington, and president of the International Union for the Conservation of Nature; and Dr Richard Foster Flint of Yale, who had crossed swords with Louis over pluvial interpretations. These eminent scientists were in the unenviable position of having to sift through Louis's incessant appeals for support for about a dozen different projects spread over three continents.

The members of the committee had to determine priorities not always in accordance with their own objective judgement, but taking into consideration Louis's emotional involvement with each particular venture. They also had to abide by the objects of the Foundation as laid down in its articles of incorporation: early man research, primate research, and educational programmes. Louis seldom had much trouble in finding funds to support his major undertakings, such as Olduvai or Miocene research; his real problem was to get support for all his marginal activities. Unable to sustain the interest of others, he would turn to what he considered to be 'his' Foundation and face the science and grants committee with horrible dilemmas. Where should their loyalties lie? Should they pursue the stated aims of the Foundation to the letter and recommend that its meagre resources be shared also with other scientists besides Louis? Or should they bend a little to accommodate the requests of the man in whose honour the Foundation had been formed?

Often they did accede to Louis's demands without adequate knowledge of the background to each particular case, since they were too far away from the scene of action to be able to judge the relative merits of bones and stones, primate behaviour, student travel grants, and so forth. By the time the Leakey Foundation was operating Louis was soliciting money to support students studying monkeys and chimpanzees, and later he added gorillas and orang-utans; he clamoured for money for Ubeidiya and for an equally costly dig in California. How could the committee argue about the worth of all these ventures when they had so little information about them? They had to accept Louis's word, and they all knew only too well how his enthusiasm was apt to run away with him.

Louis, in fact, tried to run the whole show by remote control, and to a large extent he did just that. Although the Foundation was supposed to assist any scientist concerned with the study of man, Louis's demands were such that there was little money left over for anyone else. Also, most of his colleagues on the committee had a real affection for him and could not bring themselves to disappoint him. As his health deteriorated, he was apt to take advantage of this in a form of blackmail, implying that he would have another heart attack if they did not support his projects. So it was that the committee sometimes backed him against their better judgement – and who shall blame them?

12 Syndicates and Sororities

One of the main reasons why Louis spent so much time in the United States lecturing and stimulating the Leakey Foundation into action, and why he needed so much money, was to support research on apes and monkeys. He believed that observations on living primates would lead to a better understanding of extinct ones, and that apes in particular had much to teach us about our own behaviour; but this does not fully explain why he became so absorbed in such studies and turned his back on African prehistory to the extent that he did. The reasons are complex, but basically they can be attributed to increasing physical disability, which prevented him from taking part in active field work himself; to competition from Mary and Richard; and to his reluctance to adopt modern techniques.

Mary is a more dedicated scientist than Louis ever was; although she could not rival his genius and flair, she had the perfect temperament for the attention to detail which modern archaeology demands. Much of the excitement experienced by the old selective collectors has gone and *everything* is now grist to the computer's mill, with excavation reports reduced largely to statistics. This would not have suited Louis at all. While he was interested only in the more spectacular discoveries, Mary was quite content to make exact measurements and compile elaborate tables of tool types, laboriously uncovering the evidence centimetre by centimetre.

Richard, although temperamentally more like his father, is shrewd enough to bow to the new scientific gods. At East Rudolf he has a site with practically unlimited scope and he includes every kind of specialist on his expeditions. He is a good team leader, whereas Louis, although first rate at leading students, was never happy with scientific equals. Richard is also a better administrator than his father and takes great pains to get the co-operation of ministers and other government officials; and he has proved to be as successful in raising funds as Louis.

Louis's solution was to launch into new fields of research far removed from those in which his family was engaged: it was a question of keeping up with the Joneses, but not in direct competition with them. These peripheral activities – some people called them Louis's wildcat schemes – demanded a great deal of time and energy; the emotional stresses involved and Louis's struggles to keep them going took a tremendous toll of his health, but his pride was involved and he could not let go.

There were other reasons also for Louis's 'dropping out'. His sons had flown from the nest and Mary had come to roost at Olduvai; the house at Langata was no longer a home, echoing only to the strident shrieks of the tame hyraxes and to the sound of Louis's sticks tapping round the courtyard. To ease his loneliness he would invite his favourite students to stay, and when Mary turned up she would find that it was no longer her home either.

Even when Louis was in his sixties girls in their twenties found him attractive; he clung to his immortality, and naturally he was flattered and pleased. He collected satellites like the planet Jupiter, using them to run errands and help with his writings; but he also encouraged some to pursue their own studies under his direct supervision. As Dr Melvin Payne put it, he 'had a genius for selecting young people and motivating their career aims.'[1] Their research provided a vicarious outlet for his energies, and at the same time he earned their gratitude and devotion by raising the money to support them.

Observations on living primates were a legitimate part of Louis's probe into man's origins, for their behaviour might be expected to provide clues to the way of life of the Miocene apes and the Pleistocene hominids. Ethology, the study of behaviour, was still a relatively new science and there was scope for making important discoveries; also, ethology was not shackled by technicalities, such as those which Louis found so irksome in the 'new archaeology'. He had neither the time nor the temperament to make long studies of primates in the wild himself, even if his age and health had allowed it, but he had no difficulty in inspiring others to do it for him.

As long ago as 1946 Louis had sent a young man to study chimpanzees in the wild, but he packed it in after six months. Louis always quoted this failure in support of his contention that women made more satisfactory observers than men, although he seldom mentioned the fact that a young woman he sent ten years later to study the mountain gorilla was equally unsuccessful. He had a theory that women should be better because they have more patience and powers of concentration and, being used to the responsibilities of children, they should be particularly successful in studying relationships between ape mothers and juveniles. Women also had an advantage in that they would not be threatened by male apes, but on the other hand there was the danger that they might become emotionally involved: the story is told that a certain female student customarily went around topless in the forests, but when her favourite male chimpanzee appeared she coyly pulled on her shirt.

Before sending three most successful ape-girls into the forests, however, Louis began with monkeys behind bars. For many years his primate research centre at Tigoni near Nairobi was his pet project and, because it was so close to his heart, it caused him more worry and anguish than any of his other endeavours. At Tigoni Louis could test out all his favourite theories about taxonomy, diet and fertility. There was room for several students to be employed at a time and, unlike the ape researchers, they were close enough to be under his eye. For nine years Louis had a woman with suitable academic qualifications to run Tigoni, but after she left in 1969 the young assistants were often left without a leader and the results were sometimes unfortunate.

It all began in March 1958, when Louis attended a conference on primates at Achimota, Ghana, and stayed with the newly widowed Dr Cynthia Booth. She had a double first in the natural sciences tripos from Cambridge and was professor of biology at Ghana University. With her husband Angus, who had died as the result of a bite from a monkey, she had done research on primates in West Africa for the past eight years. Louis persuaded her to come to Kenya and found her a farm at Tigoni, near Limuru, where they jointly set up the Tigoni Primate Research Centre. He found the money from the Chicago Museum, with a small grant also from the Coryndon Museum, but mostly out of his own pocket – Louis continued to draw a regular salary from the National Geographic Society, which he could spend as he liked, and a good deal of it went on Tigoni. Cages were built and monkeys collected to put in them; some animals were later imported from West Africa, which meant adding a heated block. As the monkeys multiplied more staff were needed to look after them and more food had to be bought to feed the animals. Within two years of the research centre's formation Louis was frantically trying to interest the Nuffield Foundation, the Ford Foundation, the Glaxo Laboratories in London, and the Wellcome Foundation Research Laboratory at Kabete, on Tigoni's doorstep. The situation was eventually saved by the National Institute of Health at Bethesda, Maryland, which sponsored primate centres affiliated to universities in the USA in connection with medical research. In 1959, Congress voted two million dollars for this project, so Louis's appeal came at the right moment. The NIH gave some $100,000 to Tigoni spread over a period of seven years. The accounts for the expenditure of this large sum were never very detailed, and reports on the research carried out with it were practically non-existent; it is amazing that the NIH continued to support Tigoni for as long as it did. The year that the grant was withdrawn, at the end of 1968, happened to coincide with the birth of the Leakey Foundation, and Louis's most clamant pleas to its committee members were invariably on behalf of Tigoni.

Louis's motive in setting up the primate centre was to study East African monkeys in depth before it was too late. Considering the numbers to be seen everywhere in suitable environments, this may seem surprising; but Louis was concerned at the thousands of vervets being captured every year and exported for medical research. These monkeys are widely used in the production of polio vaccines and in cancer and organ transplant studies, and it was estimated that of the 20,000 trapped annually a large proportion died in transit or soon after arrival at their destination. Louis hoped that ultimately it would be possible to breed enough monkeys in captivity to satisfy this demand, leaving the wild stock alone. Only healthy animals would be exported, thus avoiding wastage, and they would also be used to being handled and would be more amenable than wild vervets. Another advantage in the scheme was that staff wages and costs of feeding were lower in East Africa than they would be if the monkeys were bred in Europe or America. Unfortunately this scheme for Tigoni never got under way, which was a pity as the idea was good.

Another of Louis's objectives was to make taxonomic studies, as he suspected that too many species and sub-species had been made of the genus *Cercopithecus*, which embraced the vervets and guenons. Excessive splitting had been the result of studies based on inadequate samples in museums, without taking into account the wide individual variations due mostly to age differences. There were also considerable differences between guenons living east and west of the Rift Valley, which Louis believed were racial rather than specific. Sykes monkeys east of the Rift are brownish, while the rather larger Blue monkeys west of the Rift are predominantly grey; many primatologists classed them as separate species, whereas Louis was convinced they were merely subspecies of *Cercopithecus mitis*. In support of this, he pointed out that in southern Tanzania, where the Rift does not separate the monkey's range, intermediate forms are found. Cynthia Booth eventually succeeded in breeding crosses between Sykes and Blue monkeys, but under artificial conditions this has no particular zoological significance.

In general breeding at Tigoni was very successful, even with those species generally considered 'difficult', such as colobus monkeys. De Brazza monkeys, a rare and more handsome relative of Sykes and Blue monkeys, were supposed to be almost impossible to breed in captivity; but they did reproduce at Tigoni after they were fed on their natural diet of plants containing carotene (as in carrots). All the animals at Tigoni were well fed and yet some, although apparently perfectly healthy, did not breed until something extra was added to their diet: with the De Brazzas it was carotene, with bush-babies it proved to be grasshoppers.

Louis had one particular theory which he was anxious to prove concerning the relationship between diet and fertility, and he was just as besotted with this problem as he had been with the properties of zebra fat in connection with tuberculosis. He had the idea that women do not conceive in the absence of a certain element in their diet, which we may call 'X' as he did not know what it was. If only this mineral – or whatever it might be – could be identified, a perfect method of birth control would be provided simply by cutting 'X' out of the diet. Louis's extraordinary theories went to even greater lengths: he was struck by the fact that when a childless couple adopts a baby the woman often conceives soon after; this he attributed to the fact that new foods were introduced into the household when the child was weaned and the mother finished up the left-overs on the baby's plate! Louis hoped to find out the nature of this mysterious element 'X' by experimenting on monkeys; possibly, he thought, it might be something which affected the metabolism by preventing the fertilized egg from adhering to the wall of the uterus. He estimated that it might take six or more years to prove or disprove the theory, at a minimum cost of $10,000 per annum.

Louis had also noticed that Masai women who had been barren often became pregnant when they moved to another area, which he attributed to something new in their diet. By questioning friends in the United States he found that the same thing happened there, and he presumed that the answer lay in minerals in the soil. He even broadcast an appeal on the BBC and sent letters to the Press asking anyone who had had such experiences to communicate with him; he got quite a few answers, but he was no nearer to solving the identity of 'X'. Many strokes of genius and important discoveries are based on something extremely simple, but probably in this case it was *too* simple; no doubt as many factors are involved as there are letters in the alphabet, and the fact that for De Brazzas 'X' is carotene and for bush-babies it is grasshoppers did not get Louis any nearer to solving the world's population problem.

Cynthia Booth began her work at Tigoni by studying the behaviour of young monkeys and the psychological effects of separating them from their mothers, the cycle of tooth eruption, sleep patterns, vocalization, changes of coat colour with age, and the age of sexual maturity in the various species. As the breeding programme got under way she experimented with cross-breeding between sub-species and added the studies on diet and fertility.

Later still research was made on diseases, since early diagnoses would be important in any scheme to breed vervets on a large scale for export; in this, Tigoni had the co-operation of the Wellcome Research Laboratory at Kabete.

Students were trained to help in all this work, and by far the most competent assistant Cynthia Booth ever had was Meave Epps, later to become Richard Leakey's second wife. Meave had hoped to do work connected with marine biology, but she found that there seemed to be a prejudice against women in that field so she answered an advertisement which Louis had put into the English papers for an assistant to work in primatology. In 1965 she was taken on at Tigoni, where she made comparative studies of the limb bones of colobus and guenons; after writing up her thesis at the University of North Wales at Bangor she returned to Tigoni in January 1969 as acting director.

By this time Cynthia Booth had remarried and become Mrs Anthony Rivers-Thomas, and also by this time the National Institute of Health at Bethesda had withdrawn their grant owing to the balance of payments situation in the US. Because of the financial uncertainty about the future of Tigoni, Cynthia Rivers-Thomas left to take up a post in Rhodesia. The name was then changed to the National Primate Research Centre, and funds to keep it going for six months under Meave's direction were obtained from the Munitalp Foundation.

Based in Nairobi, the Munitalp Foundation supported wildlife conservation in East Africa. Its chairman, Sir Malin Sorsbie, was also vice-president of the East Africa Wild Life Society, of which Louis was a trustee, and the work of the two organizations was closely connected. The Tigoni property had belonged to Cynthia Rivers-Thomas, and Louis had persuaded the Munitalp Foundation to take out a mortgage on the place. The conditions they made were that Louis should continue as overall director, and that the title should be held by some organization connected with the Kenya Government. Louis proposed that the Museum trustees should be the legal owners of Tigoni, and they accepted this arrangement on the understanding that they should have no financial or administrative commitments. Munitalp had no wish to be financially committed either – they had done their bit in taking out the mortgage – and they agreed to support Tigoni for the first six months of 1969 more to oblige Louis than for any other reason.

Meave Epps was also reluctant to take up the appointment of acting director, not only because Louis was unable to offer her a long-term contract but also because she was more interested in working on fossil monkeys than on living ones. However, like nearly everyone who has lived and worked in Kenya, she had fallen in love with the country and she agreed to take on the job temporarily as a means of getting back to East Africa. Cynthia Rivers-Thomas officially ceased to be director on 31 December 1968, but she stayed on at Tigoni for a further two months. Tense and highly strung, she was not easy to work with; the monkeys she regarded as her personal property, which is perhaps understandable after being involved with them for nine years, and she hated anyone else having anything to do with them. She took all records and notes with her to Rhodesia on the understanding that they would be returned to Tigoni after she had written a paper, but nothing was ever published on her nine years' work. This made it extremely difficult for Louis when he tried to raise funds. He made excuses, saying that she had just started to write up her results when the National Institute of Health withdrew their grant and she was forced to leave. He even refuted the suggestion that nothing had been published: both he and Cynthia Rivers-Thomas, he said, had read papers at primate conferences in Germany and the USA and, he added triumphantly, Meave Epps had obtained her doctorate on work done at Tigoni.[2] This was hardly relevant as far as Cynthia Rivers-Thomas was concerned, and it was only a small part of the work; potential contributors naturally expected to see something in print about what had been accomplished in all those years, but they only had Louis's word about the results.

By the time Meave Epps took over, research was almost at a standstill for lack of funds. Tigoni was costing £1,000 a month to run; there were 140 monkeys, of twelve different species, housed in 65 outdoor cages, as well as twenty cages in a heated block for animals from warmer climates such as Ghana, Uganda and the Kenya coast. The heat had to be turned off, the staff reduced, and there was only just enough money to keep the monkeys fed.

Louis's troubles had really begun, and he was in such a state that the Travises and Caldwells of the Leakey Foundation produced enough money to keep the place ticking over for three months. Then the science and grants committee approved a grant to cover a further three months, out of regard for Louis personally rather than for concern about the monkeys and their scientific potential. The National Primate Research Centre continued to live from hand to mouth, but always the Leakey Foundation stepped in just in time to prevent the operation from foundering and Louis's heart from breaking.

When Meave left after her six months' stint Dr Neil Chalmers was appointed scientific director, but he fell out with Louis and departed after nine months. Some continuity was provided by a manager, who remained for more than five years, but he was not concerned with the scientific research. There was accommodation at Tigoni for five students, who got free board and lodging but no salary, and in addition there were usually two or three working on wild monkeys in various parts of Kenya. Louis was constantly pleading with the Leakey Foundation to subsidize air fares for a succession of American students to go to Tigoni, but as one of the trustees put it, it was necessary to repair damage done to a project 'with a lot of negative history and difficult personnel problems', which had been complicated by Louis's frequent absences abroad.

As usual, Louis's powers of persuasion generally triumphed and the students came. A few were qualified – one had a degree in veterinary science and another had one in primatology – but for the most part they were untrained assistants, who had applied for the work for the sake of the glamour of Kenya and of Louis Leakey. Sometimes Louis lured them with promises that they would be trained for original research in the wilds, but instead they found themselves doing office work. A few lasted the course for a couple of years, but most of them packed it in after only a few months; one girl resigned because she said she was lonely at night! The science and grants committee of the Leakey Foundation could not be expected to interview candidates personally and had to rely on Louis's judgement as to the suitability of the applicants. Money would be issued to Louis to buy the air tickets, and the members of the committee often did not even remember the names of the students. One of the board said after a visit to Tigoni: 'Girls kept on popping out of the woodwork. When I asked "Who are you?" they replied "I'm Mary Lou" or whatever, and when I asked how they had got there they all said: "Through the Leakey Foundation." I had never heard of them.'

Some of the girls were in their teens, and after Dr Chalmers's departure they were left to their own devices. Theoretically they were under Louis's wing, and when he was in Nairobi he tried to visit them every week; the trouble was that he was so seldom there for any length of time. Poor Louis, it was not that he did not want to get a scientific director – he was desperate to find one; but he never had a guarantee of enough funds to be able to offer a reasonable contract to a person with suitable qualifications.

But before pursuing the history of Tigoni, we must look at other aspects of Louis's primate research which ran concurrently.

In 1957 a slim, long-legged blonde with a turned-up nose had appeared in Louis's office at the Museum to ask for a job. Jane Morris Goodall was twenty-three and had just spent a month in Kenya with a school friend; she went to see Louis because, as she said fourteen years later in her book *In the Shadow of Man* (1971),[3] she 'wanted to get closer to animals'. Louis promptly took her on as secretary.

Soon afterwards she went to Olduvai and there, as she puts it in her book:

> Louis decided that I was the person for whom he had been searching for nearly twenty years – someone completely fascinated by animals and their behaviour; someone who could forego the amenities of civilisation for long periods of time without difficulty.

The place that Louis had in mind for Jane was the Gombe Stream Reserve on the eastern shore of Lake Tanganyika, a narrow, mountainous strip ten miles long and about three miles wide, north of Kigoma. Some two hundred chimpanzees of the sub-species *Pan troglodytes schweinfurthii* had been isolated there by surrounding cultivation for a long time and Louis was particularly interested in them because of their environment. Unlike other chimps they did not live deep in the forest but along its fringes, spending a good deal of their time in relatively open country. Their habitat, in fact, was presumably similar to that of the Miocene apes of Rusinga and Fort Ternan, or the hominids of Olduvai. And, as man's nearest relatives, they might be expected to behave in much the same way as the early hominids.

Devotion to animals and a temperament suited to life in the bush, however essential for the work Jane proposed to do, would not be enough to impress potential sponsors; Louis therefore packed her off to get some background training at Dr John Napier's primate unit at the Royal Free Hospital in London. She studied hard, learnt about primate anatomy and habits, and also worked for a time at the London Zoo, all of which took nearly a year.

Louis then had to convince a sponsor that a girl without a degree was worth supporting, and he turned to his friend Mr Leighton Wilkie of the Wilkie Brothers Foundation who was excited at the possibility of finding evidence of tool-using by chimps. He provided $3,000 with which to buy Jane a tent and a boat and to cover her air fare, after which there would be just enough to keep her in the field for six months.

Jane's mother, Mrs Vanne Morris Goodall, was to come, too – not exactly as a chaperone, more a companion. She had already been out to stay with Jane in Kenya, where she and Louis discovered that they had played hockey together as teen-agers at Boscombe. Vanne Goodall still lives nearby at Bournemouth, but she also has a flat at York Mansions in London – a large, rambling flat in a rather depressing Victorian building in the noisy Earl's Court Road. She is divorced, and the flat was used mainly by her younger daughter Judy; but it had an extraordinary capacity to expand when all the family happened to be in London at the same time – Jane and Judy, and later their husbands and children, as well as their friends. Louis was adopted into the family and a room was always kept for his use. Vanne Goodall provided a haven whenever he was in London; she helped with his writings, arranged his appointments, entertained his colleagues, and sent for the doctor when he was ill – as he was so often during the last few years of his life. She accompanied him to his lectures and they often went to plays and the ballet together. Louis seldom made other concessions to the arts: he hardly ever read a book unless it was connected with his work, nor did he look at pictures, but he loved Mozart and church music, especially King's College choir. Possibly he appreciated ballet and Vanne Goodall for the same reason–they gave him a sense of tranquillity. For years she wrote to him regularly and consulted him on every personal problem, while he poured out his troubles to her, mainly in long-distance telephone calls – his favourite means of communication. Louis's letters were usually abrupt compared with the screeds he received from his various admirers; but even so it is amazing how he found time to write as he did, let alone read his huge correspondence.

Vanne and Jane Goodall went to Gombe in the summer of 1960. Vanne kept up Jane's spirits during those first depressing weeks when the chimps would not let her get anywhere near them; all day long while her daughter was up in the mountains Vanne waited patiently in camp, doing such housekeeping as there was to be done and running a clinic for the local fishermen.

Within only a few months of their arrival Jane had fulfilled both Louis's and Mr Wilkie's hopes: she observed not only tool-making but also meat-eating among her chimps.[4] Meat-eating had never been seen among forest-living chimps, but it proved to be quite common among these animals inhabiting more open country. This was particularly significant in its bearing on the early hominids, who no doubt became omnivorous when they moved out of the forests into the savannas. On several occasions Jane actually saw chimps eating monkeys, and by washing the dung she was able to prove that meat-eating was a regular habit.

The 'tool' which Jane saw the chimps using was a grass stem, which they licked to make it sticky and then pushed into a hole in a termites' nest. Before the rains the termites were indoors waiting to fly out; by poking a sticky stem into the mass within the nest, the chimps could catch a good few at a time. They then licked off the delicacy, like a child with a lollipop. Particularly important in its relevance to hominid behaviour is the fact that the tool was sometimes *modified* by pulling off leaves and thus obtaining a bare stick.

There are, of course, other examples of tool-use among animals, including primates. Wolfgang Köhler's well-known example of chimps using sticks to lengthen their reach, and even joining two sticks together, is less impressive because the animals were in captivity and the tools were provided for them. But cases have also been reported of tool-using by wild primates. Long ago that extraordinary South African, Eugene Marais, noted in his book *The Soul of the Ape*[5] that baboons broke open the fruits of the 'sausage tree' with rocks to get at the seeds. In Liberia chimpanzees crack palm nuts with rocks; in eastern Zaire Dr Adriaan Kortlandt saw them throwing branches as weapons; and a hunter called F. Merfield even observed chimps poking twigs into a hole in an underground bees' nest and licking off the honey adhering to the 'tools'. However, Louis – and through much publicity the rest of the world – was wildly excited about Jane's discovery. If a chimp could use a stem as a tool, the bigger-brained australopiths must have had a far wider range of artifacts than the stone tools which alone have been preserved; Dart's osteodontokeratic culture got a boost, and Mr Leighton Wilkie rejoiced that he had given his blessing both to Dart and to Jane. Louis even went around preaching that the definition of man as 'the tool-maker' would have to be revised as a result of Jane's observations: but there is a great difference between modifying a stem by pulling off a few leaves, for an immediate purpose, and deliberately shaping a stone by means of another tool for use some time in the future. The intention is not to belittle Jane's work, for she did excellent work; but Louis put undue emphasis on the importance of this particular aspect of it, and undoubtedly it had good publicity value.

Just before these discoveries of meat-eating and tool-using were made, the Wilkie Brothers Foundation's grant ran out and Louis was worried that he might have to withdraw his pupil from Gombe, but the Wenner-Gren Foundation gave a small sum just in time to keep her going. After these two discoveries there were no problems; the National Geographic Society began their yearly grants and Jane has never looked back.

Louis could squeeze money out of the most unlikely sources, such as a weekly newspaper more renowned for its long-legged, extravagantly busted cover girls than for its interest in science.

39. Jane Goodall was the first of Louis's three 'ape-girls'; with her in camp at Gombe Stream Reserve is her mother, Mrs Vanne Morris Goodall

40. *Below* Jane Goodall and chimpanzee friends entertain visitors from the National Geographic Society's research committee: Dr Leonard Carmichael, Dr Melvin Payne and Dr T. Dale Stewart

41. Birute Galdikas Brindamour began her studies of orang-utans in Indonesia in October 1971
42. *Below* By 1970 Dian Fossey was completely accepted by mountain gorillas in the forests of the Virunga Volcanoes, Rwanda. 43. Dian Fossey courageously endures the cold and almost perpetual rain and mist at her camp at an altitude of 12,000 feet

During Jane's second year at Gombe he persuaded *Reveille* to pay for her sister Judy to join her there to photograph the chimps. Although Judy had had little previous experience with a camera, the excuse was that the chimps would be less likely to object to the presence of a girl looking rather like Jane than they would to a stranger; the bait was that, in return for their support, *Reveille* could have exclusive interviews with Jane when she went back to England. Unfortunately Judy's pictures were literally a wash-out owing to three months' solid rain, but *Reveille* got their exclusive interview. 'The world of science wanted to know about the secret habits of the chimp in the wild,' the article began. 'The renowned anthropologist Dr L. S. B. Leakey (of "missing link" fame) chose Jane for this challenging assignment. She logged a thousand hours of lonely vigil in the jungle' . . . and so forth.[6]

Louis was most anxious for Jane to be taken seriously in scientific circles, which meant that she must take a degree. He was able to persuade the authorities at Cambridge that her work was important enough to be written up as a thesis, without having to get an ordinary degree first, just as he had done thirty years earlier in the case of Donald MacInnes, and as had happened also with Fred Wicker of Fort Ternan. At Louis's request Dr John Napier wrote a testimonial for Jane in which he said: 'She has very well developed powers of concentration and a capacity for original thought; she is completely absorbed in her subject . . . quiet and thoughtful, but completely determined.'[7]

Jane made her first public appearance in April 1962 at a symposium on primates at the London Zoo; she spoke about tool-using among the chimps at Gombe and her assurance and clear delivery made a very good impression. In that spring term she went to Newnham College and worked in the Sub Department of Animal Behaviour under Professor R. A. Hinde. Jane resented the time spent at Cambridge, for she was itching to get back to Mr McGregor, Flo and all her other chimp friends at Gombe; but she is ambitious as well as dedicated and so she went through with it, putting in the required number of months and flying back to Africa as often as possible.

There was now an added attraction at Gombe in the form of Baron Hugo van Lawick, a Dutch photographer who had been filming for Armand Denis's 'On Safari' programme. Louis got to know him through the Denises and formed the opinion not only that he would be the right person to photograph the Gombe chimps for the National Geographic Society but also that he would be the right husband for Jane; he duly fulfilled both functions. By now a feeding area had been established, and it was possible to get close-ups of the chimps eating bananas, as well as longer shots in the forest; Hugo made some outstanding films and stills. He and Jane were married in London in 1964, and Louis's grand-daughter Alison Davies was one of the bridesmaids; the honeymoon, of course, was spent at Gombe.

In the following year Jane got her PhD and was thus doubly emancipated from Louis, who up till then had administered the chimpanzee research account and paid the salaries. Jane was now scientific director of Gombe and Hugo became administrative director. Jane's period of solitude was over and she had to accept the presence of students to carry out various lines of research.

In 1966 the Director of the Tanzania National Parks began to press for Gombe Stream Reserve to be made into a National Park, and the administrative officers at Kigoma were all for it: whereas a Reserve was completely unproductive, a National Park would mean tourists and hence profits. It might be thought that Louis would have been in favour of this idea, since a National Park would give the chimps complete protection; but in fact far from welcoming the proposal he was dead against it. He was worried that if Gombe came under the control of the National Parks the authorities might interfere with the research work or even prevent its continuation. Louis would have liked to keep it permanently closed to outsiders, but he was overruled and Gombe became a National Park.

Until Jane married and got her degree Louis had been like a proud father to her; but he could not be accused of over-possessiveness – he never even managed to visit Gombe. At first he deliberately kept out the of way so as not to interfere, and after she got established his hip was too painful to allow him to negotiate the steep slope up from the lake. He wrote to her constantly, addressing his letters 'Dear F. C.' (Foster Child) and signing them 'F. F.' (Foster Father), while her sister Judy was 'F. D.'

(Foster Daughter). Louis adopted the whole Goodall family, and he helped Judy just as much as Jane.

Soon after Judy went to Gombe in an abortive attempt to photograph the chimps, Louis introduced her to the British Museum (Natural History), where she learnt to make casts and became extremely competent. While she was working there Louis did much propaganda on her behalf: at a meeting of the Wenner-Gren Foundation he exhibited a set of fibreglass casts of twenty hominid fossils which she had made and obtained orders for twelve sets at $200 each. There had been a row over this in Nairobi: Mary was furious that Louis had taken precious type specimens of hominids to London, where they were not available for study. Richard also disapproved of them leaving the country, and he wanted the National Museum to get royalities on casts rather than have the fees go to an outsider. Richard had asked the Centre's technician, Ron Clarke, if he couldn't produce anything better than the old-fashioned plaster casts which Louis had instructed him to make; he replied that certainly he could, and proceeded to turn out some beauties in plastic. Louis then blew his top, as he wanted Judy to have the monopoly. A small enough matter, but it caused a further rupture between Louis and his wife and son.

In the summer of 1968 Judy gave in her notice at the BM and Louis helped to set her up in a freelance business; it was registered as FD Casting – not many people knew that FD stood for Foster Daughter. At first it was carried on at Vanne Goodall's flat, but after Judy's marriage to Rod Waters she operated from Hampshire. Again Louis helped, securing a loan to pay for the house through an American admirer who had already given money to the Centre in Nairobi through the Astor Foundation, with which he had family connections. The loan was eventually made over to the Leakey Foundation on the understanding that it was to be repaid in due course by FD Casting.

After Jane became famous, she put in many appearances at Leakey Foundation dinners and 'intimate parties'; like Louis, she had to pay the penalties of fame by lecturing and keeping in the public eye in order to win support for her research. As Louis became less of a novelty in Los Angeles, other members of the

Leakey syndicate sometimes held the floor on behalf of the Foundation, but although Jane in particular drew large attendances none attracted such a crowd as Louis himself; to the end of his days he continued to be *the* star. Naturally he basked in the reflected glory from Jane's success and constantly drew attention to it, as well as to the success of any of his other pupils who had made the grade. He was not jealous of anyone within the syndicate; but with anyone outside it was quite otherwise, and he frequently pointed to the supposed inadequacies of others doing primate research. He seldom criticized his pupils' work in private, certainly never in public, and if any of them were failures, as with some of the Tigoni students, he made excuses for them. If anyone within the syndicate needed help, not only with money but also in connection with their private lives and relationships, Louis would go to endless trouble on their behalf; they were not all loyal to him, but he was nearly always loyal to them. Louis's involvement with the Goodall family was exceptional and his pride in Jane was therefore greater and more personal than in the case of any of the others, but he came to have a great affection also for his second ape-girl, Dian Fossey, and an equal admiration for her work among the gorillas.

After chimps it was logical to turn attention to man's next closest kin, the gorilla. Far less was known about these apes – it seems extraordinary to think that the first successful gorilla birth in captivity did not take place until 1956 (in Columbus, Ohio), and very few observations had been made in the wild. About the time when Jane first went to Gombe Dr George Schaller had spent a year studying mountain gorillas on the slopes of the Virunga volcanoes, on the borders of Zaire, Uganda and Rwanda, but Louis felt that a far longer period of work was necessary. In the introduction to his delightful book *The year of the gorilla* (1965), Schaller mentions that Walter Baumgartel, who ran the Traveller's Rest Hotel at Kisoro in Uganda 'wrote to Dr Leakey and Dr Dart, two of the foremost students of apemen in the world, and asked their advice. As a result Miss Rosalie Osborn, a former secretary, attempted to study the gorillas between October 1956 and January 1957, and when she left Miss Jill Donnisthorpe, a journalist, continued the study until September 1957. I awaited their reports with eagerness. When they arrived and I had read them, I was truly depressed . . . the amount of information about the behaviour of the apes which these investigators obtained was minute'.[8] Louis was responsible for launching both these young ladies – Rosalie Osborn was a long-standing member of the Leakey syndicate – but they did not have the right temperament for the work, nor the perseverance to proceed with it.

It is, of course, extremely rare to find anyone with sufficient patience for long-term studies of apes in the wild, and it was six years after Jane began her work before Louis managed to find a comparable person to tackle gorillas. Jane, unlike her chimps, is no extrovert, but Louis's second ape-girl, Dian Fossey, is perhaps even more introverted than the gorillas she studies with such complete dedication. She identifies herself with them, but without sentimentality; gorillas are Dian's life, and even a short parting from them to take a degree at Cambridge was too much for her to bear the first time she tried it.

Dian is less ambitious than Jane and shrinks from publicity, but if this gives the impression of a timid person hiding from the world in the forests it is far from the truth. Dian is a strong personality, with considerable charm and humour, and unbelievable courage. She is a complete loner, very tough, with extremely high standards and is critical of herself as well as others.

Very tall, dark and handsome, Dian was already thirty-five when she began her gorilla work. Born in 1932 in California, she trained as an occupational physiotherapist and eventually became director of the occupational therapy unit at Kosair Hospital, Louisville. In 1963 she went on a trip to Kabara, where George Schaller had worked; there she met Richard's safari business partner, the wildlife photographer Alan Root and his wife Joan, who took her with them when they went into the forests to photograph the mountain gorillas. That same year, Dian visited Olduvai and met Louis for the first time; but he did not know of her deep interest in gorillas until he came across an article she wrote on her brief observations of them in *The Courier Journal* of Louisville, in March 1965. During his lecture tour of the United

States the following year Louis went to see her at the hospital where she worked and proposed that she should study mountain gorillas. Dian gave in her notice to Kosair Hospital straight away, and in August 1966 went to California to say goodbye to her family.

While waiting for the funds that Louis promised to collect, and for visas to enter Zaire, Dian prepared herself thoroughly for the task. She studied at the Primate Center at Stanford University, near San Francisco, where Jane van Lawick Goodall was later to become visiting professor; she even went to the lengths of having her appendix removed so that, as she put it in a letter to Louis, 'I won't be spilling viscera all over the mountain'. This was done at Louis's insistence, and Dian thinks he made this condition so that he would be able to weed out any applicant who was not really serious. By the time three months had passed since Dian had thrown over her job and she seemed to be no nearer to getting to Africa, she began to get impatient. The visas still had not arrived and various sources that Louis had tried for grants had turned him down. At last, in November, he wrote to Mr Leighton Wilkie, who once again came up to scratch as he had done with Jane. Louis then heard from the National Geographic Society, to whom he had applied in the first place, that his letter had never been received; the NGS put up more money, as did the New York Zoological Society who had been part-sponsors of George Schaller. Professor Fairfield Osborn, president of the New York Zoological Society, asked in a letter to Louis:

> What new breed of human beings is this? These young women go out to far places, obviously relishing the risks involved. Do you think they are trying to prove they are better than men? A subconscious motivation of which they may not be aware?[9]

As we have seen, for this sort of job Louis did think that women were better than men.

Dian arrived in East Africa just before Christmas 1966, and Alan Root offered to accompany her to Kabara, where he stayed for a couple of days to help her set up camp and engage staff. After that she was on her own, with two reliable Africans who could fetch help if necessary. During the six months she was at

Kabara she observed three groups of mountain gorillas on the slopes of Mt Mikeno and the adjacent saddle, at an altitude of over 14,000 feet; in another few weeks she would undoubtedly have been completely accepted by one of these groups, but by then she was in real trouble. Schaller had got out just before Zaire obtained independence in June 1960, and when he went back later he was able to get across the border without too much difficulty; now, six years later, the situation was far worse. The frontier between Zaire and Uganda was closed, the guards had become truculent, and the warden of the Albert National Park insisted that Dian should come down to the Park's headquarters at Rumangabo for her own safety. There she was placed under house arrest for two weeks, and her pleas to be allowed to cross the border into Uganda were rejected by the military authorities, who also had a camp at Rumangabo. Things were getting 'a bit rough', as she put it, so she made the excuse of having to go to the border town of Kisoro to get money in order to register her Land-Rover in accordance with the laws of Zaire. She was accompanied by six armed soldiers, and all she could take with her were her personal belongings, field notes and chickens; all the rest of her equipment she had to leave behind at Rumangabo so as not to arouse suspicions that she meant to leave the country. (What, one wonders, did the soldiers make of the chickens? Perhaps they had heard of the eccentricities of Western women and thought it no more surprising that a hen should be taken for a ride than a dog.) Once across the Ugandan border Dian spun the Land-Rover round into the Traveller's Rest Hotel and into the protection of its proprietor, Walter Baumgartel. Ugandan soldiers conducted Dian's armed escort back across the border and she was told that she would be shot if she ever returned to Zaire.

Six months work in getting the gorillas accustomed to her presence had been wasted, and she now had to start the long habituation process all over again on Mt Visoke in Rwanda, five miles away from her previous camp on Mt Mikeno. Mr Leighton Wilkie generously provided money for new equipment, and stores were obtainable at Ruhengiri, twenty miles from her new camp. ('Stores' is perhaps a misnomer for the very limited range available in the few *dukas* at Ruhengiri and Dian lived mostly on potatoes.)

Once again, it took nearly six months to build up the gorillas' confidence, but by that time they were letting Dian approach to within ten feet of them. The animals were much wilder than those she had known in Zaire, which were protected in a National Park; the Rwanda gorillas had been harrassed by Tutsi herdsmen and frightened by Batwa poachers setting traps for duikers. Dian was successful in being accepted because she imitated the gorillas' actions, scratching herself ('grooming'), chewing wild celery, and copying their vocalizations, which include deep belching noises.

After a year Alan Root came to take pictures, but the weather was even worse than the normal for that altitude – not just cold and misty, but teeming rain. Frustrated, he returned to Kenya planning to complete the photography later; but he was bitten by a snake and nearly died. The work was continued by Bob Campbell, who arrived in September 1968 to look after the camp while Dian went to the USA to report to the NGS. Campbell is quiet and competent, and did not bother either Dian or the gorillas; she was happy to leave the camp in his hands. There had been trouble from poachers, and Tutsi herdsmen were grazing their cattle higher up the mountains into the last remaining refuge of the gorillas; they had even been threatening Dian's guards, so it was essential that the camp should not be left unattended.

Dian saw Louis briefly on her way through Nairobi – it was more than a year since they had met, but she was always very punctilious in sending him progress reports. He persuaded Dian to go to Cambridge to see Professor R. A. Hinde of the Department of Animal Behaviour, who supervised Jane while she was working for her PhD; Louis was very keen that Dian should do the same, but at that time she felt she must stay with her gorillas. She then went on to Washington, where the National Geographic Society arranged for her to hold a Press conference; she was disgusted with most of the reports, calling them 'blatant sensationalism'. (She herself later wrote a fine and modest article for the *National Geographic*, which appeared in January 1970.)[10] Within two months Dian was back on Mt Visoke and absolutely delighted to be there; all was well, and Bob Campbell, she said, had done a good job. It took six days to find her gorillas again, but when she did locate them it was a case of greeting old friends.

44. Louis lectured many times at the University of California's Riverside campus, where he always got a big welcome

45. *Below* Students in California were inspired by Louis's talks and flocked to hear him; on this occasion he was speaking at Victor Valley College, Victorville

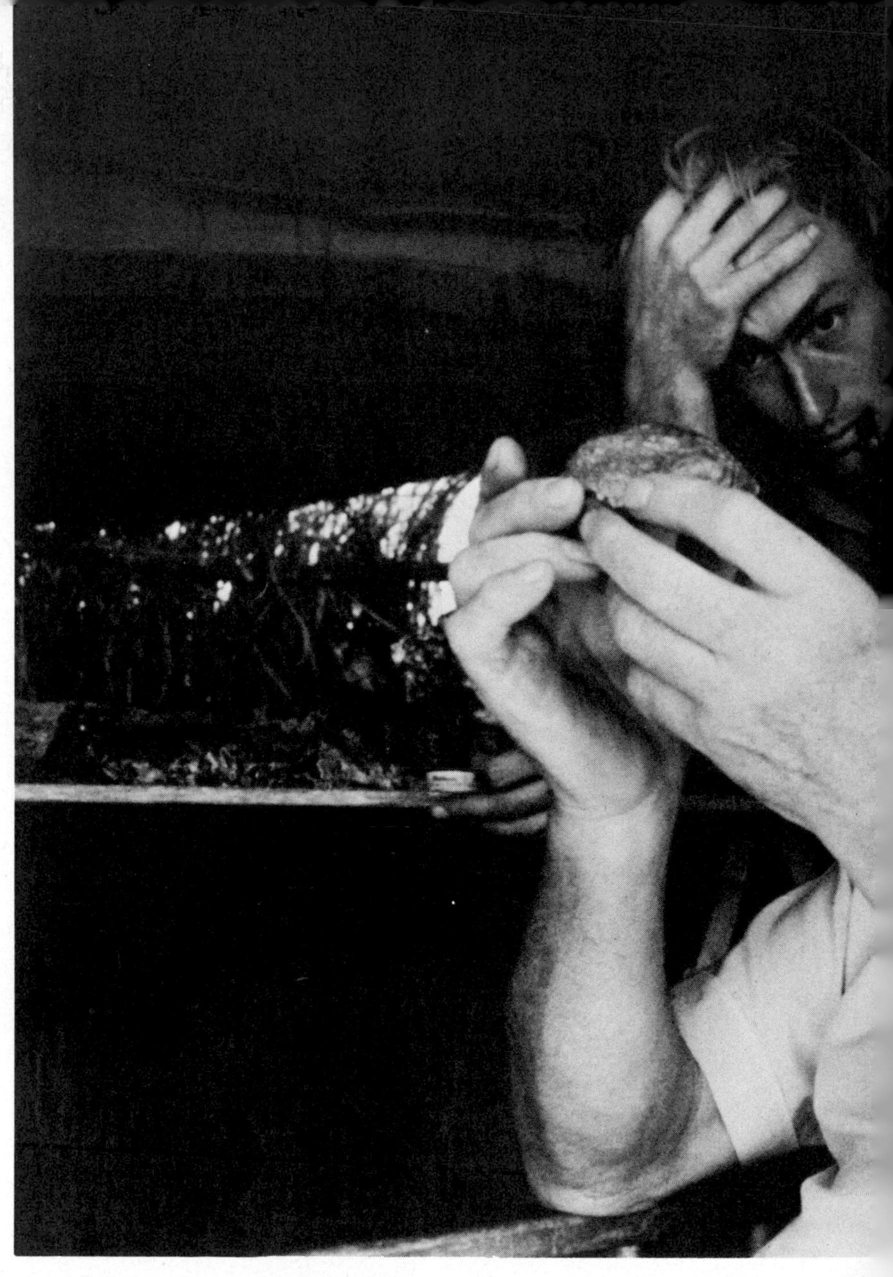

46. In his camp at East Rudolf Richard shows Louis the skull of a fossil monkey found in 1969

47. Louis engaged in a characteristic occupation – cleaning a fossil

So absorbed was Dian in her work that the presence of any visitor was a distraction she could hardly bear. In one of her letters to Louis she told him that no less than nine people turned up one day: 'But I hid in the cabin. Three were really freaked out hippies who reckoned this would be a great spot for communal living.'[11] Much as Dian would have liked to work entirely alone she needed assistants to make a survey of the mountain gorilla population of the Virunga volcanoes: Schaller estimated there were 400–500 left, but Dian reckons there are less than 300. The first candidate resigned after a very short time, a second withdrew as soon as funds were available, a third proved completely unsuitable. Dian, although an American, maintains that students are trained better at British universities and work harder than her compatriots; but when an Englishman was produced he, too, failed to come up to her exacting standards. The census work was eventually started by two girls, but they left after only a few months – and considerable expense in getting them to Rwanda. Louis had to find all these assistants, interview them and raise money for their fares and salaries; the many disappointments showed how difficult it is to find people prepared to work under such conditions – cold and misty, with a diet of potatoes and only the occasional glimpse of a gorilla to provide excitement. Louis appreciated all the more how fortunate he had been to find Dian.

He much enjoyed her letters, which usually contained amusing – and sometimes alarming – anecdotes. In one letter she told him that one of her staff had got hold of some of her hair, which he intended to take to a witch doctor in Zaire; the love potion made from it was to be slipped into her morning tea every day until she fell in love with him. On one occasion she was bitten by a dog which she suspected was rabid, but mercifully it was a false alarm. There was a more serious incident when the case containing all her money, cheque book, passport and car papers was stolen, and Louis had to send replacements.

Although there were still difficulties in crossing into Zaire by car, it was possible to walk there over the mountains. Dian wanted to see what was happening at Kabara, where she had begun her work, so she tramped for four hours in continuous rain into the country where she had been told she would be shot if she ever returned. On the way she broke more than sixty traps set by poachers and destroyed a number of huts left by Tutsi herders, who as usual had been working their way ever higher up into the mountains. Dian estimated that less than half the gorillas she had known in 1967 had survived; owing to the high prices paid by zoos, poachers were thriving, but she managed to rescue two baby gorillas destined for a zoo in West Germany and nursed them back to health. There had also been a very nasty incident when some drunken poachers hunting buffalo happened to meet a group of gorillas near a village and stoned six of them to death.

Just as Jane had won her emancipation when she obtained her degree in 1965, so Dian untied the strings which bound her to Louis after speaking at a Leakey Foundation dinner five years later. 'You will *never* know how nervous I was that night,' she confessed in a letter to him; but from that moment she gained confidence, and instead of dreading public appearances she began to look forward to them. As she was not qualified academically she was still supposed to be under Louis's supervision, but from then on she reported to him less frequently, and months went by when she did not write. As he was still responsible for raising the funds to continue her work this may seem ungrateful; but her independence was precious to her, and fond as she was of Louis she had no intention of letting their relationship go beyond a certain point.

There was a good attendance at the Leakey Foundation dinner in September 1970, and afterwards Joan Travis commented in a letter to Louis: 'I had expected her to be a super-sized rather masculine recluse; instead she turned out to be a delightfully feminine, warm human being. She won our hearts and applause. She is utterly devoted to you. . . . Her lecture and slides held us spellbound for one and a half hours. You should really be very proud of Dian.'[12]

Louis certainly was proud of her. Her letters, although infrequent, continued to be full of interest. For example, she sent this account of the gorillas' reaction to Bob Campbell, who returned to make yet more film:

I can't tell you how thrilled I am with the events of the past few months. Nothing could compare with the joy that I feel concerning the near total acceptance of not only my presence but also that of Bob Campbell and all his ciné gear. This week Digit (young blackback of group 4) literally leaned on my back, after grooming some burrs from my sock. Papoose continues to push her nose into the ciné camera in order to obtain her image more clearly; it makes focusing a problem.[13]

First chimps, then gorillas, finally orangutans – Louis was determined to sponsor someone to study them as well. Orangs are the farthest from man of the three great apes – gibbons are not counted as 'great' – and the only ones living outside Africa; they are also by far the rarest and least known in the wild. It has been estimated that only about 5,000 survive, of which one third are in captivity, and, apart from a hundred or so in Sumatra, they are restricted to parts of Borneo. Orangs are retiring creatures, living in scattered groups deep in the rain forests: not the sort of environment to tempt observers, even if warmer than Dian's Virunga volcanoes. Very few studies have ever been made on orangutans, apart from those of Dr Barbara Harrison in Sarawak and those of John Mackinnon of Oxford University; he spent three years observing orangutans in both Borneo and Sumatra, made a film of them and won his doctorate as a result of his research, but in Louis's eyes even this was not thorough enough.*

To complete his trio of ape-girls Louis found one with wide-set Slavic eyes and the beautiful name of Birute Galdikas Brindamour; the last part was added after he had chosen her for the work when she married Rod Brindamour – how fortunate that he should have a surname as poetic as her own. Of Lithuanian origin, born in 1946 at Wiesbaden in Germany, Birute is a naturalized Canadian and was educated in California. She obtained a BA degree in psychology, minoring in zoology, and an MA by thesis in anthropology; so in her case there was no need to worry about academic qualifications, as there had been with Jane and Dian. She even had a husband to protect her who was fully qualified for the role he

*John Mackinnon's book *In Search of the Red Ape* was published in 1974 by Collins.

would have to play; a Canadian, he was an air pilot, a good photographer, had experience in forestry work, and was a useful handyman. While waiting until the orangs were ready to pose for his camera, Rod Brindamour would be able to look after the camp, fetch stores, and help the Indonesians over conservation. Birute was only twenty-four, and the Indonesian authorities would certainly not have been happy if she had been alone in the remote jungle. The only slight problem was how to raise enough money to provide for a couple – it had been difficult enough to get anyone to sponsor a single person.

Operation Orang was by far the most expensive of Louis's ape projects, and his aim was to find $12,000. First he wanted Birute to look at the work that Jane and Dian were doing in East Africa, so he needed fares for her and her husband from California to Nairobi and then on to Borneo, almost the whole way round the world; and the Brindamours would have to be provided with equipment and living expenses for a trial period of at least six months to find out if the scheme was feasible. (As it turned out, when Birute got to Africa Dian could not be contacted, so she never saw the gorillas at all, but she spent a few days at Gombe with Jane.)

Dian had grown impatient at having to wait for three months before embarking on her studies, but Birute had to wait nearly two years. During this period, from 1969 until 1971, she learnt all she could about orangs in Los Angeles County Zoo and then got a temporary post at Simon Frazer University, British Columbia. She was certainly dedicated, and fortunately she was also athletic: Louis used to say that she even practised swinging from tree to tree so that she would be able to keep up with her quarry, but no doubt this was an exaggeration!

Even Louis began to get depressed at the lack of response to his fund-raising efforts, but he never gave up hope. In the end he fell short of his target by some $3,000, but the Brindamours were prepared to live on less than the proverbial shoestring. Most of the money came from a private benefactor via the Leakey Foundation, and the rest came from the Wilkie Brothers Foundation – as usual – and from the National Geographic Society. The NGS, however, made it clear that, although they were prepared to help to get the project started, they had no intention of getting involved in yet another long-term primate study. The readers of their magazine had had chimpanzees and gorillas, which was about as much as they could take on apes for the time being. (By April 1973, however, the *National Geographic* did publish a short announcement about Birute's work, accompanied by two of her husband's photographs.)

The location for the orang studies was chosen in consultation with the Nature Conservation and Wild Life Service of the Forestry Department, Djakarta. Its director advised the Brindamours to go to Sampit Reserve in southern Borneo, which was still relatively unexplored.

Two days after arriving at Djakarta in October 1971 Birute wrote to tell Louis that they had obtained visas granting them semi-permanent resident status in Indonesia for a period of three years. Although they had funds only for a short trial period they had every intention of staying for as long as it was necessary to complete the work.

Birute's next letter was written a month later from Sampit Reserve.[14] The problems, she said, were innumerable as the boundaries were not enforced and the local government had granted logging concessions along the rivers right into the heart of the Reserve. (The orangs have had to retreat farther and farther into the forest because of human encroachment, and now their existence is threatened by loggers.) Out of their meagre resources the Brindamours bought a motor boat to avoid having to depend on the whims of the logging companies when they needed stores; but one of those companies did come in useful by building them a cabin.

After they had been there a month Birute had already logged sixty-five hours of observation, mostly of one female orang and her infant. In their spare time, such as it was, the Brindamours reared three baby orangs confiscated from villagers. These animals were the nucleus of a rehabilitation centre from which several orangs were released back into the forest.

The Brindamours lived mostly on rice, sardines, bananas and tea. The constant rain meant that their clothes were always in rags and their shoes disintegrated. However, in spite of the damp, ants, leeches and occasional cobras, they thoroughly enjoyed their life of freedom and privacy. Their peace was disturbed only by the cries of the gibbons, to which they awoke each morning. They only went to 'town' once every two months, and their motor boat saved them the torture of paddling a canoe through the swamps for fifteen hours. Air mail could take up to three months to get to Kalimantan from the United States, and no less than five letters that Birute wrote to her mother in California during the first six months never arrived at all. In spite of the communications problem Louis got reports from time to time and was delighted with her progress.

He certainly picked three winners in his ape-girls; the only sadness was that he never saw any of the places where they worked. But just before the Brindamours left for Indonesia he did manage to get Jane, Dian and Birute together for dinner at Vanne Goodall's flat in London. Louis positively glowed.

13 The Calico Years

Ever since his Cambridge days Louis had had a hunch that man reached America much earlier than was generally accepted; and a chance meeting with an enthusiastic local archaeologist led him to try to prove it in the Calico Mountains of southern California. Once again he was to become embroiled in controversy, and this time it was even more prolonged than the Kanam episode thirty years earlier. For many colleagues who felt admiration and affection for Louis and his family, the Calico years were an embarrassment and a sadness.

It began in 1963 while he was visiting professor at Riverside. Miss Ruth de Ette Simpson, who worked at the San Bernadino County Museum at Bloomington, told him of primitive-looking artifacts in semi-desert country east of the Calico Mountains where, in Pleistocene times, there had been a lake. He accompanied her to the site and, in her own words, she showed him 'material in what I thought to be an important deposit, but Dr Leakey did not like it because it was a secondary deposit in a canyon'.[1] Although Louis did not like this particular site he *was* interested in the setting.

The so-called Yermo Fan is a deeply dissected alluvial deposit which accumulated in this now very arid area as a result of rain washing material out of canyons and spreading it at their mouths. As one channel became clogged another was made, and eventually a fan-shaped delta was built up. Louis's mind worked as follows. Geologists said that the fan accumulated a very long time ago during the Pleistocene, therefore it was of the right age for settlement by early man. There was suitable material for tool-making in the form of chalcedony, a milky-looking rock resembling chert. There must have been water, not only because the formation of the fan itself implied seasonal floods but also because there are high shorelines above the present residual lakes. And, as Louis put it, 'out in front was a great plain which must have been verdant green, with animals and plants suitable for food. It was ideal'.[2]

The setting was right, now all he had to do was to find tools *in situ*. Ignoring Miss Simpson's 'important deposit', he strode over the hills until his eyes lit on a clean face made by a mechanical excavator; sticking out of the side of the cutting were pieces of chalcedony which just *might* have been humanly worked. That was good enough for Louis; he stuck in some pegs on the surface of the fan just behind the cutting, saying to his astonished companion 'This is where we're going to excavate'. And that is what Miss Simpson was to do for many years to come; the local Leakey cult was to receive a tremendous boost, and some of Louis's Californian admirers were to credit him with supernatural powers.

In scientific circles, however, the reaction was noticeably cooler. The Yermo fan was dated by geologists to at least 50,000 years, probably 100,000 or even more. By the 1960s the date of the earliest American had been pushed back to some 20,000 years, although even that was by no means certain. There had never been a hint of human presence any earlier, and as for 100,000 years – it was heresy, completely unthinkable.

Rushing off to the National Geographic Society, Louis inspired them with his usual enthusiasm. Frankly, early man in America was of greater interest to them than early man in Africa. They gave money to begin excavations immediately. He then persuaded the San Bernardino County Museum that 'Dee' Simpson should spend her time digging in the place he had selected, which she did with tireless energy for the next six years. She and her crew of volunteers, mostly from the Archaeological Survey Association of Southern California, worked in five-foot squares, going down three inches at a time and using only small hand tools: dental picks, linoleum knives, shoemaker's awls and sculptors' implements. The position of every piece was plotted and a photographic record was made. The 'good' specimens were kept sitting on a pedestal of soil in the hope that Louis would put in one of his appearances before they had to be moved when the excavations got too deep. If he did not turn up in time the piece was witnessed

48. Louis's eldest son Colin, who left Uganda on 26 September 1972 with his family; Louis had been much concerned for their safety

49. *Below* Richard and his wife Meave with the '1470' skull, found at East Rudolf in 1972, which made Louis's last days particularly happy

50. Louis – a final portrait

by at least three people before it was lifted; nothing was left to chance or to possible criticism.

During the first season, which began in November 1964, nothing very convincing in the way of 'artifacts' turned up, and Louis was shown only a very small proportion of the thousands of rocks that were lifted. 'Those specimens which I particularly like,' said Dee Simpson, 'are separated and marked "special". I see them again and again, and select from those the ones that Dr Leakey sees'.[3] Of those hand-picked specimens there were only about half a dozen that Louis approved of, but these were enough for him to persuade the National Geographic Society to put up funds for a second season. Then, when the team reached the six- to nine-foot levels, 'artifacts' began to appear in significant numbers. The National Geographic Society arranged a field conference to decide whether the excavations should continue and the answer was 'yes'; but the NGS insisted that control pits should be dug to see if comparable finds turned up at random all over the fan. They did not: out of 12,000 pieces there were only twenty that Dee Simpson 'rather liked', and of these only three were accepted as possibles by Louis. 'They're not good,' he said, 'nobody will like them.'[4] Nobody did like them, and Louis had proved his point: the main excavations had – providentially – struck a concentration of 'artifacts', which were not present elsewhere in the fan.

By 1968, however, the National Geographic Society was beginning to lose interest, and Louis had to raise money elsewhere. He tapped at various times the Wenner-Gren Foundation, the Isotope Foundation, the Wilkie Brothers Foundation and the Pennsylvania Museum; there just might be something in it, these foundations thought, and if there was it would be something very important. Mr Robert Beck also gave money for the Calico dig through the Leakey Foundation; this was the very first grant made by the Foundation, in December 1968, nine months after it came into being, but it was by no means its last contribution to Calico.

Patiently Dee Simpson and her crew continued, year after year, their faith in Louis never faltering. The pits were roofed over and the excavators no longer had to toil under the broiling sun or winter snow; a generator was even installed to allow them to continue at night. A second master pit was opened, forty feet away from the original excavations; at the nine-foot level in this second pit forty-three specimens were accepted by Louis, whereas in the levels immediately above there had been practically nothing that he fancied. Then came something really exciting, something that the crew called their 'feature': a circle of nine fairly large rocks, with smaller ones in between. A Boy Scout visitor recognized their significance at once: 'Ma'am,' he said to Dee Simpson, 'I don't mean to tell you your business, but that looks just like where I cooked dinner last week.'[5]

One rock, a yellowish one likely to contain iron, was sacrificed for tests; it was sliced in half to obtain two independent measurements of the degree of magnetization, to determine whether it had been subjected to heat. One piece went to Dr Rainer Berger of UCLA, the other to Dr Vaslav Bucha of the Geophysical Institute of the Czechoslovakia Academy of Sciences. Dr Bucha cut his half into little cubes and found that those from the smaller end of the stone, the end which had pointed towards the centre of the 'feature', were more highly magnetized than the cubes from the larger end: i.e., the stone had been heated at the narrow end. 'In the final analysis', said Dr Berger, 'it would appear that in that circular arrangement of stones there must have burned a fire.'[6]

A preliminary report on the excavations at Calico was published in *Science* in 1968 by Louis, Dee Simpson, and Dr Thomas Clements, a geologist of the University of Southern California.[7] Among the 'artifacts' they distinguished many large flakes with bulbs of percussion, usually – but not inevitably – the hallmark of human workmanship; also a few 'scrapers' and some simple tools apparently worked on both faces. Casts of thirty-seven typical specimens were prepared by FD Casting, Judy Goodall's firm, for distribution to archaeologists.

For the most part prehistorians were not convinced by the casts, nor for that matter by the actual specimens which some of them saw when they visited Calico. One of the severest critics was Mary, who, if anyone, knew a genuine stone tool when she saw one. Louis was very upset by her reactions, but he was too deeply committed to retract and he had to keep up the morale of his diggers and of his sponsors.

Triumphantly he wrote to Joan Travis in 1969: 'One by one our critics are capitulating. Many scientists, including Professor Clark Howell, now agree with our findings.'[8] Professor Howell is an anthropologist, not an archaeologist, and 'many' was a gross exaggeration; but Louis did have one spectacular convert. The French prehistorian Dr François Bordes, who was an expert at manufacturing stone tools himself, visited Calico twice; on the first occasion he was doubtful, on the second he capitulated. Joan Travis described the event graphically in a letter to Louis: 'It is a strange experience to observe scientists being "objective". They examined and peered at all of the various flakes and tools – circled the table in the back room – round and round they went, in near absolute silence. Bordes gave his characteristic Gallic shrug now and then while Dragoo (of the Carnegie Institute Museum in Pittsburgh) kept saying "You really have an amazing assemblage of material here." Both as non-commital as could be.'[9] Later Bordes gave his views on tape for the Leakey Foundation's use, distinguishing between those specimens which he felt could have been created by nature and those which gave a good indication that man might 'well have been there at the time of formation of the fan'.

Encouraged by this objective view, Miss Simpson and her crew dug harder than ever; but before pursuing their fortunes it is necessary to keep abreast of events in Kenya.

Now that Louis was away from Nairobi so much it was inevitable that he should have to neglect the administration of the Centre. Each member of the staff was left to pursue his or her independent line of research, and there was little overall direction, at least so far as the bones were concerned. On the archaeolgical side Mary was in charge and things ran more smoothly, but she had no time to spare for anything other than Olduvai. One of the most efficient of those working at the Centre and always a great help to Mary, with whom she got on very well, was Richard's wife

Margaret; but in March 1969 she had a daughter, Anna, after which she could only work part-time.

For some time Richard and Margaret had not been happy together, and the reasons appear to have been very similar to those which had caused the break between Louis and Frida. Margaret, like Frida, wanted a conventional home life and found it difficult to adjust to Richard's irregular working hours and long absences.

That summer Richard went off to East Rudolf for three months on his second expedition, which was extremely successful from several points of view. As well as a great many fossil mammals beautifully preserved, the bag included a cranium almost exactly like the Olduvai Zinj; but instead of being in hundreds of pieces it was almost intact, although unfortunately lacking teeth. It was found – spotted from the back of a camel – exactly ten years, almost to the day, after the discovery of its famous relative from Olduvai. Another less complete cranium from the same level about a mile way was completely different. Richard, as already mentioned, distinguishes two lines of early hominids as '*Australopithecus*' (the Zinj-like form) and '*Homo*', and in his terminology this second skull is *Homo*.[10] The geologist Miss A. K. Behrensmeyer of Harvard tackled the mapping and correlation of the various tuffs; and samples were dated by potassium/argon at Cambridge University by Drs J. A. Miller and F. Fitch. Perhaps the most exciting find of the 1969 season was artifacts below a tuff dated to 2.6 million years; these are far older than any other stone tools yet known and about 800,000 years earlier than any artifacts at Olduvai.[11]

For about a month Dr Meave Epps joined the party; she had just finished her stint as director of Tigoni, where she had helped Richard with the paper he had prepared on a fossil colobus monkey from Baringo. Meave is intelligent and attractive, very feminine, gentle and restful. By the time the expedition returned from Rudolf Richard knew that he must sort things out with Margaret; although the break had come many months before, the love which he now felt for Meave made it final. Richard did not return to his house at Karen, and divorce proceedings were started.

Apart from the worries of his domestic problems, Richard, who hated inefficiency, was becoming increasingly concerned about the

Centre and the Department of Osteology. He made up his mind that both must be financed and administered by the Kenya Government via the Museum trustees, both for the good of the departments and for Louis's sake. Richard was fond of his father and it distressed him to see the deterioration in his health caused by the constant anxieties of fund-raising. The problem was how to persuade him to relinquish control; Richard knew it would not be easy, but probably he had no idea of just how difficult it was going to be.

Louis was becoming ever more obstinate, and the pain from his hip made him bad-tempered; he needed handling with great tact, but Richard, who was himself irritable because of his unhappiness at home, put the proposition more bluntly than he might otherwise have done. Having just returned from a long absence Louis was expecting a warm welcome, and this sudden proposal hit him like a cold shower. The situation was made even worse when Mary, who in any case was cross with Louis over Calico and other matters, supported Richard. Privately, Louis was rather relieved at the prospect of getting rid of the Department of Osteology and had to admit that logically it should be attached to the Department of Zoology at the Museum; but he could not believe that his own family appeared to be ganging up to try to push him out of *his* Centre, the Centre which he had founded and had kept going for seven years entirely by his own efforts.

Over the next few months the tension built up. The Museum trustees appointed a small committee to go into the question of the transfer of Osteology and ways of raising funds to absorb it; also, very much against Louis's wishes – and he himself was one of the Museum trustees – the committee was to discuss the future of the Centre. Since this concerned Louis so directly he had to be appointed a member of the committee; but fortunately for the others he went off to Paris and then America before it met. By the time he returned Richard had informed him that the trustees were planning to take over the Department of Osteology in two years time, on 30 June 1971. But as far as the Centre was concerned Louis said flatly that he was not prepared even to consider handing over any part of his responsibility for prehistory and palaeontology. Richard was building up a grandiose plan for the future of those departments, as told in the last chapter of this book, but for the moment he said no more.

There was yet another contretemps between father and son over the description of the new hominids from East Rudolf. When Louis said 'We must send them to Phillip Tobias,' Richard replied that he had no intention of doing so and that he proposed to give them to Professor Joseph Mungai of the University of Nairobi to describe. 'But he is an anatomist,' objected Louis, 'not an anthropologist.' 'That is the very reason why I mean to let him have them' retorted Richard. 'I want a straightforward anatomical description, I don't want an anthropologist to give them fancy names.' To which Louis, remembering the *habilis* controversy, might well have said '*touché*'.

In September 1969 Louis attended a conference in Paris sponsored by UNESCO on the theme of the origins of *Homo sapiens*. There he had several personal triumphs which took his mind off events in East Africa and family frictions. First, the 300 or so delegates unanimously accepted that the Kanjera skulls were Middle Pleistocene and around 100,000 years old; at long last, after 35 years, these fossils were officially vindicated* (the Kanam jaw was not discussed). The pundits had been influenced by the skulls discovered at Omo by Richard in 1967, which were apparently even older than those from Kanjera and yet indisputably *Homo sapiens*. Louis was elated enough over

*To those familiar with the see-saw of anthropological opinion and knowledge, it may come as no surprise to learn that within a few years of being at last accepted, the Kanjera skulls were rejected once more (happily it did not happen until after Louis's death). Radiometric assays on the human bones and associated fauna show a considerable difference in the averages of the groups: human bones 22 parts per million eU308 (uranium), fauna 136 p.p.m. Reporting these results in 1974 (*Journal of Human Evolution*, 3: 257), Dr Kenneth Oakley infers 'that the Kanjera hominids, although fossilized (Upper Pleistocene?), are considerably younger than the Kanjeran faunal stage (Middle Pleistocene).' And he concludes: 'When deposits such as the Kanjera beds become waterlogged during the wet season, bones lying on the surface readily become incorporated, so that when subsequently discovered they can easily have the appearance of ocurring *in situ*.'

this, but there was more to follow. Dr François Bordes, who was chairman of the session, publicly proclaimed that some of the Calico pieces were artifacts and must have been made at the time of formation of the Yermo fan. Louis had something exciting to report to the Leakey Foundation board meeting in October.

This was a sad occasion as Allen O'Brien had just retired as president; the reason he gave was that the position should be filled by someone in daily contact with the executive director. 'With my propensity to travel,' he said, 'I am clearly not that man.'[12] The obvious choice was Ed Harrison, in whose building the headquarters of the Leakey Foundation was housed. He duly became president while the founder, O'Brien, took a back seat as vice-president. A brunch was given in Allen's honour, and letters and telegrams of appreciation for all he had done were read. He was presented with what was described as an 'encapsulated jaw' – a cast of Louis's earliest hominid, *Kenyapithecus africanus*, encased in a plastic block. Other trustees got one too, but non-board members had to pay $1,000 to qualify for a jaw.

At the board meeting which preceded the ceremony Louis announced that the Emperor of Ethiopia had agreed to become patron of the Leakey Foundation. There were also important matters to discuss. For some time Louis had been planning an international conference on Calico so that he could, he hoped, confound his critics once and for all when they saw the evidence for themselves. The Leakey Foundation had voted $5,000 towards the costs, and it was hoped that the meeting could be held in California early in 1970. As it turned out everything had to be postponed because in February of that year Louis had a heart attack.

Earlier that month the Leakey family had reversed their usual roles; Louis remained in Kenya, while Mary and Richard reported to the NGS in Washington on the previous season's work at Olduvai and East Rudolf respectively and put forward their case for renewed grants for 1970. This was the first time that Mary had done this herself; although by now she was the undisputed boss at Olduvai, always it was Louis who had reported to the NGS research committee on her behalf.

For his part, Richard had something to be proud of – the oldest tools in the world. After Washington he went on to lecture at various universities, followed by a visit to Los Angeles to make his debut at a Leakey Foundation dinner.

Some of the officers of the Foundation, who knew about the row over the Centre and who naturally took Louis's side, had not exactly been looking forward to Richard's visit. What, they wondered, was his motive for appearing at their functions to raise funds for his father's enterprises? Was he hoping to make contacts who might be useful in financing his own projects in the future? It was with a feeling of suspicion that they turned up at UCLA to listen to his commentary on a film of the East Rudolf expedition, but he completely won them over. Students had stood outside with signs saying 'Please help me. Sell me a ticket', and two hundred of them had to be turned away. The applause after the lecture was nearly as enthusiastic as it would have been for one of Louis's talks. Richard had definitely arrived.

The Leakey Foundation dinner took place on the following night at the select California Club. It was attended by twenty-three trustees and spouses, as well as twenty-two new Fellows plus 'spouses or dates', a total of eighty-six guests. The general opinion was that Richard conducted himself with skill and dignity, and Robert Beck reported to Louis: 'Richard has come and gone in great style. He has perfected a poise about handling difficult questions in public and he exhibits an energy capacity that is extraordinary. He has a brilliant way of bringing an exciting orderliness to a set of incomplete facts.'[13]

Philip and his newly married – but soon to be divorced – Californian wife Lynn also happened to be in Los Angeles at the same time, as he was negotiating about the television showing of a documentary on a safari he had made; so the whole family, except for Jonathan, who was quietly growing melons at Baringo, was in America cut off from Louis. Louis decided to spend a few days at Olduvai, and while he was there he had a feeling that things might not be going too well with Mary in Washington; at any rate he was worried and felt unwell. He had a pain which he attributed to indigestion, but in spite of this he suddenly decided he must go to Washington himself, so he drove the three hundred miles to Nairobi and boarded the first available plane for London. During the flight he was in severe pain and had to be carried off the aircraft at London Airport; he said he must have an ambulance, but refused to go to hospital and insisted on being taken to Vanne Goodall's flat. She called for a doctor, who referred him to a heart specialist, and the ECGs showed that he had had a coronary three days ago, dating from the time of his indisposition at Olduvai. He was put into the Princess Beatrice Hospital in Old Brompton Road, where he had a far more serious heart attack. For five days he was on the danger list, after which he began sending cables to the National Geographic Society that he intended to come to Washington in a 'few days'. In fact he was out of action for nearly six months.

As soon as he was out of danger Louis began to receive a stream of visitors. Of course he was supposed to keep quiet, but he insisted on talking non-stop about the latest finds from Olduvai, from Fort Ternan, from East Rudolf. He kept this up for the six weeks he was in hospital, and all the time he fretted about what was happening at the Centre and at Tigoni, and about how soon he could get to America to sort out the Leakey Foundation. Joan Travis kept him fully informed about their activities: preparations were well in hand for the Calico conference; lectures and dinners were being arranged for Jane and Dian; and the usual fund-raising efforts were going on. 'Please stop your fretting,' she entreated him. 'Problems and anxieties always assume overwhelming proportions when you feel alone. But you are ***not*** alone – you are surrounded by people who care *deeply* and who are all working together to lighten your load.'[14] However, her soothing words did little to alleviate his anxiety about the lack of funds, especially for Tigoni and the Centre.

After Richard got back to Nairobi he had to run the Centre as well as the Museum and, while Louis was seriously ill, had to make decisions without consulting his father. Later, when Louis asked for more information, it was not always forthcoming in enough detail to satisfy him and he began to think that Richard was hiding things from him. In fact it was simply that Richard was too busy to put everything down on paper.

In the summer of 1970 Richard went to East Rudolf on his third expedition, and by the end of the season at least twenty more hominids had been discovered. Meave found a mandible which pleased Louis greatly: it appeared to resemble the Kanam jaw, thus implying that the Lower Pleistocene '*Homo*' which he had talked about for so long had existed way back on the Pliocene-Pleistocene boundary.

Soon after the expedition returned to Nairobi in October, Richard and Meave were married. Although Louis and Mary were very fond of Margaret, they were equally fond of Meave, and they were delighted to see Richard so happy. Margaret continued to work at the Centre, so they did not lose sight of Anna, a bright and charming child who was the apple of her father's – and her grandmother's – eye.

Meanwhile Louis had to find something to occupy his mind while he was convalescing in Vanne Goodall's flat in London. His energy in embracing causes was amazing: he managed to get a Society for the Prevention of Cruelty to Animals started in Ethiopia, and he probed into the activities of the Church of Scientology!

He also used this period of enforced inactivity to make a series of 16 mm colour films, with a camerman sent to London by the Leakey Foundation. The Foundation had two objects in view: one was to record some of Louis's thoughts for posterity and, it was hoped, to sell the documentaries commercially; the other was to enable him to earn some money while he was out of action. One dialogue was with Jane discussing primate research; another was with her sister Judy on cast-making; and another with Vanne Goodall on conservation, in which they discussed the anti-conifer campaign in the New Forest. This was another cause which Louis had embraced, and he had thrown himself into it with as much vigour as if the Forestry Commission had proposed to plant Christmas trees in his beloved Nairobi National Park rather than in Hampshire. In another film he talked with Michael Day on the evolution of man; and in others he spoke about prehistoric art, fire-making, and the manufacture of stone tools. One of the most appealing was the film in which he demonstrated string figures to his Davies grandchildren, accompanied by some of the African folk tales that he told so delightfully.

The total unedited footage amounted to some 13,000 feet, from which the Leakey Foundation eventually extracted about forty minutes of roughly edited material from a couple of the films. As for the rest, when Louis saw the results he had to admit that it would be necessary to add extra sequences to make the films a commercial proposition, and that some would be suitable only for schools. At the time of his death, the films were still gathering dust in the Foundation's office, but the trustees were hoping to make negotiations for the marketing of at least some of them.

In spite of his inability to relax during his convalescence Louis made an incredible recovery from his heart attack; but he had had a real shock, and perhaps even he recognized that the bell was beginning to toll. For one thing his memory was impaired, and he was unable to do a full day's work, which made him cross with himself and with anyone who tried to restrain him. The only compensation was that for the sake of his heart he had to lose weight – by the summer he had managed to shed 28 lbs – and this benefited his hip; for the first time since the operation he was able to get around with one stick instead of two.

When at last he could return to Nairobi he found that everything was running smoothly under Richard's direction and perhaps he admitted to himself, if not to anyone else, that there might be something in the idea of handing over control of the Centre. The nagging feeling that he was superfluous in Nairobi made him more determined than ever to make a go of Calico. The conference had been postponed until the end of October, eight months after Louis's coronary and only two months after he was allowed to travel; his colleagues' admiration for his courage probably made them less outspoken in their criticisms of the Calico 'artifacts' than they might otherwise have been.

During the weekend of 22–25 October 1970 about a hundred geologists and archaeologists plus spouses assembled at the San

Bernardino County Museum to evaluate the results of Dee Simpson's six years of intensive work and Louis's unshaken faith in Calico. The Leakey Foundation paid Louis's travel expenses to come to the conference and $5,000 towards the fares of others attending; the rest of the money was provided by the University of Pennsylvania Museum. Among those present who have been mentioned already in this book were Drs Desmond Clark, Basil Cooke, Garniss Curtis, Richard Flint, Richard Hay, Glynn Isaac and Kenneth Oakley. The gathering was said to be the largest scientific get-together ever convened to examine the evidence from a single site. Most of the participants came with a fairly open mind, although they were prejudiced in the sense that they were *hoping* to be convinced because of the affection and respect they had for Louis.

The delegates spent one day examining the excavations, which by now were twenty feet deep; a morning listening to papers by Louis, Dee Simpson, the geological adviser Dr Clements and others; and an afternoon scrutinising the so-called artifacts in the Museum. The geologists among them were amused at the efforts made by Dr Clements to prove that the Yermo fan was at least 50,000 years old: this they did not dispute – they were sure it was at least 100,000 years old, which made it more difficult than ever to accept man's presence in America at such a time.

Louis's case rested on five main lines of evidence. There was an unusual concentration of flakes within a restricted area; there was selectivity in the material used to make them; some specimens showed the use of several different flaking techniques; material had been imported to the site; and, above all, there was a hearth. The opposition view was summarized very clearly by Dr Kenneth Oakley, who had taken a particular interest in the problem of flaking by natural agencies, giving many examples in his popular handbook *Man the toolmaker*. He pointed out that the Calico specimens were remarkable for their heterogeneity – even Richard's tools from East Rudolf, dated to more than two and a half million years, show a regular pattern of flake scars, indicating that the tools had been worked with deliberation. Louis himself had said in the *National Geographic* of September 1960, at a time when Zinj was considered to be the toolmaker at Olduvai,

'*Zinjanthropus* clearly fashioned his own tools, the Oldowan implements . . . and *they show a remarkable consistency of design*' (my italics).[15]

Oakley also pointed out that concentrations in a small area do not necessarily imply the work of man, as the rocks could have been brought there by natural forces. If the flakes had been due to human activity one would expect to find at least a few cores from which the flakes had been removed. With regard to Louis's argument about selectivity of the best materials, Oakley said that chalcedony is more likely to be flaked by natural pressure or concussion than other rocks because of its fragility. He also dealt with the point about different flaking techniques on one specimen: when there is concussion between boulders due to torrent action, a lump of rock could be subjected to several rounds of flaking.

One of the strongest weapons in the Leakey armoury was the 'feature' in the second master pit, the so-called hearth; but the sceptics produced answers for this too. The stone showing higher magnetization at one end might have been struck by lightning or heated by a bush fire; the circle could have been a natural arrangement, produced as the result of boulders swirling round in a hollow. There was no sign of fire crackling on the stones, nor were there any traces of carbon (although these could well have disappeared in the course of time).

Quite a few of the prehistorians found themselves in agreement with Oakley's conclusions that all the Calico 'artifacts' were produced by natural processes, although few actually said so out of consideration for Louis's feelings; and because of the apparent minority of dissenters Louis took it that he had won.

On their way to the conference Dick Hay and Kenneth Oakley had stopped at a gas station and got into conversation with the attendant. 'I've dug there myself from time to time', he said, 'but I never saw anything but rocks.' This just about summed up their opinion after they had seen the site, and the opinion of many of the others. A handful of those who attended the conference were convinced, some privately rejected the artifacts out of hand, and there was the usual proportion of 'don't knows'. Many felt that more evidence was needed – but the excavations had been going on for six years and thousands of specimens had been amassed, so it is hard to see what further evidence could be produced.

A report of the conference was published by the San Bernardino County Museum Association two years later, in 1972.[16] Its title, *Pleistocene man at Calico*, was rather unfortunate: there was no doubt that the fan deposits were Pleistocene, but whether man had shaped the rocks they contained was still very much an open question. The transcripts of the sessions were heavily edited 'to reduce the verbiage' and may have been somewhat selective, but reading between the lines there can be no doubt that the issues were far from resolved. But whether or not the Calico Hills were inhabited fifty thousand or a hundred thousand years ago it would be a rash person who would bet against human remains far earlier than those known at present being found in the New World sooner or later. As Louis said, it is just a question of looking in the right place, and at least he inspired his American colleagues to go on looking.

Even those who disagreed with the conclusions drawn from Calico were unanimous in their opinion that the site should be preserved as a model of how prehistoric excavations should be conducted; even Mary agreed that the techniques had been exemplary. So far the site is protected, and Miss Simpson is praying that the pits will not have to be filled in. An ancient guard, looking and talking like a character out of a Western, emerges from his hut to conduct visitors up the steep slope and through a locked door in the cage surrounding the first master pit. Overhead is the bridge from which measurements were taken, and a witness column has been left in the centre. A tape recording echoes round the pit – Dee Simpson's voice giving an excellent summary of the whole story. Another short climb, and visitors enter the second master pit to view the original 'feature' and yet another stone 'circle' which was exposed later. Back in the San Bernardino Museum Dee Simpson is writing a full report on the 'artifacts', which now include a number of supposed cores and small blade-like flakes. She played her part with skill and loyalty and still has complete faith in the human workmanship of the objects she unearthed. Even if Louis had felt in his heart he might have been wrong it could not be expected that he would ever admit it; after the conference he just didn't talk much about Calico.

During the two years between making its first grant – to Calico – in December 1968 and the end of 1970, the Leakey Foundation had given away more than $150,000; of this over $77,000 had been awarded to projects and individuals under Louis's direction, mainly Tigoni, the Centre and Calico. When he saw these figures Louis wrote to the executive director, Gary Phillips:

> Am I to understand that the Foundation has granted more than half of its grants to projects which are not under my direction, when at the time the Foundation was set up it was especially for the purpose of financing projects under my direction, thus saving me time and energy as I grew older? I find this extremely disturbing and distressing.[17]

The repetition of words demonstrates the extent of Louis's indignation when he dictated them. The letter also shows very clearly that nothing the male members of the committee could say would budge him from his view that the whole purpose of the Foundation was to serve *his* needs and his alone. (The lady members had always shared this view.)

The explanation of Louis's egocentric attitude, as well as his obstinacy over Calico, will be apparent after reading the narrative of woe told in the next chapter. His mind had been affected by a series of physical mishaps, and anyone who did not have his indomitable constitution would have been dead long ago.

14 A Chapter of Accidents

African bees are notoriously *kali* – fierce – as they say in Swahili, but they held no terrors for Louis since his early bee-keeping experiments at Kabete, in fact he rather fancied himself at handling them; it was therefore adding insult to very severe injury when hundreds of the creatures descended out of the blue and made a completely unprovoked attack on him. It happened in January 1971 at the old Arab city of Gedi, near Malindi on the Kenya coast where Louis had bought a house. With its facilities for surf-riding, its dhows and its picturesque fish market Malindi has become the Mecca of countless package tours from Europe, but it is still possible to avoid the luxury hotels and boutiques and enjoy a private paradise. Swimming in the gloriously warm water of the Indian Ocean was the best possible treatment for Louis's hip, and it was also good for his heart to get down to sea level from an altitude of 5,500 feet at Nairobi. At his house at Malindi Louis could unwind, forget financial worries and escape from family pressures. He often invited Tigoni students and others to keep him company there, and in between his visits he could make a little money by letting the house.

One day he was resting in the shade of a tree at Gedi while the girls who were with him explored the ruins. Gedi is surrounded by thick forest and is hot and airless; no doubt the bees were attracted by Louis's sweat when they suddenly descended from the branches above. He got up to try to fend them off, over-balanced and fell heavily to the ground; the effects of this fall turned out to be even more serious than the stings, although this was not discovered for a long time. Louis used to boast that he received about eight hundred stings, which was certainly an exaggeration; but they did amount to several hundred.

This would have been more than enough to finish off most healthy people, but for someone who had suffered a severe heart attack only a year ago it was nothing short of a miracle that he survived.

Because of his heart condition antidotes would have been dangerous; and he should have had a pressurized plane to take him to hospital in Nairobi, but the Flying Doctor service provided one without even oxygen. For at least a week after he got to hospital he was unable to see or even to think; this was attributed to the massive dose of drugs he had been given but in fact was due to concussion from the fall. Louis was in hospital for over a month and once again, as he had done after his coronary, he made an incredible recovery; but he was left partly paralysed and his right hand was powerless. To someone who depended so much on scribbling down his thoughts for lectures, articles and books this was a terrible blow, and it also meant that all letters, however private, had to be dictated. Enquiries and messages of sympathy poured in from all over the world, and Louis's fans suffered agonies of anxiety when they received only formal notes of acknowledgement.

In contrast to some who moaned that they felt so cut off Dian Fossey's humorous letter must have cheered him up. 'Haven't you enough to cope with without taking on a swarm of bees single-handedly?' she asked. 'What next! If you don't start behaving yourself, you're going to find yourself in real trouble one of these days young man.'[1]

One of Louis's first thoughts on emerging from his coma had been for Dian; thinking she might be short of funds he dictated a letter telling her to contact his secretary if she needed money and he would fix it somehow. Of course, as had happened also after his heart attack, as soon as he was capable of thinking he began to worry. He wrote to Joan Travis: 'Just how I shall meet my financial commitments when I have been unable to go over [i.e. to the USA] to earn my usual money for current expenditure I don't know, but I will cope by mortgaging one or both of my plots at the coast.'[2] In fact Louis only had one: the other was Mary's.

The Leakey Foundation was going through a particularly worrying time just then – as told later – but the problems were kept from Louis until he recovered. Meanwhile Ned Munger resigned as chairman of the science and grants committee and was replaced by Clark Howell, an all-round anthropologist and an excellent chairman.

It is well known that people are prepared to be generous towards something that touches them personally, such as health, but pure science – whether prehistory or space travel – does not come into that category. The trustees were beginning to discover that the appeal of the past was limited, and they began to think about widening their scope. If the Foundation was to embrace living monkeys and apes there was no reason why it should not include also the welfare of present and future man. Conservation, for example, was particularly popular with contributors. One of the first hints is given in the minutes of a board meeting on 21 July 1970: 'It is timely for the Foundation to present to the public personalities and educational information related to man's origin, current and future environment, as well as conservation of human and natural resources.' Richard was looking for funds for conservation at East Rudolf, where a National Park was to be established, and during a visit with Meave to Los Angeles in January 1971 he obtained money for research on animal feeding patterns.

Feeding patterns of the monkeys at Tigoni, however, were less popular with the Leakey Foundation. As usual one of Louis's main preoccupations was to find a scientific director for the place. Just before the bee episode he had written to Gary Phillips:

> I wonder how you expect me to persuade any of the four candidates to give up their present work and come out to Tigoni when there is no certainty of continuity beyond June? . . . Clearly nobody but an idiot would think of accepting an appointment where there was no chance of paying him as well as the staff under him and have enough left over to feed the monkeys and pay the menial staff. . . . At the moment it is quite clear that there is no understanding at all of what the Tigoni problem is.[3]

The Leakey Foundation understood it only too well! Tigoni was like a piggy-bank that was emptied every night, and its appetite was insatiable.

Soon after Louis wrote this letter the science and grants committee approved a grant of $20,000 for Tigoni, to cover six months, under certain conditions. They proposed that the National Primate Research Centre should be controlled by a scientific board of directors; that the staff should be professionally trained; that scientific reports should be published; and that 'efforts should be made to restore past records and to maintain continuing data records on research projects.'[4] Fair enough, one would think; but Louis's reactions were predictable: 'I would first need to know,' he wrote,

> just what influenced the science and grants committee to make the recommendations which they did make without at least consulting me about them. I have made a variety of financial arrangements including pledging my property and house to secure a loan to keep Tigoni running. . . . I am also negotiating with other organizations. . . . I am sure it will be less difficult to obtain funds from them than from the science and grants committee.[5]

In insisting that Tigoni should be controlled by a board – in other words that it should cease to be dominated by Louis alone – the Leakey Foundation had hoped that the members of that board would be the Museum trustees. However, Louis argued that as they would have nothing to do with the financial or administrative side before, there was no reason why they should do so now. Very well, said the Foundation, Tigoni should seek affiliation with the University of Nairobi; but in Louis's eyes this was infinitely worse. He was indignant at what he took to be an implication that 'his' primate centre would be in a subordinate position to the University, and he was afraid that they might dictate policy. Mr Harold J. Coolidge, one of the Foundation's trustees, was brought in to act as mediator. He was used to handling far more delicate matters than this; with great tact he drew a comparison with the Serengeti Research Institute's 'connection' with the University of Dar es Salaam.[6] Louis was completely mollified; as he wrote to Gary Phillips, it all boiled down to language difficulties: 'Harold Coolidge has had a brain wave,' he said, 'and realized the conflict was because of the different use in English and American of "affiliation". In strict English, affiliation indicates a subordinate and junior position, i.e., the relationship of son to father. I most emphatically rejected that I should be "affiliated" in such a way to the University of Nairobi. Then I received Harold Coolidge's copy of the notes on the relationship of the Serengeti Research Centre [*sic*] to the University of Dar es Salaam and I began to realize that you were not using the word in our strict English sense, but rather for a formal written association between Tigoni and the University, without implying any subordinate status on our part, an association rather of equal bodies for mutual benefit.'[7] Equal? Impossible to believe that even Louis considered Tigoni to be on equal terms with the University.

In fact he must be forgiven, as his loyal friends in the Leakey Foundation forgave him, for the vehemence of his initial outburst and for these pathetic attempts at face-saving; for while these delicate manoeuvres were going on Louis had not fully recovered from the bee stings and the concussion. The end of the Tigoni negotiations will be described later in their proper place; meanwhile, true to their word and to the best of their ability, the Leakey Foundation continued to pour money into the National Primate Research Centre out of consideration for Louis.

Apart from Tigoni, one of Louis's main worries during his convalescence was the future of that other Centre. In March, Richard, as administrative director of the National Museum, confirmed formally that the Department of Osteology would be taken over by the Museum trustees at the end of June, as arranged two years previously, and the Centre would be taken over a year later, in June 1972. Although Louis was quite happy about Osteology, and even at the prospect of being relieved of the financial responsibility of the Centre, as far as its control was concerned he still had every intention of staying at the helm. His reply to Richard makes this clear: 'I would ask you to confirm the fact that although I shall be relieved of the necessity of raising the total finance for Prehistory and Palaeontology after July 1972, this does not mean that the Trustees imagine that I wish to relinquish my responsibility for research work undertaken in this department. Most emphatically I hope that I shall be able to carry out my duties as Hon. Director of Prehistory and Palaeontology much more thoroughly, unless my health deteriorates. At the present moment it is very much on the mend.'[8]

This optimistic note is typical of Louis's courage; not only was he paralysed down the right side but, unbelievable as it may seem, was actually recovering from yet another set-back when he wrote. He had taken three girls, two students and a prospective secretary, on a trip to Tsavo National Park, and he and one of the girls were afflicted with vomiting and diarrhoea; as they were too ill to move the others asked the Flying Doctor service to come and pick them up. When they described the symptoms there was panic: a cholera scare happened to be on at the time, and the thought that Louis might have this on top of everything else was extremely serious. The health authorities were informed, and an inspector, together with a doctor and a nurse, flew immediately to Tsavo; happily it was a false alarm, and Louis proved to have ptomaine poisoning.

The Government was not to take over the Centre for another year, and until then Louis had to keep it going. The current grant from the National Science Foundation was due to expire in September, and he put in a further application, stressing the need for expansion of the laboratory facilities. All Richard's material was flowing in to the Centre: 'Already', said Louis, 'he has discovered more than I have in forty years at Olduvai; carried the dating of fossil man back from 1.9 to 2.6 million years; discovered vast amounts of undescribed new fossil material and immensely rich exposures of geological deposits.'[9] In view of the strained relations between Louis and Richard at this time over the future of the Centre it is touching to read of his pride in his son's exploits and his acknowledgment of their importance. Louis also pointed out in his application that they needed more technicians to develop the fossils out of the rock, to make casts and to do photographic work. The Centre, as he stressed, was international rather than national – the French and American collections from Omo were being studied there – and its staff were underpaid. Several had already left and palaeontologists were hard to find; Louis did not want to lose any more for lack of money.

As already mentioned Richard had been 'thinking big' about these matters for some time, but he could not risk upsetting his father still further by discussing his ideas with him. However, Louis had heard rumours and eventually Richard had to admit that the Museum trustees planned to set up an Institute for Prehistory and Palaeontology which would take over all the collections and work of the Centre. Louis's retirement was an integral part of this scheme; but although Louis agreed that he might consider retiring in five or ten years time he announced that he had no intention of being pushed out in the cold at the tender age of sixty-eight. He said he would be delighted for others to raise the funds, so long as he retained control of how the money was spent. It is no secret that Louis constantly borrowed from one research fund to rescue some other project that might be foundering at the time, just as he put money out of his own pocket – when he had any – into Tigoni or other ventures; if the Museum took over obviously such shuffling from one account to another would have to stop. There was a complete impasse but, as Richard had broken the news on the eve of Louis's departure for America at the end of April, there was time to cool off before any more was said.

As soon as Louis had been able to pull himself together in hospital after the bee stings, he had cabled to Joan Travis asking her to go ahead with lecture commitments for May 'as I must raise funds'. He was determined at all costs to be fit to travel by then as he was particularly anxious to take part in a symposium in San Francisco in honour of Teilhard de Chardin. In acknowledging the University of California's invitation to give a paper on that occasion he had admitted that, although he agreed with Teilhard's philosophy as expressed during the latter part of his life, 'nevertheless I am regarded by many as an enemy of Teilhard. . . . I have the very strongest belief that in his early and somewhat irresponsible days Teilhard played a considerable part in aiding and abetting in the Piltdown forgery. Whether you are willing to have me under those conditions participate in a symposium which is in a sense in honour of Teilhard and his quest for perfection must be for you to decide. Naturally I could not during the symposium express my views about the long past episode of his youthful career unless I was specifically asked to do so.'[10] In reply the sponsors thanked him for his 'refreshing candor' and said that the programme committee saw no reason to exclude those who held controversial opinions.

With his experience in handwriting cases Louis was particularly intrigued by forgeries of all kinds. He had hinted that he believed Teilhard was implicated in that super-hoax Piltdown in the book he had written with Vanne Goodall, *Unveiling Man's Origins* (1969). He had even drafted part of an entire book on the subject, but was brought to a temporary halt by the paralysis of his hand after the bee episode. Louis had no real evidence, only a hunch: Teilhard had once told him that Dawson, the main suspect, was not responsible, but had refused to elaborate. In his writings Teilhard never referred to Piltdown, although it was he who had found the canine tooth which fitted into the jaw. Nor did he attend the meeting of the Geological Society when the Piltdown discoveries were announced to the scientific world; if he had been present and had been questioned, Louis assumed that as a priest he would have had to confess and so spoil the trap which he and Dawson had laid. Louis also believed that it was Teilhard who had initiated the hoax to test the reactions of the pundits, with the later connivance of Dawson, and the whole thing got out of hand. He had been particularly annoyed because the exposure of the forgery in November 1953 had come just too late to be mentioned in the fourth and revised edition of his *Adam's Ancestors*, which was published that year. In it he repeated the contention he had always held, and which was of course correct, that the skull and the jaw did not belong together; and in the family tree on the opposite page he had had to show Piltdown as an offshoot on its own. The three exposers of Piltdown were Professor J. S. Weiner and two of Louis's old friends, Kenneth Oakley and Sir Wilfrid Le Gros Clark, and Louis thought that they might have told him what was going on in their minds. (Le Gros Clark, incidentally, died in July, 1971, just two months after the Teilhard symposium; and Teilhard himself had died in 1955, two years after the exposure of the forgery.)

Louis would have loved to air his views on all this at the meeting in San Francisco, but he was apprehensive about the reaction of the numerous followers of the Teilhard cult if he attacked their hero; for perhaps the first time in his life Louis was also a bit nervous about possible questions from the Press. The University of California gave him a first class air fare, as well as living expenses and a small honorarium for his paper, but he used the money to cover two economy fares as his doctor insisted that he should be accompanied. He took with him from Nairobi his new secretary, Cara Phelips, who had worked for him for only one week when she was told she was to go with him to America. She was only twenty-five and it was a big responsibility; but she had been brought up in Kenya, which gave her an advantage over her contemporaries in dealing with the unexpected. Her letters to her parents give a blow-by-blow account of that harrowing trip.[11]

The first letter, dated 27 April, 1971, was written from the Westbury Hotel, New York. 'Louis is amazing; I am the one who is weary. We went to the top of two skyscrapers just for the fun of it – Louis's idea, not mine.' They then flew on to Los Angeles, where they were met by Joan Travis and spent the next two days in her house. 'She is a super person,' wrote Cara, 'and made me feel at home at once. My room opens on to a terrace with a heated swimming pool. Fresh salmon, melons and strawberries for dinner. Louis is still well and I think the trip is doing him a power of good. I like him more and more and find him easier to understand all the time.'

30 April, San Francisco:

> We were met by the Dean of the University and a representative from the Mayor's office. VIP treatment all the way, with the Mayor's car and chauffeur to bring us to the hotel. After lunch in our rooms we were whisked off to collect the Mayor and taken to a Press conference. Everyone wanted to speak to Louis and ask him questions; what a wonderful speaker he is.

The first drama took place on arrival at a dinner that night for the principal speakers at the conference; in trying to open the door of the car Louis fell out head first on to the concrete. He appeared to be all right, although bruised and shaken. The following day he delivered his paper, which was entitled 'From savanna to city and beyond' – an ambitious theme which began in the Miocene and ended with exhortations to the younger generation to adopt a synthesis between scientific truth and spiritual thinking.

Before Louis began to speak, said Cara:

> the audience rose and clapped and clapped. After he had spoken they rose again and clapped and clapped. Nobody else had half as much applause, it was all rather moving to see the following he has in this country. The majority of the speeches are double Dutch to me, and Louis agrees. The speakers use long and complicated words to say something simple.

Louis's supreme ability to use simple words to say something complicated was one of the reasons why he had such a following; he always put himself on a level with his audience, and never talked down to them.

Unfortunately, however, at the end of the day Louis had to talk down to the audience in a literal sense. Speakers answering questions had been placed round a dais on the stage to give television cameras a better view, and, as Cara describes:

> Louis didn't realise how near he was to the edge. He pushed his chair back and crash, over he went backwards. Luckily a young man in the wings rushed out from behind and managed to break most of the fall. All this happened in front of the TV cameras and an enormous audience. He was very shaken and had to lie down on the stage on pillows for about fifteen minutes before the Mayor drove him back to the hotel.

In a letter to Richard, Louis brushed off the whole incident but admitted

> I was foolish enough not to rest the next day but to go to the conference again, so that I had the most ghastly headache and was duly ticked off by the doctor. I am afraid I am working Cara very hard but she is a tower of strength. . . . She does her best to protect me but finds I am difficult to control.[12]

Two days after his fall Louis flew to Los Angeles; as a precaution he was X-rayed, but the report was excellent. At the weekend the Travises flew him to Calico in their private plane – they are both pilots. 'We had a bit of a panic,' wrote Cara, 'as his headaches started again, so we rushed him to the hotel and he was able to rest. On Monday morning we went back to the site for Louis to be interviewed by reporters . . . then we drove back for his first student lecture. He was in fine form and spoke brilliantly.'

The next day they flew to San Francisco once again, where Louis was to lecture at Berkeley. The auditorium seats 2,400 people, but it was packed to overflowing and many had to be turned away. 'The lectures cover some of the history of the evolution of man,' wrote Cara, 'with a punch line about pollution and biological warfare. All rather dramatic, but it makes one think.' So it went on, flying back to Los Angeles the next day, then a lecture at Santa Barbara, followed by a week of other talks in the Los Angeles area and Leakey Foundation meetings.

> Louis has good days and bad days depending on how much he's doing. It's impossible to keep him quiet. I have now learnt to refuse point blank to do something when he's tired, like phoning or letters. It's getting to be rather a joke now, but I think he knows what I'm doing, although it looks as though I'm trying to get out of work.

The temperature was in the eighties, which made travelling to lectures rather trying; but Louis could cool off in the Travises' pool, and on the whole he was bearing up well. Then on 25 May, three weeks after his fall from the platform, he had 'a bad setback with some rather worrying news about decisions in the Foundation and he has taken it very badly.' (This was a proposal to affiliate the Foundation with the Los Angeles County Museum, described later in this chapter.) 'He was not well, with headaches again, but insisted on driving to Riverside to give his last lecture of the tour.'

Louis always enjoyed the reception he got at Riverside; hence, probably, his determination to go through with his last lecture at all costs. As he sometimes did when he did not feel up to talking too much, he proposed to show the film 'Land of the Sonjo', about Richard's expedition to Lake Natron. On the way he felt worse and even suggested that Joan would have to do the commentary for him; however, much to her relief, by the time he got there he felt better and was able to do it himself. There was an audience of some 1,800 students and the atmosphere in the hall was stuffy; perspiration poured down Louis's face, which got whiter and whiter, and Joan and Cara were in the agonizing position of having to decide whether they should try to stop him. However, he got through the ordeal and the only concession he made was to bolt immediately afterwards before being besieged by autograph hunters. Instead of staying the night at Riverside as planned they drove the sixty miles back to Los Angeles so that the doctor who knew his history could see him early in the morning.

By the time the doctor arrived Louis was talking nonsense, asking Cara to get the slides ready for his next lecture and not taking it in when she assured him he had given the last one. He was taken to the Cedars of Lebanon Hospital, where the well-known neurosurgeon Dr Charles Carton did a brain scan which revealed a clot. In Louis's condition an emergency operation was risky, but it had to be done. None of the Leakey family could be contacted by telephone – it was a public holiday weekend in Kenya – so Joan Travis had to take the responsibility of signing the necessary form authorizing the operation. Later Allen O'Brien managed to contact Philip, who got hold of a pilot to fly him to Olduvai to tell Mary what had happened.

Three holes were drilled into Louis's skull, and after the surgeon had removed the clot caused by the fall from the platform in San Francisco, to his amazement he saw another one underneath. This one was clear plasma, and the fact that the red corpuscles had been absorbed indicated that the clot must have been several months old; evidently it had been caused by Louis's fall when the bees attacked him in January. Cara's letter of 30 May gives an account of these events:

> Yesterday was a complete nightmare. The Travises left early to go to the hospital and left me alone in the house to look after phones and meet a reporter. They were hoping to bring Louis home after tests – but I heard various disturbing bits of news by telephone that Louis had a blood clot and that surgery was necessary. The relief when Joan phoned through at 3.30 to say the operation was a success and all was well. Louis is now doing just fine. I saw him this morning and he was bright and very chuffed that the other clot had gone as well. The next twenty-four hours are critical so far as the post-operative problems go, after that we can relax. He will be in hospital for two weeks (first week in intensive care) and then will need at least two weeks' convalescence before going home. . . . He woke up this morning and first of all asked for his razor and toothbrush, and then insisted that someone should phone Arnold Travis and make sure that I got my trip down to Blythe (the Travises' ranch) as Louis

reckoned I needed a holiday. How about that from a boss who has just come round from a head operation? At least it showed that his mind was perfectly all right. His brain was not touched during the operation at all. At one stage yesterday they could not pinpoint where the clot was – inside or outside the brain – but after injecting some sort of molecule (I think) into his arteries they could find out exactly what was going on. Apparently this system of tests is still very new and the hospital Louis is in is one of very few that have had it.

After ten days Louis came out of hospital: 'He is definitely brighter and more relaxed than I have known him, and the paralysis is wearing off on his arm and leg. If he had not fallen in San Francisco the second clot might never have been found.' It was this second clot, caused by the fall at the time of the bee stings, which had brought on paralysis through pressure on the brain. The pressure had had a curious side-effect, making him uncharacteristically docile; but once it was relieved his temper returned and he began to yell at the unfortunate Cara if he was crossed in any way – an aspect which she had not met before.

Soon after, Cara reports:

He continues to make wonderful progress. . . . He is much slimmer and is watching his weight carefully. His right hand is so much freer it's quite amazing. Joan Travis and I continually pester him to use it as he still automatically reaches out with his left hand when he doesn't need to.

Although he got back much of the feeling in his right hand, he was never again able to write properly.

Louis was indeed fortunate to have such devoted friends during this nightmare period. After experiencing the Travises' kindness and care for three weeks, at last, on 29 June, Louis and Cara flew on to Washington thinking their troubles were over. But on the plane he developed a bladder infection, and by the time they reached the hotel he was extremely weak. Cara telephoned to a friend who called in a doctor:

Louis's temperature shot up to 103 and his pulse was racing. Rosemary (English friend) is just great. She's a nurse, quiet, sensible and so kind. She stayed with Louis all Tuesday night so that I could sleep. I was just about shattered by the time I got to bed at midnight.

'I haven't been out of the hotel since we arrived. I daren't leave Louis. I slept on a bed in his room last night in case he fell in the bathroom and I didn't get much sleep. However, he is much better and we are not flying now until Sunday night to give him a chance to get stronger. I am being nurse, laundrymaid, cook and doctor all at the same time. Rosemary is coming in this evening and will sleep here. Louis's room is really a flat, with sitting room, kitchen, cooker and fridge. It's so hot it's unbearable, humid and muggy, about 95°. We have air conditioning in the rooms, but that's upsetting as well as noisy.'

> The National Geographic is across the street, and Louis is held in very high esteem there so nothing is too much trouble for them. Thank heavens we are here and not in New York; at least there are people we can call on in an emergency. When we get to London Louis says I must have a rest, and I think he is very grateful for all I have done in these last two days. Oh dear, I have just taken his temperature and it's up over 100 – heaven knows why as he's on antibiotics and is taking twenty pills a day. I have to keep track and give them to him.

The next day Louis was back in hospital, his temperature fluctuating alarmingly every six hours. 'I rode with him in the ambulance,' wrote Cara, 'with the sirens and alarms screaming. There was no need to get him there in a hurry, but there was a traffic jam and the driver didn't want to waste time. American ambulances are very public and have glass sides so everyone can look in.' To crown everything, at the hospital his stretcher got stuck in the lift.

Cara tried to contact the Leakey family on the telephone, but as usual without success; she managed to get through to her parents, who live near Langata, and eventually they got a message to Mary, who had been through a harrowing time in the past few weeks. However, when she spoke to Louis on the telephone in hospital he assured her there was life in him yet. He had been away for three months instead of the six weeks he had planned.

After he returned to Kenya he had two more attacks of the bladder trouble and was on antibiotics for another month before it finally cleared up. The only bright spot in this long saga of disasters is that the Leakey Foundation had prudently taken out an insurance policy and Louis was fully covered for his operation and medical bills, which amounted to $8,000 (just under £2,750). Louis owed them his life – in the person of Joan Travis, who had got hold of the right surgeon in time – and his solvency.

By the end of September, only six weeks after fully recovering from his bladder infection, Louis set off again to America to try to raise money, for things were not going at all well. The National Science Foundation, which had supported the Centre ever since 1962, announced that they could not renew their grant after October – like everyone else at that time they were feeling the pinch from the economic situation. Louis thought he might even have to give notice to Cara and his other secretary and close down the office as well as the Centre. He also had to stop the Fort Ternan excavations, which were being carried out by some African assistants from Olduvai and a group of American students.

Louis was worried that his health might not stand another strenuous lecture tour, but with his usual courage he went ahead. He confessed in a letter to Dian Fossey: 'I had to go back because of fund-raising and was a little afraid of doing so, but it has turned out all right. I have been hard at work and am keeping very fit, but have not achieved an awful lot in the way of funds. It is more difficult than ever before.'[13] He went to Washington, New York, Chicago and Denver, then on to Los Angeles before starting on a two weeks' tour of colleges sponsored, as before, by CAPES.

The first of his lectures in California was at Caltech, on 15 October. This series, sponsored in co-operation with the Leakey Foundation, had become an annual event; Louis started the ball rolling with 'The latest evidence on the antiquity of man', and Jane and Hugo van Lawick followed a month later. By now Jane was a visiting professor at Stanford University in the department of psychiatry whose head, Dr David Hamburg, took a great interest in her work. (He became a trustee of the Leakey Foundation and a member of its science and grants committee in December, 1970.) In the words of a brochure produced by the Foundation:

> There is great promise in using chimpanzees to provide experimental models of human disorders, such as psychosis or clinical depression; but this can only be fully interpreted if there is a background of information about the normal (and abnormal) behaviour of this ape in its natural habitat. . . . It is believed that the field studies at Gombe, combined with the studies at Stanford on captive chimpanzees, will yield valuable new data on mental illness, aggression, child development and adolescence.[14]

The chimps, in fact, were to be subjected to scrutiny by a whole battery of psychiatrists, ethologists, biochemists, sociologists and statisticians, few of whom, other than Jane, had any experience of primates in the wild. The Leakey Foundation's original offices had been called 'Nairobi West', and now at Stanford the outdoor primate research facility came to be known as 'Gombe West'.

On 24 October, nine days after Louis's Caltech lecture, the Leakey Foundation staged a debate on the subject of aggression between him and the playwright Robert Ardrey. (In his book *African Genesis* Ardrey had likened Louis to a bull in search of a china shop!)[15] Like Louis, Ardrey was – and is – an outstanding popularizer of science; and, as he said in his opening remarks, they had something else in common: 'We two are probably the most opinionated men of the 20th century.' However, he continued, 'we like each other, so we ritualize our aggressions.' They agreed amicably to differ, Ardrey maintaining that man the killer appeared on the scene very early, while Louis argued that aggression was 'linked with the change of man from an animal into psycho-social man, when he simultaneously developed speech, religion, abstract ideas and magic.' Until fire had been controlled, he said, it was necessary to be silent and listen for predators, but once man had fire he could invent words and develop ideas which could lead to aggression. With speech you can stir up emotions, and with leisure you can think up things like jealousy and malice.

After the debate the speakers answered questions. One member of the audience asked what should be taught to the youth of today, which gave Louis an opportunity to expound the philosophy which he brought into so many of his lectures. His reply was as follows:

> First, encourage more mixing of people from different backgrounds

> until they realize they are all one and the same. Second, distinguish between faith as distinct from religion. Because of the destructive influence of dogmas and doctrines we are letting our young people lose faith. Having lost faith, because they confuse it with religion, they are not willing to abandon violence. You can't kill people if you feel that they also have a faith and are meaningful in this life. I took some random samples of dossiers of people who had committed violence in the US. Out of a hundred files which I was allowed to see only three individuals admitted to any faith.

The matter of dogma versus true Christianity was a subject to which Louis returned again and again, and it is typical of the thoroughness with which he went into it that he should have investigated the dossiers of criminals. Louis always did his homework, as the fundamentalists found when they questioned him on the Bible and discovered that he could quote it better than they could themselves.

The Ardrey-Leakey debate took place in Caltech's Atheneum which seats two hundred, and the fee was $40 a head. The dialogue was filmed, and eventually published, and the Leakey Foundation got some good publicity as well as useful dollars.

The Foundation badly needed a boost as both funds and morale were at a low ebb. There were conflicts and tensions among the trustees, and everyone had different ideas about the direction in which they should be heading. To cut a long story short, the five male members of the executive committee had got together to devise a plan whereby they could get the Foundation out of the social mire in which it seemed to be stuck. They proposed that the Leakey Foundation should be associated with the Los Angeles County Museum of Natural History, of which the Foundation's president, Ed Harrison, was also president. Such a move, they thought, would not only lend the Foundation an air of scientific professionalism and make fund-raising easier but would also enable economies to be made by the joint mailing of news sheets and so forth. However, the men reckoned without the ladies, who had not been consulted on the matter and were perhaps justifiably indignant, as after all, it was they who had done most of the work. It even looked as though the intention was to throw them off the board altogether, for the proposal was to limit the trustees to five, each of whom agreed to pledge $10,000 a year for the next two years. Affiliation would make the whole thing more impersonal, and Joan Travis and Tita Caldwell appealed to Louis.

Naturally enough, Louis aligned himself whole-heartedly with them. He realized at once that he would have far less control over policy if the proposed merger took place, and in addition there would be a loss of prestige. The idea of the Leakey Foundation being a mere part of the Los Angeles County Museum! He reacted with quite extraordinary vehemence, and to Ed Harrison he wrote:

> No matter how much you tell me some of your trustees are willing to pledge $10,000 for the next two years, if we come in with the Museum I will not change my mind. I am not to be bought in this way. If the trustees concerned are not sufficiently interested in our research work to give the money for it except with conditions, I would infinitely prefer them not to be trustees. I repeat, I will never agree to the Foundation being linked with the County Museum.[16]

Louis thought up a wonderful excuse for opposing the plan: he maintained that four chimpanzees exhibited in the Los Angeles County Museum had been obtained as the result of illegal collecting in the Kabale Forest of Uganda, and that he could not possibly allow his name to be associated with such activities. On 25 June, just before his brain operation, he wrote a letter to Gary Phillips which he intended to be shown to all trustees:

> The Museum had, and presumably still has, a policy of what I consider to be wholly unnecessary killing of great apes for habitat groups and I am not prepared to be a party in any way at all or to have my name linked with such activity.[17]

This might at first sight appear to be humbug: there were habitat groups in the National Museum in Nairobi containing animals killed specifically for exhibition, including rare ones; and as recently as 1966 Louis himself had asked for the co-operation of the senior game warden in Addis Ababa in obtaining skeletons of the ibex and mountain nyala for his osteology collections. In fact, the chimpanzees had been killed in 1963 with a permit from Uganda, so that there was no question of illegality; but unfortunately a private individual had made a movie showing the actual killing, which had been shown in the Los Angeles County Museum. This is really what had incensed Louis, and he obtained Ed Harrison's promise that the film would not be shown again in public.

Louis also wrote to Jane van Lawick Goodall asking her to dissociate herself from the Foundation if the affiliation went through. By this time Jane was a big noise, second only to Louis himself in her power to attract potential subscribers to lectures and dinners sponsored by the Foundation. The Foundation could not afford to lose her, nor could she afford to lose the goodwill of the Foundation, which acted as agents for her lecture tours. At the same time she did not wish to upset Louis, who had raised the money to get her started at Gombe. She therefore told him she would back him, although probably she did not mean to go through with it if it had come to the crunch.

In the letter to Gary Phillips already quoted Louis also said:

> I have clearly made up my mind that in the event of this proposal going forward I would have to withdraw my association with the Leakey Foundation completely and so would Jane Goodall and I suspect the Emperor of Ethiopia would take the same line, as well as several others.

(It seems unlikely that the illustrious patron of the Foundation would have felt particularly strongly about the killing of four chimpanzees in Uganda!) Louis's letter ends:

> If I was forced to withdraw from the Foundation, I should have to withdraw also my name from being used, at least the 'L.S.B.' part. If you persuaded some other member of my family to reinstate the 'Leakey' part, I suppose I could not prevent that.

In other words, Louis was terrified that he might have been taken at his word: the thought of it being no longer the Leakey Foundation was unbearable and he was counting on Richard to save the name, and his own face, if the worst came to the worst.

Ed Harrison was in a very embarrassing position. As president of both the Leakey Foundation and of the board of the Los Angeles County Museum he was wearing two most uncomfortable hats, and some of the other Foundation trustees were also directors of the Museum. In reply to Louis's letter to Gary Phillips, Mr Harrison said: 'While your letter was intended for all trustees, I have temporarily prevented those copies from being sent because, truly Louis, I do not think you intended to go as far as you did. If you are still of the same mind, I will see to it that all trustees receive a copy of your letter.' He ended with these words:

> Louis, while I respect your opinions and appreciate your counsel, I would like to suggest that, in future, we agree to mutually respect the Foundation's purpose and the best intentions of those who support your efforts and the Foundation's continued success. In the future, perhaps you and I should privately discuss your concerns.[18]

Not altogether surprisingly, in September 1971, just three months after this corresponence, Ed Harrison retired as president of the Leakey Foundation. He was succeeded by Dr Ned Munger, who had been involved since the beginning. At the same time Gary Phillips resigned as executive director – mainly because the Foundation was undergoing a grave financial crisis and there was no money to pay his salary. For a time the office functioned with the aid of a part-time secretary and 'the accelerated efforts of volunteers' who were, of course, Joan Travis and Tita Caldwell. The ladies, to their great credit, held the whole Foundation together. They were not dropped from the board; the affiliation with the Los Angeles County Museum did not take place; and the Foundation's title continued to bear the name of L. S. B. Leakey. As usual, Louis had got his way.

Because the proposed affiliation did not come off the five trustees did not go through with their pledges of $10,000 each, and at one time there was precisely three dollars in the Foundation's account (apart from Robert Beck's endowment fund, which was not available for current expenditure). A loan had to be arranged with the bank, and for months the Foundation had to back-pedal on the allocation of grants. The money promised for Tigoni for the six months up to August had not been paid and, although by November the Foundation managed to scrape up $2,000, an outstanding balance of $6,000 was still due. Even this covered only the basic needs; there was nothing with which to guarantee the salary of a scientific director, nothing with which to continue the diet and fertility programme. An overdraft of $5,000 on the Ubeidiya account could not be met until January 1972, and then it was obtained by Louis personally through the generosity of a private donor. Salary for the Centre's palaeontologist, Dr John Harris, could not be found and had to be paid out of reserve funds for building repairs until the National Geographic Society helped out in January. The overall picture was dismal, and it speaks much for the dedication of the Foundation's officers that they did not pack it all in.

At Christmas time each year Louis used to write to Fellows and other supporters of the Foundation reporting on progress and indicating where funds would be most welcome – which in this particular year was just about everywhere. He began his 1971 letter by assuring them that he had recovered, thanking all those who had sent letters and flowers. He had to admit that at one time it had seemed that the Foundation would have to close down, but that it appeared to have turned the corner. He stressed the urgent need for money for Tigoni, the Centre and Ubeidiya. Other projects were described as 'magnificent' – chimps and gorillas, Richard's season at East Rudolf, Mary's at Olduvai; but in fact the part played by the Leakey Foundation in sponsoring these projects was very slight. A report on the work at Tigoni was conspicuous by its absence: even Louis could not say that the progress here had been 'magnificent'.

Just before Christmas Louis and Mary attended the seventh Pan African Congress on Prehistory at Addis Ababa – their last appearance together before a large international gathering of scientists. They were surrounded by old friends and it was a very happy occasion: as organizer of the first congress in 1947, Louis was always the centre of attention at these conferences. He had been bitterly disappointed that he had been unable to get an invitation for this congress to be held in Nairobi and, as had happened also at the 1967 congress in Dakar, he was telephoning constantly to the Kenya Government to try to get a firm invitation for the next meeting. It came through eventually, but not in time for Louis to be able to announce at Addis Ababa that the 8th Pan African African Congress on Prehistory would he held in East Africa in 1975. Now it will be organized by Richard; if Louis had lived he would have been seventy-two by then, but would surely have played a very active part in it. It is sad that he was not spared to see the wheel come round full circle from Nairobi 1947 to Nairobi 1975; but at least he had the satisfaction of participating over a period of 24 years in the congresses he launched so successfully.

15 Last Journey

The last year of Louis's life, 1972, followed a familiar pattern, with an American lecture tour in the spring and an exceptionally strenuous one, even by his standards, planned for the autumn. The only difference was that he packed in yet a third visit to the US: after the Addis Ababa conference he went to London, leaving there on Christmas day to speak at the annual meeting of the American Association for the Advancement of Science at Philadelphia on Boxing day. His subject was 'Mammals (including man) and their environment in relation to conservation problems in Africa today'.

He started the new year in fairly good shape and tried to be careful, resting a certain amount in the afternoons. This did not prevent him from visiting Olduvai on his return from the United States in January, and taking some students up to Fort Ternan. After that he had a short holiday at his house at Malindi: he was still experiencing breathlessness at high altitudes, and a spell at the coast always did him good. On 14 February he left for London again en route for America.

One of his engagements was to discuss plans for the formation of a branch of the Leakey Foundation in London, and there was also an idea of forming other branches or 'chapters' in various cities of the USA. The hope was that, after deducting office expenses, each American branch would send the money it raised to headquarters in Los Angeles; but the London venture would be almost entirely independent. This suggestion had come from the artist Fleur Cowles, wife of the timber magnate Thomas M. Meyer and a Fellow of the Leakey Foundation (she became a trustee in September 1972 shortly before Louis's death). As well as being a great admirer of Louis's work, she was extremely interested in Jane's chimpanzee research.

On 17 February Louis went to see her at her flat in Albany, Piccadilly. They had corresponded about the project of setting up the first European branch of the Leakey Foundation for the past year, but because of Louis's chapter of accidents little progress had been made. They now discussed possible members for a founding committee, a board of trustees and – it was hoped – Royal patronage. Among the names suggested for the board were Sir Mortimer Wheeler, Mr Malcolm MacDonald, Dr Glyn Daniel and Sir Vivian Fuchs. Vanne Goodall and Jane were also to serve, and others who joined the board later included Dr John Napier, Dr Kenneth Oakley and Sir Julian Huxley.

Louis was greatly excited at this time because Sir Julian – at the age of 84 – was campaigning vigorously to get him elected to the Royal Society, and was getting good support. At last, after three abortive attempts in the past, it seemed as though Louis would have made it; but he died just before the new Fellows were elected.

Soon after his discussions with Fleur Cowles in London, Louis arrived at Cornell University for his second stay as professor-at-large. It was four years since his previous visit, and, as before, he had asked for a private apartment. His doctor had advised him that he should have someone with him in case he needed help, and he was accompanied by Cindy Levin, step-daughter of Robert Beck. In correspondence about the arrangements Louis had reminded the associate professor of anthropology at Cornell that on his last visit, which was also in winter, he had slept out on the verandah several times. 'Therefore I could perfectly well do so again,' he wrote, 'and move one bed outside, and I propose to take this step.'[1] For all his tropical upbringing Louis was no hot-house plant. For most of the time during his three-weeks stay it was bitterly cold, and one night while making up the fire he dropped a log on his foot and broke a bone. Louis was very accident-prone because his plastic hip made him clumsy, but he never remembered to make allowances for it. He continued his programme, giving lectures and having informal discussion with students, and he was appreciated just as much as he had been in 1968.

While Louis was at Cornell, Richard was also in the United States. For several years now he had adopted the same routine as his father, reporting to the National Geographic Society and then lecturing all over the country to raise funds. After speaking at Caltech on 22 February, he was due to appear at a Leakey Foundation dinner, but instead had to hurry back to Kenya. There were disturbing reports of a raid on his camp at East Rudolf, and he was worried about the safety of his resident staff. Fortunately it proved to be a false alarm, but the reason for his precipitate departure could not be made public as the authorities did not admit that raids across the Ethiopian border took place. Louis stepped in and deputized for his son, and 'eleven new Fellows were added to the Foundation's roster as a direct result of pre-dinner publicity or post-dinner enthusiasm,' records the Foundation's minutes.

In March the Duke of Edinburgh visited Nairobi, and Mary, Richard and Meave dined with him at the house of the British High Commissioner (Louis was still in America). Only five days before the party Meave had had a daughter, Louise, so she was unable to go with Richard to East Rudolf when he took Prince Philip there for a week, but the photographer Bob Campbell and his wife Heather shared the duties of host with Richard. Prince Philip was thrilled with the wonderful bird life thronging the lake, but on alternate days he dutifully looked at fossils.

When Louis returned to Nairobi in April he again experienced difficulty in breathing. His doctor advised him to go down to sea level immediately and then make the ascent to Nairobi in easy stages. The Leakey Foundation heard rumours that he had had another heart attack, which was indignantly refuted by Louis. But an electrocardiogram had shown that he had been overdoing it too soon at a high altitude, and he was told he must lose more weight, take gentle but regular exercise, and avoid tension – an admonition which asked the impossible of Louis.

With characteristic optimism he was planning to visit Dian Fossey in Rwanda. 'My leg is very much better,' he wrote to her, 'and I am able to walk quite a lot. My only problem is whether my heart and lungs would bear the altitude of your camp. I am very much hoping to visit you as soon as I relinquish the duties of Director of the Centre at the end of June.'[2] Dian knew perfectly well that his heart and lungs would never stand 12,000 feet – she had considerable difficulty with her own lungs – and was terrified that he might try to come.

On 30 June Richard, as director of the National Museum, duly took over the administration of the Centre for Prehistory and Palaeontology on behalf of the trustees. At least one source of anxiety for Louis was removed and, having lost the battle for its control, he was really very relieved that the onus of raising funds for the Centre now fell on the Kenya Government. For ten years he had acted the role of Atlas, carrying on his shoulders what was acknowledged to be the most important storehouse of hominid fossils in the world. The most eminent palaeontologists and leaders of international expeditions made regular pilgrimages to Nairobi for the express purpose of studying the Centre's unique collections, and for the privilege of discussing their significance with the man who had built them up.

One problem that arose was where to find the money to pay the salaries of Louis's two secretaries now that he could no longer draw on funds allocated for the Centre. He reckoned he would need to give six extra lectures to earn enough to keep them on; surely, he said to Joan Travis, some of the Leakey Foundation Fellows would be willing to help? He had already tried the National Geographic Society, but they felt that secretarial expenses should come out of the $9,000 salary they gave him every year to spend as he chose. Louis never seemed to have anything in his personal accounts in Nairobi, London or Washington as he was continually dipping into them to rescue Tigoni or other projects. There was just enough in his Washington account, into which his lecture fees were paid, to meet the secretaries' salaries for the first month, after which it was a question of robbing Peter to pay Paul. All such petty problems added to the tension which Louis's doctors told him repeatedly to avoid.

His major worry – as always – was Tigoni. Against almost insuperable odds he had managed to keep it going – *just* – for fourteen years, but he still could not offer an attractive contract to a mature person to cope with the assorted teenagers there. Tigoni was costing $25,000 a year to run, out of which the Leakey Foundation had contributed $20,000 per annum for the past two years. And yet, as Louis admitted to Joan Travis only a month before he died, 'As regards what the students are doing – most of them, regrettably, very little.'[3]

Louis had tried to gain the interest of the Ford Foundation in Tigoni; one of their major concerns was population control and this, he thought, should fit the bill in connection with the diet and fertility studies on monkeys. He was advised that in approaching the Ford Foundation he should think in terms of hundreds of thousands of dollars rather than tens of thousands; but, unfortunately, thinking big did not produce the desired results.

Meanwhile Louis had been thinking very big in another direction, and in this case it did produce results to the tune of $100,000; but this windfall was never used for the purpose for which it was intended. The story began in 1967 when Louis flew over the Suguta valley on his way to Omo. The Suguta river, which would normally be dry were it not for the fact that it is fed by hot springs, begins in practically unexplored territory north-east of Lake Baringo and peters out in a swamp south of Lake Rudolf. Louis thought that along the formidable eastern scarp of the Rift Valley in this area there should be fossil localities, and he made up his mind that someone must get there by land and take a look.

Since 1965 the East African Geological Research Unit, sponsored by Bedford College, London, in association with the Geological Survey of Kenya, had been mapping the country north of Lake Baringo. The research students, however, had stopped short of the country Louis had in mind. The whole area is dotted with volcanoes, there are no tracks, and for hundreds of square miles there is no water. It is wild, beautiful, fascinating, terrifying country, and in order to explore it one needs to be not only young and active but also to be backed by considerable resources. The part to the south was divided into a grid of about eight huge squares, each of which was tackled by one geologist. In the course of their mapping the students often discovered fossil localities – one such was mentioned in connection with Richard's expedition to rescue the skeleton of an early elephant west of Baringo. Farther to the north-west, at a place called Ngorora, another geologist had found important fossil mammals, including the tooth of a hominid, which had been dated by potassium/argon to about ten million years. Several other fossil sites of various ages ranging from Miocene to Pleistocene were known in other parts of the Baringo basin, as well as farther north near Lake Rudolf. The area, as Dr Clark Howell once said, might contain a dozen Olduvai Gorges.

The fact that no geologist had penetrated the country between the Bedford College grid and Lake Rudolf was a challenge that Louis could not resist, and he wanted a member of his own family to be the one to take it up. Richard was completely tied up with East Rudolf, so Louis turned to Philip. Although no geologist, Philip was quite prepared to do any amount of 'bundu-bashing' – a Kenya expression for bush-whacking. Louis got funds from the National Geographic Society, and in 1969 Philip had set out on a three weeks' reconnaissance. He was accompanied by Dr Emiliano Aguirre, a Jesuit palaeontologist from the University of Madrid who had worked for a time at the Bedford College site of Ngorora.

Their target was a sharp peak called Nakali, north-east of Lake Baringo and in an area which was in the process of being mapped by one of the Bedford geologists. Although Louis sometimes referred to Philip and Aguirre's 'Suguta expedition' Nakali is in fact a long way south of the Suguta valley; the Leakey Foundation used to call it 'UnBaringo', to distinguish Louis's project from the province of the Bedford geologists, and perhaps this term is more appropriate than 'Suguta'. Philip and Aguirre made a track as they went along, but eventually had to abandon the Land-Rovers and walk for the last five days. Around Nakali they collected a number of fossils, including a small and previously unknown species of three-toed horse. Louis was particularly excited by a tooth which was thought to be that of a tapir, an animal known only from Asia and America. Unfortunately when Aguirre studied it on his return to Madrid he did not have much in the way of comparative material; he was also unfamiliar with the peculiar fossil pigs of Africa – the tapir turned out to be a pig. To add to the confusion it had not come from Nakali at all but from Ngorora, where Aguirre had also worked. Perhaps Louis confused the two sites in his mind; at any rate, largely on the strength of this beast and also on the hominid tooth – which had also come from Ngorora! – he began to make preparations for a full-scale expedition to the Suguta, hundreds of miles to the north of both Nakali and Ngorora. Moreover, although he had been unable to do active fieldwork for some years, he was actually determined to take part personally in this expedition to one of the most forbidding and waterless areas in the whole of Kenya.

Louis knew that the operation would be very costly. It would involve an aerial survey, as well as air support to bring in supplies and water to the ground party, and he estimated he would need $100,000 for the first year's work, followed by $50,000 per annum for the next three or four years. After appealing to the National Geographic Society for funds he spoke enthusiastically about the potential of the area in a public lecture in Washington. *Science News* of 16 October 1971 reported:

> Leakey wants to start a new dig in East Africa that he hopes will re-write man's history. With the enthusiasm and stubbornness that have marked his career, Louis S. B. Leakey says he can prove that true ancestral man existed seven million years ago.

The deposits had not been dated, and this was guesswork, based on the appearance of the fauna; but it did seem probable that at least some of the sediments in the area would cover the practically unknown 'black hole' in palaeontological time from around ten to five million years ago.

In April 1972, apparently by an incredible stroke of Leakey's luck, a pilot dropped into Louis's lap. Mr Frederick E. Potts of Fepco Aviation, Alaska, offered himself and his Cessna plane for a period of two years to do whatever work Louis had in mind. He was a Leakey fan and wanted to go to Africa; it seemed as simple as that. Unfortunately it transpired some time later that Mr Potts required a considerable fee for his services.

Louis had hoped to use the pilot in the summer of 1972, but by the time funds for the expedition came through it was too late to collect a competent research team. Louis was thinking in terms of three palaeontologists, an archaeologist, a cartographer and a photographer, but most of those whom he approached already had commitments. He was planning that he and Philip, together with two or three Kenyan students, should go ahead to organize air-strips, roads and camps before the main party arrived. He was absolutely determined to take part in the expedition himself: it was to be his swan song, diverting the headlines from Olduvai and East Rudolf.

By June 1972 Louis had obtained the necessary funds – not from the National Geographic Society as he had hoped but, by yet another extraordinary stroke of luck, through a most unexpected source. Soon after the dialogue on aggression at Caltech in October 1971 Robert Ardrey happened to write to an old friend, Dr Henry Allen Moe, who was in hospital. To cheer him up, he told him all about the debate and the plans Louis was making for the 'Suguta' expedition. Dr Moe was an ex-director ('for goodness knows how long', said Ardrey) of the Guggenheim Foundation, and he persuaded them to come up with a grant of $100,000 for 'Suguta'. As the money was to be paid through the Leakey Foundation it would also presumably qualify for a matching donation from Robert Beck. As Ardrey expressed it in a letter to Joan Travis: 'About all I can say is Wow! If that is what comes from writing a gossipy letter to an old friend in hospital, maybe I'd better start writing more such letters.'[4]

News of the Guggenheim grant came through in June 1972, but for the time being it was kept confidential. Louis had hoped to announce it at a Press conference after the Leakey Foundation's annual meeting in October. He was setting the following January as his target for the great expedition, but in the meantime he had to obtain a permit from the Kenya Government. Louis had arranged that Fred Potts should come on ahead to do other work: although the fees involved would be an unnecessary extravagance, the glamour of having a private pilot was irresistible. Potts was actually due to leave Alaska a few days after Louis died and was only just stopped in time from going to East Africa.

Both Mary and Richard had been extremely worried about the proposed expedition, and it was a great relief that it did not come off. Not only did they know that Louis's health would not stand it, but they also realized that it would be essential to enrol a team of specialists and make a thorough survey first – which Louis had not done.

Some time before Louis's hand was paralysed he had finished writing a draft of the second volume of his memoirs, a sequel to *White African* which covered the first thirty years of his life. It ends in 1951 and is called *By the Evidence*, since a good part of it covers his experiences with the CID in the Second World War. It was to be published in the USA, and the possibility of publication in the UK by Collins was being discussed. In May 1972 Louis told Sir William Collins that he had shelved it in the hope that he would have been able to make corrections by hand, but that he was still incapable of writing more than a few lines. Soon after, he said with pride in a letter to Dian Fossey:

> Although I still can't write much my hand is improving very fast and I actually wrote a five-page memo the other day; it took me about five times as long as it would have done before the bees, but it was legible.[5]

Louis's writing had been barely legible for the past thirty years!

In April he had gone over the first part of the draft with Vanne Goodall and Rosemary Knocker (now Mrs Poole), and by the end of a week they had managed to get five chapters into final shape. Rosemary Knocker, who had recently moved to England, became a close friend of Louis's when she lived at Langata and often typed for him; she had begun the work on the autobiography as long ago as 1969. Louis had already had an advance from the American publishers, and he now asked Collins if they would give him an advance on UK royalties so that he could return to England in the summer to finish the work. It is distressing to think that even then, in the last year of his life, he was so pressed for money. 'I find I can get a cheap excursion fare,' he wrote to Sir William Collins, 'so long as I spend at least 25 days in the UK. . . . Unfortunately I am unable to afford even the reduced air fare.'[6]

In August Louis and Vanne Goodall spent three weeks at Rosemary Knocker's cottage in Hampshire. He was happy and relaxed, and by the end of his stay there was a great improvement in his health. Fifteen chapters went off to the American publishers, and the last three chapters and the epilogue were completed a few weeks before he died.

Louis was also polishing another book in which he propounded his theories about Teilhard de Chardin's connection with the Piltdown hoax. After his death Mary was very anxious to prevent its publication: Louis had no new evidence to put forward, and she felt that the imputations he made would damage his reputation – she was far more concerned about Louis's reputation than about Teilhard's.

Mary was also concerned about the distribution of the films Louis had made in London while recovering from his heart attack in 1970, when he had been tired and not at his best. The Leakey Foundation had invested $20,000 in this venture and had begun negotiations about the possibility of obtaining funds to make additional footage. Louis had always been worried that the films might be released without proper editing and updating where necessary, and now there was talk about making an entirely new series on his work and ideas. Many of his lectures had been taped, and the Leakey Foundation was anxious to protect his rights as he was apt to lend them for private use or educational purposes without getting a fee, or – worse – without keeping track of where he had lent them. The production of cassettes for distribution to libraries and universities was another money-making possibility, and Louis had plans to record talks on a wide variety of subjects for this purpose. Clearly if he could make as much money, or even more, out of films and cassettes as he did by lecturing it would be far less exhausting. Joan Travis was particularly enthusiastic about all these possibilities, which Louis intended to discuss during his October visit to Los Angeles.

Early in the year she had written to him about his programme:

> May I remind you that we will need to know your outside dates for the Fall as soon as possible, so that we can start making arrangements. I suspect that you might have to include all of October and maybe even part of September. You know, ten days for Dee Simpson, three to four days for Seattle, three to four days in San Francisco, a few days in Chicago, a few more in New York, a few in Minneapolis, Los Angeles and so on. Films, cassettes, TV, McMaster, whew! Seriously, do try to allow for these, plus lectures.[7]

('McMaster' refers to McMaster University, Ontario, where Louis had undertaken to deliver the Redman Lecture in October.)

Was this the sort of programme to be undertaken by a very sick man, a man who was still partially paralysed, who had had a very serious head operation the year before, and who had suffered several heart attacks? At first sight it might seem thoughtless, even callous, to encourage him in this way; but in all fairness it must be stressed yet again that this was not only what others expected him to do, it was what Louis himself wished to do. He was becoming increasingly restless, and wherever he was he wanted to be somewhere else. When he was in Nairobi or London he was impatient to get to the United States to raise funds; and when he was there he felt he must return to Nairobi as soon as possible to deal with problems at Tigoni and elsewhere.

In his reply to Joan Travis he said he could not be away for too long 'unless Tigoni affairs are much more settled than they are now.' He suggested cutting down the ten days allotted to Dee Simpson for Calico, but the only item he proposed to cut altogether was the few days in Seattle. There he had a cousin who was a dental surgeon and who had offered to make special dentures for him; Louis had always had difficulty with these tiresome pieces of equipment and for years had chewed on his gums rather than spare the time to get his teeth fixed. It was typical that this should be the only thing for which he would not give up even three or four days; anything to do with his health or comfort always featured at the very bottom of the list. As top priority he put the making and marketing of films, and added: 'I would very much like to have six to eight lectures if they can be arranged, and of course I would like to do a Leakey Foundation dinner.'[8] Every time, funds for research came first.

If research came first, perhaps next in importance for Louis was to have a platform for his views, whether by writing, lecturing or teaching verbally. At this time he was considering taking up one or other of the academic posts he had been offered in California, including a chair at Caltech. For several years he had lectured there and they had now booked him for something more ambitious. Originally known as the 'master class', the title was later changed to 'seminar lectures', and they were to consist of six lectures spread over two days, 11 and 12 November. They would involve a great deal of work, but Louis was to receive a guaranteed minimum fee of $4,000 plus travel expenses. Caltech's Ramo auditorium seats 400, and participants were to pay $75 for the series of six lectures; Louis was not at all sanguine that the tickets would be sold.

He proposed to call the series 'Adam's ancestors – Eve's children'; the first three talks he would devote to ancestors – Miocene apes and early hominids – and the others would be concerned with stone age man's ideas and handiwork. Louis worked tremendously hard, dictating draft after draft, collecting tapes of his previous talks, amassing slides and casts of fossil skulls. He was in a state of exhaustion before he embarked on his last journey.

In the summer of 1972 Richard led his fifth expedition to East Rudolf, returning with a trophy that made Louis's last days extremely happy. By then the professional staff, gathered from all over the world, had expanded to about seventy during the season; they were not all there at the same time, but there might be as many as twenty to thirty geologists, palaeontologists, archaeologists and physicists (to collect dating samples) at any one time. The camp was beginning to look like a delightful beach hotel on the Indian Ocean or the Mediterranean, with an airy thatched communual dining room, laboratories, a separate house for Richard and Meave, and rows of simple wooden huts as bedrooms for visiting scientists.

By the end of the 1972 season the total number of hominid fossils collected since Richard began work there in 1968 amounted to more than eighty, the proportion of australopiths to *Homo* being about 50:30. Some were mere scraps of bone, others were isolated teeth; but there were nineteen skulls or portions of skulls and – in some ways even more important – four sets of associated limb bones. It was clear that two entirely different contemporary hominids were living in the area from more than two-and-a-half million to one million years ago. Not only did the skull fragments show this but the two kinds of very distinctive limb bones told the same story. From the relatively large sample obtained at

East Rudolf it was also possible to see the extent of individual variations. There were juveniles and adults, males and females; there were even very large males and rather small though fully mature ones – perhaps the equivalent of 'silverbacks' among gorilla populations, or the dominant baboons who lord it over less well-endowed brothers.

On 27 August 1972 one of Richard's champion collectors, Bernard Ngeneo, was searching at a site about thirteen miles north-east of the camp at Koobi Fora when he noticed bone fragments scattered over the steep slopes of a gully, and which he recognized as being part of a hominid skull. After sieving the surrounding surface material at least 150 pieces of bone were collected. Although they had eroded out on the surface, the geologists agreed that they must have come from a horizon well below the volcanic tuff which had been dated to 2.6 million years.

The Leakeys had a talent for marrying women who were expert at restoring skulls: after Meave had worked for about six hours in putting the main pieces together she held in her hands the now famous skull known as KNM ER 1470. (The letters stand for Kenya National Museum, East Rudolf.) The vault of the cranium was rather steeply domed, far more so than in any of the other finds of that age from East Rudolf, or in any of the much later *habilis* skulls from Olduvai. Anatomists later estimated that the cranial capacity was about 800 c.c.; for comparison, the robust but low-browed Zinj is 530 c.c., estimates of the less complete *habilis* specimens from Olduvai range from 633 to 684 c.c., and modern man averages about 1400 c.c. When Richard reported his discovery at a meeting at the Zoological Society of London in November, only a few weeks after Louis's death, the skull caused a sensation. (In fact, it was a cast: the original, he said, would never leave Kenya.) Some anatomists criticized parts of the reconstruction, which was only a preliminary one and there were still pieces to be fitted together, but nobody disputed the size of the brain.

Unfortunately 1470 had no teeth, but the sockets show that the incisors and canines must have been relatively large, as in *Homo*, whereas in the australopiths these teeth are small in proportion to the cheek teeth. Richard also pointed out that the face and upper jaw are unlike those of any known form of hominid.[9] Several limb bones were also found in 1972 in the same general area, and the straight-shafted femur attributed to the same kind of individual as 1470 is almost indistinguishable from that of modern man.

When Richard got back from East Rudolf at the end of September he showed the skull to his parents in Louis's office at the Museum. It was a very emotional moment. Louis's whole face lit up, and he said: 'They won't believe you!' The theories he had held for so long seemed to be completely vindicated: here, apparently, was *Homo*, the direct ancestor of modern man, way back in the earliest Pleistocene.

The two secretaries, Pat Barrett and Cara Phelips, were also in the office at the time. Mrs Barrett said later, in answer to a letter of condolence after Louis's death: 'Louis's delight and enthusiasm, the expression on his face, and the way in which he handled the skull, together with his unbounded congratulations to Richard, all created a moment which was unforgettable. Louis left Kenya in a very happy frame of mind, for which we shall always be thankful.'[10]

Louis and Mary, Louis and Richard, were united by the excitement of that skull in a way they had not known for years. They were really 'together', just like they had been in the old days, the tensions and differences forgotten. Louis's last evening at Langata, and his last in Kenya, was spent rejoicing over 1470.

He had planned to leave for London on 26 September and, as usual, had been doing far too much. A new doctor had discovered that he had very high blood pressure and had put him on to stringent drugs, urging him to rest as much as possible during the treatment. Of course he did not: he was working up till the last moment on his Caltech lectures, and often during his 'rest' in the afternoons he was dictating information about the Kikuyu to an American research student.

Anxiety was the very last thing he needed just then, but unfortunately during those last few weeks before his departure he was frantically worried about his son Colin and family who were in Uganda. General Amin was expelling Asians, and the Nairobi press was very hostile to political events in Uganda.

Colin would not admit that there was anything wrong. From Makerere University, where he was doing research on beans, he wrote to Louis on 12 September:

> Thank you for your concern for our welfare. Press reports are completely untrue that any British were told to go except for British Asians and there is no anti-British feeling or action here at all other than for and from isolated individuals who have lacked tact to the point of foolishness. The University is working as normal, there is no mass exodus or sense of panic, nor any need for such. I believe the internal security of this country is as good at present as it has been at any time for the last few years. The attitude of the English papers is most ill-founded and unfortunate.

Under the new University of Cambridge status Colin had submitted a published work for his PhD and now had to appear in person for a *viva voce*. He had bought his air ticket to London before money in Uganda was frozen, after which he could not pay fares for his family, whom he had intended to leave in Kampala. Louis telephoned repeatedly urging him to bring Susan and the girls with him, since he was not at all convinced by Colin's assurances that there was no cause for anxiety. As a precaution Louis applied to the Kenya exchange control department for permission to pay their air fares to London from his bank account in Nairobi, and this was allowed. (Needless to say there was not enough in his account, but he paid on an overdraft.) On the very next day, Louis received a message that Colin and his family were arriving in Nairobi next morning, 26 September, and leaving for London that same afternoon. 'Refugees' from Uganda were not allowed to stay for more than a few hours.

Louis met the family at the airport in Nairobi and took them to lunch at Langata before they continued their journey to London. They had left Uganda just in time, driving in convoy with a police escort from Kampala to Entebbe. Only a few hours later, exhausted by the strain and anxiety, Louis himself left Nairobi.

Priscilla met him at London Airport and he seemed to be in good form, talking volubly about his plans. For the next few days in Vanne Goodall's flat he worked on the finishing touches to his autobiography, but he was definitely tired and was persuaded to put off an appointment with the BBC. On 30 September he saw Dr Grant, who had attended him so often before; although the routine ECGs were good, Dr Grant advised him to postpone his flight to New York from 2 October to 5 October so that he could get a few more days' rest.

While he was getting dressed on Sunday morning, 1 October, Louis had a coronary. Vanne telephoned to Dr Grant, who immediately put him in the intensive care unit at St Stephen's Hospital, Fulham Road. He was conscious for a little while and apparently knew he was dying. Vanne left the hospital at 9 a.m. as he was under sedation, and half an hour later he was dead.

When the hospital informed her Vanne first telephoned to Priscilla and then sent a cable to Joan Travis. Obviously it was important that Joan should cancel Louis's lectures and other appointments as soon as possible, but cables were not necessarily private and there was danger of a Press leak before Mary could be told the news. As usual she was incommunicado at Olduvai. It was a Sunday, so no one would be at the Museum; Jonathan had only a radio telephone, Richard was at East Rudolf, and Philip had no telephone at his home. It seemed unlikely that anyone would be at the house at Langata, but by a miracle Philip happened to be there when Priscilla rang. He contacted Jonathan and then flew to Olduvai to break the news to Mary; Richard heard when he returned next day from East Rudolf.

Late in the evening Michael Day telephoned to Nairobi and was told that by then Mary had returned from Olduvai and that the news of Louis's death could be released to the Press in London. An hour before midnight Colin rang Reuters and the obituaries were in the papers the next morning.

Louis's body was flown back to Nairobi on 4 October, and next day there was a simple burial service at the little church at Limuru where, in the afternoon sunshine, Louis was laid to rest beside his parents. The pall bearers were his three sons, Jonathan, Richard and Philip; Mr Mbiyu Koinange, representing President Kenyatta (who sent a personal wreath); Professor Joseph Mungai; and Mr

Joab Omino, Permanent Secretary of the Ministry of Natural Resources. A car had been sent to collect Louis's oldest friend, Heselon Mukiri, but unfortunately there was a misunderstanding about the time and he missed the service.

There had been an announcement in the Nairobi papers that the funeral was to be private, and this was also broadcast on the Voice of Kenya, successor to the vernacular broadcasts which Louis had pioneered during the Second World War. But the fact that it was to be for members of the family only had not been stressed sufficiently, and there were innumerable enquiries about the time from those who wanted to be there. They had to be content with the memorial service held the following day in All Saints Cathedral, Nairobi. Mr William Omamo, Minister of Natural Resources, gave a short address, as did Louis's brother-in-law Dr Leonard Beecher, who assisted in the service. The main tribute was from the Attorney General, Mr Charles Njonjo, who had known Louis since childhood and whose father still lives near the mission station at Kabete; it was a most moving eulogy, which perhaps Louis would have appreciated more than any of the other words that were said or written about him:

> I stand before you on this very sad occasion on behalf of His Excellency the President Mzee Jomo Kenyatta to pay this country's respects to the memory of one of the great sons of Kenya, who won for himself a world-wide lustre of affection and respect. It was always his great gift to merge himself, quite unaffectedly, into any segment or arena of the diverse pattern of mankind. And he would wish to be remembered, not in terms of any race or nationality or tribe, but as a member of the human species.
>
> Sixty-nine years ago, just a few miles from here at Kabete, a distinguished missionary of that time had a son, who was destined to become Dr Louis Seymour Bazett Leakey. As a youngster he grew up among the Kikuyu people, and remained throughout his life an authority on their language and their culture. Plans that were made for his secondary and higher education were frustrated by the First World War, but thereafter at Cambridge he showed evidence of academic brilliance. And of course in decades that followed this man was honoured by universities and learned bodies in Europe and the United States, and in many parts of Africa.
>
> His approach to the process of learning was always novel, and some-

times stubborn. While his scientific training was extensive, and his grasp extraordinary, he would never meekly accept whatever was portrayed to him as scientific gospel. Always this had to be submitted to the final test of his own observation and intellect. No man of this century has come closer to an infinite zest for enquiry. . . .

Leakey was sometimes the despair of chairmen whose job it was to try to keep lectures or meetings within the reasonable bounds of time. So refreshing and exciting was his mind that everything went on and on. Switching from stone age evolution, he could bring compassion to bear on current human problems. He would probingly relate fossil discoveries to the arguments of today for wildlife conservation. He would revel in the challenge of questions about sun-spots or volcanic behaviour, about the evolution of species or the meaning of human traditions, about pathology in flamingos, or the latest research into serum techniques.

In his wife and family Dr Leakey was a fortunate man. We share with them the memory of a mind and being who was devoted to the cause of human enlightenment. We are all a little prouder for having known him whom we commend to God's mercy.

Another commemorative service which would have given Louis much pleasure was held on 20 October in St John's College Chapel at Cambridge, the Chapel where Louis had so often attended evensong and listened to the choir with such enjoyment. Frida, Priscilla and Colin were there with their families, as well as many of Louis's friends and colleagues. Most of his closest associates from the peak period of his career were dead – Wayland, Hopwood, MacInnes, Le Gros Clark – but there were still some who had known him ever since his Cambridge days, including those who had been taught by him. One of these was Dr Glyn Daniel of St John's, who gave the address.

Of the obituaries that appeared in the British newspapers the day after Louis died one of the fullest was in *The Times*; although officially I was supposed to be its author perhaps I can say without immodesty that it was also the most remarkable since most of it had been dictated by Louis himself! As long ago as 1958 I had been approached by the obituary department of *The Times* to provide an appreciation of Louis for their files and, as he happened to be in London at the time, I rang him up and asked if he would like to write it. He chuckled and was obviously delighted at the idea, so we compiled it together. Every few years I used to bring it up to date by adding the latest Leakey discoveries.

Many of the tributes to Louis which appeared in the scientific journals were written by colleagues who had been inspired by him, and their very real admiration and affection comes through. For sheer excellence none of the other notices can compare with the one by Phillip Tobias, published in the *South African Archaeological Bulletin* in June 1973.[11] It would do it an injustice to quote from it, and anyone who has an interest in Louis is urged to read it in full.

Michael Day, writing in the *British Medical Journal* of 21 October, pointed to Louis's 'blend of courage, humour, determination, industry and humanity'. He also stressed Louis's extraordinary powers of observation:

> His uncanny sense of knowing where fossils were to be found, unfairly termed 'Leakey's luck', came from a remarkable eye for country and a wide knowledge of all the sciences that contribute towards the search for fossils. . . . His rare knowledge of animals and animal behaviour were acquired as a lifetime observer in the field. An early morning drive in Nairobi National Park in his company was an unforgettable experience.

Dr W. W. (Bill) Bishop, field leader of the Bedford College geological expeditions to the Lake Baringo area, emphasized in the *Yearbook of the Geological Society* for 1972 Louis's talents as a teacher: 'There are few teachers who in their late sixties would agree to give master classes for undergraduates at 7 a.m. in order to avoid disappointing them because of an otherwise full schedule. There are fewer still who would find such lectures crowded to the doors.'

In the *National Geographic* of January 1973 the Society's president, Dr Melvin Payne, wrote of Louis as 'a beloved friend – a powerful, brilliant, hulking man who dedicated his life to pushing back the horizons of the past, no matter what the cost to his health.'[12] On the opposite page is one of the most characteristic pictures of Louis ever taken (the photographer was Dr Melville Grosvenor). Dressed in his old boiler suit, he holds a *Deinotherium* molar in one hand and a fossil elephant tooth resting on a squashed khaki hat in the other; he is smiling, and his eyes are bright with excitement at the latest finds from Olduvai. On the cover of this same issue is a picture of another old man with white hair. From the deep-sunk eyes and spreading nose many people might take him for a typical Australian aborigine; in fact the caption reads 'Vigorous Ecuadorian, 87, still toils strenuously every day.' If Louis had lived that long, no doubt he would have done the same; but there is another reason for drawing attention to this picture. The moral seems to be that even when you have the facial features to help it is often impossible to distinguish between races: how much more so when you have nothing more than a skull.

16 Aftermath

When Louis set off on his last journey, here is what he had meant to do. After three days in London he intended to see his publishers in New York, taking with him the last five chapters of his memoirs. Then for the rest of October he was to have had meetings and deliver lectures in Philadelphia, Washington, Chicago, Los Angeles and other places in southern California, San Francisco and Salt Lake City. The first few days of November were to have been devoted to Calico, and then he had allowed himself just two days to prepare for the Caltech seminar-lectures on 11 and 12 November. After that he was to speak at Riverside and at a Leakey Foundation dinner, at which he had proposed to talk about his early life under the title of 'Louis Leakey the Kikuyu'. At the end of November he was to have gone to Canada.

After New York the first item on this daunting itinerary was a lecture in Philadelphia sponsored by the Academy of Natural Sciences and the Leakey Foundation. The initial reaction to the shock of Louis's death had been to cancel the lecture, but a large audience had booked to hear him and it was decided that it should be given as a memorial to him. Whenever there was need for an eloquent speaker on anthropological subjects the obvious choice was Dr Clark Howell. At very short notice he stepped into the breach and on 5 October, the very day when Louis was being laid to rest at Limuru, 3,500 people heard Howell pay his impromptu tribute to his old friend.

He recalled how they had first met in Nairobi in 1954 when Louis offered to show him some of the Rift Valley sites. There were still Mau Mau hiding in the forests, so they were accompanied by four members of the King's (now Kenya) African Rifles armed with Sten guns. Three years later, encouraged by Louis, Howell excavated a handaxe site at Isimila in southern Tanzania; and in the following year, 1958, he made his first reconnaissance of the Omo beds. As already mentioned, when he later applied for a permit to work there he got no response from the Ethiopian Government. After he had given up all hope, he suddenly received a telegram: 'Omo OK. See you soon. Louis.' Louis had just had his talk with the Emperor. The subsequent Omo expeditions, which in turn led to Richard's involvement with East Rudolf, pushed back knowledge of man's origins by a couple of million years and opened a new era of international co-operation in palaeontological research.

Four days after Howell's lecture the Leakey Foundation held its annual meeting at the National Geographic Society's offices in Washington, mainly in order to enable the East Coast trustees and members of the science and grants committee to attend. In the words of the Foundation's minutes: 'It was a challenge to the trustees to decide if the Foundation could sustain the fiery dedication and purpose which Dr Leakey's leadership inspired, and a unanimous and enthusiastic rededication emerged.' A Louis Leakey Memorial Fund was also established 'in response to thousands of letters which poured into the Foundation's office'. This was designed to help students to carry on Louis's work through field training, scholarships, fellowships and travel grants; it was 'the Foundation's way of perpetuating those qualities of Dr Leakey so vividly remembered by students, his encouragement of their work and faith in their future.'

Soon after this meeting Joan Travis said in a letter to Cara Phelips:

> The Foundation seems to have survived the initial shock of Louis's death much more successfully than I had thought it might. People seem to want to see his dreams fulfilled and the inspiration of his genius perpetuated. I keep getting such phone calls and letters from Louis's students (actual and hopeful), friends and colleagues, each wanting in some way to keep in touch with a memory. You just wouldn't believe how many.[1]

The immediate hurdle to get over was the seminar-lectures at Caltech which Louis was to have given on 11–12 November. Mary had cabled to Priscilla asking her to send the casts and slides which were in Louis's luggage to Clark Howell, who once again rallied round. He and six other colleagues took over the lectures, which ranged from chimpanzee behaviour to the emergence of 'psycho-social man'. If Louis had given all these talks himself, as he had intended to do, one wonders whether he would have been able to get through without a collapse. In spite of his early forebodings, only about fifty out of the four hundred seats remained unsold – and the lectures were not of the popular sort, but six solid hours of scientific facts. After covering the costs the Leakey Foundation netted $10,000, of which half went to Tigoni, as Louis would have wished.

As a result of donations by trustees of the Leakey Foundation, twenty-five Caltech students were able to attend free. There was also a student from the Niles Township Community High School of Illinois, whose pupils had raised $500 by the sale of candied apples to pay for a lecture which Louis was to have given them. Instead they turned the money over to the scholarship fund for the Caltech seminar.

A month later, in December 1972, Allen O'Brien resigned from the board of trustees of the Leakey Foundation. The reason he gave was that he felt his usefulness was at an end, and he wanted others with more experience of foundations to take over. Some people criticized him for this, feeling that he had 'quit' and left others to hold the baby that he had fathered. It is undeniable that once Allen has got something on its feet he is eager to switch his energies in new directions. He still had an insatiable urge to travel adventurously and was planning to navigate the rapids of the Omo River – something which had never been done before and which he accomplished successfully in the summer of 1973. Perhaps he was also disillusioned by some aspects of the Foundation's work, and he may have been right in saying that it was time for amateurs to step aside. Probably the most compelling reason for his resignation, however, was that his heart was not in the Foundation to the same extent now that the reason for its formation was no longer there. Louis had been the driving force – one could say the juggernaut – behind the Leakey Foundation throughout the four years of its existence, and without him the operation had far less meaning for its founder. Louis and his scientific colleagues had opened an entirely new world for Allen, as also for other members of the Foundation, and he has no regrets.

On the contrary he has every reason to be proud. In spite of its initial lack of funds and its sometimes turbulent history the Foundation has survived. In 1971 it became public, rather than private, so as to be able to campaign for members, and its articles were reconstituted. In February 1972 three more words defining its broader scope were added to the end of its already lengthy title, which then became The L. S. B. Leakey Foundation for Research Related to Man's Origin, Behaviour and Survival. At the annual meeting a week after Louis's death the minutes recorded: 'Dr Leakey's broad span of scientific curiosity enabled him to perceive illuminating new relationships between the infinity of the past and the speculations of the future,' and indeed Louis had been much concerned over man's survival.

Among the hundred-and-eighty Fellows at the present time perhaps at least half are millionaires and half a dozen are worth more than a hundred million each. They include such names as Walter Annenberg, Gene Kelly, Charlton Heston, Frank Sinatra and James Stewart; and Gordon Getty has become a trustee. Despite this galaxy only half of Robert Beck's challenge gift has been met and the endowment fund stands at half a million dollars; the motivation is no longer there to the same extent. Nevertheless the Foundation is currently distributing some $70,000 a year, of which 68% goes to anthropological research, 15% to primate studies, 10% to conservation and 7% to education. Since Louis's death grants have been given to a very wide range of subjects: new dating techniques; Jane's work at Gombe West, Stanford, and Birute's in Indonesia; travel grants for Ubeidiya; an expedition to new fossil localities in Iran; a post-graduate fellowship for a Kenyan student to work at Berkeley and afterwards to excavate at Mary's old site at Hyrax Hill. Louis would have been particularly pleased that money is still going to Tigoni; and that a grant has been given for the editing of his long-delayed book on the Kikuyu.

The Foundation is also active in organizing lectures and symposia, and not only of the popular 'after-dinner' variety. Clark Howell's talk about Louis and his work on 5 October 1972 was the first of what has become the Philadelphia Academy's annual

Louis Leakey Memorial Lecture, co-sponsored by the Leakey Foundation. Jane van Lawick Goodall gave the second of these in 1973; and on 3 August of that year there was another memorial lecture to Louis in Johannesburg. The speaker was Phillip Tobias, and it was accompanied by a showing of the film 'Dr Leakey and the dawn of man'. The sponsors were the University of the Witwatersrand, the Royal Society of South Africa, the Leakey Foundation, and the Institute for the Study of Man in Africa, which was set up by Mr Leighton Wilkie in honour of Professor Raymond Dart. Tobias's talk may be read – and, as already mentioned, it is well worth reading – in the *South African Archaeological Bulletin* of June 1973.

The Caltech seminar-lectures of November 1972 were also such a success that, like Howell's talk at Philadelphia, they established a precedent. A second two-day symposium, 'In Search of Man', was sponsored by the Leakey Foundation in conjunction with the California Academy of Sciences in December 1973 at San Francisco. Mary came over from East Africa to speak, and old friends of Louis's who gave lectures included Raymond Dart, Clark Howell, Dian Fossey, and Jane van Lawick Goodall.

Hopes for the formation of 'chapters' of the Leakey Foundation in other American cities have not yet been fulfilled, but an inaugural meeting of the proposed London branch was held in May 1973. Its organizer, Fleur Cowles, is also preparing a commemorative volume of reminiscences on Louis by his friends. And at Berkeley, Glynn Isaac is editing 'Essays on East Africa and Human Origins – a tribute to the life's work of the late Louis Leakey', to be published as volume 3 in the *Perspectives on human evolution* series; this will include a complete bibliography of Louis's publications, compiled by Shirley Coryndon Savage, and essays on behaviour, geology, palaeontology and archaeology by his colleagues.

So many different kinds of people, not only those connected with science, have wanted to remember Louis in some permanent way. At the time of his death there was a good deal of discussion in the East African Press about the renaming of geographical features, and one suggestion was that Lake Victoria should be known by its ancient name of Lolwe; an African correspondent then proposed that the Kavirondo Gulf should be called Leakey Gulf! Unfortunately the suggestion was never adopted.

Probably the projects closest to Louis's heart were Tigoni and the publication of his book on the Kikuyu people, both of which now look like having happy endings. The Kikuyu book very nearly got into print in 1968, but there were complications over the contract and the negotiations which Louis had started with a publisher in East Africa fell through. President Kenyatta personally expressed the wish that Louis's tremendous work on their mutual tribe should be made available to scholars, since most of the material it contains is as unknown to the present generation of Kikuyu as it is to foreigners. It is no secret that Mary disapproved of some of the activities of the Leakey Foundation, particularly on the social side, but she did ask for their help in subsidizing the Kikuyu book, knowing how much it had meant to Louis. His sister, Gladys Beecher, is checking the Kikuyu terms, with a grant from the Foundation, and it really looks as though at long last it may appear in print.

As for Tigoni, at first it was an uphill struggle – as it always had been. We saw how Louis had protested against 'affiliation' with the University of Nairobi, and how at first he was against the Museum trustees having anything to do with it. In the end the trustees themselves stepped in, saying that, as Tigoni was one of the research centres attached to the Museum, they had a legal as well as moral responsibility and had a right to be on the board controlling it. Louis had eventually conceded that the trustees should be represented by two members, and that a committee should be appointed to select other prominent Kenyan scientists and administrators to serve on the board, including himself. An agreement was drawn up between Louis and the trustees stipulating that if the board should cease to function the Museum would have the first option to acquire the whole complex at Tigoni at cost price. This was the position at the time of Louis's death. The articles of association had been prepared and the new board constituted, but the inaugural meeting had been postponed until his return from America.

Louis would have been the executive director, and no one else was prepared to take this on even if they had been qualified to do so; Richard therefore proposed that the idea of a separate board should be dropped. At a meeting of the Museum trustees he told them that they would have to make a decision as to whether Tigoni was to close down. To their credit they agreed that Richard should have a year in which to try to set it up on a proper basis – if he could find the money. The Munitalp Foundation wrote off the £6,000 they had put into the property and passed the mortgage over to solicitors with instructions to release it to the Museum trustees. The trustees then reverted to the old arrangement whereby they would be responsible for Tigoni as a branch of the Museum; and the National Primate Research Centre changed its name for the third time, becoming the Institute of Comparative Primatology.

At their board meeting on 9 October 1972 the Leakey Foundation decided to continue their commitment of $1,000 a month to Tigoni for the next two months, that is up until December, in deference to Louis's wishes. No money could be obtained from Louis's various research accounts, which were in his personal name and therefore frozen on his death, and the Leakey Foundation grant only just kept the monkeys fed and the place ticking over. The students – who as Louis himself admitted were doing very little – were given notice, with the exception of one young man, and the staff reduced from ten to five. The guest house at Tigoni was rented to bring in a little money.

Richard put in an application to the Leakey Foundation for a grant of $29,000: $12,000 was to cover the monkey's food for a year, and to this they agreed; $12,000 was for a director's salary; and a further $5,000 was to cover travel grants, housing and development costs. The Foundation said it would consider the question of a director's salary when a suitable candidate had been found, and that they would wish to be consulted about the selection of such a candidate. Richard interviewed half a dozen or so at various times but failed to find anyone he considered suitable. Then, after a few months, the Leakey Foundation decided that they could not continue to give $1,000 a month to feed the monkeys unless they were satisfied that real efforts were being made to find a director. It really seemed that the long struggles to keep Tigoni viable were ended and that the place would have to be closed.

In the summer of 1973 a posthumous stroke of Leakey's luck took a hand. Into Richard's office walked a young woman named Sandra Richards who had obtained a PhD in zoology from Cambridge University, having worked in the Sub Department of Animal Behaviour just as Jane had done. Her husband was a nutritionist at the University of Nairobi and she had also been offered a post there, but came to ask Richard if she could do some part-time research at Tigoni. Richard realized at once that here was the person he had been trying to find for so long; to her amazement he asked if she would like to take over Tigoni as scientific director, and probably rather to his amazement she said she would. She was interviewed and accepted by the Museum trustees, and Richard told the Lcakey Foundation he needed an immediate decision as to whether they would provide her salary. But they were wary of Tigoni, and said they could not be rushed in this way. Richard therefore borrowed the money, half of which came from Allen O'Brien from the sale of the rubber boats used in his successful navigation of the Omo River that summer.

On his way through Nairobi in September Allen and his wife Helen visited Tigoni and he said:

> We could scarcely believe the transformation. The main house which heretofore was truly disgracefully dirty and dishevelled is now freshly painted and neat as a pin. The grounds are orderly as never before. The monkeys are in miraculous condition. The cages are spotlessly clean. Tigoni never had it so good. We were given a concise, intelligent tour by the new director Dr Sandy Richards and were most impressed. What she and her husband have accomplished in only one month is more than remarkable, it's a miracle.[2]

Dr Richards was appointed for one year, after which she was to produce a report on future prospects. Then, if Tigoni is to continue, it is up to her to find the funds. 'Louis had a good idea,' Richard told me, 'and tried very hard, albeit in vain, to make it work. We may succeed yet, and if we do much credit will go to him.'

Louis's most vigorous offspring, a much healthier child than

Tigoni, was of course the Centre for Prehistory and Palaeontology. Even before June 1972, when the Museum took over financial responsibility, it had been obvious to the trustees that something would have to be done on a very big scale. Throngs of scientists were queuing up for access to its chock-full laboratories and rows of box-like rooms, where precious hominid fossils were kept under lock and key. As the scientific world as a whole would benefit from expansion it was only right that building costs should be borne by international co-operation: Kenya alone could not cope with this embarrassingly voracious hydra which Louis had produced.

Not that the Kenya Government intended to shelve all responsibility: the Museum trustees were to provide the land and meet staff salaries, but beyond that they could not go. On 12 December 1973 Kenya celebrated the tenth anniversary of independence and President Kenyatta reviewed his Government's achievements: six hundred new primary schools, seven hundred more secondary schools; the number of doctors had been doubled; and some 57,000 African families had been resettled on land formerly owned by expatriates. All this had to be paid for, and in a rapidly developing country with a large unemployment problem technological research had to have priority over pure science – such as investigations into the origins of man.

Preliminary plans for a greatly expanded Institute for African Prehistory (IAP) were drawn up as part of the Museum's overall developmental programme; estimates for the proposed new buildings were prepared by a firm of architects; and a prospectus went off to the printers. Proofs were received a week before Louis died, just in time to change the name of the Institute to The Louis Leakey Memorial Institute for African Prehistory.

For some time Richard had been putting out financial feelers in various directions, and the fact that IAP was to be a memorial to Louis gave his fund-raising campaign a new impetus. During his visit to the United States in the spring of 1973 he concentrated on untapped sources among the wealthy industrialists of the East Coast and had remarkable success. Also, as already mentioned, the Guggenheim Foundation agreed to divert into IAP the $100,000 they had allocated to Louis's 'Suguta expedition'. The building fund, for which the estimate had been $750,000, was well under way; but Richard needed far more than money merely for bricks and mortar. He needed also an endowment fund.

The plan for setting up IAP was divided into three phases. First came the construction of the buildings, the installation of the collections, and the appointment of a director and staff. Next would be the initiation of an educational programme, the acceptance of postgraduates for training, and the appointment of visiting research associates. Finally, there would be the provision of fellowships and interchange of East African students with those from American and other universities; the production of publications; and the organization of scientific meetings. Richard's target for an endowment fund to meet all these needs is $10 million. He is thinking really big and admits that he has no time for small contributions.

Unlike his father he also has little time for people as people, so perhaps it was hardly surprising that when he approached the Leakey Foundation in March 1973 he did not gain a positive response. Richard would have liked IAP to benefit from their tax-free status, their endowment fund, and the matching donations from Robert Beck; in effect his proposal was that they should turn all their money over to IAP. The Leakey Foundation did not wish to lose their independence, nor did they wish to support 'bones and stones' exclusively and sever all ties with the primate studies in which Louis had been so interested. Yet they did not want to cut off connections with the Leakey family, and they would find it difficult to continue to support projects in East Africa without Richard's approval and goodwill. It was a tricky situation, and Richard showed that he was no more inclined to compromise than his father had been on many occasions.

It seems unlikely that Richard would ever make a happy marriage with any existing foundation – particularly, perhaps, the Leakey Foundation which is so dominated by personalities – and no doubt he will go it alone. With his ambition and drive, and his powers of persuasion, he may well succeed.

Richard, if he so chooses, could spend a lifetime at East Rudolf without exhausting its riches, but there are limits to the amount of new information that can be obtained from any one area, even one as huge as this. There are also limits to the amount of fossil fauna that can be studied by the available specialists.

For six years Richard refrained from speculating – at least in print – on the status of the East Rudolf hominids beyond distinguishing between the two lines which he called *Australopithecus* and *Homo*. In 1974, with more than a hundred hominid specimens to go on, he allowed himself the luxury of expanding a little on his evolutionary theories. In *Nature* he described some of the twenty hominids found during his sixth expedition in 1973 and gave his answers to the questions that many people had been asking.[3] Where does *habilis* now stand? Does Richard regard it as distinct from the line represented by that famous, large-brained 1470 skull?

Louis had toyed with the idea of three distinct hominid lineages in the early Pleistocene, and so does Richard; but one of his lines is different to Louis's. First, they agree on *Australopithecus boisei* (Zinj), which Richard admits 'also shows similarities with *A. robustus* of South Africa.' Secondly, they both recognize '*Homo*', living contemporaneously but showing greater variability: in this category Richard places 1470 and others like it from East Rudolf, and also the original 'pre-Zinj' child from Olduvai, H7, as well as 'George', H16. Richard, in fact, includes some, but not all, of Louis's *habilis* specimens in this second lineage. The fundamental difference between father and son lies in the third line which Richard distinguishes, and which Louis had ignored: the 'gracile' type of australopith, *A. africanus*, recognized for so long in South Africa. Admitting that he had previously questioned its validity, Richard now has evidence from East Rudolf which 'reopens the possibility of its existence.' This new evidence is a small-brained, small-toothed cranium, 1813, found by the eagle-eyed Kamoya Kimeu; and with it Richard groups H24 from Olduvai, 'Twiggy' of the dished face. Her contours had always been an embarrassing contradiction to Louis's description of his new species, *Homo habilis*, and her new status resolves the problem neatly. Would Louis have agreed? No doubt there would have been heated arguments over some of these interpretations, and both father and son would have enjoyed themselves immensely in agreeing to differ.

In September 1973 Richard organized a conference at the

National Museum in Nairobi for all those who had taken part in the East Rudolf expeditions, as well as the French and American Omo expeditions. There was a good deal of argument there too, but mostly on questions of dating and correlations between the two areas. In his closing address Dr Clark Howell said that there are moments when certain branches of science come of age, and the discovery of Zinj in 1959 had been such a moment. He described as 'the revolution of the sixties' the fact that 50% of the work of international expeditions like East Rudolf and Omo is done by young people. Louis, he said, had a talent for bringing people together, especially students: 'Without Louis, none of these projects would have been realized and many of us would not have known each other.'

It is no exaggeration to say that Louis gave his life for science, and for his family and followers to carry on his scientific work. Olduvai and East Rudolf he left in good hands, as also the research on chimpanzees, gorillas and orangutans. Mary and Richard are 'still digging'; Jane, Dian and Birute are still in the forests and are training others to follow them, and all three would acknowledge that without Louis their lives would have taken a very different course. Jane, who is a professor of Stanford and also at the University of Dar es Salaam, has put in more ape-hours than the other two and commutes between Gombe East and Gombe West. Dian is taking her doctorate at Cambridge, as Louis had hoped she would; by the time he died she had already completed the longest and most comprehensive studies ever made on the mountain gorilla. She has worked mostly entirely alone, often in dangerous circumstances, nearly always under unpleasant climatic conditions; but as long as funds and the political situation hold out, Dian means to stay with her gorillas. Birute had been at work for only nine months by the time Louis died, and he said of her in a letter to Dian: 'Birute has 500 hours of direct contact with the orangutans. She is doing magnificently.'[4] By the end of 1973 she had logged 2,500 hours of observation. The Brindamours have established three camps named Leakey, Wilkie and Dart, and at their main headquarters, Camp Leakey, they have a vegetable garden and keep chickens; they intend to stay there as long as possible.[5]

Research in the Miocene deposits of western Kenya, Louis's other great interest, still goes on sporadically, and there is certainly much more to be discovered at the sites which he found and exploited. One of the palaeontologists working on the Miocene, Dr Peter Andrews, recently described two new species of apes from Songhor and Rusinga, *Dryopithecus gordoni* and *D. vancouveringi.*[6] Like several other specialists he regards *Proconsul* as a sub-genus of *Dryopithecus*; and Louis's *Kenyapithecus wickeri* is generally grouped with *Ramapithecus* – but a rose is a rose by any other name, and all this is not important: the fossils are there for all to gloat over.

Mary's splendid work on the *Excavations in Beds I and II, Olduvai Gorge*, was published in 1972 as the third volume in the new Olduvai series, and now she is preparing Beds III and IV for publication. Olduvai is her home – the round hut which she shares at night with the Dalmatians, the airy dining room, the smaller hut used as a laboratory; she uses the Langata house occasionally, but the real proprietors are the cats and the hyraxes. Louis did not leave a will – if he ever made one, it was never found – and in any case he had practically nothing to leave, certainly no money: his sole assets were the house at Langata and one at Malindi. At Langata there are memories of Louis everywhere: in the library, with its magnificent collection of Africana, copies of his own books, shelves full of scientific journals and offprints; in the replicas of his medals on the sitting room mantelpiece; in the cupboards full of slides; in the empty fish-tanks. In an outhouse there are tin trunks full of Press cuttings and letters dating back to the Cambridge days. They contain an interesting assortment of natural history specimens which Louis would have appreciated – spiders, silverfish, even a squashed gecko.

Like the ancestral *Homo* which he sought for so long, Louis was remarkable for his lack of specialization. Nothing, and nobody, was too insignificant for his attention. People are remembered for their beliefs and sense of involvement, never for their indifference; Louis made such a deep impression on so many people because he cared for them both collectively and as individuals. In his lectures he used to say: 'I have become more and more concerned not only with man's past but also with his present and future.' And he would go on to discuss over-population, pollution and violence – which he attributed not only to overcrowding and insecurity but also to loss of self resepct.

Louis's life had not been easy, and very often he was disillusioned by the behaviour of his fellow men, but he never lost his basic faith in humanity.

Glossary

Acheulian: Palaeolithic culture named after St Acheul, France, characterized by handaxes. From about one million to 100,000 years ago.

Australopithecine: Member of the Australopithecinae, a sub-family of the Hominidae. Upright-walking hominids, known mainly from South and East Africa. From about 5 to 1 million years ago.

Carbon-14: See Radiocarbon.

Handaxe: Pear-shaped stone tool pointed at one end, characteristic of the Acheulian culture.

Hominid: Member of the family Hominidae.

Hominidae: Family that includes the australopithecines and extinct and modern forms of man.

Hominoid: Member of the super-family Hominoidea, which includes apes and hominids.

Homo erectus: Extinct forms of men with heavy brow-ridges, including Java Man, Peking Man, etc. From about 1 million to 500,000 years ago.

Homo habilis: New species of man named by Leakey from Olduvai Gorge. From about 5 to 1 million years ago.

Industry: Assemblage of artifacts from a particular site which, together with other industries, forms part of a culture.

Interpluvial: Period when rainfall was less than at present over a considerable time.

Miocene: Fourth period of the Tertiary era, from about 25 to 5 million years ago.

Oldowan: Earliest named culture, first recognized from Olduvai Gorge, Bed I, characterized by choppers and other simple stone tools.

Pleistocene: First period of the Quaternary era, from about 3 million years ago to 8,000 B.C.

Pluvial: Period when rainfall was higher than at present over a considerable time.

Potassium-argon dating: Method of absolute dating of rocks rich in potassium, based on the rate of disintegration of K-40 into Ca-40 and Ar-40.

Radiocarbon dating: Method of absolute dating of material containing carbon, based on the rate of radioactive decay of the C14 isotope.

Simian shelf: Bony projection at back of symphysis of lower jaw serving as a reinforcement, present in apes but not in hominids.

Tuff: Fine material ejected from a volcano into a lake and then consolidated.

'Zinjanthropus': Name given originally to a hominid skull from Bed I, Olduvai Gorge, renamed *Australopithecus boisei.*

References

White African (1937, Hodder & Stoughton, London; reprinted 1966, Schenkman, Cambridge, Mass.) is Louis's account of the first thirty years of his life; I have used it for the background to Chapters 2–4.

By the Evidence (1974, Harcourt Brace Jovanovich, New York) is the second volume of his memoirs, covering the years 1932–1952; it includes many stories of his experiences with the CID during the Second World War, particularly handwriting cases, which I have not repeated here.

A bibliography of Louis's writings has been compiled by Professor P. V. Tobias (*South African Archaeological Bulletin*, 1973, 28: 8–12). A more detailed bibliography, prepared by Mrs Shirley Coryndon Savage, is to appear in G. Isaac & E. R. McCown (Eds), 'Essays on East Africa and human origins – a tribute to the life's work of the late Louis Leakey', *Perspectives on Human Evolution*, vol. 3, Holt, Rinehart & Winston, New York (in press). References to Louis's scientific work up to 1962 may be found in my book *The Prehistory of East Africa*, 1963, Macmillan, New York.

Chapter 2.

1. Rev. H. Leakey to CMS, 7 January, 1903.
2. *ib.*, 31 December, 1910.
3. Rev. H. Burt, Mission Secretary, Mombasa, to CMS, 21 February, 1902.
4. Rev. H. Leakey to CMS, 31 December, 1910.
5. 'Family in search of prehistoric man', *National Geographic*, February 1965, p.209.
6. *White African*, p. 28.
7. *Kenya: Contrasts and Problems*, new edition 1966, Schenkman, p.59.
8. *White African*, p. 87.
9. *ib.*, p. 89.
10. *Sunday Times*, 30 November, 1952.
11. *White African*, p.161.
12. 'Digging for dinosaurs', *Illustrated London News*, 17 January, 1925, p.98.

13. W. E. Cutler, field diary, 18 October, 1924.
14. *ib.*, 15 June, 1924.
15. *ib.*, 30 June, 1924.
16. *ib.*, 26 December, 1924.
17. 'A new classification of the bow and arrow in Africa', *Journal of the Royal Anthropological Institute*, 1926, 56: 259–99.

Chapter 3.

1. L. S. B. Leakey, field diary, 9 May, 1927.
2. 'Stone Age man in Kenya Colony', *Nature*, 1927, 120: 85.
3. *White African*, p.190.
4. *ib.*, p.205.
5. *S. African Journ. Sci.*, 1929, 26: 749–57.
6. *The Stone Age Cultures of Kenya Colony*, 1931, Cambridge.
7. A. C. Haddon to L.S.B.L., 10 October, 1929.

Chapter 4.

1. A. T. Hopwood (obituary of H. Reck), *Nature*, 28 August, 1937.
2. L.S.B.L. to the Master of St John's College, 1 March, 1931.
3. G. Schaller, *Serengeti, a Kingdom of Predators*, 1973, London, p.11.
4. *By the Evidence*, 1974.
5. E. J. Wayland, unpublished MS, 2 September, 1932.
6. L. S. B. Leakey, A. T. Hopwood and H. Reck, 'Age of the Oldoway bone beds, Tanganyika,' *Nature*, 1931, 128: 724.
7. E. J. Wayland, unpublished MS, 2 September, 1932.
8. 'The Oldoway human skeleton', *Nature*, 1932, 129: 721.
9. *White African*, p.313.
10. L.S.B.L. to A. T. Hopwood, 8 September, 1932.
11. *ib.*, 14 August, 1932.
12. A. T. Hopwood to L.S.B.L., 16 August, 1932.
13. 'Early human remains in East Africa'. Report of a conference at Cambridge convened by the Royal Anthropological Institute, *Man*, 1933, no.210.
14. 'The status of the Kanam mandible and the Kanjera skulls', *Man*, 1933, no.210.
15. L.S.B. Leakey, field diary, 17 February, 1935.
16. *ib.*, 17 January, 1935.
17. A. C. Haddon, to L.S.B.L., 21 March, 1935.
18. P. G. H. Boswell, 'Human remains from Kanam and Kanjera, Kenya Colony', *Nature*, 1935, 135: 371.

19. 'Fossil human remains from Kanam and Kanjera – a reply to Professor Boswell', *Nature*, 1936, 138: 643.
20. *The Stone Age Races of Kenya*, 1935, Oxford, p.9.

Chapter 5.

1. G. Caton-Thompson and E. W. Gardner, *The Desert Fayoum*, 1934, Royal Anthropological Institute.
2. Rev. H. Leakey to L.S.B.L., 16 May, 1934.
3. K. P. Oakley and M. D. Leakey, 'Report on excavations at Jaywick Sands, Essex (1934)', *Proc. Prehistoric Soc.*, 1937, 3: 217–60.
4. L. S. B. Leakey, field diary, 14 April, 1935.
5. *ib.*, 3 May, 1935.
6. *ib.*, 30 July, 1935.
7. P. E. Kent to L.S.B.L., 3 August, 1935.
8. L.S.B.L. to Sir Henry Dale, 1 November, 1935.
9. Sir Henry Dale to L.S.B.L., 28 June, 1936.
10. Mrs Harry Leakey to L.S.B.L., 28 June, 1936.
11. *Sunday Times*, 3 June, 1934.
12. Sir Arthur Keith to L.S.B.L., 2 May, 1934.
13. Mrs Harry Leakey to L.S.B.L., 18 January, 1936.
14. 'The Kikuyu problem of the initiation of girls', *Journ. Roy. Anthrop. Inst.*, 1931, 61: 277.
15. J. Murray-Brown, *Kenyatta*, 1972, London, p.192.
16. *Kenya: Contrasts and Problems*, p.101.
17. *ib.*, p.102.
18. C. van Riet Lowe to L.S.B.L., 22 November, 1937.
19. Chief Secretary, Dar es Salaam, to L.S.B.L., 27 July, 1936.
20. M. D. Leakey and L. S. B. Leakey, 'Report on the excavation at Hyrax Hill, Nakuru, Kenya Colony', *Trans. Roy. Soc. S. Afr.*, 1945, 30: 271–409.

Chapter 6.

By the Evidence, 1974.
Reports from L.S.B.L. to Director of Intelligence and Security, Nairobi, 1940–44.

1. M. D. Leakey, W. E. Owen and L. S. B. Leakey, 'Dimple-based pottery of Central Kavirondo', *Coryndon Mus. Occ. Pap.* no.2, 1948.
2. W. E. Owen to L.S.B.L., 1937 (n.d.).
3. H. J. Allen Turner to L.S.B.L., 14 May, 1934.
4. C. G. Richards, *Archdeacon Owen of Kavirondo. A memoir*, 1947, Nairobi.

5. J. W. Gregory, *The Great Rift Valleys and Geology of East Africa*, 1921, London, p.221.
6. L.S.B.L. to Secretary of Trustees of Coryndon Museum, 16 May, 1945.
7. *ib.*, 16 November, 1945.
8. L. S. B. Leakey (Ed.), *Proc. Pan Afr. Congr. on Prehist. 1947*, 1952, Oxford.
9. L.S.B.L. to Chief Secretary, Nairobi, 7 March, 1946.
10. *Pretoria News*, 17 April, 1951.
11. 'Tentative study of the Pleistocene climatic changes and stone culture sequence in North-eastern Angola', Museu do Dundo, no.4, 1949, Lisbon.

Chapter 7.

1. A. T. Hopwood, 'Miocene primates from British East Africa', *Ann. Mag. Nat. Hist.*, 1933, ser.10, 11: 96.
2. A. Owen to W. E. Owen, 16 May, 1934.
3. 'A Miocene anthropoid mandible from Rusinga, Kenya', *Nature*, 1943, 152: 319.
4. 'Notes on the East African Miocene Primates', *Journ. E. Afr. & Uganda Nat. Hist. Soc.*, 1943, 17: 141–81.
5. L.S.B.L. to W. E. Le Gros Clark, 10 October, 1948.
6. 'Skull of *Proconsul* from Rusinga Island', *Nature*, 1948, 162: 688.
7. L.S.B.L. to W. E. Le Gros Clark, 10 October, 1948.
8. Chief Secretary's files, National Archives of Kenya, 1948.
9. Chief Secretary to L.S.B.L., 18 May, 1951.
10. *ib.*, 12 August, 1959.
11. L.S.B.L. to Chief Secretary, 15 December, 1948.
12. *Proc. Geol. Soc. of London*, 22 April, 1953.
13. G. L. O. Grundy to L.S.B.L., 29 November, 1943.
14. L.S.B.L. to J. Owen, 23 February, 1949.
15. Mrs W. E. Owen to L.S.B.L., 19 April, 1949.
16. 'British-Kenya Miocene expeditions: interim report', *Nature*, 1955, 175: 234.

Chapter 8.

1. *Observer*, 18 July, 1954; 23 January, 1966.
2. M. H. Cowie, 27 May, 1953.
3. *Mau Mau and the Kikuyu*, 1952, London.
4. *Defeating Mau Mau*, 1954, London.
5. *ib.*, p.52.

6. *Time and Tide*, 3 January, 1953.
7. *Times Literary Supplement*, 26 December, 1952.
8. *Observer*, 10 January, 1953.
9. A. Somerhaugh to L.S.B.L., January, 1953 (dated 'Kitale, Wednesday').
10. Attorney General to L.S.B.L., 27 May, 1953.
11. J. Murray-Brown, *Kenyatta*, 1972, p.210.
12. L.S.B.L. to R. Wainwright, 6 November, 1953.
13. R. Wainwright, to L.S.B.L., 1 December, 1953.
14. C. Boise to L.S.B.L., 30 November, 1953.
15. L.S.B.L., broadcast of 19 October, 1954.
16. *The Times*, 25 September, 1954.
17. *The Economist*, 4 December, 1954.
18. *Defeating Mau Mau*, p.133.
19. W. N. Edwards to L.S.B.L., 22 November, 1951.
20. E. White to L.S.B.L., 14 August, 1958.
21. Ylla and L. S. B. Leakey, *Animals in Africa*, 1953, London.
22. *Animals of East Africa*, 1969, National Geographic Society, Washington.
23. H. B. S. Cooke, 'Observations relating to Quaternary environments in East and Southern Africa', *Geol. Soc. S. Afr. Bull.*, 1958, annex. to vol.60.
24. R. F. Flint, 'On the basis of Pleistocene correlation in East Africa', *Geol. Mag.*, 1959, 96: 265–84.
25. K. P. Oakley to L.S.B.L., 26 December, 1957.
26. W. E. Le Gros Clark to L.S.B.L., 1 January, 1958.

Chapter 9.

1. *Olduvai Gorge*, 1951, Cambridge.
2. *Olduvai Gorge 1951–1961. Fauna and Background*, vol.1, 1965, Cambridge.
3. *Illustrated London News*, 2 November, 1946, p.502; 19 June, 1954, pp.1074–51.
4. A. W. Gentry, '*Pelorovis oldowayensis* Reck, an extinct bovid', *Fossil Mammals of Africa*, No.22, British Museum (Natural History).
5. 'A new fossil skull from Olduvai', *Nature*, 1959, 184: 491.
6. M. D. Leakey, *Valley of the Wild Sisal* (in press).
7. Commentary in film 'Dr Leakey and the dawn of man'.
8. 'The Kanam jaw', *Nature*, 1960, 185: 946.
9. *Guardian*, 8 October, 1959.

10. *Vancouver Sun*, 3 September, 1959.
11. L.S.B.L. to M. M. Payne, 19 August, 1960.
12. 'Finding the world's earliest man', *National Geographic*, September 1960, p.433.
13. *Olduvai Gorge*, p.160.
14. *Illustrated London News*, 9 January, 1960.
15. 'Recent discoveries at Olduvai Gorge', *Nature*, 1960, 188: 1050.
16. 'New finds at Olduvai Gorge', *Nature*, 1961, 189: 649.
17. 'Exploring 1,750,000 years into man's past', *National Geographic*, October 1961, p.574.
18. M. B. Grosvenor to Armand Denis, 31 January, 1961.
19. L.S.B.L. to National Geographic Society, 2 June, 1960.
20. Miss J. Hess to Armand Denis, 27 February, 1961.
21. *The Lancet*, 23 December, 1961.
22. *The progress and evolution of man in Africa*, 1961, Oxford.
23. 'A new Lower Pliocene fossil primate from Kenya', *Ann. Mag. Nat. Hist.*, 1962, ser.13, 4: 689–96.
24. *Current Anthropology*, 1961, vol.2, no.3.
25. L.S.B. Leakey, J. F. Evernden & G. H. Curtis, 'Age of Bed I, Olduvai Gorge, Tanganyika', *Nature*, 1961, 191: 479.
26. G. H. Curtis, 'A clock for the ages: potassium-argon', *National Geographic*, October 1961, p.590.
27. J. R. Napier, 'Fossil hand bones from Olduvai Gorge', *Nature*, 1962, 196: 409; 'Profile of early man at Olduvai', *New Scientist*, 1964, 22: 86–9.
28. L. S. B. Leakey, P. V. Tobias & J. R. Napier, 'A new species of the genus *Homo* from Olduvai Gorge', *Nature*, 1964, 202: 7–9.
29. W. E. Le Gros Clark, *Discovery*, 1964, 25: 49; L.S.B.L., *ib.*, 25: 48.
30. L.S.B.L. to P.V. Tobias, 8 April, 1967.
31. P. V. Tobias & J. R. Napier, *The Times*, 5 June, 1964.
32. '*Homo habilis*, *Homo erectus* and the Australopithecines', *Nature*, 1966, 209: 1279.

Chapter 10.

1. M. M. Payne, 'Family in search of prehistoric man', *National Geographic*, February 1965, p.209.
2. *Animals of East Africa*, 1969, p.134.
3. Chancellor of the University of California to L.S.B.L., 6 June, 1963.
4. L. S. B. Leakey & M. D. Leakey, 'Recent discoveries of fossil

hominids in Tanganyika: at Olduvai and near Lake Natron', *Nature*, 1964, 202: 5–7.
5. M. MacDonald to Sir Frank Soskice, 2 November, 1964.
6. Sir Frank Soskice to M. MacDonald, 2 December, 1964.
7. W. A. B. Hamilton to M. MacDonald, 25 June, 1965.
8. L.S.B.L. to Mrs Lita Fejos, 15 January, 1965.
9. W. W. Bishop & J. A. Miller (Eds.), *Background to evolution in Africa*, 1967, Chicago.
10. R. E. F. Leakey, 'New Cercopithecidae from the Chemeron Beds of Lake Baringo, Kenya', *Fossil Vertebrates of Africa*, 1969, 1: 53–68.
11. J. S. Boys Smith to L.S.B.L., 8 October, 1966.
12. L.S.B.L. to J. S. Boys Smith, 15 October, 1966.
13. Secretary of CAPES to L.S.B.L., 24 February, 1967.
14. F. J. Mchauru to R. E. F. Leakey, 13 April, 1967.
15. H. Chopeta to L.S.B.L., 20 January, 1966.
16. R. E. F. Leakey to L.S.B.L. and M.D.L., 20 June, 1967.
17. L.S.B.L. to M. M. Payne, 31 July, 1967.
18. L.S.B.L. to P. V. Tobias, 24 November, 1966.
19. L.S.B.L. to F. Wicker, 10 December, 1964.
20. 'An early Miocene member of the Hominidae', *Nature*, 1967, 213: 155–63.
21. 'Bone smashing by late Miocene Hominidae', *Nature*, 1968, 218: 528–30.
22. 'Upper Miocene primates from Kenya', *Nature*, 1968, 218: 527.
23. L.S.B.L. to L. D. Cuscoy, 20 January, 1965.

Chapter 11.

1. Vice-Chancellor, University of the Witwatersrand, to M. D. Leakey, 5 December, 1967.
2. L.S.B.L. to P. V. Tobias, 24 February, 1968.
3. M. D. Leakey, 'Recent discoveries of hominid remains at Olduvai Gorge', *Nature*, 1969, 223: 756.
4. M. D. Leakey, R. J. Clarke & L. S. B. Leakey, 'New hominid skull from Bed I, Olduvai Gorge, Tanzania', *Nature*, 1971, 232: 308–12.
5. J. K. R. Thorp to L.S.B.L., 16 March, 1943.
6. *Life*, 12 September, 1969.
7. L.S.B.L. to R. Ascher, 11 September, 1967.
8. W. A. Stini to L.S.B.L., 12 November, 1971.
9. L.S.B.L. to Mrs Joan Travis, 15 June, 1967.

10. Mrs Tita Caldwell in report of annual meeting of trustees of Leakey Foundation, 1 October, 1971.
11. Mrs Joan Travis to L.S.B.L., 8 May, 1969.
12. *ib.*, 6 June, 1969.
13. R. Beck to E. Harrison, 23 August, 1969.
14. L.S.B.L. to A. O'Brien, 11 April, 1969.
15. *ib.*, 15 September, 1969.
16. A. O'Brien to L.S.B.L., 19 September, 1969.

Chapter 12.

1. M. M. Payne at annual meeting of Leakey Foundation, 9 October, 1972.
2. L.S.B.L. to E. Harrison, 12 January, 1971.
3. Jane van Lawick Goodall, *In the shadow of man*, 1971, London, p.17.
4. Jane Goodall, 'Tool-using and aimed throwing in a community of free-living chimpanzees', *Nature*, 1964, 201: 1264.
5. E. Marais, *The soul of the ape*, 1969, London.
6. *Reveille*, 25 April, 1962.
7. J. R. Napier to Principal of Newnham Hall, 21 February, 1961.
8. G. Schaller, *The year of the gorilla*, 1965, London, p.22.
9. F. Osborn to L.S.B.L., 31 July, 1967.
10. Dian Fossey, 'Making friends with mountain gorillas', *National Geographic*, January 1970, p.48.
11. Dian Fossey to L.S.B.L., 13 February, 1972.
12. Mrs Joan Travis to L.S.B.L., 18 January, 1970.
13. Dian Fossey to L.S.B.L., 8 November, 1971.
14. Mrs B. G. Brindamour to L.S.B.L., 12 November, 1971.

Chapter 13.

1. Miss R. Simpson in *Pleistocene Man at Calico*, W. C. Schuiling (Ed.), 1972, San Bernardino County Museum Association, p.35.
2. L.S.B.L., *ib.*, p.10.
3. Miss R. Simpson, *ib.*, p.36.
4. *ib.*, p.40.
5. *ib.*, p.42.
6. R. Berger, *ib.*, p.68.
7. L. S. B. Leakey, R. Simpson & T. Clements, 'Archaeological excavations in the Calico Mountains, California: a preliminary report', *Science*, 1968, 160: 1022.
8. L.S.B.L. to Mrs Joan Travis, September 1969 (n.d.).

9. Mrs Joan Travis to L.S.B.L., 30 March, 1970.
10. R. E. F. Leakey, 'In search of man's past at Lake Rudolf', *National Geographic*, May 1970, p.712.
11. R. E. F. Leakey & M. D. Leakey, 'New hominid remains and early artifacts from Northern Kenya', *Nature*, 1970, 226: 223.
12. A. O'Brien to trustees of Leakey Foundation, 8 October, 1969.
13. R. Beck to L.S.B.L., February 1970 (n.d.).
14. Mrs Joan Travis to L.S.B.L., 11 February, 1970.
15. 'Finding the world's earliest man', *National Geographic*, September 1960, p.433.
16. W. C. Schuiling (Ed.), *Pleistocene Man at Calico*, 1972, San Bernardino County Museum.
17. L.S.B.L. to G. Phillips, 13 January, 1971.

Chapter 14.

1. Dian Fossey to L.S.B.L., 29 January, 1971.
2. L.S.B.L. to Mrs Joan Travis, 10 February, 1971.
3. L.S.B.L. to G. Phillips, 7 January, 1971.
4. E. Harrison to L.S.B.L., 5 January, 1971.
5. L.S.B.L. to G. Phillips, 7 January, 1971.
6. H. J. Coolidge to L.S.B.L., 26 January, 1971.
7. L.S.B.L. to G. Phillips, 24 March, 1971.
8. L.S.B.L. to R.E.F. Leakey, 18 March, 1971.
9. L.S.B.L. to National Science Foundation, 1971 (n.d.).
10. L.S.B.L. to S. M. Farber, 23 December, 1970.
11. Miss C. M. Phelips to Mr & Mrs J. Phelips, 27 April to 6 July, 1971.
12. L.S.B.L. to R. E. F. Leakey, 14 May, 1971.
13. L.S.B.L. to Dian Fossey, 28 October, 1971.
14. Leakey Foundation 'News Notes', July 1973.
15. R. Ardrey, *African Genesis*, 1961, London, p.246.
16. L.S.B.L. to E. Harrison, 5 August, 1971.
17. L.S.B.L. to G. Phillips, 25 June, 1971.
18. E. Harrison to L.S.B.L., 23 July, 1971.

Chapter 15.

1. L.S.B.L. to W. A. Stini, 2 February, 1972.
2. L.S.B.L. to Dian Fossey, 10 May, 1972.
3. L.S.B.L. to Mrs Joan Travis, 11 September, 1972.
4. R. Ardrey to Mrs Joan Travis, 4 July, 1972.
5. L.S.B.L. to Dian Fossey, 12 August, 1972.
6. L.S.B.L. to Sir William Collins, 9 May, 1972.

7. Mrs Joan Travis to L.S.B.L., 31 March, 1972.
8. L.S.B.L. to Mrs Joan Travis, 14 April, 1972.
9. R. E. F. Leakey, 'Evidence for an advanced Plio-Pleistocene hominid from Lake Rudolf, Kenya', *Nature*, 1973, 242: 447–50.
10. Mrs P. Barrett to Mrs B. G. Brindamour, 28 November, 1972.
11. P. V. Tobias, 'Louis Seymour Bazett Leakey 1903–1972', *S. Afr. Arch. Bull.*, 1973, 28: 3–7.
12. *National Geographic*, January 1973, 142–4.

Chapter 16.

1. Mrs Joan Travis to Miss C. M. Phelips, 30 November, 1972.
2. A. O'Brien to trustees of Leakey Foundation, September 1973 (n.d.).
3. R. E. F. Leakey, 'Further evidence of the Lower Pleistocene hominids from East Rudolf, Northern Kenya', *Nature*, 1974, 248: 653–6.
4. L.S.B.L. to Dian Fossey, 12 August, 1972.
5. Mrs B. G. Brindamour, report to Leakey Foundation, November 1973.
6. P. Andrews, 'New species of *Dryopithecus* from Kenya', *Nature*, 1974, 249: 188.

Index

Index